Porgy's Ghost

Porgy's Ghost

The Life and Works of Dorothy Heyward and
Her Contribution to an American Classic

by Harlan Greene

The University of Georgia Press
Athens

© 2025 by the University of Georgia Press
Athens, Georgia 30602
www.ugapress.org
All rights reserved
Designed by Mary McKeon
Set in Minion Pro by Mary McKeon

Most University of Georgia Press titles are
available from popular e-book vendors.

Printed digitally

EU Authorized Representative
Easy Access System Europe—Mustamäe tee 50, 10621 Tallinn, Estonia, gpsr.
requests@easproject.com

Library of Congress Cataloging-in-Publication Data
Greene, Harlan author
Title: Porgy's ghost : the life and works of Dorothy Heyward and her
contribution to an American classic / by Harlan Greene.
Description: Athens : The University of Georgia Press, 2025. | Includes
bibliographical references and index.
Identifiers: LCCN 2025019870 | ISBN 9780820375090 hardback
| ISBN 9780820375106 paperback | ISBN 9780820375113 epub | ISBN
9780820375120 pdf
Subjects: LCSH: Heyward, Dorothy, 1890–1961 | Dramatists, American—20th
century—Biography | Heyward, Dorothy, 1890–1961. Porgy | Gershwin,
George, 1898–1937. Porgy and Bess. | LCGFT: Biographies
Classification: LCC ps3515.e97 z65 2025 | DDC 812/.52 [B]—dc23/eng/20250512
LC record available at https://lccn.loc.gov/2025019870

CONTENTS

Overture | *vii*

Preface. Naming Names | *ix*

CHAPTER 1.
Dorothy Kuhns of Canton, Ohio | 1

CHAPTER 2.
Apprentice Playwright | 6

CHAPTER 3.
The MacDowell Colony | 14

CHAPTER 4.
Nancy Ann | 20

CHAPTER 5.
Porgy: Origins | 28

CHAPTER 6.
Porgy: Novel to Play | 38

CHAPTER 7.
Stops and Starts | 50

CHAPTER 8.
Porgy: Revisions | 56

CHAPTER 9.
Porgy Abroad | 72

CHAPTER 10.
Three-a-Days | 77

CHAPTER 11.
"Our Next Play" | 88

CHAPTER 12.
Credit and Credibility | 95

CHAPTER 13.
Mamba's Daughters | 107

CHAPTER 14.
The Dock Street Theatre | 120

CHAPTER 15.
War and Worries | 126

CHAPTER 16.
Legacies | 137

CHAPTER 17.
The Tragedy of Denmark Vesey | 141

CHAPTER 18.
A Candle for St. Jude | 152

CHAPTER 19.
A Case for St. Jude | 162

CHAPTER 20.
Operatic | 167

CHAPTER 21.
Porgy and Business | 172

CHAPTER 22.
Home | 183

Afterword | 195

Acknowledgments | 199

Notes | 201

Works Cited | 229

Index | 235

OVERTURE

It will always happen.

In the dark, music will swell, suggestive, wild, exotic, and exhilarating. The curtain will rise, and the magic melding of words and music that has been transfixing audiences for nearly a century will commence. A story of hope and redemption, of terror and fear, and one of triumph and tragedy will grip people in their seats until, at the transcendent end, they will sit stunned before leaping to their feet applauding.

And then many, leaving, may wonder how this miracle of art came to be. What brought these creative artists together, under what circumstances, to create the operatic masterpiece *Porgy and Bess*?

That is what happened to me when I first heard the opera performed in its, and my, native city in 1970. As a teenager, I began searching for information, a curiosity that actually led me to becoming an archivist some five years later, affording me the chance to handle and catalog the very manuscripts and correspondence of DuBose Heyward, author of the novel *Porgy*, and the musical composer George Gershwin. This only whetted my appetite to know more; there was much to read, and as the number of books grew over the years, my knowledge did, too. Then, in the late 1980s, more documents arrived at the South Carolina Historical Society after DuBose Heyward's daughter Jenifer's death; these contained the papers of her mother, Dorothy, and they told another more nuanced story, one that I had not encountered anywhere else.

As the opera celebrated anniversaries, and more books were published, I came to realize that despite the onslaught of biographies, monographs, and documentaries, no one knew the full story, or at least had not tapped the resources I had seen. No one knew or seemed to care to find out the part that Dorothy had played in the opera's creation, its sustaining, and its history. And part of the reason, I saw, was that Dorothy desired it that way.

It haunted me (why would she want to so obscure herself?), so I started to investigate the story of Dorothy Heyward's life; but there was little interest in it *from publishers, and so as other projects presented themselves, I abandoned it. But in October 2019, at the Metropolitan Opera House in New York, it happened again, as it always will. The chandeliers went up, the music came out of the darkness, and for a few hours I was again rapt, lifted to a different reality where time dissolves, and art, as pure as a note from a soprano, enslaves and enthralls and holds you, till you are changed when it finally lets you go.*

It was then that I decided that I had to add my mite to the mighty story of how this masterpiece was created. It would never have happened without the woman the world saw as a fragile, somewhat befuddled slip of a girl from Ohio, an artist dismissed in her time and forgotten by history. Even though she did not want it told, this is her story.

PREFACE

Naming Names

In the 1950s the great political drama unfolding on the national stage focused on the investigation conducted by the House Un-American Activities Committee. In the glare of popping flashbulbs, congressional investigators queried artists, activists, and ordinary citizens on their loyalty to America. The insistent question hurled at witnesses was if they, then or previously, had ever been members of the Communist Party. Gavels slammed and orders were barked; the pressure was intense to name names of fellow travelers and collaborators.

At the same time, there was another, less public drama being played out. Naming names of collaborators was part of this battle, too, but in reverse. The cause taken up by elderly, arthritic Dorothy Kuhns Heyward centered on her determination to get a collaborator's—her husband's—name restored to a classic work of art that, even then, was touring the world, soon to be deployed by the State Department abroad as a weapon against communism.

Dorothy Heyward (1890–1961) had everything against her—the overpowering name, fame, and power of the opera's other collaborators, her age, her health, and her sex. But she took on those who were billing the work as the creation of George and Ira Gershwin (in just a few years, the film version of the opera would be advertised as Samuel Goldwyn's *Porgy and Bess*). To get her husband the credit he deserved, she enlisted attorneys, editors, agents, and anyone else she could draw to her cause. In her decades-long attempt, she met with some success, but while achieving justice for her husband, she denied it to herself.

For an examination of the record shows that it is unlikely that *any* version of *Porgy* (novel, play, opera, or film) would have ever come to pass without Dorothy Heyward. Now decades after her death in 1961, and even longer after the opera's 1935 premiere, her role in it remains unexamined and obscure. Of all the collaborators, she remains the odd man (and the sole woman) left out of its story. There have been entire volumes dedicated to the opera and its impact.[1] Books on the Gershwins fill shelves. The story of DuBose Heyward's life (1885–1940) has been told at least three times.[2] Rouben Mamoulian, who directed the opera and the play, has garnered a scholarly tome or two dedicated to him, with one focused entirely on *his* contribution to the work of art.[3] Cheryl Crawford, who was a coproducer (and the first to strip Heyward's name from the work), has garnered both a biography and an autobiography that touch on the topic.[4] Even Sammy Smalls, the real-life Charlestonian upon whom the character Porgy was based, has not escaped investigative scrutiny.[5] Yet Dorothy Heyward, whose work and words structure the opera and who was legally and contractually recognized as a coauthor, has been left out. Besides that, she had six other shows produced on Broadway (two in one year), authored two novels and a children's opera, but has never received more than glancing mentions, often just in passing, in works on the opera and in other contributors' biographies. While she appears in a few summaries of American women playwrights, most are inaccurate and, at best, incomplete.[6] Despite a self-effacing nature and this lack of attention, she knew her worth. "I have a flair for the theatre," she wrote in her autobiography left in shambles, unpublished at her death; when wondering if she was to blame for this lack of prestige, and specifically for the failures of some of her plays, she demurred, proclaiming, "no, it never occurred to me; and I'm afraid it never will."[7]

While she was credited (correctly and not) with some of the fluffiest flops ever seen on the Great White Way, she also knew that she had opened up opportunities for Broadway actors of color including the likes of Juano Hernandez, Rose McClendon, Ethel Waters, and Canada Lee, while offering the American public serious investigations of race in dramas praised for their bravery even as specific productions were panned. Almost two generations before Denmark Vesey, a free person of color charged with fomenting a slave rebellion in Charleston, became an obsession of American scholars and triggered a small publishing industry, Dorothy Heyward, a white woman from Ohio, cast him as a hero in a play on Broadway. While her failures outnumbered her successes, and professional betrayals by some of the greatest names of the day plunged her into madness, still she held her ground. Although her other contributions were minor, she knew she had played a major role in the creation of a world classic.

There is an irony at work here. In the opera itself, it is Bess, appearing in the first act and disappearing before the end, who prompts the action and gives the drama its raison d'être. Similarly, the novel, certainly the play, and thus the opera could never have been written if Dorothy Heyward had not appeared. And, like Bess, she's vanished from the scene.

The aim of this book, then, is threefold. It offers a short, straightforward biography, attempting to reconstruct the details of her life (and inferring some of her reasons for what she did), while also presenting summaries and analyses of her mostly minor other works, all out of print or never published, and thus fairly unavailable. Simultaneously, in chronological sequence, extended chapters investigate her specific contributions to the novel *Porgy*, the play *Porgy*, and the opera *Porgy and Bess*.

Porgy's Ghost

CHAPTER 1

Dorothy Kuhns of Canton, Ohio

"In many ways, my life began at the [MacDowell] Colony," Dorothy Heyward wrote in an autobiography left unfinished at her death. The time was the summer of 1923, and at the age of thirty-three, she was realizing a long-deferred dream of becoming a playwright. What happened all those formative years before that summer, she summed up swiftly and almost dismissively, as if just the details of her life in the theater mattered.

She tried to suggest it had been her destiny. The daughter of Herman Lyties Kuhns and Dorothea Virginia Hartzell, she was christened Dorothea Hartzell Kuhns, born June 6, 1890, in Wooster, Ohio, where her father presided over a tractor- and plow-manufacturing business. (As if in collusion to make her youth difficult to document, her birth certificate erroneously gives the date as the seventh, and it also misspells her father's and mother's names.)

Up to that point, Herman Kuhns's professional life had been both varied and peripatetic; he had switched from manufacturing wagon springs to hotel management, as he moved from his birthplace in Lynchburg, Pennsylvania, to Cleveland, Ohio, and then to St. Paul, Minnesota. Eventually settling in Canton, Ohio, he reconnected with the light soprano Dora Hartzell, having performed with her in a local production of *HMS Pinafore*. With odd talents, Herman could conduct even while, from the pit, he occasionally dubbed in the low notes for a less accomplished singer on stage.[1]

Soon after their second meeting, Herman proposed; Dora accepted. They were married in Canton on September 10, 1881, and it was there that their daughter, Dorothy, and two older brothers, Wilbur (born 1884) and Louis (born 1889), were raised. "Canton . . . was . . . the home of my parents, my grandfather, my uncles and my brothers," Dorothy would explain, as if feeling

1

she had to apologize for being born in Wooster, instead of where her family became established.

As the editor of Canton's newspaper *The Repository*, Dorothy's mother's father, Josiah Hartzell, often featured his granddaughter and her family's activities in the social pages. Herman's father, Dr. L. M. Kuhns, an ordained Lutheran minister, had given up the church and the Midwest for a position in the pension office in Washington, D.C., to be near one of his daughters. It was there, visiting family at the age of two, that Dorothy first saw an African American, when she was placed in the care of a Black nurse. Noting the irony, "Whenever I am asked to collaborate on a play," she'd say years later, "I know without seeing it[,] it [will be] a Negro play."[2] While she did not grow up with African Americans, she also did not grow up with bigotry; for her, race was not a prejudicial issue.

Both the Hartzell and the Kuhns families moved in the same social circle as Canton's most distinguished citizen, President William McKinley, who also had an enlightened attitude on race for the times. As a young boy, Dorothy's father had carried love notes between the future president and his future wife, Ida Saxton. Years later, Ralph Hartzell, Dorothy's uncle, would marry Mrs. McKinley's niece Mary Saxton Barber. Dorothy was six when McKinley took office in 1897.

Since the president's wife was often ill (and possibly epileptic), retreating into deep depressions following the death of her two daughters, many of her nieces, including Dorothy's aunt Mary Barber, fulfilled social obligations for the First Lady and acted as hostess at the White House. Cementing the bond further, when the McKinleys left for the inauguration, Dorothy, her parents, and older brothers moved into the president's Canton home on North Market Street. They were in residence during his 1900 bid for reelection too, when the house had police protection from souvenir hunters pilfering pieces of the fence and plants from the gardens. "Our old play-room was the President's Office, and I knew the corner where he often sat at his desk," the thirteen-year-old wrote for *St. Nicholas Magazine*'s "My favorite character in history," Dorothy's first published piece.[3]

The Kuhns household "throbbed with music." Dorothy's older brother Wilbur published musical compositions in his teens; Dorothy took piano lessons and was fascinated—even obsessed—with the theater, musical and otherwise, attending melodramas like *Uncle Tom's Cabin* and three-a-day vaudeville shows barnstorming through Canton and nearby cities. Seeing Maude Adams perform *Peter Pan* in Cleveland convinced Dorothy she wanted to spend her life in the theater. She participated in church pageants, created a cardboard stage in her backyard where she authored and directed plays, the only opportunity, she'd quip, of seeing her work produced as written. She saw her first opera, *La Bohème*, at age thirteen, as Mrs. McKinley's guest. Yet with a characteristic false modesty, she wrote that of all her family, she alone lacked musical talent, a claim contradicted by her ability to sing and dance in a Broadway roadshow, authoring a play and a novel about musicians, and having a major impact on *Porgy and Bess*.[4]

In 1898, to martial music, Herman Kuhns marched off to the Spanish-American War, quartermaster of the Ohio Volunteer Infantry, the Eighth Ohio, dubbed the "President's Own." His letters back home were published in the local press, and when his service ended, he returned broken in health. About five or six years later, again changing professions, Herman was posted to Puerto Rico to work for the U.S. State Department, serving as enrolling clerk of the executive council of the colonial legislature. His wife's brother Charles S. Hartzell, no doubt, had been instrumental in getting him the post. Already there, Hartzell was soon offered the position of secretary of state in the colonial government by President McKinley, just before the president was felled by an assassin's bullet in September 1901. While Hartzell was officially confirmed by McKinley's successor, Theodore Roosevelt, the new president ultimately replaced Hartzell with his own choice. Undaunted, Dorothy's uncle stayed in Puerto Rico, serving as an attorney for many of the island's sugar corporations, affording his niece a chance to spend formative years on the island. She'd trade on this in the future, claiming that U.S. territory as her home instead of Ohio to make her seem less Midwestern and less hidebound.[5]

Although everyone knew Captain Kuhns's health had been compromised in Cuba, it still came as a shock when he suffered an apoplexy and died in San Juan on May 14, 1904, at the age of forty-nine. Herman's own father, Dorothy's grandfather, had died just a year before, and Dorothy's twenty-year-old brother Wilbur died the next year, 1905, of typhoid when Dorothy was fifteen. After these three successive losses of husband, father-in-law, and son, Dora, the songbird of the light operatic voice and church choir member, never sang again. Dorothy, her mother, and surviving one-year-older brother Louis withdrew into mourning, living in Grandfather Josiah Hartzell's house.[6]

Coming into her teens, Dorothy periodically visited her Washington, D.C., aunt, Mrs. Hamilton Bayly, and was mentioned in the city's society columns. In 1907, at age seventeen, she spent a year perfecting her Spanish staying with her uncle Charles Hartzell and his wife and their son Charles "Junior" in Puerto Rico. There, she continued to enjoy free reign of the governor's mansion. In San Juan, she bonded with Junior (her "twin cousin"), finding him more of a brother than her sibling Louis.

While the widowed Dora was not wealthy, she was rich with relations. Dorothy had five uncles and even more aunts devoted to her, while her tuition to the National Cathedral School in Washington, D.C., was apparently paid for by a suitor of her aunt Grace. (Aunts would become one of the themes of her romantic comedies.) In that Episcopal school, she learned skills such as curtseying, and as a student she was frequently invited to White House functions, learning manners that would serve her well in the coming years in socially conservative Charleston. While "confusing [her] teachers by writing [her] essays in play form," the slight young woman excelled in all subjects, including "tricky math," receiving the highest grades on record in astronomy. Years later, she'd note that despite this skill, her husband, who dropped out of high school and confessed to being bad with numbers, nevertheless sometimes negotiated her contracts behind her back, assuming it his male prerogative and duty.[7]

In 1908 Dora suffered a stroke; it took a full year and a half before she could speak again. Dorothy had planned to attend Wellesley, but as more strokes followed, Dora and Dorothy's grandfather needed care. Dorothy managed to finish high school, but with brother Louis living with family out west to help his asthma, she stayed home, the good daughter and lone family caretaker. Yet she still had time for tennis, winning doubles championships at the local country club, and every now and then she left the sick rooms for charity balls and other social events in Washington, D.C. In Canton, she starred as the heroine in the local DAR play *The College Hero* and attended suffragist lectures. A 1911 news clipping shows a fragile young beauty said to be back from a trip to the Philippines, which she said she did not like.[8]

As her grandfather's and mother's conditions worsened, Dorothy's orbit shrank. Josiah Hartzell died at age eighty-one in 1914, and her mother's precarious health continued its decline. In one two-year period, Dorothy rarely left her bedside and virtually saw no one. This lack of socializing with people her age resulted in a sort of social "arrested development." Looking younger than her years, she acted younger as well, seemingly wrapped in a "pristine innocence" and adolescently clueless in some social situations. This made her come across as naïve, childlike, and guileless. Upon Dora's death in 1917, Dorothy, at twenty-seven, had been kissed once and proposed to once (by the same man). Idealized by her extended family as the good girl, selflessly living for others, she was cast as the brave little woman, a role to be forced on her again and again, a to-be-pitied spinster in the making, perhaps.

But Dorothy embraced her unmarried status, longing to "embark . . . on [her] belated youth" at last. But her extended family, scattered geographically, all agreed on one thing: "Dorothy should be curbed." Her aunt Grace, whose suitor had paid for her schooling, demanded that dear Dorothy come for an extended stay in La Jolla, California; when that visit was over, as Dorothy put it, "my Minneapolis uncle . . . felt that I was not yet up to bucking the world on my own."

Ever dutiful, passively accepting what was expected of her, she enrolled at the University of Minnesota in fall 1917 as a freshman. She was a full decade older than other students, hiding it successfully, aided by her petite size and doe-eyed appearance. After a frozen semester, Dorothy begged off and was handed over to her uncle and aunt and "twin cousin" in Puerto Rico. There she fought against the role assigned to her by her loving and possessive, but suffocating, family.[9]

CHAPTER 2

Apprentice Playwright

In her lonely years in Canton, serving as nurse and companion, Dorothy had indulged in a secret and vicarious emotional life, reading, attending plays, and sitting in darkened cinemas. The flickering black-and-white silent images of dramatic lives in exotic settings were in stark contrast to an existence immured in her hushed Ohio home.

Still obsessed with the theater, starstruck with the movies, Dorothy had begun drafting film scenarios with complicated plots, often about struggling artists, mailing them off hopefully, and one suspects secretly, to agents or producers. She was convinced a few less reputable companies pirated her ideas, returning her scripts but stealing her plots. One success came in 1915 when the Excelsior Film Company offered thirty-five dollars for *The Ghost of Moorsdown Manor*, a complicated affair of a man wrongly accused of murder, hiding in his English mansion. Mistaken for a ghost, he is somehow recognized by a Native American woman who knows his innocence and loves him. But it was still playwriting that mostly held her attention.

In an era of much-publicized writing contests, Dorothy entered all the ones she could. Since family kept her sequestered, the postal service may have been her only avenue of outreach to the wider world she longed to join.[1]

There were many successful women playwrights on Broadway to emulate, but the question remains whether Dorothy was aware of them: she never mentions them in her autobiography or any of her writings. In 1921 Zona Gale would become the first woman to win the Pulitzer Prize for drama; she and many others such as Rachel Carothers, Zoë Akins, Edna Ferber, and Rose Franken (all but Franken older than Dorothy) were by then or would soon be national figures, creating strong roles for women, and often criticizing the social restrictions on them, promoting social justice and feminism. Clare

Kummer, whose plays Dorothy's early ones would favor, was many a critic's darling as early as 1916. So, to be a female playwright was not necessarily seen as bohemian (although Susan Glaspell with the Provincetown Players, due to a "scandalous" divorce, was judged that way). Whether she was aware of such a successful sisterhood or not, she longed for a career like theirs. When Broadway impresario Winthrop Ames offered a $10,000 prize for the best American play, Dorothy produced "pounds" of manuscript titled *Siberiaward*, a lugubrious tragedy of Polish dissidents in exile, something she knew absolutely nothing about. Not surprisingly, nothing came of it.[2]

Learning of the MacDowell Fellowship at Harvard University, Dorothy tried again and wrote another play. Admission into George Pierce Baker's justly famed English 47 class required the endorsement of Baker himself, reputed to be the best playwriting teacher in the country. The class was limited to a dozen women from Radcliffe, Harvard's "women's annex," where the program had originated, and a similar number of Harvard men (all inevitably called Baker's dozens). There were always more candidates than openings, so the slots generally went to already enrolled students. Dorothy nevertheless blithely sent Baker her second opus, adapted from a 1911 L. J. Beeston short story. The melodramatic pulp tale "Christina" is set in a convent, its heroine a young girl wanting to renounce life, eventually embracing it instead.

Her sprawling two-act play, *Cello, Harp, and Violin*, begins with a novice about to take vows as a nun, then flashes back to Paris before World War I. Set in an atelier, the action focuses on Patricia, an American harpist; Paul, a French violinist and composer; and Karl, a German cellist, caught in a plot that veers from drama to melodrama, suspense, and light comedy. This buffet of genres, not unheard of in popular plays of this era, offers up spies, swapped documents, a case of amnesia, one duel, temporary blindness, mistaken identities, and the mention of writing an opera.

In July 1918 she received word that, astonishingly, this overstuffed play, with its meandering plot, wooden dialogue, and a few flashes of vividness, was in the running to win a MacDowell Fellowship. She was asked to supply three recommendations, expound on her theory of playwriting, and explain what she had been doing in the ten years since she had left National Cathedral School. (Her answer, unfortunately, does not survive.) The news of her loss came in September, but Professor Baker, in a personal note, was encouraging.[3]

Behind his distinguished New England façade, eyes intensified by a pince-nez, Baker was very approachable, with a national reputation for mentoring and discovering talent. It did not matter if the work was tragedy, farce, or comedy; Baker did his best to lead each particular student to success. He often voiced the opinion that drama was all about action, action, action, and there was certainly a lot of it in *Cello, Harp, and Violin*.

In his September 1918 rejection letter, Baker softened the blow by telling Dorothy she had probably disqualified herself by submitting a play adapted from another work. He also tried to gently acquaint her with the reality of the theater, noting how difficult it would be to cast an actor who was also an accomplished violinist in a play with an enormous ensemble. Baker would have probably been appalled to discover that although Dorothy had made inquiries about acquiring dramatic rights for the Beeson story, she never actually succeeded, which would have put her in a ticklish situation had she won; and Baker, in turn, no doubt would have to reverse his advice upon seeing that over sixty actors would later fill the stage in her play *Porgy*.[4]

The tiny whiff of encouragement from Baker suggesting she try again galvanized Dorothy and apparently was enough to satisfy her aunt and uncle. Aged twenty-eight, she left Puerto Rico for New York, where, to make up for lost time, she enrolled in every class in every university she could find on playwriting. Under Professor Clayton Hamilton at Columbia University, she wrote the one-act *Mr. Pygmalion*. When Hamilton suggested she reconfigure it as a three-act, she followed up on it under a different Columbia professor, Minor Latham, who also suggested that Dorothy get some experience in the theater. This launched her haunting of casting offices, an experience she'd mine in future works. "Today I know as much about theatrical waiting rooms as I know about aunts," she'd later say. She auditioned for popular producer George M. Cohan, and he expressed an interest in her acting and in one of her works in progress, but neither merited a callback.

While enrolled in Latham's class, she also took a class in acting, and possibly one on playwriting, at the American Academy of Dramatic Arts sometime around 1919. For one of her writing assignments, she adapted Rebecca West's World War I novel, *The Return of the Soldier*, similar in some ways to *Cello, Harp, and Violin*, with no way of knowing she and West would eventually become friends. On her own for the first time in her life, she roomed with other female students in a five-bedroom apartment on 122nd Street.[5]

Professor Latham chose Dorothy's three-act play, retooled from the one-act *Mr. Pygmalion*, now rechristened *Have a Good Time, Jonica*, for a student production. It was so poorly staged, however, that Latham walked out of the performance, but as Dorothy recalled, "The rehearsals, re-writing, and eventual disastrous Columbia production of *Jonica* taught me more about how not to write a play than years of study and observation."

Despite the failure at Columbia, or because of it, she felt confident enough to submit *Jonica* to Professor Baker. The eponymous heroine of the amusing fast-paced romantic farce leaves her convent school to go to New York to be a bridesmaid for family friends she has not met. Incredibly naïve, she accepts a gun from her schoolmates who tell her it's necessary for women to protect their virtue. In the Pullman sleeper car, the setting of the first act, she meets a woman with a past and two gentlemen. The audience realizes the latter are the groom and his best man on the way to the same wedding, but clueless Jonica does not. The gun goes off accidently in the hands of the woman with a past, who flees, fearing she has killed someone. She disguises herself in Jonica's dress and is picked up by the wedding party, who have been instructed to meet a girl wearing that particular garment. Jonica, an innocent in a big city, is bereft.

The long second act is set in the apartment of Don, the bride-to-be's brother. Knowing the address, Jonica gets in on her own. Missing her clothes, she puts on the only covering she can find, the gauzy drapery used by Don in a portrait he has painted of his ideal woman, the original idea of *Mr. Pygmalion*. She hides when Don and the bridegroom, Ben, enter. Complications ensue when the bride, Alice, and her aunt arrive. Doors open and shut, while people run back and forth as the men try to keep the women from seeing an unexplained girl in the apartment. Jonica thinks the men are crazy, and Don wonders if his portrait has come to life. A detective is eventually called, and Alice is so upset with the shenanigans that she calls off her wedding. Just when the men and Jonica are going to be caught, Ben turns off the lights. Back on, the detective has disappeared, and Alice leaves in disgust. Ben releases the detective he has tied up but is resultingly arrested and taken to jail, leaving best man Don to wonder at the identity of the mysterious perfect woman as Jonica flees and the curtain descends.

In the third act, she turns up in Alice's aunt's house for the wedding, where the woman on the train, assumed to be Jonica, is about to act as bridesmaid. But Ben, the bridegroom, is still jailed. The detective is present, as all learn the pistol shot did not kill someone after all. Ben is released from jail, and he takes

Alice down the aisle, as Don and Jonica, their identities revealed, express their love. In the play's final line, the heroine is asked if she's had a good time, the advice called out to her as she departed by train in the first act.

Implausible but with witty dialogue, and a Keystone Cops sense of pacing, it would succeed as an evening's light entertainment with the right director and cast. And in a twist as unlikely as any in its plot, *Jonica* won the MacDowell Fellowship. Dorothy was invited to Harvard and George Pierce Baker's class.

Arriving in Cambridge, Massachusetts, for the beginning of the 1919–20 academic year, she dizzyingly found herself in the company of the "elect," the best and brightest playwriting students in one of the best universities in the country. Men students, taught at Harvard, and women at Radcliffe all met in the rambling and ramshackle wooden Massachusetts Hall.[6]

Although they studied "the history of the theatre, and ... were reasonably well grounded in Sophocles, Shakespeare, Molière, and the other great playwrights," they were not just interested in the past. "What made the 47 Workshop such an unforgettable experience for all of us who entered it," one attendee wrote, "was the fact that Professor Baker, a forceful and eager man, took us, for the first time in our limited experience, out of the academic atmosphere and thrust us into the electric excitement of the professional theater." So observed Theresa Helburn, a founder of the Theatre Guild, who would have an enormous impact on Dorothy's career. "He treated us not as students but as responsible adults to whom the contemporary stage was extremely important. He talked not in terms of classical literature but in terms of Broadway. What he was discussing and sharing with us was immediate; it was actual; above all it was professional.

"We weren't there to fool around with pretty, 'artistic' theories. We were there to learn to write for the living stage. And we wrote. How we wrote! The man inspired everyone who took his classes to try to write plays that could actually meet the competition of the professionals and make their way on Broadway."[7]

In this heady atmosphere, Dorothy again found herself in a curious situation: she was older than most, and not just less educated, but also less worldly. Many of her peers were working on advanced degrees; she had only a high school diploma. "I was young at a rather mature age," was how she put it. Her classmate, Thomas Wolfe, ten years younger, taller, and more gregarious than she, often flagged down Baker for a conversation, as she shyly hung back, trying to catch his eye.

All the plays she worked on with Baker were romantic comedies. She had discarded heavy works like *Siberiaward* and *Cello, Harp, and Violin* once having discovered the immensely popular Broadway show (and silent film) *Peg o' My Heart*. Dorothy was taken with this sentimental story of an orphan girl, trying not to fall in love with a titled nobleman, with lots of plot twists and the inevitable happy ending. (It had already influenced her heroine in *Cello, Harp, and Violin*, for Patricia is both naïve and steadfastly determined not to marry a wealthy titled man, which she eventually and tragically does.)

As part of his teaching, Baker made his students adapt a prose work into a play, something she had already done with "Christina" and *Cello, Harp, and Violin*, giving her some more of the experience she'd need adapting *Porgy*. An original one-act she wrote for class, *Love in a Cupboard*, a farce about two collaborators, male and female, writing a complicated love story, getting entangled in many of the same incidents they were writing about, was published and licensed in 1926 by Samuel French; it would eventually win the Columbia, South Carolina, Town Theatre's Playwriting Contest's fifty-dollar prize. The three-act play she'd write for Baker in class, *Poor Paulette*, focused on a waiflike young woman getting into social tangles while trying to reconnect with her father.

With the year over, Dorothy was set to return to her family, but a peremptory note from the august director of the MacDowell Colony, Mrs. Edward MacDowell, who had founded the artists' colony in memory of her deceased composer husband, brough her up short. Whether it is true or not, Dorothy claimed to have never heard of the prestigious retreat to which aspiring artists fought tooth and nail to gain admission. Mrs. MacDowell demanded the young woman call at her hotel. Brooking no nonsense, the older woman told her to get a raincoat and a wool dress—it could be cool in New Hampshire. As winner of the MacDowell Fellowship, she was required to work on her craft at the remote, wooded, 600-acre site.[8]

Wide-eyed and a bit apprehensive, Dorothy nervously latched on to another young woman upon arriving. Dorothy Kuhns and Dorothy DeJagers soon discovered they had more in common than their first names. It was the first time there for both writers, and they were among the youngest in residence. Put in the same room on the first night, they decided, as rooms became available the next day, not to separate but to stay together. Sharing space led to sharing confidences. DeJagers, Dorothy saw, was a "clown who wanted to play Hamlet." Although DeJagers had achieved success with short stories featuring clever wordplay and O. Henry–like plots, which highly remunerative magazines like *The Saturday Evening Post* eagerly published, she wanted something different. Banking her cash, she'd embark on darker stream-of-consciousness "eruditions" that no one would buy. So, she'd return to her more lucrative lighthearted pieces, a tension, Dorothy believed, and a precipitating factor and/or symptom of a looming mental illness. But that summer, there was nothing but lighthearted bubbling companionship as they gathered in large Colony Hall in the evenings. Flipping through the phonograph records, they ignored the dirges and fugues, choosing instead more modern tunes. On the sidelines was an older man, whom other colonists held in awe, but whom Dorothy chatted up obliviously, later claiming, embracing the naïve role others cast her in, that she had never heard of the poet Edward Arlington Robinson.

During the day, colonists were expected to stay in their solitary cabins and work on their own projects. Dorothy's was her farce to be called *Poor Paulette*. She had sent an early draft of the new play to George M. Cohan, who told her she had a "honey" of a third act; the first two, he said, needed work. Professor Baker, however, believed the reverse. Reading the manuscript, DeJagers agreed with Baker and also agreed to help rewrite it, pointing her to playwriting. DeJagers would go on to dramatize some of her own stories, publish plays, and write at least one successfully produced Hollywood screenplay.[9]

By the time the summer was over, *Jonica* had caught the eye of a New York producer, proving Baker right: she *had* written a very commercial play. Adolph Klauber optioned it in March 1920, and it's likely that's why Dorothy lingered in the Northeast.[10]

It's also likely that while waiting for *Jonica*, Dorothy continued to frequent casting offices, eventually getting a role in a touring production of a popular romantic farce. *The Girl Behind the Gun*, its book cowritten by P. G. Wodehouse, had opened in New York in 1918. Transferred to London the next year, the revised play was renamed *Kissing Time*. It is set in France, as the prologue to *Poor Paulette* would be, and both have cross-generation mistaken love affairs and mistaken identities. In October 1920 the musical returned to the States and went on the road. One of the chorus girls leaving the show opened up an opportunity for Dorothy.

Joining the production in Detroit, Dorothy sang and danced in too-large lavender shoes left by the actress she replaced. At a performance in Chicago, her knee gave way, but she soldiered on despite its ominous creaking. By the time the production returned to New York, she was in agony. Almost unable to move, her hands and knees swollen with arthritis, she not only had to drop out of the show but had to be hospitalized. Terrified that illness, again—this time her own and not her mother's—would sidetrack her theatrical career, she was dismayed by her family's demand that she give up Broadway.

She refused, but her "twin" cousin, Charles Hartzell Jr., and his wife, Anne, happened to be in New York, and they "captured" her. His parents paid her hospital bills and demanded she recuperate with them in the sun. In debt emotionally and financially, she capitulated and returned to Puerto Rico. After a short rest, once the symptoms that would frequently cripple her for the rest of her life temporarily abated, she made plans to leave. Dr. Baker had invited Dorothy back for a second year, something he did only if he felt the student showed great merit.

But the Hartzells told her in no uncertain terms that if she went and did not stay for an entire year and possibly get this theatrical nonsense out of her head, they would disown her. Faced with this emotional blackmail and demand for loyalty from those who had been kind to her, in a pattern she'd repeat, she capitulated.[11]

She obediently stayed a year with the Hartzells. But as soon as it was over, she left Puerto Rico to restart her life and return to the MacDowell Colony.

CHAPTER 3

The MacDowell Colony

On her first visit in 1920, Dorothy had met and befriended Dorothy DeJagers. This time a man, another future collaborator, claimed her attention.

He came up to her one night, politely standing when she entered the room, something other men at the Colony rarely did. He held out his hand and said, "'I am DuBose Heyward.' I thought he was very good looking and had a charming deep resonant voice. As I took his hand, I was surprised by its extreme thinness." He was as frail in health as she, having suffered polio as a teenager. "His well-padded coats concealed the damage to his arms and chest," however. He was fond of music, and when she spun records on the phonograph, she discovered that he was a good dancer as well. In an alternate version, she contradicted herself, saying they met when she asked the first person she saw for directions. That was the "very delightful and brilliant DuBose Heyward, scion of an old Charleston, SC family," she claimed to have been told.[1]

However it happened, there was an instant attraction; his first impression of her, later fictionalized in a scene set at a dance, "was one of eyes, dark brown, and very intent.... Then she smiled, and he knew ... daring and mischief was there.... And beauty, too.... Even in that very first casual moment of meeting, he knew that she was deeply motivated." Besides that, they must have realized what else they had in common. Although he was there as a poet, Heyward had earlier flirted with film scenarios and playwriting. An early amateur artistic triumph of his, a one-act play called *An Artistic Triumph*, had been produced for one night at a social event in his hometown in 1913. Like her *Cello, Harp, and Violin*, it was about struggling artists, set in an atelier, inevitably, in Paris.

DuBose Heyward (Edwin was his first name, but no one ever called him that) was five years older than Dorothy; as was the case for her, his father had died early, when DuBose was about three. While Dorothy had been able to finish school before taking care of her mother, DuBose, never good at lessons, dropped out voluntarily to help support his family, which was as aristocratic as it was impoverished. Instead of owning rice plantations like his ancestors, one a signer of the Declaration of Independence, DuBose's father, Edwin ("Ned") Watkins Heyward, had worked in a rice mill and lost his life there in a freak accident on May 20, 1888. DuBose's mother, Janie Screven DuBose Heyward, spoiled by her young husband, retreated into widowhood and never remarried. A woman of conviction but also of convention, she felt limited to pursuing only those genteel ladylike things one in her station could do to support DuBose and his younger sister Jeannie: she could take in guests, paint china, versify, and publish poetry, along with amusing sentimental essays about the local Blacks.[2]

Janie raised DuBose to be a Southern gentleman, which translated into his obligation of doing almost everything for her, which in turn, by all appearances, he was more than happy to do. She, for instance, would not consider walking half a block alone without his protective male presence, and decades later DuBose would astonish women in New York insisting on accompanying them to the curb and hailing a taxi. Earlier, Janie had worried in her diary whether anyone would cut her fingernails for her after her husband's death.[3]

DuBose had visited the MacDowell Colony the year before, not as an official invitee but as a guest of a promising young poet, Hervey Allen, who had been championed by imagist Boston poet Amy Lowell. Born in Pennsylvania, Allen had ended up in Charleston after serving and being wounded in the First World War, teaching at a local boys school while pursuing his writing. Heyward and Allen hit it off and began submitting their verse to an older author named John Bennett who quickly became their mentor. Born in Chillicothe, Ohio, in 1865, Bennett had come south for his health at the turn of the century and married into a prominent local family, relocating there permanently. As a young man back in Ohio, Bennett had supported himself as a journalist, cartoonist, and deft silhouette artist before writing children's stories. He was beloved for his classic juvenile novel *Master Skylark*, set in Elizabethan England and featuring Will Shakespeare; but after settling in Charleston, he had riled some of the local gentry and their paternalistic and racist attitudes by becoming an amateur folklorist and linguist very much interested in, and very respectful of, African American culture, an anomaly in the Jim Crow era. Bennett enjoyed mentoring Heyward and Allen as much as they did learning from him; the three men joined with a band of women who were meeting to discuss literature on their own to launch the Poetry Society of South Carolina in 1920. Its aim was to bring people together in a social setting to specifically encourage the writing and appreciation of poetry, in the "ancient, beautiful city" (as DuBose would have it in *Porgy*) suddenly being "discovered" by the national press, tourists, and artists.[4]

For a living, Heyward ran an insurance company with a partner. Although others have claimed he sold burial insurance to poor Blacks, extracting endless weekly payments to assure paid-for funerals, he did not. More prosaically, he insured the homes, cars, and belongings of his white peers, using his vast social connections in town as an entree. In another example of his successful salesmanship, he was traveling the South giving readings and serving as an evangelist for local-color poetry, a volume of which, *Carolina Chansons*, he published with Hervey Allen in 1922. He annually escaped the torrid and humid Lowcountry summers for a primitive shack in the cooler North Carolina mountains. "I have set myself the task of earning in eight months sufficient to support life for twelve, so that I can write for four," he explained. Now he was an officially invited MacDowell colonist in the bracing air of New Hampshire and in the equally bracing company of well-known artists like the beautiful, sexually alluring, and bohemian Elinor Wylie, "just about the most brilliant woman I know," the poet E. A. Robinson, and the winsome playwright Dorothy Kuhns.[5]

The attraction to Dorothy was strong, "the first real romance in the life of either," she believed; they slipped into each other's studios to visit during working hours, a sharp violation of the rules. When caught, Mrs. MacDowell blamed Dorothy, judging her a "siren" or vamp trying to tempt the young poet from his muse; both DuBose and Dorothy feared that, if not expelled outright, they might never be asked back. Mrs. MacDowell did not like women, another colonist theorized, especially young attractive ones. Those who were invited were "rather mousy, rather neuter, and rather past youth. They were usually small and graying and rather twittering," descriptions that fit neither Dorothy nor Elinor Wylie, putting Mrs. MacDowell on high alert. Fortunately, the Colony's official greeter, a kindly older woman named Lou DuBose, was sympathetic to DuBose and covered for him. A native of South Carolina, she'd claim DuBose as kin, demanding he call her "Cousin Lou." (Once back south in Camden, South Carolina, when the Colony closed for the winter, Cousin Lou would pay a visit to DuBose's mother, Janie.)⁶

At the Colony that year, poet and playwright Belle McDiarmid Ritchie's one-act farce *His Blue Serge Suit* was staged July 28, 1922, as a fundraising benefit. Dorothy was cast as the female lead; composer and future Pulitzer Prize winner Douglas Moore played her husband, and other cast members/colonists included the Irish poet Padraic Colum and composer Arthur Nevin. DuBose's part was to play Dorothy's brother, an expert casting call, for, as many would suggest in the coming years, there was an uncanny resemblance between the two; "they seemed more like twin brother and sister than husband and wife," a friend wrote, comparing "their [similar] apparent fragility and four very large, very luminous, very brown eyes." A "Hansel and Gretel lost in a wood, perhaps of their own making" is the phrase editor Emily Clark would mint in an essay about them.⁷

The play's plot twist centered on the borrowing of a man's suit, something DuBose knew firsthand. While Janie had thought it wonderful her son could wear the clothes of an older cousin, at one wedding, DuBose dared not sit, the hand-me-downs being too tight to allow it. In the play, the stage directions had Dorothy's character throwing her arms around her brother and kissing him. Rehearsals went without a hitch. "At the performance," however, "he kissed back, and not a brotherly kiss." He was thirty-seven, she thirty-two. While no words were exchanged, each had the understanding that they would meet again and continue the romance that, fittingly for a playwright, began on a stage.

Being the Southern gentleman Janie had raised him to be, Heyward broke Colony rules by going AWOL, accompanying Dorothy on the train to Boston, before he went on to New York to take the Clyde Line steamer home. Again, Mrs. MacDowell blamed "siren" Dorothy.⁸

They wrote to each other often, he addressing her as "Little Dorothy" and "the bravest little person in the world," and signing himself "Always" or "With Love." After a time, DuBose's mother began writing, and courting, Dorothy as well. In his first letters, he complained of working in the still steamy Charleston, while Dorothy, in the heady atmosphere of Radcliffe, during her second year with George Pierce Baker, worked with the Harvard Book Shop Players and soon was focusing on another play she dubbed *The Dud*. DuBose expressed many concerns for her health and gave her advice on how to extricate herself from an engagement to another man somehow foisted on her against her will. (How that happened is not known—she kept DuBose's letters; did he not keep hers? They don't survive.) He also warned her about getting too friendly with an African American woman she had met, assuming the other woman would want something, perhaps even equality, from Dorothy.[9]

The year passed swiftly, Dorothy consumed with her work and studies, DuBose taken in by the social whirl and business demands of Charleston. She finished *The Dud* under Baker's enthusiastic direction, and he loved it, sharing Dorothy's same sense of humor. As summer approached, DuBose was reinvited to the Colony, while Mrs. MacDowell, Dorothy was convinced, "jolly well didn't want me back." Dorothy also took it in her head, erroneously, that visits as a colonist were limited to two, and she had reached the limit. Yet, hopefully, she took a job as drama coach in a summer camp in Maine to be in the area. That she was finally invited she attributed to DuBose, who, some claimed, was one of Mrs. MacDowell's favorites. She'd never deny DuBose anything, Dorothy believed. The machinations of "Cousin Lou" had to have been helpful, too.[10]

John Bennett, DuBose's mentor, came to New Hampshire for a brief visit. Observing how often the "youngsters" socialized, taking moonlit walks together, he dashed off a letter to his wife, Susan, telling her that DuBose and Dorothy, "a young girl, slight, bobbed dark hair, attractive face and vivacious," were, in the words of Hervey Allen, "dangerously and fatally involved in mutual regard."

On the night Dorothy was sure Heyward was going to propose, he spoke instead of a visitor arriving the next day. Knowing how attached he was to Janie, Dorothy had every reason to believe it might be her future mother-in-law. But "a Charleston girl is arriving tomorrow" is all the stammering Heyward got out.[11]

The next day, a coolly poised and arresting woman appeared.

Five years younger than Dorothy, much more sophisticated, and wealthier, the new arrival, introduced as Josephine Pinckney, was as aristocratic and as well placed in Charleston society as DuBose. She was a budding poet and had been involved with the group of women who joined with DuBose and others in founding the Poetry Society. The question was—and always would be—how much, and in what other way, were they, DuBose and Josephine, involved with each other?

They had known each other for years, although Pinckney's life had never been cramped by poverty like Heyward's. While he adored and took care of his mother, Josephine often escaped hers. Camilla Scott Pinckney, "Camilla the Gorilla," as she was sometimes dubbed, had the reputation of being overbearing, a woman who would have no scruples in keeping her daughter away from bachelors and bridegrooms considered unworthy, as Heyward might have been, disfigured by polio and disqualified by poverty.

Ever curious, Dorothy was intrigued by Josephine; she was not a beauty and, in fact, looked a bit like Janie, square-faced, frank eyes, and close-cropped wavy hair; but over the years distinguished men would flock to her, including presidential candidate Wendell Willkie. Pinckney would become such the doyenne of Charleston society that people would choose the day of their parties based on her availability. Sizing up the situation, Dorothy concluded Josephine could have had DuBose as a husband at any moment, had she wanted him.

This, no doubt, was an anxious moment for Heyward, wondering if two of the most important women in his life, other than his mother, would take to each other. Josephine surely represented his past, the cultured and closed elite society of Charleston, Dorothy perhaps a symbol of future things.

To his immense relief, all got along well during Josephine's brief visit. And immediately upon her departure, DuBose deliberately invited Dorothy out for a walk. On September 4, 1923, in the middle of a field at the MacDowell Colony, he got down on one knee and proposed. She said yes, later making it more dramatic: condensing her stay to one day, September 4, at the Colony.

They walked back to share their engagement only to find that a message had come with equally exciting news. Dorothy's play *The Dud* had won a prize, and producers summoned her to New York immediately. It was for these two life-altering reasons that Dorothy would always say her real life began the summer of 1923 at the MacDowell Colony.[12]

CHAPTER 4

Nancy Ann

Now Dorothy was faced with developments coming as quickly as some of her farce's plot twists. Dorothy and DuBose's wedding was announced by Dorothy's aunt, Mrs. William Hamilton Bayly, less than three weeks before the ceremony. They were married September 22, 1923, at the Church of the Transfiguration in New York, popular with show people and artists. Bayly herself was unable to attend, being abroad for an extended stay in Europe, where, she let it be known, she had been presented at court. Josephine Pinckney could not make it either, sending a telegram that she was "dreadfully sorry," including best wishes from her mother, Camilla. William Van R. Whitall, a Pelham, New York, book collector and expert on E. A. Robinson who had founded a Poetry Society prize to honor Hervey Allen, was recruited as best man.

Dorothy, daunted by her prematurely graying hair, decided to touch it up. But in what would become a characteristic gaffe, she had it dyed so dark the groom did not recognize her, passing her on the way to the ceremony.

Nuptials concluded, the newlyweds opted out of a honeymoon. Heyward reluctantly returned to his job in Charleston to face the raised eyebrows and questions of friends and relations asking why his bride had not accompanied him. She had stayed to meet with producers in New York City.[1]

It was the Belmont Prize, sometimes called the Harvard Prize, *The Dud* had won. Newspapers trumpeted the story of an "authoress" of a three-act play "of character" who had come to Radcliffe from the National Cathedral School in Washington, D.C., omitting the ten-year gap in between. The contest, with its cash award of five hundred dollars, open only to students in George Pierce Baker's English 47 and 47A classes, was presented to the work deemed best suited for professional production. The previous year's winner, *You and I* by Philip Barry, had run successfully for a season in New York and was still on stage in Chicago.

The judges were R. G. Herndon of the Belmont production company, thus explaining the prize's name, drama critic and former Baker student Robert C. Benchley, and Professor Baker himself. Their choice was unanimous. Augustin Duncan, one of the founding members of the Theatre Guild and lesser-known brother of his famous dancing sister, Isadora, was chosen to direct. Billie Burke, the ethereal actress later to enchant millions as Glinda the Good Witch in *The Wizard of Oz* film, would star. Dorothy and Burke met, but the plan fell through and negotiations dragged on: the contract was not signed until November 23, 1923. That concluded, Dorothy went south.[2]

Telling everyone she was from Puerto Rico and not the Midwest, Dorothy charmed Heyward's friends and family, prompting John Bennett to report that she "quite won the hearts of the Charleston folk," something not necessarily easily accomplished in a city where manners, breeding, and place of birth—the closer to Charleston the better—were paramount. Only Josephine Pinckney, Bennett reported, was said to be "put out."

No record exists of what Dorothy thought of her mother-in-law. Janie would be a constant presence in her life over the coming years, and yet the sole surviving letter between them is one of Dorothy's to Janie making much of the flowers the latter sent her to perk up a dull brown hat. DuBose's mother was bosomy, with an alert look in her eyes, smiling like a benevolent Boston terrier.[3]

Janie would live on and off with them, but neither of them would ever be tied down by domestic duties. In Charleston in these years, and throughout the South, nearly every white household could afford African American servants to cook, clean, and free up the matrons for socializing. "When I went to Charleston after my marriage I found in the kitchen Maria, heroine of many of the stories in Jane S. Heyward's 'Brown Jackets,'" Dorothy wrote, giving a shout-out to her mother-in-law with a mention of one of her locally published books in *The New York Times*.

> Maria had come to Charleston from the sea islands and had brought with her a pure and uncompromised Gullah. [Gullah, the only native creole language in the country, had evolved over centuries of slavery, created by a mélange of English and African languages and grammars, the language of the characters in *Porgy* and *Porgy and Bess*.] For the first month she might have as well spoken Chinese to me, and I to her. . . . Maria was always most attentive and polite, but a certain light in her eye betrayed the fact that my dialect amused her greatly.

After a month or two we found that we could each understand the other to a certain degree if each spoke very slowly. But no amount of slowness would convey some of my ideas. Then I would call for my husband's assistance, and he would go into the kitchen and there would immediately issue forth a wild and swirling flow of language—his explanations and Maria's ready acceptance. Then her voice would go on alone with a chuckling accompaniment and I knew that she was telling him what I had said—that I had called the 'butts meat' (her favorite diet) white salt pork, or that I had seemed to say that we wouldn't have rice for dinner because we were having white potatoes [a gastronomical faux pas since all Charleston dined on rice].[4]

To neighbors and family, this seemed only natural; after an unconventional start, a new Heyward wife had come to learn local ways and to settle down in her husband's ancestral city, almost directly across the street from the mansion, now derelict, where Thomas Heyward, the famous ancestor who signed the Declaration of Independence, had lived. But Dorothy was not following the script, for soon she was back in New York City.

It wasn't just that the original actress slated for the part fell through. Although Duncan was credited as director in the early March 1924 tryouts, Clifford Brooke supplanted him in later programs, and his name would appear in the published acting version, suggesting Brooks might have replaced Duncan right before the Broadway debut.

The name of the play had also been changed from *The Dud* to that of its main character, *Nancy Ann*, a giveaway that the romantic comedy was being pitched as a vehicle for an actress. This was something Dorothy would get used to; in fact, none of her comedies would debut under the names originally chosen for them. "Each dealt with a charming teen-age heroine of amazing unsophistication—me."[5]

Audiences meet Nancy Ann Van Cuyler Farr in her New York aunt's brownstone as three more aunts assemble for her debut. A mousy, colorless thing, Nancy Ann presents in an odd dress she has designed herself, knowing one aunt will want to lower the hem while another will want it raised, something that had happened to Dorothy herself on a visit to different aunts in Minneapolis, Washington, D.C., and San Juan. There are other true-life parallels: Nancy Ann admits to having imprinted on Maude Adams as Dorothy had as a child, and she's absent-minded and obsessed with the theater. As for aunts, as the playwright would confess in an interview, "I am a connoisseur of aunts. I've got eight of them, in place of Nancy Ann's meager four. . . . it was actually one of my aunts who suggested the idea of the play to me." It is to her aunts that Nancy Ann admits that she is a dud (a word they do not understand), not only a failure at society's rules, but worse still, she admits to wanting to be an actress. Just as the guests arrive and before the curtain falls on act 1, Nancy Ann flees her debutante party and the role chosen for her by her family by exiting through a window, perhaps a metaphor for Dorothy's own escaping their clutches to go to New York City.[6]

And just as Dorothy did, Nancy Ann shows up in a theatrical impresario's office the next day, as the curtain rises on act 2. In the outer office, various auditioning actresses take verbal potshots at each other, while in the inner officer the impresario, Sidney Brian, based on George M. Cohan, brushes off a lugubrious playwright dedicated to sagas as dreary as Dorothy's first play, *Siberiaward*. Some of the seasoned chorus girls pity Nancy Ann, while others make fun of her. She manages to snag a dress one wants to sell, and she transforms herself a bit, but here, too, at her first chance to plea for a part, she is a dud.

By misadventure, she is locked in the office suite after the other girls have been ushered out and is alone with impresario Sidney. Desperate to impress, she starts screaming, playing a scene as if she is being manhandled by a brute. Sidney panics, thinking she is trying to blackmail him as a seducer. He calls the police, and she dissolves into tears, crying out for her aunts at the end of the second act.

They appear in the third act, having trailed her to the theatrical office. The police arrive, and in a comedy of errors, Sidney starts to see that Nancy Ann might be the sort of unspoiled girl child he needs to cast. As in Dorothy's earlier farce, *Love in a Cupboard*, Sidney and Nancy Ann start acting out in real life the play he is having trouble writing. The play revolves around a murder in a haunted house, and it calls for the actress to scream, a skill Dorothy herself claimed to have; and it's heard by Nancy Ann's aunts in the waiting room. They rush in, and Nancy Ann, convinced more than ever that she is a dud, escapes just when Sidney realizes she is perfect for the part in his play and in his life. She is brought back by the police; Sidney and Nancy Ann act out the curtain line of his play; and as the real curtain falls, they kiss.

Casting for this light, farcical romantic comedy called for a young ingénue, a small slip of a girl who could shed her dowdiness to bloom into a beauty. Herndon, the producer and contributor of the award, felt he needed a "name" to carry a play by an unknown author, a not unreasonable idea; it was common for playwrights to think of an actor for a particular part. But Dorothy had no say in his choice: film and Broadway actress Francine Larrimore.

Born in France into the distinguished Adler Yiddish theater family, including Stella Adler, Larrimore, however, could never pass as a fragile debutante. Her forte was slightly bawdy glamour and sex appeal, and as a star she could make demands. The producer was willing to give into them, and Dorothy, in her first experience on Broadway, despite disagreeing, gave in helplessly. In her script, she had called for seventeen parts, noting that "one actor may play [all] the [five male] 'bits'" (including a dialect-speaking blackface butler); also, one actress could take two minor roles, reducing cast members and thus salaries. But by opening night, nineteen actors and actresses filled the stage, all, according to Dorothy, at Larrimore's request. This drove up production costs, but there was worse to come.[7]

The sultry actress had the habit of referring to herself in the third person, thus telling Dorothy that the script "didn't give Larrimore a chance to do the things that Larrimore's audiences expect her to do." Larrimore then directed Dorothy to write a scene that would show her in a bedroom, in her lingerie.

When Dorothy objected, the producer took her aside and called her "little girl.... You are always little girl," Dorothy soberly realized, understanding the term was "not [said in] affection." Capitulating, against her better judgment, she rewrote the scene five or six times, only to have it revert to her original by opening night March 31, 1924, after tryouts in Pennsylvania and Atlantic City.[8]

The august critic Alexander Woollcott divined Dorothy's disgust: "it is not difficult to picture Mrs. Heyward envisioning a dainty, fragile . . . kind of primrose swaying in delicate winds of her comedy. Thus, the casting of Francine Larrimore for this role must have bewildered the authoress not a little." On opening night, Larrimore slouched around and presented herself more like a slovenly hoyden than a shy and overwhelmed debutante. Refusing to disguise her physical charms, she displayed them, in a stunning scene, nearly disrobing and showing the audience her panties, something shocking at the time on Broadway. Dorothy's stage directions called for the shy heroine to modestly withdraw behind an open door to change into a different dress. Larrimore, to get her "lingerie" scene in, played it bawdily and openly, leaving audiences and even some jaded critics aghast. "Pink Undies in Harvard Play: Francine Larrimore Gives Audience Thrill in 'Nancy Ann,'" ran one headline.[9]

In a fuller description, another critic wrote, "Miss Larrimore's disrobing act in Miss Dorothy Heyward's Harvard Prize Play . . . is as astounding in retrospect as it was thrilling at first blush. It is stuck mid-way in a play which does nothing to prepare for so liberal an event, and nothing thereafter to equal it." *Life* magazine's critic savaged Larrimore's acting, calling it terrible throughout. Focusing on the play, Percy Hammond was particularly vicious in his assessment, finding it "the cheapest, tiniest, falsest and most obsequious example of professional dramaturgy that I have seen this week." He panned Larrimore for her presentation as a cross between a kitten and a she-bear and dismissed *Nancy Ann* as something more from "a prep school for minor mountebanks" than Harvard.[10]

The *Chicago Evening Post*, however, praised the play for its "Gilbert and Sullivan touches," which must have pleased Dorothy, since her parents had met in a production of *HMS Pinafore*. "It is astonishingly good comedy and this newest alumna of Professor Baker's 47 Class at Harvard swings easily into first place with a real Broadway success," opined the *New York Telegram and Evening Mail* critic. Alexander Woollcott disliked the first act but found the final two "full of engaging foolery" in his review that appeared on April Fools' Day.[11]

But the bad reviews and the miscasting had their effect. "The main thing that is wrong with 'Nancy Ann,'" wrote the observant critic of the *Christian Science Monitor*, "is its label [as] the Harvard prize play. If this play had slipped into New York quietly without any heralding other than the announcement of an author's first play, it would have been accepted as the work of a novice, and not much expected of it, but Harvard prize play is a phrase that has rather a distinguished ring to it." The sheer weight of the award worked to sink the fragile farce.

"It is a rather awful feeling," Dorothy wrote. "Here's a gay, inconsequential little bunch of fluff that's apparently saying all the way through, 'None of this really matters' . . . and a dozen austere critics bend portentous glances on it and say, 'Here's something labelled "Harvard Prize Play." Let's all pull its ears. . . . Let's begin our treatises by warning the public that they will find her play totally unlike the contemporary efforts of Mr. Galsworthy and Mr. Shaw.'" She wanted them to realize that the prize was not for a great piece of art but for a play "best suited to Metropolitan Production"—the aim of Professor Baker's class.[12]

But with critics divided, audiences dwindled, and producer Herndon asked the author and actors to accept reduced royalties and salaries; he had already been neglecting to pay Dorothy what was already owed. For advice, she contacted a more experienced playwright friend, who told her to demand the sums and, if not delivered, to void the contract and have all rights revert to her. *Nancy Ann* closed at the 49th Street Theatre in May after forty performances.

But it went on the road, and in 1925, a year later, Dorothy, returning to Charleston, encountered what it had become. In a brief talk to Agnes Scott students, to whom DuBose had lectured as well, Dorothy had spoken with despair of what had "happened to 'Nancy Ann' in her transit from my manuscript to the New York stage."

In visiting the semiprofessional Kramer players now rehearsing it in Charleston, Dorothy saw fresh horrors. Unlike the bloated Broadway show, this version was so much of a sadder, stripped-down version that she doubted her own authorship. "Instead of being harassed by four aunts in the first act, now [she] has only two. . . . And the girl reporter has mysteriously changed into a man." Other changes were "quite baffling. I cannot see why Nancy Ann should announce her departure at the end of the first act by a letter instead of making her escape through the window in the eyes of the audience but behind the backs of her unsuspecting aunts." John Bennett wrote sympathetically of the fiasco as Dorothy went down to the Victory Theatre to do what she could to save herself from embarrassment locally.

Another odd change was the alteration of the name of the male lead. Dorothy had dubbed her theatrical impresario Sidney Brian originally, but in New York he had become James Lane Harvey, perhaps sounding more like George M. Cohan, upon whom it was based. As soon as she got rights back, she reverted to the original name of her hero, and that's how it was published in 1927, licensed and distributed by Samuel French. It was this popular, often-staged amateur version, closer to the spirit of the original, that would eventually be restaged in Charleston's premiere venue, the Academy of Music, about a decade later, with the title role assumed by a much more apt and better-cast actress, Alicia Rhett, soon to win worldwide fame as India Wilkes in the film *Gone with the Wind*.

With this vindication yet to come, Dorothy, reeling from the dismal failure of her lifetime ambition, nevertheless picked up her pen and immediately started to write a new play. But now an unanticipated, immovable object blocked her way. DuBose, either upset by the play's failure or concerned for his wife's health, forbade her to continue. In his courtship letters, he had written that she needed someone "to take you in hand and make your decisions for you," something he apparently still believed, despite the fact that he knew she had hated it when her family had tried to do just that. One wonders how much of this came from him thinking she was as weak as she looked, or from his desire to have Dorothy conform to what Charleston husbands expected their wives to be.[13]

She gave in, wanting to keep DuBose from worrying, especially now since it was his turn to write. *Nancy Ann* folded just as summer approached, the time for his annual trek to the North Carolina mountains. To give her husband peace of mind and allow him to concentrate on his work, she agreed to stop writing. But behind her docile façade, honed by years of experience placating her family, she merely pretended to have capitulated. Dorothy instead was concentrating intently on what she heard DuBose read to her—fresh bits of his work in progress—each evening. It was the story soon to be known to the world as *Porgy*.

CHAPTER 5

Porgy

ORIGINS

DuBose was at a crucial point in his life, a crossroads. He was thirty-nine, a partner in a successful business, married now for not quite two years, no children. More than anything else, however, he longed to write full-time, but Janie and his traditional Charleston gentlemanly upbringing were front and center, urging him to shoulder male responsibilities and support his family. While Janie did make some money on her own, giving lectures, she was not quite the literary sensation other biographers have made her out to be; in fact, she depended on "son," as she called him, emotionally and financially, even living with him and her daughter-in-law for periods at a time. And DuBose's sister Jeannie's husband, Lieutenant Colonel Edwin Register, had died fighting a typhus epidemic in Poland, so DuBose was now helping her financially too. He had some investments, his business income, a tiny house he owned at 76 Church Street in downtown Charleston as well as Orienta, the primitive frame house in North Carolina where he spent his summers writing.

The thought of the season coming to an end and returning to work was heartbreaking. If only fall would not come, when his old life, like a jailer, would be waiting for him. In Charleston, pursuing the arts was considered, if not exactly feminine, then definitely not manly. George Herbert Sass, possibly the best poet in Charleston in the early years of the twentieth century, had published under an assumed name while supporting himself as a lawyer and the master-of-equity. And John Bennett, regarded as the only "professional" writer in town, really lived on the money and shrewd investments of his wife, Susan Smythe Bennett. DuBose did not cast a particularly virile presence but had a delicate, weakened frame, and this was worrisome.

Dorothy had to understand what he was feeling, for she, too, had suffered ill-health and yearning, having her ambitions dismissed and thwarted by a well-meaning family that tried to straitjacket her. A creative artist and woman determined not to be dependent on, nor be supported by, a man, even as she got along with her very male-dependent mother-in-law, Dorothy was a subversive force in her husband's life. Unlike most women of her day, she was not worried about stability or being supported. Instead, she encouraged DuBose to gamble and follow his dream, which would really be following her lead. This made her not just *Porgy*'s first audience but also its midwife, bringing it into being.

Their journalist friend Emily Clark cast it melodramatically: "In June 1924 Dorothy . . . suggested that he give up his job [as a co-owner of the Heyward and O'Neill Insurance Company, not just for the summer—but completely] and write . . . *Porgy*. Tragedy faced them if the book failed, for every bridge had been burned behind them. Dorothy was eager to take the desperate chance." With a bit of trepidation, DuBose took her advice, straying from the sensible, gentlemanly, Charleston thing to do. He quit his job, sold his house on Church Street, and decided to write full-time.

Had he married Josephine Pinckney, he would never have deigned to live off her money and would have had to support her. Josephine's argument for not marrying—ever—was her conviction that if she did, it would clip her wings. She'd be forced to surrender her independence and bend to social conventions dear to her family and her city, settling down to domesticity with a husband. And it's hard to imagine the raised-in-wealth Pinckney, who summered in Europe or New England, roughing it in the North Carolina mountains as Dorothy did. The Heywards wrote in ramshackle wooden cabins; Josephine eventually would have her maid cater to her while she wrote in a protected third-floor study. Seeing him leave the insurance company, Pinckney wrote rather acidly to Boston Brahmin poet Amy Lowell that DuBose had given up his business, with "noble recklessness . . . in spite of a delicate wife," a wife, she neglected to add, who was setting her husband free.[1]

The inspiration for his work that summer had come from a newspaper article published in March 1924, right before *Nancy Ann*'s debut. It was brief, a police blotter vignette, describing how African American street beggar Sammy Smalls had fired a gun, fighting over a woman. Handicapped, Smalls had tried to escape the police in the goat cart he used for transportation. This pitiable figure, laughed at by many, suddenly became a hero to Heyward, the object of an epiphany. "Thinking in terms of my own environment, I had concluded, that such a life could never lift above the dead level of the commonplace." But Smalls had opened his eyes to human and dramatic possibilities. "In that brief paragraph one could read passion, hate, despair," emotions rawer than Heyward himself had ever perhaps felt. The idea of a man who could not walk using any means possible to outrun fate must have resonated with someone who had sat on the sideline for years, too timid to take a leap.

He and Smalls shared another unacknowledged link that Charlestonians were too polite to mention. Heyward had been crippled by polio and had a skeletally withered left arm. Smalls had likely been crippled in his legs by polio, too. ("When Gawd make cripple, He mean him to be lonely," would be a motif recurring in the *Porgy* story.) Heyward, although well placed into Charleston's social network of cousinship and sociability, was finding himself alienated as an artist, seeing things differently, adhering less to the city's values. Marrying Dorothy and not Josephine had been a token of an inner rebellion brewing.[2]

At the Colony, where they were both invited back, DuBose wrote feverishly, using his skill as a poet to color his story. It was not until after he finished his manuscript, however, and signed a contract for it, that he changed his main character's name from Porgo to Porgy, the former having come from a real-life, crude wooden doll brought from Africa, clutched in the hands of a small, captured girl sold into the DuBose family. In her lectures to entertain tourists for a fee, Janie assured her audience that everyone in her family knew the story of Chloe and her doll Porgo. It was either modesty or for a more euphonious sound, as well as Porgy being a local fish sold by African American street vendors, that prompted DuBose to change it from Porgo; Janie, following suit, thus helping to start the rumor that she had written the novel and not him, changed Porgo to Gobo when she continued to tell her quaint tourist stories.

As he wrote, he read his work daily to Dorothy and soon began to include other artists at the Colony. Chard Smith, biographer of Edwin Arlington Robinson, was there that summer and later recalled "beautiful DuBose and Dorothy—both semicrippled, he by polio, she by arthritis" at the gathering. "I remember [other colonists] Constance Rourke and Rose Cohen [too]—down in their Barnard studio to hear his experiments in prose. He [DuBose] plied us with personal charm, orange juice and so-called gin, but to small purpose. We all agreed that the story of the little crippled Negro beggar was atrocious, and that he and Dorothy . . . would be wiser to starve" than to continue to write such stuff.[3]

But Heyward refused their advice, cleaving instead to Dorothy's and his own mounting self-confidence. If leaving his job behind to write had been daring, so, too, was the "atrocious" subject of his novel, for in writing it, he was moving beyond his mother's and his city's dismissive and, at best, sentimental and stereotypical depiction of Blacks. His "contemplation of [Sammy Small's] real, and deeply moving, tragedy" was now nudging him from noblesse oblige and condescension to empathy for Blacks, which in the 1920s, in the American South, was a tad dangerous and trailblazing.

Heyward's own peer, Octavus Roy Cohen of Charleston, was growing rich publishing racist stories of shiftless Blacks aping white culture, portraying them as comic stereotypes or lowlife fools. Heyward had avoided that by fortuitously falling under the influence of Ohioan John Bennett, who had already seen Blacks—and utilized them—as the legitimate basis for high art. Furthermore, neither Bennett nor Dorothy, also from Ohio, had any historical ties or vested interests in slavery. They did not feel the need to defend the institution or mourn its Lost Cause passing. Neither had grown up in a Southern way of life dedicated to segregation or seeing Blacks as second-class citizens. Locally bred Josephine Pinckney, to become a novelist herself, would never write directly of Blacks or race but only of social changes in white Charleston society.

DuBose would always pay his literary debts promptly. He had dedicated his first collection of poems, cowritten with Hervey Allen, to their joint mentor, John Bennett; his first solo volume of verse was a tribute to Mother Janie; and when done with *Porgy*, he gave credit where it was due: the book, he noted, was "For Dorothy."[4]

The novel, passed to a publisher by John Bennett, appeared in late 1925, and to everyone's astonishment, it was not only a critical success but began to ascend some bestseller lists, proclaimed as a new note in Southern literature, applauded by both Black and white literary and social critics. In a single work, he had not only broken from years of established literary racist traditions but had also made a leap from promising poet to praised novelist. Many in the literary world took note of this sudden new arrival, looking at him with wonder and astonishment. Back in Charleston, those who had known him, his friends and family, began a reassessment, too.

Dorothy noticed a change in their neighbors, like watercolor artist Alice Ravenel Huger Smith, of a great family and pedigree, who lived in a splendid mansion across the street from the newlyweds. Dorothy noted that their whole house could fit in Smith's drawing room. Smith, once friendly, was now more diffident. She and many others in town were pleased for DuBose, of course, financially at least; but did he have to sell out to achieve it? And DuBose's mother's friends, Dorothy recalled, "would meet me on the street and say, 'Can't you persuade dear DuBose that there are so many good books to be written about white people. It is a shame for him to waste his talent.'" Why couldn't he have remained a Charleston gentleman selling insurance, publishing lyrical poems about the legends and lore and the beauty of the Lowcountry?[5]

What, they wondered, had prompted him to change and go to the gutter for a story about poor Blacks, instead of celebrating the white traditions of their proud and lovely old city? To many, this was a betrayal; he seemed to be deserting his class and abandoning the bedrock belief of white supremacy in favor of celebrating and dignifying the loud, noisy, and allegedly immoral Negroes who lived in the slum up the street, the model for Catfish Row, the book's fictional setting. When these neighbors had taken up a petition to shut down the slum and evict them all in 1922, Heyward had not signed it. What had come over the old DuBose they had always known?

The most obvious answer, of course, was Dorothy, the woman from off, which meant anywhere beyond the Lowcountry. Ohio might be bad enough—but Puerto Rico! She was not the simple, sweet woman she had appeared to be on first meeting but instead had unconventional ideas and did not do conventional Charleston married-lady things. (In the future, when Judge J. Waties Waring would challenge segregation and abandon the local point of view and rule for integration from the federal bench, people in town would similarly blame the new Michigan woman he married for "infecting" him with liberal ideas.)

American impressionist Lilla Cabot Perry, a friend of the Heywards from the MacDowell Colony, was living in Charleston in the early 1920s, recuperating from diphtheria, and recovering from some family crises, a virtual recluse. One local scene she produced, *On a Balcony, Charleston, South Carolina*, features a woman she and scholars have never identified. The petite subject stands in a dark dress with white cuff and collar, prim as a pilgrim, in contrast against the background flowering trees. Yet the woman's red cloche worn over her bobbed hair is vivid and arresting; her tired brown eyes, slightly shadowed, with care or ill-health, stare soulfully. Her self-possession is evident, nevertheless, present in her confident smile, her grit and determination seen in the lift of her chin—that motivation DuBose had noted at their first meeting. In 1925, the year *Porgy* was published, Perry caught the spirit (if not the best likeness) of Dorothy Heyward, both fragile and determined simultaneously.[6]

Dorothy was not just defying the Charleston order and an order from her husband but staying true to her calling. Against DuBose's wishes, she was dramatizing *Porgy*.

"While the novel *Porgy* was still in process of being written, I began to see it as a play," she'd reply to a query of how the adaptation came to be. The letter writer had addressed his query to DuBose, but he turned it over to his wife as being the true authority. From the very first, "it seemed to me that the novel *Porgy* was drama as it stood and lent itself to quite kindred dramatization."

"DuBose," she acknowledged, "did not agree with me and tried to persuade me that there was no play in it." "In fact, he not only withheld encouragement, he went further; he was dead set against my dramatizing it. Ten years later he was to be utterly convinced I should not try to dramatize *Mamba's Daughters*. But I did."

> DuBose was not an unreasonable man, [she was quick to note;] he had two reasons for why I should not dramatize *Porgy*. First I had demonstrated that I was not the stuff of which good theatre people are made. When my first play flopped, I had flopped with it. As a result, DuBose wanted no more plays in the family. Secondly, no sane producer would ever produce my play. DuBose thought that a Negro review, such as *Shuffle Along* [or Octavus Roy Cohen's *Come Seven!* the standard fare on stage in those days], could be successful, but [not] a large scale, expensive, serious drama! And here I was, talking about actually putting Catfish Row [her idea for a name for the play]—a great, crumbling, three-story mansion—on Broadway! Even more absurd, I wanted faces in every window. I would certainly be wasting my time.
>
> When the book *Porgy* was published and critics spoke of it as the first novel to portray the Negro simply as a human being, instead of a comic, a devotee of Ole Massa, or a social problem, DuBose was happy. But he assumed that his complete break with tradition rendered *Porgy* non-commercial. He was wholly unaware that he possessed a property of great value.
>
> As for me and my writing ambitions, the doctor prescribed a rest cure [those shadowed eyes in the portrait]. DuBose prescribed that, if I *must* write, I write a mystery. (Interestingly, I don't remember his ever having read one.) He thought, no

doubt, that the writing of a mystery story would be a pleasant form of relaxation—for the person who could abide them. I never abandoned for a minute my intention of dramatizing *Porgy*, but in the interest of family peace, I began to make passes at writing a detective story.[7]

Interestingly, the detective novel, later to be published, focuses on literary collaborators, and specifically one who steals the other's idea. "As the best method to winning him to my point of view I began to write it. I think that I worked about five months on the first draft [of the play], during all which time he thought I was writing my mystery."

As she followed her real desire in secret, "he was only a few jumps ahead of me." Once the book was published, letters arrived from authors asking permission to adapt it, none of which apparently survive. DuBose, to her dismay, "had nothing whatever against" letting others who "were so foolish as to wish to dramatize PORGY" to work on it. While denying her, "DuBose nearly gave the rights . . . to three would-be dramatists," the only one she'd name being Lynn Riggs, whose *Green Grow the Lilacs* would be the basis of the Broadway musical *Oklahoma!* With competition like that gaining on her, "I chucked the mystery story into the cupboard and got to work on PORGY."

But there were complications. "I am, I am afraid," she qualified, "a very slow worker . . . but also I was unable to give all my time to writing." While it's not possible to determine what else consumed her, it may have been her health—or a miscarriage, one she was known to have suffered but never divulged the date of. That could have also prompted DuBose and a doctor to tell her to rest, and possibly accounted for the tired look in the Lilla Cabot Perry portrait. With the first draft finally done, she chose her moment strategically.[8]

"DuBose's uncle had come for supper that night. After the meal, we sat around the fire," suggesting, if in Charleston, it would have been the colder months of late 1925 or early 1926 after the book's release in November. "Uncle Edwin, DuBose's mother, and DuBose were stoically set to listen to my opus, so I read them the first draft of the play *Porgy*," she being canny enough to show her hand only in front of beloved Janie and Janie's brother. To her great relief, they liked what they heard. Courting her, DuBose had once suggested an idea for a comedy they could cowrite; she had declined that opportunity then, but now the time for collaboration had come.

She'd always minimize her contribution. "I had worked for months on the original draft, but we completely rewrote it in two weeks," she wrote in one place, while in another, closer to the actual time of its composition, she contradicted that, saying, "After I had read the first draft to DuBose, I worked another month or two with his help and suggestions." He was otherwise engaged, working on his second novel, *Angel*, to be published in 1926, the manuscript of which shows signs of her editing. "DuBose joined me as a working collaborator during the final stages." Out of the glare of print and beyond earshot, she admitted that the play was 95 percent her work, something she'd reveal only in notes to herself.[9]

She also minimized other conflicts that emerged as they worked together. "I always over-write horribly," she confessed, "then cut and cut and cut—and then never get them short enough." DuBose, on the other hand, often achieved his end product with not much more than a first draft. Furthermore, he "wrote very fast—for three hours a day."

"We were geared to very different speed limits," is how she put it; and he, as the man in the household, was in the driver's seat. "He felt about writing in the afternoon the way a Pilgrim Father felt about plowing a field on Sunday. Not only did he refrain, but he required that his neighbor do the same." DuBose, "who was not handicapped by ever having read a book or taking a course in playwriting," dictated how things should go in the rewriting and collaborating and ended their sessions at noon. "He concentrated on my 'ho-hum' . . . Gullah language. I had had to make up most of the lines as there is very little dialogue in his novel." Yet "he laughed at my *Porgy* crap game. He said I had them all talking like fairies. *Perhaps* he rewrote every speech in that scene: they would have flowed from his pen. . . . But he left the structure as I had built it. The important speech in the play and opera that begins, 'Lor' I'se tired dis night—' is still said or sung at the moment I chose as the most effective—but I *may have* first written something like: 'I sure am tired tonight' [*emphasis* added, showing her constant belittling of her contribution]. DuBose reworked scenes I had built without changing my building but giving them a touch of brilliance I do not possess."[10]

While he was alive, Dorothy never varied from her claim that DuBose was the main author. She cleaved more to the conventions of what was expected of a wife, after all—or perhaps she gave him what he needed, understanding that her utter confidence in her skill might conflict with, and undercut, his. For in writing it, she had flagrantly "disobeyed" him, something Janie would never do: to minimize this, she seems to have taken the tack that dramatizing

Porgy was really not a creative act. In the novel and in the play, the character Porgy, unable to walk and stand on his own, constantly feels the need to prove his manhood to Bess, and she builds him up repeatedly. Dorothy was doing the same for DuBose, and Janie, in her seeming total dependence on him, may have been doing it, too. In interviews, letters, and short essays dashed off before his death, Dorothy never upstaged her husband but always said she was just the helper, adapting his story, not changing it. "All the dramatic scenes in the play were right there in the novel," she'd repeat as late as 1939, a statement that is patently untrue. Dorothy discarded many scenes from his narrative and created others on her own; and as for the order of those scenes, again, skirting the truth, she claimed, "We used them for the play in the same sequence," which ignores the shuffling, editing, and eliding she did.

In another memorable phrase, she spoke of sticking to his work like a "leech"; she was so insistent on that, repeating her claim endlessly, that most came to believe her without examining the matter. The woman who could play a naïve waif, being buffeted by aunts and fate, had convinced others, and possibly even her husband as well as herself, of her ineffectiveness. In this manner, very early on, she began the process of erasing herself from the play's and the opera's history. When she had first created *Cello, Harp, and Violin*, based on a short story, George Pierce Baker had informed her it could disqualify her as a playwright in his contest. It's possible she really did believe that adapting an existing work was not playwriting.

But scholar Frank Durham, who knew them both, disagreed. "Dorothy Heyward had had academic training and firsthand experience in the theatre, as a playwright, and, briefly, as an actress. Her knowledge of theatrical effectiveness, her gift for dialogue, her sense of dramatic form supplied the technical skill her husband lacked," he wrote. "Heyward collaborated with others—Hervey Allen, George and Ira Gershwin, and Josephine Pinckney—but only with his wife did there seem to be the complete merging [or submerging] of egos which results in the ideal integration of two talents."[11]

DuBose, as less experienced than the more published Hervey Allen, had deferred to him in the production of their book of poetry, *Carolina Chansons*. Arguing over their collaboration, Josephine Pinckney, after some "stormy— almost violent—sessions," flatly walked out on DuBose, and discarded every word he had tried to help her with on her historical novel *Hilton Head*. Heyward would soon insist Ira Gershwin's name be put on lyrics Dorothy believed Ira had not improved. With Dorothy, however, it was the reverse.[12]

While she did most of the work, he accepted her insistence that he was the genius behind it. As time passed, he would allow the story to be repeated. Possibly he did not even notice, or maybe he even believed that the work was his, and she was just the craftswoman making it happen.

But her fingerprints and her creative genius are all over the play. All one has to do is compare his novel to the script and libretto that came from it to realize that it is not his, but Dorothy's version, that played on Broadway, and in opera and movie houses all over the world. While, yes, it is a story based on her husband's book, she truly transformed it. In the play and in the opera, Bess, on being granted a divorce, is said to have gone from woman to lady with the stroke of a pen. With Dorothy's pen, *Porgy* underwent a truly similar and remarkable transformation.

CHAPTER 6

Porgy

NOVEL TO PLAY

The novel is episodic, centered on Porgy and secondarily on those in the teeming African American slum called Catfish Row. After a poetic invocation, the action starts with a murder in a crap game; the perpetrator, the stevedore Crown, escapes after killing a man named Robbins. When the white police come, they accuse an innocent old man named Daddy Peter of being the culprit. He says Crown committed it; but with cruel prejudice, the police lock him up as material witness until Crown can be found. There is a brief sketch of a scene as Porgy attends a saucer burial to pool money to get a decent funeral for Robbins, and a following one of bathos and farce in the graveyard. As soon as the service is over, the mourners scramble over each other to exit, believing that the last one left will be the first to return in a casket.

Porgy is lost without Peter to take him out in his horse and cart and deposit him on street corners where he can beg. In a stroke of genius, Porgy finds a mobility solution through a goat cart, and his world is enlarged with every hope for success.

Sometime after the murder, a devastated Black woman, Crown's girlfriend Bess, turns up, and needing a home, she slips into Porgy's room and his life. The religious "God-fearing" women of the court spurn her, especially Serena, the widow of the murdered Robbins. Maria, the matriarch of the neighborhood, periodically relents and accepts Bess.

The court is menaced by Simon Frasier, who "sells" illegal divorces, and a dope dealer named Sporting Life, who brags about the glamor of New York. Like Bess, each enters separately in the novel. Sporting Life loses money to Porgy in a crap game and starts the rumor that Porgy cheated, triggering Bess to stand up for her man and attack the women for repeating the rumor. The resulting tumult leads to Bess's arrest. She suffers in jail under the indifferent and callous eyes of her white jailers. The conditions are so appalling that Bess comes back to the court delirious and feverish; a few scenes ensue where various neighbors turn to Jesus to cure her, while others seek a conjurer's charm. After some back and forth, Maria comes to realize the charm was never delivered; yet, unaccountably, Bess got well. Despite this, Maria concludes that Jesus is not strong enough to have done it. She shows her own strength by eventually pitching Sporting Life from the court, and he disappears from the pages of the book, never to return, something dramatist Dorothy would see as a lost opportunity.

Porgy changes in his love affair with Bess, as she does too; they join the members of a church group on a picnic to a nearby island, where Bess is accosted by Crown, who has escaped there to hide from the law. He tells her he will come for her in the fall when the cotton crop has been harvested. Porgy, also on the picnic, with a sort of sixth sense God gives to outsiders like cripples, guesses what has happened and asks Bess if she wants to stay. If he can keep her, she will stay, but if Crown comes for her, she knows she is too weak to resist.

A hurricane sweeps in while many of the fishermen are out at sea. The residents huddle together against the storm. In a dramatic scene, Crown returns from Kittiwar Island, the site of the picnic, to seek shelter in Catfish Row. He shocks people with his unholy talk about how he and God are friends, and belittles folks, especially Porgy, for not being man enough to brave the storm to go after Clara who has run out, seeing that her husband's boat has capsized. Clara entrusts her baby to Bess until she returns. But she is lost in the storm along with her husband; Bess claims the baby as her own.

Crown, however, does return, slipping in one night to come for Bess and to murder Porgy. Although the latter has no strength in his legs, he has strong arms. He manages to kill Crown and dispose of the body with Maria's help. He feels he is free at last. (In poignant contrast, Heyward's withered arm was skeletally thin.)

Earlier in the book, a buzzard, symbol of ill omen, has rested on Porgy's house. The doom it foretold comes when white policemen come searching for Crown's murderer; earlier, through the kindness of a white attorney, Alan Archdale, old Peter has been released from jail. As a cripple, Porgy is not suspected of the murder but is summoned to identify the body, which terrifies him. He suspects it is a trick, being told that if a murderer enters the room with his victim, the corpse will bleed, and the truth will come out. In some of his most moving prose, Heyward describes the ludicrous, but tragic, flight of the beggar trying to outrun the police in his cart, the true-life episode reported in the press. Porgy is captured and jailed for a short time for contempt of court, refusing to look on Crown's face. He returns with presents for everyone, won in poker at jail, only to find that Bess has taken solace in drugs and reverted to her old ways. She's been taken off by some men on a riverboat to Savannah. The season of love is over. Maria goes into her room, unable to look at Porgy, now an old man, standing alone in "an irony of morning sunlight."

DuBose had written a powerful and colorful story, but it had to be changed drastically to work as a play. Dramatizing it, Dorothy condensed all the action into nine scenes (which the opera would cling to like a "leech"). Time is condensed from the six months of the novel—April to October—to the play's six weeks, now beginning in summer, allowing a lullaby called "Summertime" to be conceived. And the setting is tied down from the novel's mythical time in an unnamed city to the present in Charleston, South Carolina, with sounds of the bells of St. Michael's Episcopal Church and a view of Fort Sumter, glimpsed from the entry to Catfish Row, in the distance.

To further tighten the story, there is no longer the dribbling in of major characters one by one. Porgy enters Catfish Row after the curtain rises, his locomotion issues already solved, driving his goat cart emblazoned with the ironic phrase "Wild Rose Soap, Pure and Fragrant"—perhaps a tribute to mother-in-law Janie's book *Wild Roses*. Crown and Bess arrive together after him; Sporting Life is already present, too. All main characters are introduced in the first scene. All the minor characters now have names and personalities with lines to say. Their action is blocked and choreographed in the fight that leads to Robbins's murder, Crown's flight, and Bess seeking refuge in Porgy's room.

Before the opera was an idea in Gershwin's mind, Dorothy's dramatization included music and song. Stage directions have it in the very opening with the men singing about the feckless nature of a woman running off for Savannah, leaving her lover for dead, a nod to the novel's ending. Some of these songs would provide both DuBose Heyward and Ira Gershwin with future lyrics.

DuBose had given but a few short pages to the residents of Catfish Row raising money to pay for Robbins's burial, to keep the body from dissection by white medical students. But Dorothy, realizing its dramatic possibilities, plumbed it for all it was worth for her act 1, scene 2, creating a staggering scene of grief, operatic in its intensity. In Serena's room, Porgy and Bess sing a spiritual together about meeting in the Promised Land, which survives in the opera. Drama is added and padded with Peter also being arrested while they mourn, not later as in the novel, doubling the murder's tragic impact, taking away both victim and a witness to it. The novel's next comic and condescending scene, of stereotypical mourners racing from the graveyard to avoid being the last one left, longer than the preceding depiction of the wake, is discarded. "Turning the novel into a play moved the characters farther away from stereotypes to complex human figures," a critic would opine long after both playwrights' deaths, ironically and erroneously crediting DuBose for this change rather than Dorothy.[1]

With these two first scenes the drama is off to a rousing start, in effect a small play within a play—the murder of Robbins and his mourning—setting the plot in motion and giving the viewer a sense of the Row's communal life and beliefs. In the next scene (act 1, scene 3), a month later, we see life returned to normal. The fishermen are getting ready to go to sea. When Jake explains the necessity for such hard work, his lines are all Dorothy's. How else will his son get a college education? he asks, something she had never achieved, and nothing DuBose could have articulated or conceived for his illiterate Black characters. People speak of the upcoming picnic, as Bess moves about majestically, scorned by Serena. Maria dresses down Sporting Life for pushing cocaine, or "happy dust," and for putting on airs of faux sophistication: he is really from Charleston and had only been in New York City for six months. Porgy is told that a white attorney named Archdale will be coming to see him about getting Peter released. Then, as in the book, a Black pseudo-attorney, Simon Frazier (a change from "Frasier" in the novel, perhaps a nod to local pronunciation), enters.

DuBose obviously knew that the state of South Carolina did not sanction divorce; it would not do so until after World War II. Before then, to quash a rumor inspired by the ever-present Josephine Pinckney, DuBose and Dorothy would stage a party to proclaim they were not getting a divorce but were still happily married. In his novel in a few throwaway lines, Frasier's divorce mill is mentioned, and Archdale tells him to stop. It's not known who decided to magnify and enlarge it, while reducing the characters' dignity and turning it into a burlesque similar to the discarded graveyard scene. Suspicion for its inclusion points to DuBose, despite Dorothy's claim for being the architect of the play's structure. Not only is it the same sort of humor as the scramble from the graveside, it also prefigures another distressing episode of low comedy Heyward would concoct in his final novel, *Star Spangled Virgin*, showing Blacks staging a parade of the unmarried, another spin on the institution. He'd further reduce his characters to buffoons in his last novel by having them hoodwinked into believing that there was a man, not a program, coming to help them, named Noo Deal.

In this scene Frazier offers to divorce Bess from Crown to marry Porgy; no wedding ceremony follows, however. But because she was not actually married to Crown, that "complication" costs more money. When Alan Archdale calls foul, he nevertheless philosophizes that it's a pretty fair price to gain respectability and go from woman to lady for just a dollar and a half. This sort of indulgence in a "superior" white narrative voice reflects positions DuBose periodically took in his book, and in an even earlier essay about Blacks, "And Once Again—the Negro," and does not seem to reflect Dorothy's personal point of view. She would fight to keep a somewhat similar descent into bathroom humor from being injected into one of her plays on Broadway by a collaborator. Yet the divorce, vestigial in the novel, is expanded in the same manner as the saucer burial scene, so it may be her construction, after all—perhaps she felt more action was needed to keep up the pace of the play, having honed her skills on writing farces.[2]

In this same scene, Archdale is used as a foil as he asks why people fear a buzzard appearing; it foretells your doom, he is told, if the shadow falls on you. With Archdale gone, the topic switches from panic to picnic. The local Jenkins Orphanage band is heard. Departing from the plot of the novel, Bess, now accepted by Maria, who calls her "Sister," leaves Porgy back in Catfish Row. He has a moment of contentment knowing Bess is happy, but the buzzard descends. On this ominous note, after a death, a burial, a blooming relationship budding between the main characters, and an ill omen threatening them, act 1 concludes. Equitable in her construction, each of Dorothy's three acts would have three scenes.

Act 2, scene 1 is brief. On Kittiwah Island—changed from Kittiwar in the novel, perhaps again a guide to pronunciation—the picnic is over. In the opera, it would become a bloated scene with the insertion of Ira Gershwin's lyrics. As people leave, Bess feels eyes peer at her. It's Crown. She tries to resist him, explaining she's now a respectable woman, living with Porgy, but in a battle of wills between sacred and profane love, he touches her and she melts, and into the thickets they disappear, bringing down the curtain.

It rises again back on Catfish Row, in action that combines, rearranges, and omits scenes from her husband's novel. In DuBose's version, Bess caught a fever and became delirious after a bout in jail. Dorothy's Bess is never imprisoned; Dorothy uses the fever episode to greater effect in transposing it here. Bess lies in Porgy's room giving out hints in her delirium of what happened with Crown on Kittiwah, based on the Lowcountry's then-undeveloped Kiawah Island, where DuBose sailed on outings with Hervey Allen and John Bennett. Her illness is described to Peter, who returns from jail through the ministrations of lawyer Archdale, and the same debate as in the novel occurs. Has Bess been cured by a conjure or by Jesus through Serena's praying? Counterpointing this are the fishermen pulling out to the blackfish banks, with Clara worried about her husband, Jake. The scene ends dramatically with gusts of wind and the hurricane bell ringing twenty times. A storm is coming.

The next scene, the last of this act, is in Serena's room, a nice balance: the first scene of act 2 transpired outside of Catfish Row, on Kittiwah, and the last is acted in the Row's interior. (This reverses the pattern of act 1, with the first and last scenes set in the exterior of Catfish Row, with the middle one, an interior.) The plot of the novel is followed with the addition of many spirituals and dramatization of Crown's bawdy and braggadocios behavior, flaunting God and the storm. Bess, who has told Porgy she wants to stay with him in the previous scene, rejects Crown, who laughs. There is a descent again into demeaning stage business as Crown demands that Maria and some elders dance, showing his mastery, as they mimic the chaos of the outside elements. It ends with him rushing out to try to save Clara, who has seen her husband Jake's overturned boat. The curtain comes with the hurricane's crescendo.

Act 3, after the storm, begins quietly, with the residents mourning the dead, singing their names, including Crown's, who stealthily appears. Maria begs him to stay away, but a few minutes later he is seen creeping into Porgy's room. She overhears a tumult and then Porgy's laugh and his triumphant cry to Bess that she has her man now. He has proved his manhood to Bess and the world by strangling Crown. Maria rushes in to help move the body as the curtain goes down.

Scene 2 follows the novel with white men—a coroner, a detective, and police—arriving to investigate the murder, Crown's body having been dumped beyond Catfish Row. There is banter about how to scare and browbeat the "colored" people, but Maria bests them at their own game. They try to get a confession from Serena, the widow of Crown's victim; and then they accuse Porgy. He and Bess coolly deny it, saying their floor is always clean and there is no spot of blood there. Porgy is told he must come to the coroner's office to identify the body. The whites leave, and the court resumes life. But when the police return to take Porgy away, everyone, including Sporting Life, suggests he flee. Maria tells Porgy that if a murderer enters a room, the victim will bleed. Terrified, Porgy gets his goat, and the whole episode of the flight from the police that so moved DuBose is narrated by the residents of the court, who describe how Porgy is getting away as the laughing police hunt him down. Porgy is caught offstage, and Sporting Life turns to Bess telling her, just as he predicted, it is now just the two of them left standing. It's an ominous foreshadowing on which the scene ends, Dorothy's doing, since Heyward had dropped the dope peddler pimp from his novel long before this point in his story.

The final scene is brief. Porgy happily returns from jail with his goat after five days of imprisonment for refusing to look at Crown's face, charged with contempt of court. He is so happy, in fact, that he does not see that others can't face him, and they drift away. When he asks about Bess, Maria tells him she was not good for him. Serena is now singing to the baby Clara thrust in Bess's hands, and she tells him Bess has gone to New York. The original typed line has her taken there by some men. That is crossed out and "Sporting Life" is inserted in DuBose Heyward's distinctive handwriting, but whose idea it was is not known. Porgy immediately decides on a course of action. His friends assure him he will never find his beloved, but determined, Porgy sets off to do just that; he leaves in his goat cart as the gates close on him.

It is here that Dorothy makes her most significant impact, demonstrating not just her superior understanding of drama and her knowledge of the status of African Americans in the North and South, but also, most importantly, the workings of high art and the human heart. Her husband had looked at love and loss, and there he had left it. With Porgy's defeat, he closed his book, the saga over.

In his correspondence with Dorothy after meeting at the MacDowell Colony, DuBose had lamented how hard it must be to work toward a dream when one is handicapped, specifically meaning her work and her continuing battle with rheumatism and arthritis, not his own polio and frequent illnesses. His mother, Janie, had repeated the same thing to Dorothy almost verbatim. Heyward believed his wife could overcome handicaps to accomplish her dreams; he thought the same of himself. But for whatever reason, he did not allow the dream to continue for his crippled character Porgy.[3]

But Dorothy did; having lived in Boston, having haunted the theatrical world of New York, she knew of the teeming population of African Americans who had left the South for the North. Dorothy was not just nodding to that cultural shift but endowing Porgy with one thing her husband had not granted him: agency. He'd learn from her on this, spinning her idea into the kernel of a story of Northern migration in his next novel, *Mamba's Daughters*.

Dorothy, unlike her husband, did not see Porgy's life as over. Having felt the transcendence of something bigger than himself, she saw how Porgy could be transformed by the experience, enough to summon courage to fight his fate and not fatalistically accept it. This was what Sammy Smalls had done in real life, defying society's expectations and rushing off against all odds in his goat cart. In real life, DuBose was much more of a fatalist than hopeful Dorothy.

In a poem prefacing his novel, Heyward had spoken of a "terrible" new instrument, change itself, being thrust into his characters' hands, demanding different tunes from them, instead of the simpler ones played before. "God of the White and Black / Grant us great hearts on the way / That we may understand / Until you have learned to play" is the not very hopeful way he closed the invoking poem. He saw no solution other than toleration and hope—off in the future; and on that note, he opened his tale.

In refusing to leave Porgy wept over by Maria, closing a door on a scene she cannot bear to see, Dorothy did something remarkable. Her stage directions have the gates literally open for Porgy, empowering him to seek his impossible dream.

The final closing of those same gates of Catfish Row behind him as he leaves signals that the old world and the old ways are lost to him, and a new horizon beckons for any Black man or woman overcoming handicaps, not settling for the status quo, migrating north. The story is more resonant, suggesting that it is more than one man's journey. Indeed, critics would say, and some would complain, that Dorothy's story was not DuBose's; it was not the novel any longer, not the tale of one person, but the story of a whole community. Dorothy had known this early on, suggesting that the play be differentiated from the novel by calling it *Catfish Row* instead of *Porgy*.[4]

Yet it is more than the plot that is altered; her contribution counters the tepid prayer of her husband's opening poem and changes the tone and tenor of the work. While he had called for patience until understanding evolved, she understood all too well that people could not and would not wait, as some, even then, were moving beyond the world of Catfish Row. In watching Porgy leave, residents are witnessing an inevitable change as he reaches for the heroic. Her play is no longer just a peep over the color wall into an "exotic" community of simple people working out their fate amidst joys and sorrows. With Porgy's departure the whole trajectory of the piece is changed, uplifted to loftier art and social commentary. Just as George Gershwin would raise the story to another level with his music, so here Dorothy is elevating it, changing acceptance of defeat and loss into a transformative, but tragic, hope for triumph.

When she read her new ending to her husband, DuBose was more than moved. He sensed she had hit on something remarkable. How had she ever thought of it? he asked. She replied that her new ending was really old and was his after all. He was the brilliant one, she insisted. To convince him, she referenced a stray thought he had jotted down in pencil when he had been an author in search of an ending. And it's quite possible she typed the manuscript for him as she would *Mamba's Daughters*. Porgo, he had mused on one page of his manuscript, "had gone where no one knew—where shadows go in twilight, where the morning stars go in the crucible of day." One wonders if on this slender peg Dorothy managed to hang the heft of evidence to convince her husband of his brilliance. It's such a flimsy, vaporous phrase of vanishing and a great leap to change it into a torturous trek to the metropolis of New York City. She'd compound the lie years later, denying her contribution further, writing to newspaper editor Tom Waring, "we thought it [the new ending] up just in time for the final curtain," "we," including her husband, a good story perhaps, but one contradicted by the copyright date of her script with the new ending: August 2, 1926, more than a year before the play's opening.

The copyright application itself also bore Dorothy's forceful imprint. DuBose, at first, declined to have his name as a dramatist on it at all, remarking that he had contributed too little to take credit. But like Bess determined to bolster her man, Dorothy insisted. As a result, the play's typed title page noted that *Porgy*, a play, was by Dorothy and DuBose Heyward from the novel by DuBose Heyward, giving him two mentions on the page to her one. It was copyrighted just that way, too.

According to Dorothy, they then sent off three carbons from their cabin in North Carolina, without using an agent, to various producers in New York and eagerly awaited the response. It did not take long. All three came back, all saying, "Yes."[5]

Two are known.

The first reply came just over two weeks after the script had been copyrighted, the Actors' Theatre of New York immediately optioning it—in an odd way. Although her name had preceded DuBose's on the title page and in the copyright office, that's not how the contract read when presented for their signatures on August 19, 1926; DuBose's name was above Dorothy's.

The Equity Players (to become the Actors' Theatre) had been founded in 1922 by a group of distinguished American actors backed by funds from Rockefellers, du Ponts, and Morgans. Their goals focused on ensemble acting (certainly necessary for the large cast in *Porgy*), staging plays deemed too risky, or avant-garde, to be mounted commercially (again a plus for *Porgy*), and producing works by American playwrights (a bull's-eye for the Heywards), with a hope the plays would express the life of various American cities (a sweep!). The company included many of the reigning stars of the day, such as Ethel Barrymore, George Arliss, Paulette Taylor, Katherine Cornell (a future nemesis of sorts), Dudley Digges (to star in a DuBose Heyward film adaptation of *The Emperor Jones*), and even Augustin Duncan, fleetingly associated with Dorothy's *Nancy Ann*. The six-month option lasting until February 19, 1927, brought an advance of $250.

Dorothy and DuBose went north immediately to be on hand for rehearsals, settling in Atlantic City "where it is quiet enough to work, and near enough to N.Y. to come over when necessary."[6]

As time passed with nothing happening—no casting, no rehearsals—Dorothy was nevertheless kept busy when her earlier play *Have a Good Time, Jonica* was optioned by prolific Broadway producer William Friedlander, who planned to turn her romantic comedy into a musical. Glad to oblige, she worked on its libretto for weeks while waiting for *Porgy* rehearsals to start. Once again, however, she found herself frustrated by the producer; "he would think nothing of writing me to come from A[tlantic] C[ity] . . . on a certain day and then when I reached N.Y. telling me that he was too busy to see me. I think I must have sat one hundred hours in his office trying to keep different appointments that he made with me." "This was in the pre-*Porgy* days, and I was very hard up but at Mr. F's request I went . . . and staid [sic] for two weeks at a N.Y. hotel at my own expense and worked steadily on the book." Despite her passivity and refusal to complain, Friedlander dropped the project, letting his option expire. She, in turn, refused to refund the $250 he had advanced. And now with the Actors' Theatre plans for *Porgy* stalled, the Heywards preemptively, and possibly not quite ethically, signed a contract with another production company on February 3, 1927, a few weeks before the original Actors' Theatre's option would lapse. Eliding the truth, and apparently not keeping a copy of the first contract, they'd both uniformly state that the first and only deal they ever considered was with their first choice, the Theatre Guild.[7]

Similar to the Actors' Theatre (soon to be absorbed by another Greenwich Village company), the Theatre Guild had been founded by a core of progressive people unhappy with the state of contemporary Broadway. Theresa Helburn, a veteran of Professor Baker's workshop; Lawrence Langner, an English patent attorney; Phillip Moeller, a hopeful playwright; and a few others had started meeting in each other's apartments in 1918 to read scripts the Schubert, Erlanger, and Klaw syndicates that owned all the theaters would never consider. "The Moscow Art Theatre and the Abbey Theatre in Dublin were both flourishing," Theresa Helburn reflected. "The Theatre Guild was to be something new in the world, an unendowed art theatre."

They came up with a novel plan; they'd announce plays they'd stage and sell subscriptions before the season began, thus having money on hand to produce a few experimental works of new playwrights. Guild management was so sold on the importance of the Heywards' script that they told the authors they were willing to lose money on it.[8]

While this was hardly encouraging, the Heywards understood their play would open no matter what; furthermore, it was guaranteed a minimum of a four-week run. In the unlikely scenario that it proved popular, it could continue on Broadway, as the next scheduled Guild play went into production in another venue. Better yet, the Guild had not balked at the playwrights' demand that *Porgy* "would [have to] stand or fall with a Negro cast." This was not a commercial move and is quite possibly the reason the first attempt to produce it fell through. As its name suggests, the Actors' Theatre was actor driven: If the Heywards had refused to sanction any "blacked-up whites" onstage in *Porgy* (something Ethel Barrymore would do with disastrous results in an adaptation of Julia Peterkin's all-Black novel *Scarlet Sister Mary*), the roles could not have been assumed by members of the company. Furthermore, with a serious lack of plays about Black life, and because Black actors were not hired for them, there was a dearth of suitable actors, making the use of Black actors challenging.

DuBose's peer from Charleston, Octavus Roy Cohen, had recently sidestepped that issue in adapting his own novel *Come Seven* by employing white actors in blackface in "distinctly a negro comedy for white folks—[concerning itself] mainly with those characteristics of the negro which are most readily identified by white audiences." That meant: "Their shiftlessness, their pompousness, and their pretensions"—about as far away from *Porgy* as possible. Yet audiences howled, and the play received rave reviews.[9]

Four years later, the first actor to step foot on stage in *Nancy Ann* had been a white actor portraying a butler in blackface. Things were now changing swiftly, and in the vanguard stood Dorothy Heyward. Her insistence, along with her husband's, that the Guild employ Blacks was proof of her prescience in embracing changes for African Americans. And she also got top billing in the Theatre Guild contract.

But she kept her role from the public. Back in Charleston, she and DuBose were subjects of an article in *The Bookman* magazine. The author described what happened one night when the Heywards' apartment went dark. "We admired her calm," the writer said of Dorothy, hosting in her red dress, as the lights came back on, "and we continued eating anchovy sandwiches and chocolate leaves."

When the columnist asked about their upcoming play, he noted how difficult it was to "find out who had done most on the dramatization of 'Porgy' for DuBose says Dorothy is the dramatist and Dorothy says she did only the typing and the hurricane in the play version." The likely author of *The Bookman* piece was John Farrar, who had bought the novel and obviously knew Dorothy's history with *Nancy Ann*. Referencing it, he noted that "although certain actresses are said to be more than temperamental, she is eager to jump into the fight again." She and DuBose went back to Atlantic City in early 1927, ready for Theatre Guild rehearsals to begin.[10]

CHAPTER 7

Stops and Starts

By this time, the drama regarding George Gershwin, "the great menace," had already played out. While waiting in Atlantic City for the Actors' Theatre to mount their play back in 1926, Dorothy and DuBose had searched for possible actors to cast in *Porgy* by attending shows like Paul Green's *In Abraham's Bosom* and the jazz opera *Deep River*, by Laurence Stallings. At the same time George Gershwin was rehearsing his play *Oh, Kay!* in Philadelphia, commuting back and forth to New York, before its eventual opening in the theater that *Deep River* would vacate on closing. One night, Gershwin had reached for a book on his bedstand in the hopes of relaxing; *Porgy* kept him awake instead. Gershwin had been searching for a subject for an opera, having failed to acquire the rights to *The Dybbuk*, a play on medieval Jewish themes, and he had not followed up on an earlier suggestion from Carl Van Vechten, a white cultural critic fascinated with Harlem and Black cultural life, to collaborate on a Black jazz opera. *Porgy* now seemed perfect for his needs, and so he set about contacting DuBose. Either for a better story or due to lapses of memory to come from a looming mental tragedy, Dorothy would later write that Gershwin's inquiry came while she was secretly dramatizing the novel, flushing her out into the open, provably untrue. It's well documented that Gershwin did not read the book until September or October 1926, by which time the play had been completed, copyrighted, and optioned. In an interview with a local Charleston magazine, DuBose told a more likely story: that Gershwin had first contacted him through their mutual friend Laurence Stallings, possibly when all three were in New York in late 1926. However it happened, in late summer or early autumn, Gershwin came to Atlantic City to visit Dorothy and DuBose.[1]

Gershwin, wildly successful as a commercial Broadway composer, brimming with self-confidence, arrived on the boardwalk along with his older brother, Ira, and Ira's new wife, Leonore, nicknamed Lee. Those three trailed behind DuBose and George as the two men spoke; that Dorothy, the prime author of the play, was not involved in the discussion is telling. It was up to DuBose and George, she saw, to decide if her play would see the light of day or be surrendered to the composer, if the first option fell through. No doubt she was nervous, but eventually relieved, for "far from objecting to a *Porgy* play," Gershwin, once his talk with DuBose was over, told her that "he was all for it. He thought it would be a good forerunner for the opera."

And he was right. "It is an adage among opera buffs that operas based on plays have a greater chance of success than operas based on novels," *Porgy and Bess* scholar Wayne Shirley attests. "On the legitimate stage the authors have the chance of experimenting with changes needed to rework a novel into a drama. . . . (You can rewrite Act III of a play two nights before the opening; an opera you can only cut.)" Shirley concluded that "It is probably fortunate that Gershwin decided to defer his operatic version until the play *Porgy* . . . was produced." For, as Dorothy herself realized, "if the play had been . . . awful, it surely would have dulled George's enthusiasm. It might even have extinguished it." Gershwin, on seeing the play, would cheer it, noting his "feelings . . . gained from that first reading of the novel, were confirmed when it was produced as a play," one that "audiences crowded the theatre . . . for two years."

In early 1927 the Guild hired Russian-born director Robert Milton to take charge of *Porgy*. But not sanguine of its success, Milton dragged his very cold feet, so much so, in fact, that Guild personnel came to wonder if Milton had even finished reading the script; and so production was postponed to the following season. That left the Heywards with no reason to stay in the New York area, even cheaply in Atlantic City. They had sold the tiny house at 76 Church to launch DuBose's writing career; their North Carolina shack was not winterized, and Mother Janie was on her own, most likely staying at My Old Kentucky Home boarding house in Hendersonville, North Carolina.[2]

Having had to defer it due to Dorothy's career, now was the perfect time for a honeymoon. By April 1927 they were aboard the S.S. *Majestic*, crossing the Atlantic, encountering at least one passenger unimpressed with them. Writing from the ship, misspelling their names as the "DuBois Haywoods" (no doubt what a Charleston accent sounded like), an unimpressed fellow traveler confided, "I don't care for them much," explaining that the couple of writers were "so unhealthy looking." Lilla Cabot Perry had portrayed Dorothy with dark circles under her eyes; waiting in New York as productions fell through had tried their patience, pocketbook, and nerves. The ever-thin DuBose and Dorothy determined to rest, gain weight, and restore health.

Once landing in England, at the suggestion of novelist Hugh Walpole (who shared a publisher with DuBose), they found a quiet place to stay in Polperro, Cornwall. Heyward wrote Janie of the cold, describing the long, invigorating walks along the cliffs and visits to Norman churches. He and Dorothy were so impressed with the singing of some fishermen in one particular religious service that they later incorporated it into rewrites of *Porgy*. DuBose also wrote of the "gentry"—the wealthier professionals and retirees who invited the couple to tea in their gardens overlooking the ocean. He gave them his highest possible praise, comparing them to Charlestonians, grateful that their English reserve gave him the privacy he needed for writing.[3]

DuBose was behind schedule in finishing and delivering his third novel, *Mamba's Daughters*, a tale of three generations of a Charleston Black family, climaxing in a migration to New York with a parallel white family's story. He gloried in telling Janie of his sale of serial rights to *Woman Home's Companion*, mentioning in an aside that Dorothy was working on a "story," too, but sharing no details. It likely was "The Young Ghost," a trifle of a tale based on the mysterious death of her friend Rose Gollup Cohen, whose autobiography, *Out of the Shadow*, detailing her childhood in a Russian Jewish shtetl and her later union work on Manhattan's Lower East Side, had earned her admittance to the MacDowell Colony. There, in the summer of 1924, she had been one of those clustering around DuBose as he read from his novel *Porgo*. Not long after, Cohen had been cut off from her family for her affair with a much younger non-Jewish man, and her sudden death confounded everyone: was it a despairing suicide, or an accident? One of Cohen's peers, the celebrated Russian Jewish emigrant writer Anzia Yezierska, saw it as a tragedy and used suicide in her short story based on Cohen.

Dorothy, ever the optimist, turned that on its head, instead creating a romantic tale of a ghost haunting a house, trying to let it be known to her grieving young husband that she had not killed herself but had died accidentally. "The Young Ghost" came out in the popular *McCall's* in February 1928, a full year after Yezierska's tragic "Wild Winter Love" was published in the more literary *Century* magazine.[4]

With that tale done, it's likely Dorothy set to writing a novel of her own, hoping she, too, might sell serial rights as DuBose had, and she was also busy typing *Mamba's Daughters* when a letter dated June 27, 1927, arrived from the Theatre Guild's Theresa Helburn.

Although Dorothy was the playwright, and her name was first on the contract, "Dear DuBose," is how Helburn began her letter. After cataloging the director Milton's missteps, she reported that the board had fired him, and she was now introducing his replacement, a young man soon to need no introductions due to his meteoric rise in the ranks of Broadway and Hollywood directors. Not quite thirty, Rouben Mamoulian had been born to Armenian parents in Tiflis, Georgia. A disciple of Stanislavski, he had fled Russia after the revolution for Paris before he was brought to America in 1923 to work at the Eastman School of Music in Rochester, New York. There, through hard work and self-promotion, he had quickly come to the attention of the Guild. Not only were they gambling on the Heywards, the producers were now gambling on Mamoulian: *Porgy* was to be his Broadway directing debut.

Helburn wrote that Mamoulian loved the script but had a few suggestions to improve it. "None of the changes . . . are . . . basic," she assured DuBose. "Indeed, it's a great play," Mamoulian would soon tell the press. "It loses nothing that is in the book and is in many ways more dramatic. It is really a marvelous piece of work."[5]

In the future, however, with no one surviving to contradict him, he'd revise history, aggrandizing his role, mostly at Dorothy's expense, and while both Dorothy and DuBose admired his skills, they would always avoid him, feeling little respect for him personally. Interviewed decades after the fact, Mamoulian would reference a lengthy fifteen-page memo supposedly sent to DuBose with dramatic changes. No trace of it survives in any archive, and if DuBose, who did not often keep letters, managed to hold on to the one from Theresa Helburn, he surely would have done so with Mamoulian's. In her missive, Helburn managed to convey both Mamoulian's and the Guild's critique in less than *three* pages, along with other news and greetings. In the future, many would comment on Mamoulian's megalomania, often behaving as if he had created the whole world of theater himself.

"I have decided to write to you about them at length," Helburn explained, referencing their suggestions, "because you will have time and leisure to think them over this summer, and none of them . . . are the sort which would rouse controversy." The first one was "entirely superficial." Mamoulian, Helburn explained, found the first act too long, with its three scenes comprising the crap game and murder, the saucer burial wake, the time in Catfish Row with Porgy getting a divorce, and Bess leaving for the picnic. Helburn believed it an "excellent suggestion" to change Dorothy's three acts with three scenes each to four acts. The first act would consist of two scenes; act 2 would contain the last scene of act 1 and end with her original scene 2 of act 2, the picnic where Bess encounters Crown. Act 3 would follow Bess delirious in her room in Catfish Row, getting well, and the hurricane beginning. It would end with the hurricane scene. Act 4 would survive as Dorothy's original act 3: Crown coming after the hurricane and being killed by Porgy; the police arriving and arresting him; and the final scene with Porgy's return to find Bess gone. The nine scenes would survive entirely, with now two of them in the first three acts, and three scenes in the final one.

The other advice was minor as well. Helburn suggested that Porgy's character be built up, restoring a tad of his centrality to the play; it might be advantageous to show his interest in Bess from the beginning. Dorothy had already moved in this direction by putting all the main characters together at the crap game. Helburn's third suggestion again built on an element sensed and enlarged by Dorothy. After her husband had dismissed him two-thirds of the way through his novel, Dorothy had retained Sporting Life as the instigator of Bess's tragic end. The Guild liked that and just wanted it enhanced a bit more. "Sporting Life and Happy Dust should be made a menace. . . . We must know he is a real danger," was how Helburn termed it. It could be achieved, she thought, by just adding a line or two of dialogue about "Sporting Life and some accomplices threatening to abduct Bess to New York" earlier in the play.

In closing her letter, Helburn asked Heyward to "think over these points and make whatever changes or notes you think wise." It could wait till rehearsals, due to start September 5, "but you may have inspiration in the peace of Cornwall," she added, signing off condescendingly with "warmest greetings" to "Mrs. Heyward."[6]

DuBose never wrote the other Mrs. Heyward, his mother, about the arrival of this letter, focusing instead on the progress he was continuing to make on *Mamba's Daughters*, leaving any changes to the script to Dorothy.

They worked on their projects in Cornwall till August 9, then going on to London and Paris where they'd rendezvous with world-traveler Josephine Pinckney. They were due back in New York September 1, and whether they made a quick trip south to see Janie is not known. After "one mad scramble since . . . return[ing] to America," the couple, DuBose wrote, were ensconced in Hotel Manger on Seventh Avenue between 50th and 51st Streets "doing a considerable amount of preparatory work on the script" before rehearsals would begin. "It is now commencing to take form," Heyward told his old friend Hervey Allen, "but needs more attention than new-born twins."[7]

Dorothy and her mother, ca. 1895. Courtesy of the South Carolina Historical Society.

Dorothy Kuhns as a young woman. Courtesy of the South Carolina Historical Society.

Mrs. Hamilton Bayly, one of Dorothy's formidable aunts. Courtesy of the South Carolina Historical Society.

DuBose Heyward, ca. 1920s. Courtesy of the author.

Jane (Janie) Screven DuBose Heyward, ca. 1920s. Courtesy of the South Carolina Historical Society.

Josephine Pinckney, ca. 1934. Courtesy of the author.

Portrait of Dorothy Heyward, ca. 1924, by Lilla Cabot Perry. Courtesy of the South Carolina Historical Society.

Dorothy and DuBose Heyward, ca. 1927. Courtesy of the author.

Original 1927 *Porgy* program with Dorothy as lead author. Courtesy of the author.

Later (ca. 1928) *Porgy* advertisement with DuBose as lead author. Courtesy of the author.

Dorothy and DuBose Heyward's bookplate. Courtesy of the author.

DuBose, Dorothy, and Jenifer Heyward in North Carolina, ca. 1930. Courtesy of the author.

The Heyward's home, Dawn Hill, in North Carolina. Courtesy of the South Carolina Historical Society.

CHAPTER 8

Porgy

REVISIONS

It was quite easy for the Heywards to restructure the play in the four acts as Mamoulian had suggested, all nine scenes intact and in order; after that, the first changes they made came in the very first scene. (These additions and emendations can be seen in the 1927/1928 published "Acting Edition" of the play.)

Through added dialogue, Dorothy's forte, the people in Catfish Row tease Porgy of being sweet on Crown's Bess, just as the couple enters. He swears he never swapped two words with her, but his attraction is apparent. Sporting Life is seen clearly as the evil instigator of all that will happen in the play. He is the source of Crown's liquor and happy dust (cocaine), both of which fuel the fight and murder of Robbins, setting the tragedy in motion. After Crown flees and Bess is searching for safety, Sporting Life offers her happy dust and invites her to come with him to New York, but she replies she hasn't sunk that low yet, setting up the end at the beginning. In this heightened version, following Dorothy's impulse to keep him in the drama, Sporting Life functions very much like the shark Maria is seen cutting up in her cookshop: out for blood, alert to any vulnerability. He also is the serpent in the Eden of Catfish Row, the man who has gone off and has returned to corrupt it. This scene also has more of the suggestion of an initial lullaby that would morph eventually into "Summertime."[1]

Scene 2 follows the original almost exactly as written. Ending the act here, after the intensity of the drama of the murder and wake, as Mamoulian suggested, makes it literally a hard act to follow. There is an inserted five-minute intermission.

In the new act 2, scene 1 (Dorothy's original act 1, scene 3), action and dialogue proceed very closely to her original version. There is a bit more interaction between the white attorney, Alan Archdale, who asks Porgy to refrain from begging with his odiferous goat in front of his office. A line of dialogue originally spoken by Black attorney Simon Frazier about gaining power over white people, or at least gaining their favor, by making them laugh, is now Porgy's, rounding out his philosophical character. The divorce sequence is integrated a bit more into the action. As before, the scene ends with Bess leaving without Porgy for the picnic and the buzzard landing on his roof to predict doom. Daddy Tim, a character present in the first draft of the play, has disappeared, with his lines mostly given to Jake, the fisherman, and Peter, the honey man, obviously based on the real-life vendor Ralph Bennett, whose song for selling his wares was now included as well. The Peter mentioned in the novel was not given a profession; nor was he noted to be hard of hearing as he is in the play.

The Kittiwah Island scene (now act 2, scene 2) is longer and has some additions and changes. The boat is leaving, and people say they don't want to be left behind. Bess is now searching for a pipe Maria has lost. The latter claims she dropped it because she saw a spirit, Plat Eye, a folk belief Heyward would use very soon in his ghost story, *The Half Pint Flask*. This sets up what Bess will soon sense: Crown staring at her through the thickets. When Maria is told that Plat Eye is not in the Bible, the dialogue suggests the conflict of the song "It Ain't Necessarily So" that would prompt Ira Gershwin's added opera lyrics in this scene. And there is additional dialogue between Bess and Crown when she asks, "What you want with Bess?" She reflects on how sad Porgy will be when all go back to Catfish Row and she is not there, lines that would transfer verbatim to the opera.

In the next scene (Mamoulian's act 3, scene 1), Bess recovers from the fever almost exactly as originally written. There is less dialogue among the denizens of Catfish Row speculating about what happened on Kittiwah, with more direct talk about it between Porgy and Bess themselves. A line about cripples being able to understand things others can't appears; and when Peter returns from jail and goes out again on his rounds, he now sings his wares.

In the hurricane scene (now act 3, scene 2), some cuts have been introduced. In the original version, Bess went out and saved Porgy's goat, but that is gone.

In fact, all scenes with the goat, except Porgy's arrival in the first act and his departure in the last, were eventually cut; and missing again is Daddy Tim who originally heard Death knocking at the door, his lines now given to the slightly deaf Peter. The lurid "ragtime song" that Crown sings to defy the wrath of God, only mentioned in the original version, is now spelled out, a boast also of his prowess with women. As in the original version, the people huddled in Serena's room discuss what they witness as Crown rushes out: a wharf collapses, and he disappears. Porgy's and Bess's eyes lock over Clara's baby.

The published, or "acting version" of the next scene, act 4, scene 1, pumps up the role of Sporting Life in a very dramatic way. As the mourners sing, intoning the names of the dead, as Crown's is mentioned, he is seen creeping into the court. Sporting Life witnesses the ensuing battle. He hears Porgy's cry as he kills Crown and his later triumphant call to Bess that she now has her man. Maria slips in to help clean up and move the body. The scene ends with the flare of a match, showing Sporting Life downstage, lighting a cigarette, sinisterly taking it all in.

There is less dialogue between the white men coming in to investigate Crown's murder in this revised version, act 4, scene 2. Now the coroner engages with a character named Lily Holmes who once worked for him. There is a bit asking her why she got married but never took her husband's name. She explains that she married Daddy Peter, aged eighty-two (old enough to have been born in slavery). If he sickens, he will not linger as a younger man might. (This, too, was based on the real life of honey vendor Ralph Bennett, whose second marriage to a younger woman was reported in the local press.) Again, the whites leave, and the Blacks take back the court, singing "I can't sit down!" a phrase that appeared in the novel and which Ira Gershwin would take up in one of his songs. When the whites return to take Porgy away to identify Crown's body, Sporting Life manipulates and predominates the dénouement, saying falsely that although he doesn't know who killed Crown, police can trick a suspected murderer in the presence of a corpse. If the body bleeds, the police know the suspect is guilty. The line had previously been Maria's, consistent with her belief in superstition over religion. After planting that fear in Porgy's head, Sporting Life malevolently suggests and engineers Porgy's escape in the goat cart. As in the earlier version, the Black people watch in hope, while the whites make sport of Porgy and his inevitable capture.

With him gone, Sporting Life tells Bess her man will be locked up for a year. There's a boat soon to leave for New York; the Clyde Line steamship pier was just a block or so away from where Heyward put Catfish Row in his imagination. Bess spurns his happy dust and goes into her room. Maria triumphantly tells Sporting Life he doesn't know Bess, but the dealer has the last word in the scene. "You don't know happy dust." This is a literal following of what Mamoulian had suggested: Sporting Life, doom, and happy dust all linked. This bit, however, would be cut by opening night, reverting to Dorothy's original version, her portrayal of Sporting Life apparently malevolent enough, with the forced focus on drugs—and not the willpower of Bess to resist them—now deemed unnecessary.[2]

The final scene is a bit longer than it was originally. Porgy comes in, driving his goat, with tales of how he won at craps in jail, even taking the shirt off the jailer. Now he has gifts, a hat for Lily Holmes, a dress for Bess, and one for Clara's adopted child. When he sees the infant in Serena's arms, he inquires as to Bess's whereabouts.

His friends tell him that Sporting Life repeatedly exaggerated to a dejected Bess how long Porgy would be jailed. First drunk and dispirited, she then succumbed to his happy dust and left with him. When Porgy understands that she has gone to New York, up North, past the U.S. Custom House, he is decisive. Since he has come from jail with his goat, there is no need to call for it. In his cart, he leaves, and the child Scipio opens the gate for him. Porgy turns in the direction Lily pointed. St. Michael's church chimes the hour, and the gate clangs shut. Serena is still singing the lullaby to the baby.

That is how the play *Porgy* has come to be known over time, frozen in print in its published form, available in orange paper wraps as the Theatre Guild Acting Edition just as the play premiered, and out in a trade edition hardcover with a dust jacket, an introduction by DuBose on "the American Negro in Art," and illustrated endsheets the next year. That version, however, is not what the audience saw opening night, or in all subsequent productions, including what Gershwin witnessed. The *Porgy* they saw was more memorable and dramatic—and much closer to the opera that would result. It had evolved in the crucible of rehearsals, through agonizingly long nights, and rewrite after rewrite, with the playwrights, primarily Dorothy, amending the script daily. After one particularly grueling five-hour script conference, with "mostly hard-boiled, commercially minded Jews," as DuBose described them to his mother, the playwrights "saved most of it, and frankly, built up some bits, to advantage."

Heyward also wrote despairingly to Janie about how painful it was trying to get the actors "scarcely more than amateur" to follow Mamoulian's direction. He could not understand why they held back. It went deeper than the fact that many lacked serious experience: many were from families that had escaped the South. The much-praised Rose McClendon, their Serena, for instance, was from Greenville, South Carolina. Just a generation or even less removed from the Catfish Row–like poverty and prejudice, they were now being asked to revert back to those roles that whites cast them in on stage and in real life. The actors and actresses who were used to performing professionally were confounded by and distrusted Mamoulian, who talked down to them as "children" in rehearsals, even as he tried to break them out of the stereotyped Stepin' Fetchit behaviors that most white directors and audiences usually demanded of Black actors (or those in blackface) on Broadway. This was something jazz singer Ethel Waters, later a friend of the Heywards, understood. In her view, the actors could never give up signaling they were acting. "There was no 'I'm a bitch!' and 'I'm a whore' in it. The characters in *Porgy* kept apologizing for being themselves."[3]

Many on that stage were not actors at all. In the huge cast were men and women who were just there for the fun, including budding Harlem Renaissance writers Robert Bruce Nugent, Wallace Thurman, and Dorothy West, as well as Harlem social arbiter Edward G. Perry. West would note that these chorus members, as a group, were disliked by the rest of the cast; yet Wallace Thurman would lead a strike to get the cast higher wages than their seventeen dollars a week.[4]

Heyward would write about—and praise—some of the cast members, but often with left-handed compliments. In his foreword to the published play, he'd explain how his belief in the rhythm of Blacks, or at least of "primitive" Black bodies and societies, had guided him. In a too subtle and not very successful attempt to tamp down Mamoulian's claims that he alone was the genius behind this, DuBose emphasized that he and Dorothy always believed that "the background itself must be an active, significant factor, a powerfully flowing stream of movement, colour, and sound, upon which the story [would be told] as though it were a dominating human force." All reviewers, critics, and historians would credit Mamoulian for such movement and vitality on stage, ignoring Heyward's claim, only published after the play opened. That Mamoulian *was* a master at this, there is no doubt, and after his debut, he'd take his trademark mass rhythmic storytelling skills into future theatrical productions and films for which he'd become justly famous. His direction was superb, but it must be acknowledged that he did not add anything to the play that the authors had not expected him to bring forth. His genius of choreographing movement and action is best seen in *Porgy*'s final scene: it is ushered in with his "symphony of sounds" as people hammer, sweep, snore, and iron in a wordless aria of communal life before the action commences.

"Our Porgy and Bess are developing marvelously and play the love scenes with such beauty, simplicity, and purity, that one forgets they are Negroes, and loses that unpleasant feeling about them," DuBose wrote Janie, possibly the only person with whom he could share such distaste. In the same letter he reported that when Cleon Throckmorton's set and the goat appeared in rehearsals (the latter on September 18, the former a few days before), it made an incredible impact.

Both Throckmorton and Mamoulian had gone to Charleston to seek inspiration and soak up atmosphere and ideas. Because the Heywards had been in Cornwall at the time, they had relied on DuBose's mentor John Bennett to show them around, and it was Bennett who was instrumental in suggesting that the local Black orphanage's band, sent around the city and the country to raise funds, be used in the production. Heard offstage in the first iteration of the play, after many back-and-forth communications and dickering with New York City officials over child labor laws, the Guild succeeded in having a Jenkins Orphanage Band appear on stage. The compromise worked out required performers to be at least fifteen years old, and information in the program offered patrons a way to make financial contributions to the orphanage if desired. One cannot but wonder how Throckmorton in particular got along in staid Charleston; he was known for organizing the very libertine Krazy Kat Klub, with a marked homosexual presence in his native Washington, D.C., and he was also active in encouraging theatrical programs in segregated Black schools.[5]

His set saved the show, Dorothy firmly believed. "One night, a week before the opening, everything looked terrible. DuBose and I had no expectations beyond the proposed four-week run, but we did so greatly want the curtain to go up on the opening night. Lee Simonson, then of the Guild executive directors, was storming up and down the aisle. . . . Lee would cry out in pain [as scenes were repeated] 'Not again. I can't stand it!'"

"It was a lovely night for the authors," Dorothy reminisced. "I was sitting by Theresa Helburn. Lee Simonson—not seeing me in the dark theatre—bent over her and said, 'How much money have we sunk in this blank blank thing?' She whispered, 'Too much to go back now,' and gestured towards the massive set. . . . Without it, I believe PORGY would have died in rehearsal." Getting little sleep, the cast, director, producers, and authors plugged on. DuBose confessed to Janie, "I am a poor hand at this rewriting work, but Dorothy is wonderful and has worked like a horse, and has done most of it."

While Dorothy was rewriting *Porgy*, DuBose was closing in on the end of his novel *Mamba's Daughters*, witnessing events that would appear in its pages. "I wonder what Grannie would have said if she could have seen me singing at the piano with the cast today, and calling them ladies and gentlemen," he wrote Janie. "We drop the 'Mr.' when we talk among ourselves, but colored are always 'Mr.' and 'Mrs.'"

In the forthcoming novel, he'd dramatize a scene of cultivated Blacks in Charleston addressing each other that way; and one white character based on Heyward wondered if it would be so horrible after all to use "Mr." when addressing a Negro.[6]

More to the point, Kate Wentworth, a stand-in for Janie, while watching Black cast members perform in a *Porgy*-like play, assumes the actors would "expect to be addressed as Mr. and Mrs. no doubt—No, I couldn't manage that."

Even more significant than the "mistering" episodes in his novel are *Mamba's Daughters'* closing scenes, when Saint Wentworth, the stand-in for DuBose, is also in the audience of that musical Negro drama with his mother and wife, Valerie. That may sound like "Dorothy," but there the similarity ends, for in the novel, she is Dorothy's antithesis: Valerie prompts Saint to *give up* his artistic dreams for business. Critics have wondered how prophetic DuBose could have been, seeming to describe a work like *Porgy and Bess*, which would not debut for another seven years after his novel's publication. Heyward, in reality, was not seeing the future but recording what he was seeing daily in rehearsal on the Theatre Guild stage. As opening night grew near, he felt in his bones that *Porgy* was going to be like nothing ever seen before. And he'd have the benefit of critics and their comments to help him clinch his forthcoming novel's climax. In it, Saint Wentworth overhears audience members discussing the spectacle of Black actors triumphing on the stage. "What's it anyway, a play—an opera—a pageant?" they ask. There is authorial ventriloquizing when a character responds, "Can't you feel that it's . . . something that Stallings and Harley got a glimmer of in 'Deep River'—that the Theatre Guild caught the pictorial side of in *Porgy*; that Gershwin actually got his hands on in spots of in 'Rhapsody in Blue'? It's epoch making, I tell you."

The play that premiered on October 10, 1927, with a star-studded audience attending the night before, was different in many ways from the two previous versions discussed, Dorothy's original copyrighted 1926 script and the later Guild and Mamoulian-prompted rewrite that appeared in print as the authorized acting version. Preserved in the Theatre Guild Archives at Yale University is a copy of the prompt script, the master copy used during the run of the play. It alone presents what audiences saw: the version of *Porgy* rewritten mostly by Dorothy that made people realize they were witnessing a landmark event in American theatrical history.[7]

A textual analysis is necessary to understand the historical play *Porgy*.

Act 1, scene 1 has a few additions from the acting version. All the extras are named; and the stage directions suggesting that dialogue begin in true Gullah, an idea present from the start, takes on substance and resembles Dorothy's own acculturation in the kitchen with their Gullah-speaking cook, Maria. In the transition from Gullah to English, Maria wonders how Porgy got his name; Jake assumes it is because he eats so much fish, Porgy being the name of the local blackfish, obfuscating the evolution from Porgo. Then the Gullah subtly becomes closer to standard English with invitations to a crap game.

To learn Gullah, and to give local inflections to the dialogue, some actors had turned to reading Ambrose Gonzales's *The Black Border*, a compilation of tales in the vernacular. Dorothy had encountered Gonzales in 1925 when the Columbia, South Carolina, newspaper he edited awarded her a prize for her play *Love in a Cupboard*. Other cast members were tutored by a friend of the Heywards, Sam Gaillard Stoney Jr. of Charleston, who stopped by the theater during rehearsals and stayed to help the cast with the "rhythm and feel of the language[;] he talked to them in Gullah, spicing his talk with amusing anecdotes. . . . They laughed until Jack Carter, who played Crown [and who was so light-skinned he had to be 'blacked' up], actually rolled on the floor." "The actors' one objection to the play was a six-letter word meaning "Negro." Dorothy had employed it in the play, as her husband had in the novel, not as a pejorative hurled by whites but by Blacks as "one person speaking to another." Her husband, she reminisced, never used the word and would not speak to whites who did. Later productions of the opera would replace the N-word totally.

There is also more of a suggestion of a lullaby being sung, and all in all, there is much more singing in this scene, with many extras taking up the song Jake had initially sung alone. The next scene of the saucer burial or wake (act 1, scene 2), greatly expanded by Dorothy from the novel, follows her earlier two versions very closely, again with more singing and, as to be expected, more stage directions, more lyrics written out, to be used in the operatic version.

Act 2, scene 1 cuts some of the stage business of Bess haughtily ignoring other women in the row but inserts language that the opera would use as neighbors note how happy she and Porgy are, singing in their room. Then something that was never in any script but was suggested in the novel appears. Reminiscent of a scene in the book, Lily Holmes hints Porgy might be cheating at dice; Bess fights her, saying she, Bess, is fair game, but Porgy is not; Maria praises a woman for standing up for her man. Then lawyer Frazier enters to give Porgy a message from Alan Archdale to please not beg in front of his office. He sees Bess, and the issue of a divorce is brought up. Annie says she wants one too, suggesting that was needed to tie it more closely to the story. With strategic cuts, the scene continues as before, but now the Jenkins Orphanage Band comes on stage. "I'm so happy, I can't sit down," people sing as they leave. But the whole sequence about the buzzard being the bird of ill omen, leading to Porgy's doom, has vanished. It would be inserted and then cut from the opera as well.

The Kittiwah Island scene (act 2, scene 2) has also changed. Gone is Maria's talk of plat eye, while the debate between superstition and religion has morphed into an argument between Annie and Jake, who asks her if this is a picnic or a prayer meeting, possibly leading Ira Gershwin to "explore the possibilities" of giving Sporting Life lyrics "with a cynical and irreligious attitude" to sing in his "It Ain't Necessarily So" song. (In his telling, Ira omits the fact that the play had a song about Satan in this scene; in his insertion, Ira would have Sporting Life doubt the devil as evil.) Heyward, in his introduction to the play, gives credit to actors Ella Madison and Wesley Hill entirely for this interpolation. It's more important to note that in this version, as in all the others Dorothy wrote, Sporting Life does *not* attend the picnic as he uncharacteristically would in the opera; he has put on his city airs and disdains such provincial doings; more importantly, there is no sound dramatic reason for him to attend. This scene ends act 2.

Act 3, scene 1 begins after a ten-minute intermission. Bess is delirious; the fishermen are setting out; Maria's conversation about suspecting Bess has seen Crown on Kittiwah is cut, having Porgy speak of it to Bess directly instead, once she is "cured," the business whether prayer or a charm effected it retained. But language originally in this scene, describing the effect Crown has on Bess, referencing his hands on her, has been cut and inserted earlier, in the previous scene between Crown and Bess on Kittiwah, not only making that scene longer and more pointed, but freeing up time for the addition of a new character created by a member of the cast, Leigh Rollin Whipper of Charleston.

Born there in 1876 of families dedicated to Black education and politics, he studied law at Howard University but gave it up for acting. He'd have a long career on Broadway and in films, becoming the first Black member in Actors' Equity and a founder of the Negro Actors Guild. He also had previously directed an entirely Black play on Broadway.[8]

Cast as the undertaker, with just a few lines in the saucer burial scene, Whipper decided to quit the show. When Mamoulian asked why, he told the "mad Armenian" that his rigid directing style was alienating the cast. Many called Mamoulian a genius, and Dorothy may have agreed, but her definition of "genius" was someone who could be rational one minute and completely irrational the next.

Whipper took Mamoulian under his wing in a tour of Harlem one evening. They went to a trade union meeting, met attorneys and physicians, and then went to the Harlem YMCA, before entering Smalls Paradise, run by another Charleston expatriate, African American Ed Smalls, no known relation to Sammy Smalls. Mamoulian was spellbound by the whirling done by the waiters with their trays. They ended up at a storefront church service, where the plate was passed, perhaps reminiscent of the saucer burial scene. Mamoulian, ever the egoist, never acknowledged this, not just minimizing both DuBose and Dorothy's role but that of others as well; the story only came out when a scholar interviewed Whipper in the 1960s. The next morning after their rounds, however, Mamoulian no longer called the actors children but "folks." He immediately let them weigh in on the saucer burial scene. Whipper stayed on.

While Mamoulian did not acknowledge Whipper's contributions, DuBose did—in print. On the day Whipper introduced himself to DuBose and Dorothy as a fellow Charlestonian, "We got him to help us check the atmosphere of the play," Heyward explained. "Then he asked me if I remembered the old crab vendor who had been a figure about the streets years before. I did remember him only vaguely. [Whipper was nine years older than DuBose.] Our undertaker then illustrated him for us. 'Go ahead and put him in Catfish Row,' we told him," making him "not only the actor, but playwright as well." The "bit" does not appear in the printed acting version, yet "crab man" is listed as a character with information on actors and credits; the crab man character would survive into the opera as well.[9]

With compression needed, cuts being made even up to opening night, the hurricane scene was made tighter, with the rather demeaning bit of Crown making specific characters dance cut. It ends with him chasing Clara into the storm, without the running commentary of the frightened men and women looking out the window describing his fate. In this scene on opening night, a vital cue was missed, with Crown taunting God, and the thunder not coming when it should have to answer him back.

In Mamoulian's act 4, scene 1, the mourning of those lost in the storm continues as before; the previous pumping up of the role of Sporting Life as witness to Crown's attack on Porgy has been cut. The first revision's addition of a conversation with Sporting Life suggesting to Maria that Crown might still be around, and that two men involved with one woman will mean tragedy for someone, is retained as Dorothy intended it. The scene ends with Porgy's triumph over Crown, crying out to Bess that she has her man now, instead of focusing on Sporting Life watching it happen, inserted after Mamoulian's suggestions. This keeps the attention on Porgy and gives him his moment of joy and triumph, without having Sporting Life upstage him. Dorothy's dramatic instincts were better than Mamoulian's here.

The next to the final scene (act 4, scene 2) has many cuts, reducing the roles of the white men invading the Row, as they go directly to putting Serena through their questions if she witnessed Crown's murder the night before. Turning to Porgy, they question him about it and eventually take him away as Peter had been carried off in the first act; it's much cleaner and direct. Thus, the description of Porgy running away from the police, the real-life occurrence that had fired Heyward's imagination, ironically disappears from the play.

Sporting Life again gives the line about the trap being set by whites, luring a murderer to view his victim, making the body bleed; and he lies to Bess on how long her man will be gone. Tempting her with New York, he offers happy dust. She gives in but then thinks better of it, calling him a rattlesnake, and goes to her room. The scene ends with the wily Sporting Life saying he'll leave her a dose, which he does, saying maybe she will change her mind. She opens her door to retrieve it and the curtain descends, a more nuanced and haunting behavior pattern, taking the Mamoulian-inspired focus off of happy dust and putting it back on Bess as Dorothy had intended.

The final scene (act 4, scene 3) begins with the symphony of sounds created by Mamoulian, showing his genius in orchestrating a normal day on Catfish Row through the sound effects of its busy inhabitants. When Porgy returns, he is not in his goat cart because he was arrested and taken away from Catfish Row, not chased down the street. The police return him in the paddy wagon, or Black Maria, offstage. Once he realizes that Bess is gone, he calls out, "Bring my goat," sparking the question as to why he needs it.

If statements made by and for Mamoulian are to be believed, he has to be credited with not just changing the first part of the final scene with his symphony of sounds but changing its ending as well. Joseph Horowitz in his book on Mamoulian quotes *Porgy and Bess* scholar Wayne Shirley's praise of the added line "Bring my goat" as being one of the most moving in theatrical history. (It's changed to "bring my coat" in productions that have no goats in them.) Horowitz attributes its brilliance to Mamoulian; but with no goat present in this version of his return to Catfish Row, the cue *has* to be given, and the line *has* to be said to allow Porgy's exit at the end of the play to match his beginning entrance. And it's not so much the words themselves (more moving, according to Shirley, than well written) as what they convey: Porgy is not going to stay; he is going to defy fate, which was Dorothy's contribution and not Mamoulian's. Mamoulian has also been credited with the addition of lyrics by those surrounding Porgy sing as he leaves, "I'm on my way to the Heavenly Land." Horowitz writes that this addition to the script is in Mamoulian's handwriting, acknowledging that this is not necessarily confirmation that he was their author. DuBose would soon be credited as sole author of those lines in the opera, however, and Dorothy, in an offhand remark, noted their similarity to the play's, so her testimony suggests her husband and not Mamoulian as the author. Mamoulian would direct the opera, and so could have claimed credit then for those lyrics had he wanted to.

Horowitz does suggest that these lyrics somehow change the ending entirely. "It bears stressing," he'd write in an article in the *American Scholar*, "that the opera's ending and its re-visioning Porgy, do not originate with Gershwin, or his librettist brother, Ira. Nor does either originate with Heyward and his wife, Dorothy," a statement that seems to fly in the face of facts: Dorothy revised the ending and copyrighted it a full year before Mamoulian ever read the script. Certainly, Mamoulian brought his musical insight to the play, and the song heightens the drama of the moment. It is an inspired addition, icing on the cake perhaps, but not sweet enough to clinch Horowitz's main argument in his book *On My Way: The Untold Story of Rouben Mamoulian, George Gershwin and Porgy and Bess*. Not only does his title leave out Dorothy and DuBose, his text nearly does the same. Horowitz argues that Mamoulian was the unsung hero of the play and the opera, that it was Mamoulian who made it into a different piece of art entirely with his added "I'm on my way" musical ending. The Heywards would always try to avoid Mamoulian in the future, never stating why. And years later, Dorothy would object strenuously to the direction, begun by Mamoulian, that would lend the play, which she knew was tragic, a happy ending.[10]

When opening night came on October 10, 1927, the authors thought it went wonderfully well, better than the dress rehearsal that many dignitaries attended the night before. It's not known when Gershwin saw it, but he loved and "cheered it enthusiastically," obviously realizing that his opera now had a successful structure to compose upon. When the Heywards left the theater that night, they were too exhausted, exhilarated, and excited to sleep. "The hotel at which DuBose and I were staying generously presented each guest with a morning *Times*," she later reminisced. "About dawn a boy would walk along the corridors and hurl a paper at each door.... DuBose and I were still trying to get to sleep when the boy's nearing thuds on the doors of our neighbors sounded like the approach of the 'Gods of the Mountain.' ... We pulled in our 'Times' and read what the critic thought of us." It was not really a bad review, "but to two exhausted playwrights at 5:00 a.m.... it looked terrible."

In his review, Brooks Atkinson expressed mixed feelings about the play, saying it was uneven; another critic would say when it was good it soared, but when it was not, it stumbled, which was the basic substance of Atkinson's critique. He was thrilled with Dorothy's saucer burial scene, which another critic called "one of the most electrifying scenes New York has offered in years," but thought most of the play did not live up to it. "With a cast of twenty-three [speaking] characters, countless neighbors in the bustling alley, and nine fairly disjointed scenes, 'Porgy' emerges as an ebony carnival of crap-shooting, murders, blaring picnics, comedy bits, passionate spirituals, a hurricane storm—a thread of story running timidly through a sprawling production." Yet he called it "always true" and complimented the authors for never deserting that veracity for "showmanship." Other reviews were raves, and Atkinson himself would later return and revise his first qualified opinion. But at the time, the other reviews trickling in, according to Dorothy,

> consoled but did not reassure us, nor did they reassure the Theatre Guild. We were called in conference and it was decided that we should condense and amalgamate and bring the new script to the Guild office at two o'clock on Thursday. [The play had premiered on a Monday; they were given the ultimatum on a Tuesday]. We shut ourselves in our hotel room and worked all Tuesday night and all day Wednesday and Thursday morning, and started for the Theatre Guild dejected carrying a manuscript we did not like. We knew that our story rambled; everybody had told us so. But we feared that the hasty revisions had not improved it. And it was raining.
>
> Our dejection was so deep that we were only mildly curious about all the umbrellas outside the Guild Theatre. There seemed to be a long line of people stretching down the block, foolishly standing in the rain. We knew that the box office for Tuesday and Wednesday nights had not been encouraging, and theatre lines, I think, rarer in those days. Besides we were totally unprepared for anyone to like PORGY.
>
> We went up to the Guild offices and presented our revised script. They looked at us as though the revision were some strange idea of our own in which they never shared. They said, "You're crazy to want to change it. We're a hit," they said. "We would have told you only we just became a hit." The tide had turned without any discernable rhyme or reason. They had not loved us Wednesday, they loved us Thursday.[11]

If one detects a trace of faux naïveté on Dorothy's part, her husband's letter to his mother, however, confirms the fact. In his note datelined "Thursday," he confirmed that on Tuesday they were told the last act was flat, and that for two days, Dorothy and he "had been writing ourselves blind on a new arrangement. We carried it over today but do not know if it will be used." It wasn't. For true to Dorothy's statement, the tide had turned, but not inexplicably perhaps. In his note to his mother, DuBose reported that the reviews were now "splendid" and "the popularity seems growing."[12]

Dorothy had to be aware of what had changed since opening night; yet she never claimed or flaunted the fact that, again, her instincts proved better than Mamoulian's and the Theatre Guild's. For the only change possible to document opening week, other than scene changes going more smoothly, is the alteration in the number of acts, from Mamoulian's four to Dorothy's original three, which would certainly have streamlined the play, cutting out a full intermission.

Brooks Atkinson in the very first review had noted it was a play in four acts; and that was how the first week programs were printed. The programs dated the next week, and all the following ones, showed that the play had been reduced back to three. Those new programs showed two scenes in the first act, four in the second, and three in the third. Surviving evidence in the program Dorothy and DuBose signed to John Bennett reveals that a sheet was inserted during the first week's run, possibly during the two days they had shut themselves up in their room rewriting. Headlined "PROGRAM CORRECTION," it states, "The play will be presented in three acts as follows" with one ten-minute and then a twelve-minute intermission. The prompt script, which served as the manual for the play during its run, with all its technical cues for lights and sound, is in three acts, but one page of technical cues survives from what had been the fourth act, evidence confirming it started that way, all suggesting a change occurred very soon after opening night. While Mamoulian is constantly praised for his streamlining and his contributions, no one has commented upon the fact that the play that became famous was in three acts, as Dorothy had conceived it, with just one variation: two scenes in the first act, four in the second, and three in the third, instead of her original three in each act. The fact that *Porgy* was published as a four-act play in 1927, almost simultaneously with the opening, has further obfuscated the change. All subsequent printings, in 1936, in 1955, and in 1959, with various reprints going on for decades, would also be in four acts.

"The play is so entirely satisfactory now," DuBose wrote his mother on Saturday. "I am sure that the reason for the impression in some reviews that it dragged was due to the long waits between curtains. [And with one less act, there was one less wait.] Now they change like magic, and that effect is gone. The house is always full and the audience is delightfully responsive." Even he did not speak of the play's restructuring to his mother, so it has slipped out of notice. "Standing Room Only now at Porgy!!!!!!!" he wrote to Janie that next Thursday, October 20.[13]

With *Porgy* on its way, and with the play to be acclaimed and anthologized (in four acts) as one of the best plays of the 1920s, the exhausted authors headed home, which then was rented quarters in North Carolina shared with a very proud Janie. She, too, had seen the play, as would her friend Leila Leeds.

Leeds soon raved to Janie how wonderfully true to life the action was and congratulated her on all the splendid newspaper notices. But she was puzzled. "What surprises me about the write-ups," Leeds observed, "is that Dorothy has no praise whatever in her part of it. It is all DuBose Heyward. . . . I hope she does not feel bad about it," Leeds mused. "She certainly did her part splendidly."

While it's interesting that it took another woman to recognize Dorothy's disappearance, equally noteworthy is that Dorothy Heyward never returned the letter to her mother-in-law, but kept it close her entire life. No one else at the time commented on the fact that DuBose would probably never have written the novel without her encouragement, nor would the play have been possible without her, with scenes added, characters created and built up, along with music introduced and a new ending, all hers. *Porgy* may not have been the play and the way she had imagined she would leave a lasting and unalterable mark on American theatrical and operatic history, but that's the way it turned out. Silently and splendidly, Dorothy helped create a classic. If her life, as she stated, began at the Colony, it reached its "glamorous" peak with *Porgy*.[14]

A scant six months later, she almost lost it.

CHAPTER 9
Porgy Abroad

"I have been in a terrible state," DuBose wrote Hervey Allen. It was the Ides of March 1928, and he had just returned to North Carolina after a visit with his old friend. In his absence, he told Allen, "Dorothy ran up a terrific blood pressure and had to be rushed to the hospital for a week. It almost finished me as well as her," he continued, "but she responded immediately to treatment and with care will come through all right now."

Her kidneys had been affected, he added later. Returning from the hospital, Dorothy "was in bed from then until early May, where her little son was born, and went again, without breathing. . . . It was hard on both of us, but the fact that she is spared to me makes me deeply grateful." "The DuBose Heyward baby was born dead," John Bennet's wife, Susan, wrote on May 6, amazingly cutting Dorothy out of the story again. (Was it that she was so tiny and self-effacing that she lacked gravitas?) "I know no more than that but agree that one could hardly expect any stamina for any baby in that couple," she concluded unkindly. In her grief, Dorothy stayed silent and turned to creative work, a project begun long before. But not DuBose. "I am not going to start another book for a year," Heyward vowed right there and then, "and see if we cannot get some joy out of life before we get any older."[1]

True to his word, after turning in his long-overdue *Mamba's Daughters* manuscript, he laid down his pen. He returned to Charleston briefly in mid-January 1929 with Dorothy, dutifully fulfilling the request of the Poetry Society to greet Rouben Mamoulian, who had come to lecture. Mamoulian made no friends referencing the cockroaches and red bugs that had terrified him on his initial visit. A few weeks later, the Heywards, who were having a house built in North Carolina with their new *Porgy* royalties, were back in New York, celebrating *Mamba*'s sale to the Literary Guild. DuBose was reluctant to live there, John Bennett reported, because he feared he would continue to be too associated with Harlem culture and Black actors and literati. Before leaving again, there were literary parties and other pursuits while Dorothy paid visits to doctors and checked in on her playwriting career. More pressingly, however, she was now overdue delivering a manuscript to the Century publishing company. But DuBose, intent on taking time off, left New York at the end of January, taking her with him. They embarked aboard the ship *Providence* for the first leg of a two-month cruise through the Mediterranean and southern Europe.[2]

Sitting in the sun on deck, DuBose wrote to his mother that both he and Dorothy no longer resembled ghosts after New York and the "upset" (probably a reference to her miscarriage). They stopped at Naples, went on to Constantinople and then to the Holy Land, visiting Jerusalem, Bethlehem, Haifa, and the Dead Sea. After Palestine, they went to Egypt, with stops at Alexandria and Cairo, dutifully posing on camels in front of the pyramids. Onboard again, they stopped in Madeira and ended their cruise in Marseilles around March 14, 1929, going by motor coach to Cannes and then to Paris. According to evidence in two of her scripts, it appears that Dorothy spoke French fluently.

DuBose had proudly told Janie that he and Dorothy had been recognized as celebrities, getting a cabin upgrade, and, inevitably, running into Charleston connections. Before landing in France they had authored a vaudeville script based on *Show Boat* that other passengers acted out, while Dorothy and DuBose shouted their lines to them through megaphones.[3]

All this led them to their real destination, London, to witness the European premiere of *Porgy*. On March 26, most of the original New York cast, including the Jenkins Orphanage Band as well as the original goat, left the United States, posing for photographs in Atlantic City, to reassemble for rehearsals and an opening set for April 10, 1929, at His Majesty's Theatre. Special dispensation had been required and granted for the goat to bypass quarantine laws as long as it stayed in the theater. Despite the edict, the goat was stealthily taken out at night to frolic in a park. Mamoulian's direction would be followed, and the Cleon Throckmorton set rose again.[4]

The London program featured prominent photos of Dorothy and DuBose and offered patrons the opportunity to buy copies of the British editions of the play and of *Mamba's Daughters*. Many of the cast members, like Rose

McClendon (Serena), Georgette Harvey (Maria), and Lee Whipper (the crab man), were photographed and featured, too. In this less racist country, Black actors were given more attention, credit, and respect.

To help with Gullah and some elements and customs strange to the British public, explanatory notes were inserted in the program; another thing those flipping through its pages encountered that American audiences had not was Dorothy's diminishment. DuBose now enjoyed top billing as the leading author of the play; and that's how it would remain the entire six-week run, setting a precedent for years to come. In the following decades, she, who would rage at those who dared minimize DuBose's role in *Porgy and Bess*, would write anthologists and others, saying, "If you prefer to shorten [*Porgy a play by Dorothy and DuBose Heyward dramatized from the novel Porgy by DuBose Heyward*] you could use: 'PORGY by DuBose and Dorothy Heyward.'" She was obviously complicit in her own minimizing.[5]

English audiences did encounter some trouble with Black English and American accents, but the play took London by storm. Critics praised its drama, novelty, actors, and music, as international press coverage from Austria, France, South Africa, and beyond confirmed *Porgy* as the cultural phenomenon it was. The play was translated into French, and a Paris production was imminent, but according to its translator, "Mamoulian kept delaying his decision . . . he had several talks with . . . a theatre manager . . . [but] his contract with Paramount [Pictures] did not allow of his directing anywhere else."

Charles B. Cochran had given an opening-night fete, affording absent-minded Dorothy the opportunity of embarrassing herself in a wardrobe mishap worthy of Nancy Ann. "On opening night in the theater and at the supper party that followed, I met almost every literary celebrity of whom I had ever heard. The night was also the debut of the most beautiful dress I have ever owned. . . . I was so cold, and Sir Charles Cochran, the producer, had rushed us so from lunch to an interview to supper that I had no chance to look in the mirror. I only knew I was freezing to death; I had forgotten the dress was backless," and her "woolies"—her undergarments—were in full view to all the guests. (Did no one tell her of her gaffe?)[6]

Publishers Theodore Bayard of Heinemann's, publisher of the British edition of *Porgy*, and Russell Doubleday, "in honour of Mr. and Mrs. DuBose Heyward, whose *Porgy* is the admiration of London," threw another party and gave Dorothy the opportunity to wear the dress again—correctly. The guest list included many women, including popular novelists Clemence Dane (aka Winifred Ashton), Marie Belloc Lowndes, Enid Bagnold, Gladys Bronwyn Stern, Shelia Kaye-Smith, Elizabeth von Arnim, then Lady Russell, and Rebecca West, whom DuBose had met previously, and whose work Dorothy had adapted as a play. According to West, yes, Dorothy's dress was lovely, but so was she: "very beautiful indeed, like a picture by Alfred Stevens, the Belgian, with her dark curling hair which restrains itself from curling too much, and her pallor which is like an exquisite physical form of reserve." West and Dorothy would become friends, and Dorothy would also later befriend Elizabeth von Arnim in her Lowcountry visits, too, perhaps unaware that both women had been mistresses of H. G. Wells. Many of those she'd met in 1929 would eagerly seek her out when she'd return years later. "In fact, Rebecca West devoted a chapter of one her books," a collection of pieces originally published in *The Bookman*, to the party in her honor, but Dorothy once again slipped from the center of attention, as West, instead, spent her energy "concentrating chiefly on Max Beerbohm."

"More invitations poured in for thrilling opportunities including lunch at St. James Palace [with the king and queen], and a weekend with Lady Astor." She who had known presidents in her youth was now to meet royalty. "But I was able to accept none of them," she wailed. Unimpressed with royals and nobility, DuBose, believing a man's own home was his castle, insisted that they leave to check on the progress of Dawn Hill, the house being built in North Carolina. Weeks before arriving in London, he had told Janie, but possibly not Dorothy, that after the premiere, he planned to find a ship to take him home immediately and not linger, a royal invitation notwithstanding. "DuBose led me firmly aboard ship for home" was how Dorothy narrated it flatly in her autobiography. "Our house . . . was under construction, and he wanted to supervise." Ironically, the house, a two-story colonial-style residence rising outside of Hendersonville (for the sum of $7,017) was being financed by royalties from the play, made possible by Dorothy. But she deferred to her husband, and while he could focus on brick and mortar and the swimming pool, she also had something to consume her attention. A message had come to Dorothy when abroad from Broadway producer Harry Frazee, the former owner of the Boston Red Sox who was despised by many for trading Babe Ruth to the New York Yankees. He, like at least two other producers, had fallen for her early play *Poor Paulette*, copyrighted by Dorothy back in 1920; Frazee wanted to stage it but felt it needed improvements. Was she easy to work with? he inquired of the Century Play Company. The answer had come back yes, so preparations were made for them to meet and collaborate.[7]

The farce, rechristened *The Cinderelative* (similar in name to a 1922 Gershwin song), had first been bought in 1924 by John Patton Russell of the Art Theatre, Inc. Russell had been so bowled over by it he asked Dorothy to help him rewrite a play of his. Russell's option lapsed, however, and interest came again in 1928 from the producer John Golden, who had a string of successes on Broadway. The nibble had not led to a bite; but now *Paulette / Cinderelative* seemed destined to see the light of day. But Frazee's sudden death in June 1929 put an end to it. Meanwhile, other personal and professional opportunities beckoned.[8]

CHAPTER 10

Three-a-Days

The failure to mount *The Cinderelative* might have been for the best since another of Dorothy's plays was now attracting attention. The option on *Jonica*, which William Friedlander had bedeviled Dorothy about before the opening of *Porgy*, had not been resolved; it had lapsed, but he was still interested, and another production seemed likely at any moment.

Complicating it further was that she was in hot water for being late in delivering a manuscript by that name to the Century Company. The work, *Hot Water*, had evolved from her earlier, complicated three-act play, the overwrought *Cello, Harp, and Violin*, which had brought her to the attention of George Pierce Baker. She had completely rewritten it, however, freeing her one female and two male musicians from their mired European tragedy by turning them loose as insouciant young artists in New York City. She sometimes used the original play title for this revised narrative and at other times called it *The Curtain Must Rise*. With *Porgy*, she had turned a novel into a play, and now she was attempting the reverse. Literary agents Brandt and Brandt had originally thought the tale could be boiled down into a short story, and maybe in that guise, or installments, it had been sent to *Century Magazine*. But in November 1927, just after *Porgy*'s launch, Dorothy got word from the Century Publishing Company that it wanted it expanded into a novel; a contract for *Hot Water*, later *Toots Ensemble*, was signed in December 1927, with a publishing date set for the coming year; Dorothy would retain all dramatic rights.

"Since leaving New York immediately after the opening of 'Porgy,' Mr. Heyward has been in Hendersonville, N.C. with his mother, Mrs. Jane Screven Heyward and his wife who is working upon her first novel," the *Charleston News and Courier* had noted back in January 1928. But that year had brought on her health crisis and a miscarriage. Then, when she could focus on it, DuBose had taken her off to Europe. The Century Company's deadline was June 1929, but, traveling abroad, she again missed it. She could only work on it in earnest now, back in the States, a full year and half after the contract had been signed.[1]

The curtain rises, or the book opens, on an empty stage at Carnegie Hall, with a full house waiting for a violinist named Ric to appear. When he doesn't, his manager goes to tell him he is in hot water, only to find him literally soaking in a tub full of it, having whimsically given up his concert to think about a concerto he wants to write. The manager tells Ric his professional life is over, and Ric, frivolous and young and unconcerned (there's a lot of Gershwin in him), says he is fine with that.

A year and a half later, Ric takes up lodging in a boarding house as he works on his composing; he meets Jan, an earnest young harpist living next door, slim, gamine, and lovely. A performer her whole life, she has been longing to be a "serious act" on the vaudeville "three [performances] a day" circuit, the basis for the book's eventual title. Recognizing Ric's talent, Jan understands she has a chance of success if they can form a trio with a flutist. Ric is taken with her seriousness and pluck as well as her musical skill. She, in turn, finds the attentions of the young man Tad, heir to a department store fortune, inconvenient. Tad is disinherited by his father for refusing to go into the family business, and so, when, to gain Jan's favor, he picks up a flute and masters it, she bends both men to her will, and a trio, the Jadrics, is born.

Successes and failures follow, informed by Dorothy's experiences in Broadway agents' offices. Ric is amused that he, a prized performer, is unrecognized. Tad, the ham, is always trying to learn as he tags along, with Jan being the only serious one intent on refining their act. Both men inevitably fall for her, Ric vowing not to propose until his concerto is finished, while Tad proposes regularly. Their conversations, befitting a playwright, may sparkle, but as for action, Dorothy tells too much, failing to dramatize it. Ric composes songs for the group; Tad introduces comedic touches and sings occasionally. They rise and soon get top billing.

For Jan, "It was ecstasy to have years of patient labor so gloriously rewarded. . . . Her whole life had been one untiring, gallant effort to perfect herself in her chosen art," Dorothy wrote, revealing a bit of her own story. "Her lofty estimate of herself was not genuine conceit. She had always believed in herself, and now at last the world was coming to believe in her, too." For Jan, as for her creator, this brought "no desire to brag or be puffed up, but . . . expressed itself in a buoyant step, a singing heart, a capacity for harder work than ever before, and a great yearning to be kind to everybody." This is an apt description of the author, giving into the whims of her husband in London after a triumph in *Porgy*.

Success is within reach as the Jadrics are booked at New York's Palace Theatre. But Ric misses the first performance listening to a "great conductor" rehearse his concerto at Carnegie Hall. In these pages, Dorothy's skillful description of the concerto's orchestration and programmatic elements belies her denial of being musically inclined. Jan is frantic, worried about what tragedy might have befallen Ric as she sees her professional dreams vanish. At this wrong moment, Tad's father approaches Jan to buy her off from supposedly pursuing his son for his money. As in her farces, entanglements ensue, perhaps not so well played on the page as on the stage. Jan is so angry she tells Tad's father she will marry his son just out of spite; and so, when Tad proposes again, she accepts. When Ric turns up, not in the least contrite for losing Jan's big chance, confident she will give up her victory at the Palace for his at Carnegie Hall, she, in a fit of anger, does something very un-Dorothy-like; she stands up for herself and then elopes with Tad.

The marriage ceremony almost happens, but Jan remembers the Jadrics are scheduled for a second performance that night at the Palace. Ironically, Ric makes it, while these two, rushing back, are too late and can only watch Ric from the wings wowing the audience with his solo talent. Jan leaves angrily, disappearing from both men's lives. Tad believes she's off to become a success on the West Coast; Ric believes Jan and Tad have married.

If the chapters on the Jadrics' ascent are pleasant and harmless, if a bit too long, those on Jan's financial and artistic decline, after the trio's breakup, verge on the tragic, the jarring shift in tone perhaps reflecting the sad time after her miscarriage. Jan is forced to give up more and more, eventually even having to sell her harp.

Some of the most dramatic, honest, and effective writing comes in Dorothy's taut, unnerving, and almost harrowing description of women desperately auditioning for chorus girl parts and their winnowing down one by one, a humiliation she might have experienced in her own attempts to be cast. There is a further flash of autobiography when Jan dyes her hair to look younger, but it backfires, as it did for Dorothy on the eve of her wedding. The change in tone from the whimsical early chapters to her heroine's being "ruthlessly discarded" is stark.

The scene shifts to Ric's return from a successful tour of Europe. Looking up Tad, he realizes Jan did not marry him, and no one knows where she is. The hunt is on till she's found still relentlessly pursing her dream, now playing in a low-class "tent" circuit down South. When she takes her place onstage that night she is startled to discover that Ric and Tad have replaced the no-talent musicians with whom she has been playing. With the performance over and with a blackface minstrel act in the background, she is cold and brittle as she berates them for foolishly and unprofessionally paying off her coworkers for one silly dramatic gesture.

"Who said anything about playing for one day?" Tad replies. "I bought out their whole booking." With that, she and the readers realize that the men are not slumming to witness her shame but have come back to be a trio with her. Just then their cue comes for their next three-a-day performance. "The effect on Jan was automatic; a marionette on a string that was suddenly jerked stageward [the metaphor explaining the dust jacket illustration of three musical puppets]." "And she gave that sudden bob of her head and, obedient to her leadership, the Jadrics went into their old routine." The vaudeville curtain rises on them as their story concludes.[2]

When *Three-a-Day* was published in April 1930, it was not just Dorothy who had changed since signing the contract. The stock market had crashed some seven months before, and the hopeful, lighthearted ease of the 1920s, marking the first two-thirds of the book, had given way to the later chapters' darker tone and downward spiral to melancholy. Yet the reading public wanted light entertainment, and most reviewers focused on the novel's more winsome qualities, uniformly praising its lighthearted fun. Noting that her characters were not flaming Jazz-age youth, the critic for the *New York Herald Tribune* called it pleasant and tender. "The heroine is a bit prim.... The young men, in spite of slight whimsical touches, might be Mr. Alger's heroes." Perhaps the story was better suited to a few hours' entertainment on Broadway than a 300-page novel.

The New York Times praised it as "a nicely contrived story marked by deft characterization and a rich flavor of theatrical goings-on." But, it had to be noted, "Those who anticipate an important or significant novel ... by the coauthor of 'Porgy' will be disappointed." Her first play, *Nancy Ann*, had been condemned for not standing up to the heavy mantle of the Harvard Prize, and now her first novel was being dismissed as something unworthy of the dramatist of *Porgy*. The play's huge success would haunt her, and the shadow it cast would obscure her later efforts, *Porgy* becoming something of a liability used by critics to taunt and condemn her for not repeating work she had no desire to.

Dorothy took it on the chin, never claiming the book to be literary—she'd leave chapters about her novels blank in her autobiography. And if written as a deliberate attempt to make money to recoup losses in the stock market, it did not work; sales were poor and the Century Company did not advertise it, even when she offered to pay for promotion herself. And when she asked her husband's publisher to take it on, he declined. It did sell to Warner Brothers in 1935, however, and it could have made a good screwball comedy, had it ever been filmed. Still, the $2,000 purchase price (about $40,000 in the 2020s) must have been welcome.[3]

There were other chances for moneymaking on the horizon as well; for just as the book was published, her two plays *Have a Good Time, Jonica* and *The Cinderelative* both went into production. Her claim that the ultimate failures of both were due to the poor productions they received does have merit, but Dorothy became an active collaborator in their demise, her blind trust in others and lack of business sense betraying her.

As in the past, not standing up for herself, she became an easy target for producers to ignore. Other women playwrights of the day were stronger, quite shrewd, and some became their own producers. It probably did not help Dorothy's situation that she was pregnant and later marooned in rural North Carolina when much of this was going on, so all she could do was write desperate letters and telegrams, have emissaries represent her, or take quick visits to New York City.

Have a Good Time, Jonica opened first. William Friedlander, who had tied up the rights and frustrated Dorothy with his shenanigans years before, was back on the scene, apparently also desperately trying to get some income in the Depression. He presented another contract, still determined to make it into a musical. This time, without her participation, he began to rewrite it, casting himself as a coauthor. Dorothy, horrified at what was happening, protested and made a claim against him with the Dramatists Guild, but there was little she could do. In the contract he had presented in 1929 and which she, with DuBose's approval, had signed, Friedlander had tricked her into abandoning some of her rights by literally pasting over standard contract language with added text of his own. "My husband and I went together [to the producer's office], but neither of us knew anything about musical contracts," she explained, noting that Friedlander "swore to us that the contract he was offering was in keeping with the Dramatists Guild requirements, that these requirements were very different for musicals, than for straight plays."

Friedlander was taking her play into a direction she disliked, yet she had no rights to approve the cast and, by signing, had given him carte blanche to create music for the play, while also agreeing to less than standard royalties. One of the stipulations she most regretted was clause 4, which noted, "The name of the author of the book shall be announced as joint author thereof." Now despite the fact she did not want her name on the musical and tried to have it pass under the pseudonym of Joyce Farr, she was blocked. Friedlander may have been unethical, but he was no fool; he knew the value of having the coauthor of the triumph *Porgy* associated with his travesty. While Friedlander kept Dorothy's name in high relief, he changed just about everything else. He shortened the play's name to *Jonica*, changed her three acts to two, invented scenes, including one set in the convent school, added singing and dancing, and left gaping holes in the plot.[4]

The play opened in tryouts in late March in Washington, D.C., which Dorothy made it up to see, before moving to Atlantic City. As late as April Fool's Day 1930, she, knowing the musical was due to open on the seventh, was arguing with Friedlander through the mail, sending him specific suggestions to get the script back on track. She wanted dialogue changed and scenes reworked. She may never have seen the final script; it does not exist in her papers, but what she saw she did not like.

In the opening first act on the Pullman car, for instance, with Jonica going off to New York and losing her gun, the addition of a bit involving a constipated child named Millie appalled her; a pun on the gun going off and Millie's constipation being solved ended the act. Dorothy was incensed at the vulgarity and tried every legal recourse available to get it removed, but Gertrude Workman, the mainstay of the Century Play Company, wrote of what she witnessed in the audience a few days before. "The offensive line is in just as it was before you made your protest," she reported, "but from a very practical standpoint, I do not advise you to insist upon its being taken out because it brings the heartiest laugh of the evening and laughs of this kind have financial value." Workman reported that other people she consulted did not find it as offensive as Dorothy did, "coming as it does from a drunk, and concerning a child."

For the author, perhaps a "bit prim" as a critic called her *Three-a-Day* heroine, it was *Nancy Ann* all over again, her play highjacked and pitched more vulgarly. The only positive things Gertrude Workman could report on was that although plot holes about a pearl necklace Dorothy had assiduously worked out still existed, some of her suggested changes and directions *had* been adopted. "So, you see, Mr. Friedlander paid some attention to your letter, at least."

Paying attention was one thing, but paying royalties another. Others, besides Dorothy, not being paid might have included William Moll, the lyricist, never again to be credited in a Broadway show, and so possibly a pseudonym. But there were others, more famous, also on the creative team. Joseph Meyer, to become an acclaimed writer of future songs, was credited with the music, and future Pulitzer Prize winner Moss Hart, although noted in the program as coauthor of the book, denied it vehemently throughout his life and in his memoirs; yet his biographers note that he was indeed involved, and probably rewrote his past, denying rewriting *Jonica*, possibly because of the poor job he did on it and probably because it flopped; he liked to state that his real debut on Broadway came later, in September 1930, when his and George Kaufman's *Once in a Lifetime* became a great success. Dorothy and Hart would meet face-to-face for the first time five years later at the *Porgy and Bess* premiere. Since he denied his involvement, although he even kept clippings of it, she'd remain forever mystified, believing "some unknown ghost rewrote it."[5]

If Dorothy winced and tried to look away, critics, of course, did not. Yet one who saw the March tryout in Washington, D.C.'s National Theatre thought *Jonica* just missed being fine and came across as "an amusing and often ribald production" and noted that some lines needed to be cut, something with which Dorothy vehemently agreed. *Variety* concurred, seconding Dorothy's belief that the play opened too soon; the play would have been better if it had more time on the road to get the kinks out. The critic noted weaknesses in the script and direction, and another reviewer pointed out the unresolved subplot of the pearl necklace.

But desperate for cash returns, with not enough preparation, Friedlander launched *Jonica* on Broadway. The *New York Sun* on April 9 called it "a musical farce—and a good one. . . . Hardly anybody sang very well and nobody cared" was its verdict; what carried it along was its "bright book" and "youthful naivete—everyone danced and had a good time." Meanwhile, the *New York Herald Tribune*, perhaps unwittingly unaware of Dorothy's novel of the same name, praised the musical for its "certain unpretentious three-a-day touch."

As the play went on, more changes were made; its future looked bright, but in mid-May, after about forty performances, the unpaid musicians refused to enter the pit for the matinee, and a backstage operator also refused to work. Not paying the faraway author was one thing, but stiffing performers at the theater was something else. It was Friedlander's financial precariousness that ultimately doomed the show, not the show itself, which was gaining grudging respect. "I've a feeling that 'Jonica' isn't the musical comedy it might be. But I've another feeling that it may be later on," a New York critic had opined. And though Dorothy and DuBose dunned Friedlander for months, he apparently never paid the money she was due.[6]

Just a few months after this debacle, *Poor Paulette*, rechristened *The Cinderelative*, also debuted on Broadway. Dorothy's central character is in search of the father she has never really known, following an early divorce. He, Paul, has been happily remarried to Agatha for years. Given the opportunity to meet him, Paulette figures out a scatterbrained way to spend time in his presence without revealing her identity to determine if he likes her for herself and not just out of paternal duty. His brother Penfield, her uncle, is to be married, with his fiancée, Marcia, due to come from Paris. That's where Paulette has been living, coincidentally in the same apartment building as the fiancée. When Marcia is delayed at the last minute, Paulette rushes to New York, quickly convincing her uncle to allow her to pretend to be his betrothed. But an obstacle is Agatha's younger brother Jimmy who, in the play's prologue, was stuck in an elevator (yet another coincidence) with Paulette on his way to meet his future aunt. That meeting did not happen, but in their brief time together, Jimmy fell for Paulette, who never gave him her name. So, when she turns up pretending to be Marcia, betrothed to someone else, he is jealous and distraught.

Eventually, Paulette feels her father really does sincerely like her, and when she is ready to reveal herself, the real fiancée's arrival is announced. Agatha has been troubled by Paulette, who does not seem at all in love with Penfield, her supposed intended, instead lavishing too much attention on both Agatha's husband (Paulette's father) and Agatha's brother. Paulette overhears Paul agreeing, saying she reminds him of his first wife, a flirt, who thought only of herself. This, of course, horrifies Paulette, who, failing to impress her father, wants to leave.

When confronted and asked who she really is, she denies she is even Paulette, but her reaction to a Topsy Turvy doll she had adored as a child betrays her true identity. Her uncle Penfield and his fiancée, Marcia, will marry, with Paulette and Jimmy soon to follow, a happy ending with Paulette, the Cinderelative, restored to the bosom of her family.

The script had been making the rounds for years, until a community theater in Harrisburg, Pennsylvania, decided to produce it in the spring of 1930; its director, Adele Eichler, rewrote it extensively, especially the last act, and in changing its name, rejected *The Prodigal Daughter* for *And Arabella*, a reference to the renamed double-ended doll, Liz and Arabella. In the original play, the doll, Black with her skirts in one direction, and white with its dress flipped over, had just been called Topsy Turvy. *And Arabella* was staged successfully in Harrisburg with Dorothy DeJagers listed as a coauthor, since she had worked on it with Dorothy when they first met at the MacDowell Colony. DeJagers had recently taken it up again, smartening up the dialogue, which the Heywards' theatrical friend, Daniel Reed, reading it in Hollywood, thought completely unnecessary. He found Dorothy's original version fine, "a charming light comedy." But Dorothy let some of DeJagers's edits remain to give her friend theatrical credit.

The Pennsylvania production, successful though it was, seemed to lead nowhere, although Broadway producers had swooped down on it, ultimately disappointed because they were seeking a "negro drama" like *Porgy* instead of the frothy farce it was. Eichler herself, however, was responsible for raising their expectations, since she had used DuBose Heyward's name ostentatiously in the program, noting he would be in the audience, connecting him to Dorothy and *Porgy*.[7]

That had been in March 1930, just when *Jonica* was opening in Washington; in August, a newly established production company decided to stage the play, not Eichler's version, but the one done by the two Dorothys. The Hyman brothers, Dorothy realized, were the "rankest shoe-stringers," but a sale was a sale, and here was a chance to get it produced and possibly wring income from it, which both *Three-a-Day* and *Jonica* had failed to deliver. Desperate to reverse her luck, she appears to have blinded herself to the obvious or again was just being terminally optimistic. "Dorothy DeJagers and I would never have consented if practically every reputable producer in New York had not already turned *Poor Paulette* from their doors," she explained. DeJagers agreed to the sale, although she, like Dorothy, had had bad experiences with producers. When her *Saturday Evening Post* story "The Average Woman" had been filmed as a silent back in 1924, she had sued the producers for not honoring her contract and had won. Due to marry soon and down on her luck, not having published much recently, she craved a Broadway credit, which Dorothy was glad to supply. Both were aware, however, their chance of success was low. For not only were the producers not reputable, the Dorothys lent the Hyman brothers money they had made from the $1,500 sale of the play's amateur rights. Samuel French would publish it the next year as *Little Girl Blue*, deliberately obscuring any of the play's earlier productions or names.[8]

Things were moving much too unprofessionally and much too quickly with these "speedsters," as Dorothy described them. The contract for *The Cinderelative* was signed at the end of August, although the Century Play Company advised that a better title would be *Page Mr. Ripley*, a continuing gag in the play based on *Ripley's Believe It or Not*. A scant few weeks later, newspapers reported that brothers Jack and Lionel Hyman were laying the foundations for a subscription series similar to the Theatre Guild, with membership dues to defray the production costs. Amazingly, with rights just secured less than a month before, the brothers announced that the play would open on September 18.[9]

There was no way a crew, actors, or technicians could come together so quickly in an untried production company. The impending debacle was so obvious that Dorothy, in New York for rehearsals, seeing that there was no set or costumes, actually skipped the second dress rehearsal to take in Marc Connelley's *The Green Pastures* instead. She knew the play would fail, but having learned from her jousts with Friedlander, she had inserted a protective clause in the contract stipulating that her name and that of DeJagers could be removed from the production if they so desired. They had come up with pseudonyms like "Hugh Hartzell or Heyward Hughes." "The Hyman Bros., however, would like to use both [real] names," a representative of the Century

Play Company wrote Dorothy, "and naturally, your name does mean something from a publicity angle." Dorothy refused to have her name associated with the looming flop, but the Hyman brothers broke the contract.[10]

"Come Home to Papa," DuBose telegrammed when she wrote him of the nightmarishly amateurish production. By then, the critics had circled, each trying to outdo each other in their condemnation of the play. "'Cinderelative' is about as bad as its title might lead you to expect," was the comment of one reviewer, calling it "dismally flat and tiresome." Yet *Billboard*'s critic realized, "If the play had been better mounted and perfectly cast, the Hymans would have in *The Cinderelative* an attractive little offering, dear to the hearts of a predominately feminine public given to sterilized drama in which the milder form of expletives are used on the greatest provocation, and only in the face of having them washed out of the mouth with strong yellow soap." No doubt, what hurt most was critic Gilbert Gabriel's comment in the New York papers: "It is so poor and so little a play that Dorothy Heyward, who is one of its authors and who once upon a time helped [!] her husband, DuBose Heyward, write a play by the memorable name of 'Porgy,' must undoubtedly know it as well as everybody in last night's audience did." Indeed, the shock of it was intense; DeJagers found her coauthor weeping but reluctantly agreed, at Dorothy's insistence, to never tell DuBose. Once again as author of *Porgy*, Dorothy was being haunted by its success, with her role now demoted to "helper" status, inferring she could not achieve success on her own.

The play folded after two nights, and despite DuBose's dictate, she did not run home to be comforted. Instead, she fought further collapse by lingering for a few days in the city to do some work, and to take the time needed to compose herself. With her emotions back in check, Dorothy returned to her husband and mother-in-law, Janie, and the newest member of the family.[11]

Having suffered two miscarriages, as a precaution she had spent the first few months of 1930 in New York during the last stages of her pregnancy, in the care of specialists. In a year of three crises, two Broadway flops, and a stillborn novel, she nevertheless experienced joy and a profound personal triumph. On February 15, 1930, Dorothy had given birth to Jenifer DuBose Heyward in New York City.

CHAPTER 11

"Our Next Play"

One of the first people DuBose contacted was the director of the MacDowell Colony, where he and Dorothy had met and where he had proposed. Addressing her as "Mother MacDowell," he wrote, "A small, but healthy, daughter arrived yesterday afternoon. . . . Dorothy and new arrival both are doing finely."

"We were awfully sorry not see you before leaving New York," he apologized on March 28, "but we wanted to get to this lovely fresh air and sunshine [at their home in North Carolina] as soon as the doctor would let them travel. Both are model patients." The christening was hurried, wedged between *Jonica*'s failure and *The Cinderelative*'s. Dorothy had stayed with Jenifer until the end of March when she went up to Washington, D.C., for the *Jonica* tryouts, coming back almost immediately. On the evening of April 5, in Hendersonville, Dorothy stood in as proxy for Marian MacDowell, who had consented to be Jenifer's godmother, and DuBose doubled for Dorothy's "twin" cousin, Charles Hartzell, as godfather. Josephine Pinckney, an extra godmother, had told them her schedule allowed her to "come to Hendersonville at once or not at all." That had determined the date; "Godfine" is what Jenifer would call her (while Mamoulian had recently dubbed her "the Princess" when he had visited her in her palatial mansion in Charleston). The officiating minister was DuBose's good friend Moultrie Guerry. The Heywards now had an heir; Dorothy, fragile and forty, was not going to bear any more children.[1]

As she adjusted to the requirements of motherhood and reviewed the failures of the year, Dorothy knew they were facing a new fiscal reality. Most of the money from *Porgy* play royalties left over from the construction of their North Carolina house had been lost in the Depression. It was supposed to have served as their summer residence, but now as the only home they owned, living in it year-round, they wished they had spent more money on a better furnace instead of a swimming pool. To raise cash, DuBose turned to films, working on a script for Eugene O'Neill's *The Emperor Jones,* adding scenes very similar to ones Dorothy had crafted for *Porgy*. In building a back story for Brutus Jones, the central character, he'd add a crap game, a murder, and make singing central to the story, very *Porgy*-like. No doubt, it was his fame associated with the play that had landed the film deal. And he'd do a brief stint in Hollywood for *The Good Earth*, while his play of miscegenation and murder, *Brass Ankle,* drafted swiftly, as was his habit, without Dorothy's keen eye, died in 1931 after a few weeks on Broadway.

Dorothy had no luck either with her attempt to rush to market the mystery story she had lackadaisically been making passes at since secretly dramatizing *Porgy*. She signed a contract for *Nightmare House* with Farrar and Rinehart, DuBose's publisher, about eighteen months after Jenifer's birth.[2]

In it she rehashed the idea of Rose Cohen's death, the basis of her "The Young Ghost" short story, and a device DuBose would quietly borrow for his 1936 novel *Lost Morning*, another attempt to make money, with its central male character left to wonder if the woman he loved had killed herself or died accidentally. In her work, Dorothy laboriously introduced references to an old unsolved case of murder versus suicide in a conversation between two men in her book's early pages. The men are writers, who, like DuBose and Hervey Allen, had once written books together, with one of them, like DuBose, having been in insurance. That character, Chalders Vane, is the famous author of *Farrabee* (sounds like *Porgy*), a Pulitzer Prize–winning novel turned into a play and a film (and film rights for *Porgy* were sold early), an overshadowing success never repeated.[3]

But there, similarities stop. Vane is haunted by something in his past, sensed by all around him including his old writing partner, Vane's children, and his attorney. All end up, with the attorney murdered, at Delamare House, the original Nightmare House, a writers' retreat, somewhat based on the MacDowell Colony. Simultaneous to the signing of the contract, Dorothy found herself enmeshed in a real-world literary gathering of Southern writers in Virginia, including the likes of Ellen Glasgow and William Faulkner, one of the few spouses allowed to attend the literary gatherings as a creative artist.

That Virginia affair was apparently dull, hampered by banalities, formalities, and too obvious politeness, but in her Delamare House, Dorothy struggled to dramatize the opposite. The lights go out, deathlike faces appear at windows, and loose shutters bang; midnight searches, with characters running in and out just missing each other, share the same frantic pacing that fueled her farces. And as such, they seem more suited to staged slapstick than to a tense mystery story.

Furthermore, the diverse characters' actions are not dramatized; rather, they are recapitulated in dialogue, and the plot ticks along as creakily as Delamare House's ancient grandfather clock that mysteriously chimes only before a death. As the story finally gels and secrets come out, Chalders Vane admits to having stolen the Pulitzer Prize–winning manuscript from the writer who founded the colony; another colonist is revealed as the very detective trying to resolve the old murder or suicide case, and many there are implicated. As in her comedies, Dorothy kept piling complication upon complication, finally allowing the various knots of the mystery to work free. While more corpses pile up, a happy ending comes for Dina Delamare, the standard Dorothy Heyward heroine, young and plucky, characterized by an "element of naïve improbability."

The book, retitled *The Pulitzer Prize Murders*, was published in early 1932 to surprisingly good reviews. *The New York Times* noted, despite it being Dorothy's "first detective story," that its many mysteries entitled "her to an honorable niche in the mystery hall of fame." *The Toledo Times* called it one of the best mysteries of the year; and the *Chicago Evening Post* deemed it above average, saying the "plot is satisfactorily baffling." Others commented on the atmosphere, comparing it to Poe's "The Raven." "The novel would have been better if shorter and compact," was the verdict of the *Newark (N.J.) News*.

But in the Depression, at a cost of two dollars, with little advertising and faint praise, the book, like *Three-a-Day*, soon sank from sight and today is something of a rarity. Dorothy would never attempt a novel again, returning to the more familiar terrain of playwriting as she mulled over the life of another African American man who had walked the streets of Charleston. Sammy Smalls, the basis of *Porgy*, had by this time "vanished like a ghost," his death depriving her of seeing him in the flesh. Her new subject had inexplicably disappeared from history, too; something that baffled both Dorothy and DuBose as they worked to recover the extraordinary life of Denmark Vesey.[4]

Somewhat of a cottage industry today, with book titles bearing his name, a statue raised in his honor, and debates swirling in his wake, Dorothy and DuBose felt, circa 1930, that they were among the very few who had ever heard of this once-enslaved man who had purchased his freedom in 1799 after winning a lottery. After that he disappeared from sight for twenty years, then emerged in the summer of 1822 as the rumored leader of thousands of enslaved people intent on destroying the white population of Charleston. The conspiracy, which some scholars suggest was an overreaction to vague murmurings, making it more a white plot than a Black one, was foiled, and Vesey was hanged before any uprising took place.

Dorothy had discovered Denmark Vesey after DuBose had been tapped by a group of descendants of plantation gentry to write an essay for a book for the Society for the Preservation of Spirituals. DuBose, and Dorothy too, it seems, were members of this group that periodically donned frock coats and hoopskirts to sing, for a fee, Gullah spirituals, such as those used in *Porgy*, songs and tunes and pronunciations these whites believed were in danger of disappearing. The book was to be a lush affair, with contributions from various authors and artists identified with the cultural movement called the Charleston Renaissance. DuBose, due to the phenomenal success of *Porgy*, was seen by many as the leader of this movement, and the society had chosen him for the essay "The Negro in the Lowcountry." It was a task, he'd declare in its opening sentence, of "insurmountable difficulty." Neither scholar nor historian, he appealed to published experts and started doing research; as usual, he turned to Dorothy.

"I remember very clearly, though it's a long time ago, that we were sitting under the huge pine trees by DuBose's North Carolina studio. [They each had their own spot where they pursued their writing.] I was reading my lesson aloud to him: a book on early American Negro history. It gave one-and-one-half pages to the story of Denmark Vesey, who wanted to set his people free. As I finished the one-and-one-half pages DuBose and I said simultaneously, 'That is going to be our next play.'"[5]

The story amazed Heyward, a lifelong Charlestonian. He had never heard of Vesey, even though his first books of poetry had mined the legends, lore, and history of the Lowcountry. He was further startled, no doubt, to discover that one of the judges condemning Vesey had been his direct ancestor's brother. This was definitely not the sort of loyal "darky" tale Mother Janie would share with tourists in hotel lobbies in the spring. Rather, the concept of Blacks conspiring to kill whites was an explosive idea for a white Southerner to pursue. He had included a similar murderous scene in his *Emperor Jones* script, but censors had cut it, so he must have realized how taboo it was viewed. In his 1932 eponymous novel, DuBose's white hero, Peter Ashley, would come to ponder some of the horrors of slavery before going off, nevertheless, to fight for the Confederacy. Dorothy, unconflicted, thought Vesey "the greatest leader the Negro Race has ever had."

DuBose had previously been drawn to the life of another freedom fighter, the white Ella May Wiggins, who was shot dead in 1929 on her way to support the Loray Mill strike in Gastonia, North Carolina. DuBose saw her as a Joan of Arc figure and began writing of her, changing the name of her Sevierville, Tennessee, hometown to Merrivale, a name lifted from Dorothy's manuscript *Three-a-Day*.[6]

It's not possible to pin down why or when he abandoned the manuscript, but it was certainly while researching Vesey, whose story, also ending with a martyr's death, had to be more appealing. It was set in Charleston, after all, and critics were already suggesting he wrote better of Blacks than whites. Besides, *Strike!*, a novel based on Wiggins, had appeared in 1930. Doing his due diligence, he encountered no major work on Vesey, who seemed to inhabit only footnotes in these years. The field was clear.

A few years before their discovery, author Joseph Hergesheimer, whom the Heywards knew, had employed elements of the Vesey saga in a nightmarishly surreal short story, "Charleston." In the 1927 *Saturday Evening Post* tale, collected in *Quiet Cities* in 1933, Hergesheimer had not named Vesey but literally resurrected one of his lieutenants, Mingo Harth, bringing him back to life in Reconstruction, portraying him as evil incarnate, involved in voodoo and the like, a central element to come in one of DuBose's and Dorothy's scenes.[7]

Hergesheimer made a tidy profit off the sale of the story to the *Post* and even more off the trade, boxed, signed and numbered, printed-on-various-paper-stock editions of *Quiet Cities*. Other writers drawn to Vesey would not be so lucky. In a few years Paul Bowles, who'd contribute incidental music for one of Dorothy's plays, would compose a score to accompany eccentric gay Southerner Paul Henri Ford's unfinished libretto, only to have it lost in manuscript and never produced; and in the following decade Jewish poet Aaron Kramer would write a poetry cycle on the leader. Set to music by Waldermar Hill, the oratorio, used in civil right protests in the 1950s, would not prove popular. If foiled in the nineteenth century, Vesey would nevertheless succeed in frustrating white artists and scholars in the twentieth and twenty-first who'd expend vast amounts of ink and energy trying to convince others to their point of view, some believing the conspiracy had been a white fantasy born of fear, others seeing it as a noble, or despicable, Black reality. Dorothy believed in it and in Vesey implicitly.[8]

With the die cast, her curiosity piqued, there was no going back; she may have been left in Hendersonville with Jenifer, when DuBose drove down to the Charleston Library Society where he found two pamphlets about the insurrection. She herself had tarried in New York after *The Cinderelative*'s failure to do research on Vesey there. In his essay for *The Carolina Low-Country*, DuBose would describe how "the faded pages of the official reports" stunned and caught his "imagination by the sheer power of its drama." With his article done, he dashed out some pages of a script, but, with his savvy eye to economics, he turned research over to Dorothy, as he turned to a surer moneymaker, his Civil War novel *Peter Ashley*.

At about this same time, DuBose's mentor, John Bennett, forwarded a letter from an old friend, Broadway producer George C. Tyler, looking for an author to write a play about Blacks serving in World War I. Heyward demurred, noting other commitments and confessing his failure to have participated in the war. DuBose next tested the waters regarding Vesey, explaining that he and Dorothy had "been studying for and preparing material upon [him] for several years." "The play we have in mind is concerned with the life of Denmark Vesey who directed the evil-starred insurrection in 1820 [*sic*]." Not only was Vesey a "very moving character," but the play's themes would take up conflicts of past and present, the differing worldviews of those born enslaved in America and those born free in Africa, as well as differences between voodoo and Christianity; "the play would probably have . . . as much music as *Porgy*." In strictest confidence, Heyward confessed "that George Gershwin for several years has been interested in the question of doing a Negro opera with me and has taken the matter up in earnest within the past fortnight." Heyward went out on a limb suggesting, "I think he [Gershwin] might be seriously interested in working with me on the incidental music" on Vesey.

The work would not be an opera but a play with music; "we are quite full of it," he wrote Tyler, but he was unsure if the "whole idea is too remote from Broadway to justify the huge outlay of labor and money that would go into production." What did Tyler think?

Gershwin, in a letter to DuBose less than a month before, had indeed signaled that he was still interested in *Porgy* but needed another year or so to clear his desk of projects. This gave time for Heyward to work on Vesey, and Tyler, in fact, wrote back he found such a play "a grand thought. I only wish I were in the position . . . to undertake the financing of it." Had he the cash, and not so many debts, "I'd grab at the chance of going in." But with no money to back it, Heyward returned to *Peter Ashley*, leaving Dorothy to raise Jenifer and work on Vesey.[9]

This is what she was doing when Gershwin signaled he was ready to begin. She shelved Vesey for *Porgy*.

CHAPTER 12

Credit and Credibility

The Theatre Guild was enthusiastic about an opera based on the play from the very beginning, so much so, in fact, the directors were willing to sign a contract and commission the work sight unseen. According to one scholar, they were even ready to finance an Al Jolson musical version before a Gershwin/Heyward work was in hand. The Jolson blackface version never materialized, and the first contract for the Gershwin/Heyward collaboration, dated October 26, 1933, stipulated that George was to write the music and DuBose the book and lyrics; Ira was to be included as well, which, according to Dorothy, upset DuBose, who, not having been consulted, believed Gershwin was including his brother so as to "not throw him out of work for two years." But once "he got to know Ira and found what a fine fellow he was," DuBose changed his mind.[1]

Dorothy was also a direct participant. While not mentioned, she was recognized as part of the creative team, and all involved knew it. Gershwin himself, in his March 1932 letter to Heyward, emphasizing his excitement for the project, had called *Porgy* "the most outstanding *play* I know about colored people" (emphasis added), and although later noting he would reread the novel, it was Dorothy's play adaptation that lingered in his and in the public's memory. The contract specified George would get 5 percent of the royalties and Ira would get 1 percent, while Dorothy and DuBose would share 4 percent, an obvious acknowledgment of her status. Her outranking of Ira from the start would be a sore point in the future when the opera would be dubbed the Gershwins' *Porgy and Bess*. And as to film rights, to have an even greater impact, Gershwin was to have 30 percent; Dorothy and DuBose would share the same; Ira's share was only 6⅔ percent, the remaining 33⅓ percent going to the Guild. Yet when the contract was drawn up there were only signature lines for Warren Munsell of the Guild and for George, Ira, and DuBose, all men, two of them with no history with the work. But on the contract that the Heywards kept in their personal files, Dorothy adamantly drew in a line on the bottom and signed her name, acknowledging her claim. The Heywards' version also has an addendum that other surviving copies apparently lack. It notes that the Theatre Guild would not sanction a production of the play by the Heywards without the Guild's consent. The producers were already trying to avoid unwanted confusion or competition between the two versions, knowing even then how closely the opera and play would be linked. It was DuBose who'd solve the problem of keeping the versions distinct by suggesting that the opera be called *Porgy and Bess*. Yet opera and play were always to remain very close kin; "cousins" is how Dorothy would describe them.[2]

Work was supposed to have been completed by July 1934, but when it wasn't, the Guild executed another contract extending its interest "until the opera is completed." Only Munsell, George, and Ira apparently signed that agreement, although there is a blank line for another signature; the majority of the work that needed to be completed was George's. He had returned to New York from having spent time in North Carolina and on Folly Beach near Charleston with DuBose and Dorothy, and still needed time to orchestrate. By then, DuBose's libretto was nearly, if not totally, complete, except for some arias and lyrics to be added. This contract, like the original one, noted that the opera was based on both the play and the novel.

When DuBose had started work on the libretto, it was not his novel to which he turned, he and Gershwin agreeing that the *play* had to be cut by 40 percent with the original dialogue "re-arranged for musical treatment." So, it was more with scissors and paste rather than with a pen that the libretto for *Porgy and Bess* was crafted. DuBose mostly edited a piece that was nearly all Dorothy's work.

There were three versions of the play from which to choose: the earliest one copyrighted in August 1926 for which he claimed he did not deserve credit; the published acting version, easy to access, which included some of Mamoulian's and the Theatre Guild's suggestions; and, lastly, the prompt script, the true acting version with some Mamoulian and Guild suggestions removed, along with changes and rewrites dating from the final weeks of rehearsal, work that was mostly Dorothy's. Evidence in the libretto suggests that this latter version was the one DuBose used, either from a copy he had at hand or in his head from memory. In 1938 Mamoulian would go on the record saying that he had been reluctant to be involved in the opera, because he "felt the play was so complete in its form, had such direct simplicity and strength, that any attempt to translate it into operatic form might spoil it."

In multiple places, bits of business and dialogue in the printed version but cut in the prompt script, and thus in the production, failed to show up in the libretto, and since the prompt script was the leanest version available and had pleased audiences for years, it made perfect sense to use it. In act 2, scene 3, for instance, Dorothy had originally had some of the folks in Catfish Row whispering that Bess had been with Crown on Kittiwah Island while Bess lies delirious in Porgy's room. That had been cut from the final production and does not appear in the opera libretto. Lily Holmes being questioned by the coroner, present in the next-to-final scene in the printed version, vanished from the prompt script and would not appear in the opera.

In fact, there seems to be only one small "bit" cut entirely from the prompt script and not present in the libretto, focusing on Maria's interior debate if Jesus or conjuring had cured Bess from the fever she caught in the thickets of Kittiwah Island. All cutting, of course, allowed for extended vocal enlargements, duets, choruses, and arias. The play, which many critics said rambled, was nevertheless taut enough in spots that, in some scenes, like that of the hurricane, as DuBose told George, there was little for him to do other than add spirituals with suggestions of how they should be staggered and sung.[3]

Dorothy and DuBose's fine writing, "far beyond that of the run-of-the-mill Broadway play and most classic operatic librettos, too," according to one critic, survived into the opera, the prose making itself quite adaptable for recitatives. In the opening crap game scene, Jake's "Seem like these bones don't gib me nuttin' but box-cars tonight. It was de same two weeks ago, an' the game broke me. I ain't likes dat luck" survives almost totally, with only "seem" changed to "seems," "de" changed to "the," and "ain't" changed to "don't," perhaps a typing mistake or perhaps Dorothy, the typist of the opera, did it deliberately. A few lines later, the comments about the dice being the "same cock-eyed bone whut clean de gang out las' week," became the more euphonious "same cock-eyed bones what clean the game out last Saturday night."

Ira agreed, noting that his brother often could just lift dialogue from the libretto for songs and recitatives "with scarcely a syllable being changed." Yet an even more compelling—perhaps the most compelling—argument and proof of Dorothy's impact as coauthor (and even primary author) of the libretto is actually more obvious. The entire dramatic structure of her play survived unmolested and intact in the opera. Her successful play only needed editing: the nine scenes of *Porgy* became the exact same nine scenes of *Porgy and Bess*; and Mamoulian's misstep in making it into four acts was walked back. DuBose kept it in three as his wife had planned, following the shift that had occurred after opening night, grouping two scenes in act 1, four in act 2, and three in act 3. And of course, vitally, her transcendent ending was retained.

Playscript and libretto are such close kin, in fact, that the simile Dorothy used to describe her sticking like a leech to the novel is actually much more apt in describing what DuBose did in sticking to her script. He rewrote virtually nothing, just cut, and sometimes moved her lines, while following her structure scene by scene, dramatic action by action, almost verbatim in spots, working more as an editor than an author as he inserted his wonderfully crafted lyrics. Even the one addition he did suggest can be traced to Dorothy. One day he excitedly told Gershwin of a fresh idea of his. He added a scene between the overture and the opera's beginning (cut before opening night but reinstated in later years). It shows a dance hall featuring jazz musician Jasbo Brown, with couples dancing, a scene that dissolves to become the opening scene on Catfish Row, men gambling and Clara singing "Summertime."[4]

In the play version, Dorothy had begun with cast members speaking throwaway lines in pure Gullah, incomprehensible to the audience, slowly bridging to a more familiar language that could be understood. Her husband seems to have seized on the thematic idea and translated it, suggesting to Gershwin that he do the same musically, starting with one musical vocabulary (jazz—perhaps seen as a native "tongue" of Blacks) bridging to more operatic idioms.

When the opera premiered, those who had seen the play caught these and many other subtleties, realizing exactly how aligned the two works were. (Later critics and scholars, never having seen the play, did not have this ability, and if they relied on the published version for comparison, many similarities were lost to them.) "Essentially, it is the play 'Porgy' in opera form," Elliot Norton would write in the *Boston Post*, after seeing the initial tryout; "everyone knew that Heyward and his 'Porgy' were good," he continued. "The question was, was Gershwin good at opera." "The dramatic strength of the story was one factor in the success won by the opera," noted another reporter for the *New York Herald Tribune*. "The task which George Gershwin set himself in making an opera out of DuBose and Dorothy Heyward's play 'Porgy' was none other than adding music to one of the most striking plays of our generation," yet another observer at the time concluded, "a play which in its choral episodes was already provided with sufficient music for its actual needs." This was not an uncommon, if not totally correct, comment from critics who knew Dorothy's play.

The Guild producers had come to this realization of Dorothy's importance to the work as it progressed. On June 28, 1935, a few months before the opening, a new and apparently final contract was drawn up, laying out all the percentages and credits, naming all members of the creative team, this time finally and legally acknowledging Dorothy as a coauthor. This last version was between the Theatre Guild, as manager with "GEORGE GERSHWIN, Composer, IRA GERSHWIN, Lyricist, and DuBOSE and DOROTHY HEYWARD, Authors of the book, hereinafter designated 'Authors.'" While DuBose's role as lyricist was cropped out apparently for the ease of legal language, Dorothy was clearly and finally recognized as coauthor of the book, or libretto. This time there was a line for her to sign her name.

The irony was, and is, few people have ever seen this document. Apparently, there is not one in the Gershwin archives, and the early photostat in Dorothy's papers has been ignored. It appears that only one version was signed, possibly when all the principals were in one place at the same time. And then the original vanished, unknown until the summer of 2022 when the contract came to auction, provenance undeclared, and sold. Whoever purchased it has the original of the most compelling legal evidence proving that everyone at the time, including producers, DuBose, and the Gershwins, acknowledged Dorothy as a full partner in creating one of the world's most popular operas.[5]

But why, in programs and advertisements, she was not credited as coauthor of the libretto but only acknowledged as coauthor of the play upon which the libretto was based, remains a puzzle. Perhaps if credit for the play had not already shifted toward DuBose, perhaps if they had not been married, and crucially, if Dorothy had not already begun minimizing her role, and definitely if they had different agents, instead of sharing Audrey Wood, Dorothy's name very likely would have been attached to the libretto as coauthor, and she would have been on the stage at openings and been acknowledged in print. She could have demanded it but continued on with her casual approach to business and credit, helping assure her own erasure, content (for some unknown reason) with being *Porgy and Bess*'s ghostwriter, paid for her contributions with royalties but not named. For decades now, the story has been that DuBose and George alone conducted most of their collaboration through the mail, with Dorothy on the sidelines, DuBose sending drafts and ideas and adding songs where he and George felt they were needed. Yet for many of their lyrics, DuBose and Ira went back to her script; DuBose's magical lullaby "Summertime," for instance, called one of the most perfect songs of all time and covered as frequently as any other in America's songbook, was made possible by Dorothy shortening the timeline of the play and opening it in summer; DuBose took the first line, "hush little baby don't you cry," from the initial line of the lullaby in the play to end a stanza. In the same scene he is credited for the song "A woman is a sometime thing"; while he did write the lyrics, it's likely he had heard that turn of phrase on the streets of Charleston, since it had been recognized as a standard Gullah aphorism as far back as the 1880s.[6]

Dorothy may not have been aware of that bit of inspiration, but she knew her play and thought she knew her husband. While she was content to keep quiet about her contributions, she was angry and outspoken when DuBose allowed others to take credit for his work. "Whenever Ira would change a single word in a lyric, it then appeared under both their names," something Dorothy thought unfair. Having seen DuBose write "'I Got Plenty o' Nuttin', then seeing Ira's revisions which seemed to me not to help at all I protested to DuBose that I thought Ira made changes just to get his name aboard. DuBose said, 'absolutely not.'" Yet George Gershwin himself, possibly unknown to Dorothy, would inform Ira that DuBose felt he was doing most of the lyrics and demanded more credit.

Because she knew "DuBose was a stickler for the truth," she realized "He was troubled with Ira Gershwin inserting an 'Okay' into DuBose's first draft of 'I Got Plenty o' Nuttin'. He said no Gullah would ever have said, 'Okay.'" But he himself okayed that and let it stand in the song, and he gave Ira credit as coauthor. It was she and Ira together, she told a PhD candidate in the 1950s, and not just Ira, who had worked out the dummy lyric for this song for DuBose to use for a tune Gershwin had already composed; DuBose had a bad memory for tunes, something, she with a musical background, could help him with. "I feel quite sure if DuBose were alive and repeatedly given credit for work Ira had done he would make some sort of protest," she'd come to say. She liked Ira personally, but the most important change he introduced into the opera she did not like at all.[7]

It was she who had reinserted Sporting Life into the action of the play after her husband had dropped him early in the novel, she who precipitated his transformation into the role of nemesis to Bess. With encouragement from Mamoulian and Theresa Helburn, she portrayed him as the instigator of all the action, getting Crown high in the first act to prompt a murder, enticing Bess all along, hanging out like the buzzard whose shadow augurs doom, starting the rumor that the coroner was going to trick and convict Porgy when he looked on Crown's corpse, and then luring Bess off to New York City. In all this she had never included him in the Kittiwah Island scene, simply because he was neither necessary nor integral to Crown's seduction of Bess. In fact, she knew it would have been out of character for him to have attended. In all versions of her rewrites, Sporting Life makes fun of the picnic and refuses to go, saying he, a sophisticate with time spent in New York, is above such small-town doings. DuBose hewed to this tactic as well. "Picnics is all right for these small town n——rs, but we is use to the high life, you know," DuBose put in the libretto, following the text from the play. (In later versions, the N-word would be changed to "suckers.") "Why with your looks, Bess, an' yo' way wid de boys, dere's big money for you an' me in New York."

The opera changed that, bloating it to some extent, when cuts were needed. And scholars who study the first draft of the libretto know that one scene is missing in the Library of Congress's copy—the Kittiwah scene—missing, basically because Dorothy's version was almost entirely discarded. Worse yet, the one responsible for the new scene actually embedded contradictions in it, something that has generally escaped notice. Although in act 2, scene 2, Sportin' Life (his name in the opera) says he is not going to the picnic, he illogically turns up in the next scene. He is not just present but front and center, stepping into star mode. His song "It Ain't Necessarily So," with lyrics by Ira, following the chorus "I Ain't Got No Shame," picks up the theme that had just been previously expressed in a line or two of dialogue, as residents of the Row debate if the picnic is for saints or for sinners, a retreat for pleasure or piety. With Ira's addition, the tiny scene, only a few pages long, the shortest in the play, ballooned. Sportin' Life's song is a showstopper in more ways than one. The lyrics are clever, the music rousing and crowd pleasing; but it does nothing to advance the action. In fact, it slows down the inevitability of Bess being manipulated by Crown, and it impedes the progress of the drama. If it was inserted to give an audience more insight into Sporting Life as a character, it fails and, in fact, backfires, for it changes him from a menace into something close to a mischievous scamp. With sympathy built up for the devil, he no longer is seen as the demon leading Bess to her downfall, which now appears less tragic, since her betrayer has been portrayed more positively. George Gershwin obviously saw the contradiction and felt he had to comment on it to defend his brother's insertions, noting, somewhat disingenuously, that in the opera, "the character of Sportin' Life, instead of being a sinister dope peddler, is a humorous, dancing villain, who is likeable and believable and at the same time evil."

"Humorous" and "dancing" is the opposite of how both DuBose and Dorothy saw him, but that is what he often became. The man who first interpreted him in the opera, vaudeville actor John Bubbles, set the standard for others to follow for decades, moving him from arch unsympathetic villain to a wily, clever, and sly, almost likable, rascal. On stage he wins over the affections of some of the Row inhabitants as the rousing number also wins the audience. Since Bubbles could not read music and would mistakenly shift rhythms unaccountably, he played the role so broadly in rehearsal that the musical director, Alexander Smallens, wanted to fire him; Mamoulian, whom the Heywards did not want to direct, loved him, however, as did the Gershwins. Bubbles was directed to tap-dance during the picnic scene to help keep him on point, but for the story it was pointless, the happy scene diluting the tragic inevitability of the end. Since so many other actors would follow this pattern, giving the character a sort of less naturalistic, more cartoonlike quality, Dorothy, in the future, would plead longingly for the "pre-Ira version" of the story with Sporting Life having no charm to redeem him, and allowing Maria's and Bess's assessments of him to ring true, both calling him a rattlesnake.[8]

George's family loyalties not only gave Ira the opportunity to add something to the libretto, but it also won out when cuts had to be made after the opening to keep it from running too long. Gershwin cut the song of doom, the buzzard song (good, but unnecessary for the plot) that Heyward had composed; out went his Jasbo Brown opening as well (perhaps with more reason); but George did not touch any song or lyric of his brother's, even though "It Ain't Necessarily So" was truly not necessary to the action. And as if to prove how Ira's character differs from the original conception, their names are spelled differently. What was "Sporting Life" in the novel and the play is "Sportin' Life" in the opera, more familiar, rounded, more friendly, and further proof that the play's character and the opera's are of a different stripe, cousins, possibly, but certainly not close ones.

Dorothy saw her husband defer more and more to Ira as the project went on. After all, Ira was there in New York, when DuBose wasn't, and Ira had years of expertise that her husband lacked, knowing that a word which might sound good on the page often would not when sung. Dorothy watched as DuBose suggested that Ira write the lyrics to the sacrilegious song ("A Red Headed Woman") that Crown belts out in the hurricane, seeming to defy God. He got total credit for that, but when asked about another song, "Bess, You Is My Woman Now," "I'm pretty sure I took a line from the text," Ira acknowledged, "and probably used three or four other lines from the libretto," words that Dorothy had written. That lyric was eventually credited to DuBose and Ira, a rarity according to Dorothy; she believed that the formula that a DuBose/Ira collaboration followed did not always hold for an Ira/DuBose collaboration.

"DuBose . . . worked longer and harder on the libretto and lyrics than on the original novel," Dorothy would protest, and she insisted *Porgy and Bess* was really by "George Gershwin and DuBose Heyward (with assists from Ira Gershwin and me)." She never said if she did more than Ira, but the contracts and their royalty structures suggest she did; she also recalled her agent, Audrey Wood, telling her that Ira had once agreed that his name could be omitted from billing and advertisements. "I want Ira, who is one of the finest and most generous men I have ever known, to have credit for his fine work. But to call 'Porgy and Bess' 'the George and Ira Gershwin opera' simply isn't so," she'd complain bitterly in the 1950s when advertisements were claiming that to be the case, and Ira stayed silent. After his brother's death, Ira had written DuBose, "It was a great honor to be associated with you, however small my contribution." Perhaps more telling than that is the photograph of DuBose and Ira that appears in the published vocal score of the opera: DuBose faces forward with a friendly arm outstretched, while Ira, uneasy in his skin, looks down; there is an awkward gap between them, as if they were expecting George to bridge it. One can only wonder if Dorothy ever came to realize that the trait she so disapproved of in DuBose, in allowing others to claim credit for his work, was exactly what she was doing to herself to a much greater degree. In her conflict (and she always tried to avoid conflict), perhaps it was easier to focus her ire on Ira, instead of protesting what her husband was doing to them both. She would lie awake at night in the coming years trying to puzzle it out.[9]

As for George, above the fray, Dorothy was amused and charmed by him, agreeing with her husband that he was, indeed, a genius. She had been present in Charleston for Gershwin's first brief visit in December 1933 and in January 1934 when the newspapers were already (!) naming Ira and not DuBose as the opera's lyricist, and again later that summer on Folly Beach. Once downtown, when rude cocktail guests talked over Gershwin's piano playing in a Charleston drawing room, she saw DuBose blow his top at the unsophisticated bad manners of his fellow Charlestonians, while the pianist kept his cool, not even noticing as he went on playing.

She visited Gershwin in his apartment in New York as well and was present for his thirty-sixth birthday in 1934 when DuBose was "immediately surrounded by beautiful young girls," and she sat by. By this time, she and particularly DuBose had broken the ice with the genius by teaching him about ice. They liked their cocktails, but Gershwin was not much of a drinker, and so DuBose had to take Gershwin in hand. Though the latter liked to entertain and kept a fully stocked bar, he did not have ice on hand for his guests until DuBose told him of its necessity. And ever polite, DuBose also taught George some manners, especially regarding the use of RSVPS. When Deems Taylor hosted a party for him, George refused to say if he would come or not until DuBose told him he had to attend since he was guest of honor. So, George agreed but arrived at midnight when other guests were leaving.

One of her most vivid memories of George was his act of "seizing my arm as I was leaving a rehearsal to go to the hairdresser," proof that she was present as the opera was being mounted and the creative team was on hand for suggestions. "George would not let me get away until he explained in detail that his *Porgy and Bess* was the greatest music yet written in America."

Dorothy agreed, even as someone much closer to George did not. It was Dorothy who would be saddled with George's mother, Rose, when she and her son visited Charleston together—he was as devoted to his mother as DuBose was to Janie. It was Dorothy's lot to listen to Rose complain about George giving up his lucrative career to write an opera that would never make her any money, a completely tone-deaf comment to the wife of the man who had kept pleading with George to get on with the opera because he needed the money. It was because of Rose, Dorothy believed, that George delayed as long as he did.

She saw things differently from her vantage point on the sidelines and was a dissenting voice about some of the experiences that George, her husband,

and others always put in a positive light when recounting visits to Black congregations to research music and folkways. The received story has been that all the congregants were delighted to have George and DuBose drop in, while Dorothy more coolly, and perhaps more empathetically, believed that the church communities would have preferred to have gone uninterrupted and unobserved, but when asked if they could enter, ministers were unfailingly polite and consented, George and DuBose salving their consciences via their contributions in the collection plates. And from where she was standing in church with them, she thought George found the Holy Roller congregation they dropped into in North Carolina not so much inspiring as frightening.

She continued to stay on the sidelines and stay quiet as the opera approached its premiere set for October 10, 1935, at the Alvin Theatre, exactly eight years to the day after the play's premiere. Preceding that were dress rehearsals, with invited celebrities in attendance, first at Carnegie Hall and then during tryouts at the Colonial Theatre in Boston. "When the final curtain dropped [at that first Boston performance], the audience went wild. . . . As they cheered, almost everyone who had any part in forming the opera came to the stage." Conductor Alexander Smallens was called up, Rouben Mamoulian, director, bowed, and then George Gershwin, the clear favorite, appeared; "the audience was worked up to such an emotional and enthusiastic pitch that it would have probably battered the seats down with pounding, had it been disappointed. This fever-pitch ovation must have been sweet music to the ears of the genius who set DuBose Heyward's tragic primitive tale to such strangely beautiful music."

That night, there were cries for the author of the libretto, too, if from no one else than the Charlestonians present in the audience. And if there was any doubt as to whose presence was demanded, it vanished when chants of "Heyward, Heyward!" filled the hall. But neither DuBose nor Dorothy mounted the stage that night; and in a few weeks, DuBose would hang back and barely be seen at the New York premiere.[10]

No record survives as to why he did not take his rightful place onstage that night in Boston; Dorothy apparently never put down her thoughts on it either. No matter the cause, it set an unfortunate pattern and precedent. Whether from modesty, stage fright, humility, or graciousness, or possibly his distress over the neglect of his wife, DuBose let others enjoy the limelight, shunning it himself. In the future, producers and, to some extent, Ira, too, would step into the vacuum and take advantage of his absence, while taking credit for his and Dorothy's work. If her husband, whose name was on the program and the marquee, would not accept accolades from a public that wanted to crown him, how could she step forward to claim her ghostwritten contributions? She couldn't—not in 1935 and not as time passed. It was only after the stripping of his name from the opera began that Dorothy, no longer standing in the wings, moved to center stage, fighting to restore credit to DuBose. She knew the truth of her own contributions, but that was not an issue; the world, she felt, had to know of DuBose's.

CHAPTER 13

Mamba's Daughters

The years after the opera went swiftly for Dorothy and DuBose, although he, in particular, was slowing down. The hoped-for boost to his career and his finances had not materialized. Although the opera had gained international attention and ran for 124 performances on Broadway, phenomenal for an opera, but not long for a musical, he lost the few thousand dollars he had invested in the production, not to mention the years of deferred work and the energy and hopes he had put into it. "I think George knew they had written a masterpiece," Dorothy reflected, "but to the best of my knowledge DuBose never realized that in *Porgy* he possessed a property of great value." She, on the other hand, knew how good it was, sure to bring financial rewards and renown, but she was never able to convince her husband. Still, he had wonderful memories of working with the Gershwins, and he and George made vague plans to get together in the future on another collaboration. In the meantime, he turned his attention to Janie, Jenifer, and Dorothy and ways to make money.

In 1936 he published an unsuccessful novel that never earned its advance. *Lost Morning* is the story of an artist who, realizing he had sold out, determines to start again upon gaining inspiration from a younger woman. In it, he not only employed the plot device Dorothy had used in her story "The Young Ghost," but it also bears some striking similarities to the 1931 novel *The Golden Vase*, published by ex-Charlestonian Ludwig Lewisohn. If the less than thrilling drama of an artist's midlife crisis did not excite critics or readers, the story of *Lost Morning*'s Felix Hollister's failing marriage nevertheless may have sparked rumors; talk at the time in Charleston had it that the Heywards were splitting up. Dorothy and DuBose promptly threw a party to report that the stories were untrue. A few years later, Josephine Pinckney, at the center of it all, would be involved in other whispers of divorce swirling around her paramour, Wendell Willkie, a 1940 and 1944 Republican candidate for president.[1]

The Heywards were now spending more time in Charleston. They had bought a house they christened Follywood on Folly Beach years before, and Gershwin had rented a house across the street, since lost in a hurricane, when working on the opera. If the Heywards came to town, they sometimes stayed with DuBose's remarried sister, Jeannie Register Haskell, at 98 Church Street. After *Porgy and Bess*, however, they decided to commit to the city, purchasing a mansion, albeit the smallest of its neighbors, at 24 South Battery Street, across from White Point Garden, at the dramatic tip of the Charleston peninsula. It was where one would announce one's arrival in society, something DuBose, with his background and favorite-son status, did not need. Yet the foothold did prove to him, if to no one else, that he had arrived financially, something dear to a man who had been raised in genteel poverty.

The reason for the move was Jenifer. She had been born in New York and raised in North Carolina; before it was too late, her father wanted her to have a traditional Charleston upbringing. Earlier, at age two, he had her name put down for Miss Sadie Jervey's school. Jenifer did attend briefly, but almost immediately her parents enrolled her in Charleston Day School, founded, conveniently, in 1937 on South Battery Street, just as they bought a house nearby. When it moved a few blocks away, Jenifer could still walk there, and the little girl, who was always on her toes, prompting all to think she would be a ballerina, forced her teachers to be on their toes, too. Never, they said, had they encountered such a vague, dreamy girl; DuBose had been a dreamy child, too, and Dorothy was known for scatterbrained faux pas, but Jenifer surpassed them. She also had a penchant for making up stories, no examples known, that set the city "agog."

Jenifer was closer to DuBose than to Dorothy, who was a terrible cook, not at all domestic, and often off writing. To satisfy his daughter's love of bunnies, DuBose crafted a bedtime story for her that, when published, became a perennial children's classic and the most lucrative professional two hours of his life. *The Country Bunny and the Little Gold Shoes* was illustrated by Marjorie Flack, soon to marry William Rose Benét, both friends of the Heywards from the MacDowell Colony.

Dorothy, as always, longed to get back to playwriting; she had time on her hands: Her mother-in-law ran the household, answered the phone, did the ordering and supervised the cook, a chambermaid, and a man of all skills, an African American whose name has come down to us only as Gerald. She was still excited about the Vesey project, but DuBose, less so. Perhaps prompted by *Lost Morning* and the divorce rumors, he went ahead with a collaboration with his wife on a fairly lighthearted play about a long-married couple, icons of the American theater, no longer able to keep up the façade of being *America's Sweethearts*, the play's projected title.

DuBose wrote a draft with characters named Wally and Lee, which Dorothy would change to Kit and Kat, as alliterative as Dorothy and DuBose. Ever the businessman, before proceeding further, he asked friends in Hollywood and agent Audrey Wood about the commercial aspect of it. In the play's pivotal first act, the press would gather for a "lovey" story about the couple when "the woman explodes by announcing dramatically that the team is finished—they are separating." The play was going to end with them reuniting, with the conclusion that it might be necessary to accept life's banalities, perhaps not the typical terrain of Broadway comedies, sweetened a bit with the announcement of a pregnancy. But their work stalled and was never finished.[2]

DuBose was more at loose ends than Dorothy, longing for what, he was not sure: connection, friends, inspiration. Before returning to Charleston, he had tried to get friends like Hervey Allen to move closer to him in North Carolina. "Cool summers and no mosquitoes, air bracing for work," he had written, with "enough nice people to be interesting without being run to death," with the larger Tryon about forty minutes away.

Still looking for inspiration, he agreed to be part of a two-month cruise put together by Huntington Hartford, one of the country's wealthiest men, whose mother had a house in Charleston. There'd be scientists and botanists on board who'd do work at the islands they stopped at in the West Indies, and society people, too, a sort of floating house party on a vintage square-rigger wooden ship, the *Joseph Conrad*. DuBose had visited the Virgin Islands once before with Dorothy and had been struck with the similarity of local speech there to the Lowcountry's Gullah. He left the ship to spend more time there to gather ideas for a story that could be a novel, a collaboration with Gershwin, or both, like *Porgy*.[3]

Ironically, Dorothy had collaboration on her mind, too; she thought she could interest DuBose in a project that would allow them to join forces again. But just as she had with *Porgy*, she disobeyed him and proceeded secretly.

His novel *Mamba's Daughters*, published in 1929, had been partially written during the rehearsals and run-up to the smashing success of *Porgy*; it could not be anything but a positive memory. But *Mamba* would make a terrible play, DuBose thought. He had resisted its dramatizing, thinking it too sprawling, a saga of white and Black families, taking place over two decades, in Charleston, in a bleak phosphate camp outside of town, and in New York City.

But with him abroad, Dorothy set off to prove him wrong.

She had been brooding over it, working it out in her mind, if not on paper, for some time. Its actual first glimmers had come during the "glamorous" *Porgy and Bess* era, in fact at a *Porgy and Bess* party. The hostess was Georgette Harvey, the original Maria in the play, the only principal recast in the opera in the same role. The party was in honor of another veteran of both productions, Rouben Mamoulian. Not especially fond of him but wanting to be polite, Dorothy and DuBose had attended. Jazz singer Ethel Waters rode up to the party with them in the same elevator. "The white lady asked if I remembered her," Waters wrote in her 1950 autobiography. "She'd [Dorothy] been a guest at a society tea where I'd sung some years before." That had been at writer and novelist Katherine Brush's house where Waters had performed "I've got a man now, I've got Porgy." Earlier, Dorothy had seen Waters in a review on Broadway called *Blackbirds*, which parodied *Porgy*, something *Porgy and Bess* scholar Wayne Shirley called a ghost *Porgy*. "Afterwards she'd come up and complimented me on one of my songs, a take-off number on 'Porgy' that Dorothy Fields and Jimmy McHugh had written. I could recall her exact words," Waters reminisced, "'Miss Waters, it's wonderful how you manage to convey the whole story and meaning of "Porgy" in that one little song.'"

As DuBose and Dorothy (who had no trouble addressing Waters as Miss) and Ethel Waters sat together on a couch, Dorothy asked her what she had thought of the opera. Waters replied she had liked it better than the play. Apparently feeling more comfortable with Dorothy, Waters, being told they were the authors, changed the subject to a book she had read some time before, telling her "how and why *Mamba's Daughters* had held me spellbound. Yet I did not know that DuBose Heyward had also written that novel as I explained that Mamba's family was just like my own. . . . 'To everyone else, I know, Mamba is the main character in the story,' I told Dorothy Heyward, 'but not to me. Hagar is the main character. . . .' Hagar, fighting on in a world that had wounded her so deeply . . . was all Negro women lost and lonely in the white man's antagonistic world.

"Dorothy listened as I talked all about this.

"'If we ever decide to dramatize *Mamba's Daughters*,' she said, 'We'll see you.'"[4]

Now two or so years later, with DuBose off on his cruise, Dorothy honored her pledge to Ethel Waters and began dramatizing the novel, not just making it a play, but riskily turning it into a vehicle for a Black woman who had no real acting credits, viewed only as a vocalist. She had given her word to Waters despite what producers would think.

In keeping her word, she used all her innate dramatic skills, slicing away most of the subplots and white characters, focusing on the women in three generations of a Charleston African American family: Mamba, a shrewd old woman from a slum neighborhood like Catfish Row; Hagar, her hulking, slow-witted, oversize daughter; and Hagar's petite, pale-skinned daughter Lissa. Dorothy had to manipulate the passage of years from Lissa as an infant to her leaving Charleston as a young woman to become a famed singer in New York City, achieved through a series of dramatic flashbacks after an initial prologue. Set in the present, people gather in Mamba's downtown Charleston room, Hagar vexingly not there, all excited to hear Lissa sing nationally.

After the prologue, the action of act 1 draws the audience back in time twenty years before; Lissa is a baby in Mamba's arms as Hagar is in court, getting sentenced for almost killing a man for cheating her out of money for her washing. Mamba, desperate not to separate mother and child, uses her wiles to connect herself to a white man in the courtroom, Saint Wentworth, a character based on DuBose, and one described by Dorothy, perhaps slightly tongue in cheek, as "the type of Southern gentleman that the city of Charleston is convinced no other community can grow." Giving into Mamba's pleas, Saint prevails upon the judge, his cousin, to hear Hagar's story, and instead of sentencing her to five years in prison, the judge craftily remands Hagar to Saint's custody, banning her from Charleston, to work for Saint in the Ediwander (Edisto) Island commissary. In the next scene, the five years of parole have nearly passed. Hagar has been accepted by the Black community and is seen to be longing for her daughter, whom Mamba is raising strictly, hoping her light skin color, and her singing talent, inherited from Hagar, might move her up the social ladder into the Black middle class of the city. In this scene, Mamba is supposed to bring her for a visit, but Lissa does not show up, nearly breaking Hagar's heart. In the next scene, in church, where Hagar sings to lift her spirits, the island's minister is shown to be hypocritical, and Gilly Bluton, the island's wily seducer of other men's wives, a sort of Sporting Life figure, is knifed. He's despised by all, so no one comes to his aid. But Hagar, the outsider, is the only one who will take him to a hospital in Charleston. This has transpired in the next scene when Hagar, recognized by the police and chased for breaking her parole, flees to see her mother and get a glimpse of Lissa, who is scared of her. Hagar dumbly surrenders to the police who come for her, ending act 1.

Subsequent scenes in the four-act play move forward in time. Hagar, out of jail, now back in the commissary, still slaves away for her daughter who is advancing in age and talent. When Lissa, as a beautiful young teen, finally comes to the commissary with friends, the awkwardness and distance between mother and daughter are dramatized. Lissa hears that her mother was once in prison but realizes how much Hagar has suffered and labored for her. The play so far, a fairly straight narrative drive, offset with a lot of singing, follows the main developments in the book. In a departure from the text, collapsing time and place, it is in this scene that Lissa is seen by Gilly Bluton, the man Hagar saved earlier. A few hours later, Lissa has been drugged and raped by Gilly, and Hagar, the personification of brute mother love, nearly kills him. Mamba excoriates her for that: it would have gotten Lissa's name in the papers and tainted her career. Lissa is spirited away to New York, and as time advances, her triumphant debut on national radio is announced. Before the performance, Saint, back at the commissary, asks Hagar why she continues to live in poverty chopping cotton, when her daughter is so successful, and she reveals that Gilly has been blackmailing her out of the funds Lissa sends, demanding more and more hush money to keep mum about her baby born after the rape, and dying right after, something not in the novel. The melodrama ratchets up as Hagar confronts Gilly who, unimpressed, declares he's off for New York to "headquarters" to confront Lissa personally for even more blackmail; she can be tried for murder, he says, for burying her baby illegally. To further defend the child for whom she has sacrificed her life, Hagar kills the man she once saved. In the final scene at the commissary, after Lissa's heartful tribute on the radio to her mother, Hagar, "free as Gawd," buys everyone what they want, as she makes the final sacrifice. To save her daughter's name, Hagar confesses that she killed Gilly because he was her lover and betrayed her, something no one believes despite the confession she signs. She then kills herself offstage as a spiritual is sung. Doing this, she has earned grace, transcendence, and, finally, fulfillment and a sense of self. Always being scolded by Mamba for having done the wrong thing, getting herself and others in trouble, Hagar has finally figured out something on her own, a way forward for everyone she loves.

Back from his cruise, DuBose joined Dorothy at Dawn Hill, and they went over the play together, now definitely more of a melodrama than a tragedy. The script was imperfect but had many strengths, with its forward motion, swift passage of time, and the inclusion of music, including Ethel Waters's singing. There was the hope that, although some scenes were tangential to the plot, the Black actors and actresses, singing spirituals provided by the Society for the Preservation of Spirituals, and Waters's voice combined, would add some of the same sort of excitement audiences had loved in *Porgy*. And in the song "Lonesome Walls" that DuBose wrote for Waters, with music by Jerome Kern, he recycled some lines such as "one of these mornings," and "spread your wings" from "Summertime."

In the first week of August 1937 (he returned from his voyage in May), DuBose, although not the primary author (Dorothy later claimed she wrote three-quarters of it), was now taking charge, writing to the Theatre Guild's Warren Munsell that their script would be available in a week or ten days. "The white story has been cut out," he summarized, "and, like *Porgy*, it stands as a great Negro Story." If the Guild wanted to do it, it would have to decide quickly to accommodate Ethel Waters. "She has read part of the script, and . . . is dying to cut loose," he told Munsell. "At this moment, she is holding off possible engagements for the approaching season in the hope that we can get the play accepted in time for her to book up with it." He further acknowledged that Waters's motives were not financial; "she does not expect . . . as large a salary as she gets in musicals. She wants to do this . . . 'for art.'"[5]

"I was thrilled and I was scared when I read the play," Waters recalled. "It was easy for me to visualize the staggering emotional impact *Mamba's Daughters*, written by a Southern white man and his wife would deliver in the theater. In the theater it is the knockout that counts, and *Mamba's Daughters* was all knockout." Not everyone agreed. The Theatre Guild turned it down, and the

Heywards shared the news. "The Heywards, Dorothy and DuBose, [Waters one of the few to put Dorothy first] were fine people," Waters wrote. "They always played straight with me. . . .

"One main reason the moneybags men refused to put up the financing . . . was because the Heywards insisted I play Hagar. 'Ethel Waters, are you kidding?' was what they got whichever way they turned. 'Ethel is a good singer, but no actress.'"

Finally, a call came from the Heywards' agent that the play would be produced, and Waters was called to their hotel room in New York, only to be told the deal suddenly fell through. The authors were disheartened, but Waters was not, having been told by a fortune teller to expect such news.[6]

This was one of a series of setbacks for DuBose. He had wanted to work with George Gershwin on a libretto based on his novel of the Virgin Islands; but Gershwin's tragic death of a brain tumor ended that and also cut short a valued friendship. DuBose would work on it with Arthur Shwartz, and Dorothy would work on the libretto as well. Nothing would come of it, however, and the novel, *Star Spangled Virgin*, published in 1939, would get deservedly poor reviews. If Heyward had started out to write a satire about the impact government programs, like the New Deal, had on the rural Black population of the American Virgin Islands, he badly miscarried, instead creating a demeaning and condescending look at the islanders; perhaps as a libretto, he may have had something in mind similar to the Gershwin brothers' earlier Pulitzer Prize–winning musical of political shenanigans, *Of Thee I Sing*.

But if Heyward was deflated, Waters was not, having been assured by her fortune teller that 1938 was not to be her year, but 1939 would be. Then producer Guthrie McClintic, who had once optioned Heyward's earlier *Brass Ankle*, contracted to mount it. McClintic had strings of successes to his credit, many starring his wife, Katharine Cornell, dubbed the leading lady of the American theater, and well known for her portrayal of Elizabeth Barrett Browning in the rather maudlin play *The Barretts of Wimpole Street*. The Heywards had to have been cheered because of who he was, what he had done in the past, and the fact that he had accepted Ethel Waters as the Heywards' Hagar. In his autobiography, however, he'd cut the Heywards from the story and take full credit for casting Waters in the part. Waters herself credited McClintic for allowing her to find her way in the role and for agreeing to some of her casting suggestions, landing positions for personal friends and young singers whose careers she wanted to advance. Georgette Harvey, at whose apartment the match had been made between Waters and the Heywards, was cast as Mamba; and the small part of Lissa's friend Gardenia was played by none other than Anne Brown, Gershwin's original Bess. White actor José Ferrer got an early start in his career playing Saint, and the up-and-coming Black actor, Canada Lee, later to menace Dorothy's career, got a boost here as well. Spirituals were once more supplied with the aid of the Society for the Preservation of Spirituals, and McClintic, considered an eccentric, if not a genius like Mamoulian, was expected to direct with his usual color and flash.[7]

The omens were good, but pretty much nothing else was, leaving Dorothy flummoxed and at a loss as to how to describe what transpired. She and DuBose showed up for rehearsals, pen in hand, time set aside for the rewrites they knew were necessary for the play to make its transition from the page to the stage. She herself had many ideas of how to improve it. And someone else familiar with the book had suggested cutting the melodrama of birth and secret burial of the baby to reduce plot complications and to "strengthen the last half of the play immeasurably." The scene of the murder could also be rewritten to make it as harrowing as it was in the novel. Not at all necessary, either, was the charade of Gilly also being called Prince, a plot device needed in the novel but not in the play, despite it being written in. Many of DuBose's condescending and flat-footed pronouncements about Blacks could be cut as well. There were phrases about Negroes finding solace in singing, and in the novel he had inferred it was a shame that Blacks were now colliding with a strange new world, similar to his opening poem in *Porgy*—so tragic, in fact, that some Blacks were actually committing suicide, something Heyward thought African Americans never did.

Dorothy was itching to rewrite. But she was stunned when McClintic would not allow it, even when she forcefully told him how bad she believed the play to be in spots. McClintic was a man with a violent temper known for screaming obscenities at wrong numbers on the phone and flinging cards at bridge partners who did not do what he thought best. When she tried to change a maudlin scene, he raged at her for insulting his wife. He told Dorothy she was a "nitwit" because she did not "agree with her [his wife, Katherine Cornell] that every line was magnificent." And then he threw a chair at her.

Dorothy had crossed into an odd emotional territory, something for which her rather straightforward life had not prepared her. The psychological dynamics of McClintic and Cornell presented an emotional minefield. He had grown up poor and uncultured, and rose into society and notoriety when he married the wealthy and socially prominent Cornell, whom he had first met at an early meeting of people who eventually founded the Theatre Guild. Although he had successes as a producer and director, her fame outranked his, and she had a penchant for bad plays, melodramas that would not get the playwright any attention but which would be vehicles for their stars. Having had an abortion, which she regretted, and never having children, might have drawn her to the story of Lissa losing her child, which others wanted to rewrite.

She also relished being in plays with violence and ploys like knockout drops, as in *Mamba*. If she had been Black, Hagar would have been the role for her, and so that apparently affected her judgment. She always vanished when her husband threw a fit, or chair, as he had at Dorothy, seeming to deliberately miss her.[8]

It made its mark, nevertheless, and she got the message; yet again, she became the "little girl" at the hands of a powerful director. It was not so much that she was a woman, since other female playwrights like Lillian Hellman at the time stood up to producers and directed and cast their own works. Dorothy seemed to have no ability or backbone at such times, always deferring action and preferring peace, even while knowing that she and her play would suffer. Yet DuBose was curiously absent, too. Dorothy made no mention at all of her husband weighing in on these issues, which she at least protested. He had not stood up for himself with Ira Gershwin, as she thought he should have. McClintic obviously was not a gentleman, but DuBose was. Not weighing in or insisting on changes would have a profound impact on him, too.

As rehearsals progressed, Dorothy knew the play would bomb; having no tryouts out of town did not help the production either. Marian MacDowell, Jenifer's godmother and head of the MacDowell Colony, seeing them right before the play opened, noted of DuBose that "he sounded so tired and sort of discouraged."

While Dorothy's explanation of not being allowed to rewrite may seem farfetched, analysis of available texts verifies it. Unlike *Porgy*, the published version of this, her fifth play on Broadway, veers just a few dozen words from the original play she and DuBose finished at Dawn Hill in the summer of 1937, so much so, in fact, that an error in local geography in the typed version about a corner of streets that could never meet in Charleston, Elliot and South

Battery, was not caught and appeared in the printed version. In fact, the play as produced was actually worse than the original written script.

For one thing, as the surviving script apparently used in production reveals, the prologue was dropped. In the published version, there is this note: "The play stands up without the Prologue," but "in the opinion of the Authors, its inclusion heightens the drama of the scenes that follow." They were right, but Ethel Waters noted that McClintic thought the play was too long. He retained all the other scenes but made Dorothy's four acts into two.

Most of the dialogue is almost exactly as originally conceived; every now and then, however, Dorothy's original subtleties are blunted in the printed version, as the audience is constantly reminded of how much time has passed from scene to scene, and there are frequent reminders of what consequences Hagar might face from her actions, as if the director did not trust his audience's, or his playwrights', intelligence. Saint lectures Lissa about her mother's self-sacrifice, which is perfectly obvious to anyone in the audience, and the whole play is weakened, as the one transcendent line granted Hagar—regarding her happiness that she has finally made a smart decision without Mamba's interference—is no longer in evidence, removing any catharsis. This further reduces Hagar to a symbol of dumb motherhood, allowing her no growth as a human.[9]

The play opened January 3, 1939, and Waters's performance electrified the audience and entered theatrical history. For the first time, a Black woman's name appeared above the title of a straight play, and Waters transitioned from a singer to one of America's finest dramatic actresses overnight. "That [was the] night I'd been born for," she wrote in her autobiography. (The play also made Broadway history in another way: Perry Watkins, the scenic designer, became the first African American to gain such credit.)

When Brooks Atkinson, the sole critic who did not think Waters's performance a benchmark in Broadway history, criticized her in his opening-night review, many in the theatrical world protested. They took out an advertisement in the press, stating, "We . . . feel that Ethel Waters's superb performance in *Mamba's Daughters* . . . is a profound emotional experience . . . a magnificent example of acting . . . moving on a plane of great reality, that we are glad to pay for the privilege of saying so," with Judith Anderson, Tallulah Bankhead, Oscar Hammerstein, Burgess Meredith, Carl Van Vechten, and both of DuBose's publishers, John Farrar and Stanley Rinehart, among the signatories. "That ad so startled Mr. Atkinson that he hurried back for another look at our show," Waters wrote. "And he did a complete whirlabout. Yes, that second time, he liked it.

"The reaction of women who saw the play was amazing. . . . Each night they'd come back to my dressing room. Always I had to stay in my stage clothes until after they were gone. They had come to visit Hagar and would have resented finding Ethel Waters in her place." Hagar was a character for the ages, and Waters would play portions of the role for the rest of her life. The play would be revived at a theater in the Bronx in 1953, and again off Broadway in 1998, winning the actress Heather Gillespie, playing Hagar, an Obie.

Mrs. MacDowell went to see the play soon after it opened and agreed that Waters was magnificent. "Poor DuBose," she wrote, "people will go to hear the players, if not to hear the play." Displaying her distrust of women at the Colony, she went on with "a mean thing to say, but one can't help wondering about his wife's work." When *Porgy* triumphed, DuBose was credited, but when *Mamba* failed, Dorothy was blamed. "She never had anything of her own succeed." Yet, reading the reviews, MacDowell found "certain faults that the newspapers overemphasize." While admitting the script was "thin," she found all the criticism "not quite fair, for DuBose Heyward made a wonderful part for her [Waters]," now suddenly crediting DuBose for anything good in the play. As for Dorothy, "she looked a wreck last night. The papers have been cruel about the play—rub it in. . . . It just makes one sick."[10]

Yet *Life* magazine, one of the most influential periodicals in the country, thought the play important enough to give it a several-page spread, showing images of various scenes, and white Harlem Renaissance leader Carl Van Vechten wrote that "I cannot quite convince myself that any play which offers us a character of such unforgettable proportions can be regarded as insignificant or unimportant."

While Waters triumphed, the Heywards did not. And one wonders if it was about this time that Dorothy changed the name of the characters in their embryonic play *America's Sweethearts* to Kit and Kat. Kit is what McClintic called his wife, and maybe Dorothy saw through the fraud of their marriage, he gay, she lesbian, both pretending to wedded bliss for the public. If so, it shows Dorothy standing up a bit for herself, a tad wickedly perhaps, for the play was going to end with Kit becoming pregnant, suggesting that Dorothy knew the backstory of Cornell's abortion and regret. It would have been her one way of getting back at the architect of her destruction, if *Sweethearts* had seen production—which it did not.

Mamba lingered on into May. The year 1939 was not a good one for Broadway according to their agent, Audrey Wood, and soon, to help recoup the funds he had put up for its production, McClintic was asking players and authors to take a cut in their royalties, to which they all agreed. Earlier, however, DuBose had told Dorothy not to do that when her own plays had been in trouble. Attendance perked up when Eleanor Roosevelt, wife of the president, attended, but it closed after about 160 performances, before going on the road.

The Heywards' return to Charleston after the opening had many consolations. Soothingly, the local press had loyally called the play a triumph. Janie and Jenifer were there, and the old solidarity between mother and son was restored. But worse for DuBose than any professional failure was what happened just a few months later. He was in the North Carolina mountains in June 1939 when Janie died at age seventy-four of heart failure. Shocked and heartbroken, he accompanied her body back to Charleston and attended the funeral at St. Philip's Church cemetery, where she was laid to rest next to his father, a man he barely remembered. She, however, had been a mainstay of DuBose's life.

Her loss left him stunned, and he wrote to Hervey Allen that he was "too shot to work." But as he finally began to focus, he recalled the humiliation he and Dorothy had suffered with McClintic, seeing how unfair it had been to them as playwrights; it would be shameful if it happened to others. He was now toying with the idea, as Paul Green had with his Carolina Playmakers in North Carolina, of creating a lab for new, upcoming talent. "I am beating the bushes along the Carolina coast for potential Eugene O'Neils [*sic*]," he was soon reporting to a friend.[11]

New York had turned on him and he returned the favor, turning his back on it. He was now back in Charleston for good.

CHAPTER 14

The Dock Street Theatre

DuBose wasn't nursing his wounds, or not exactly, but he was changing his focus as a writer, from novelist to playwright. He had authored and acted in a small play for locals in 1913 and had also written a skit for an anniversary of the Charleston Museum ten years later, in which he had played his ancestor, Thomas Heyward, a signer of the Declaration of Independence. He made mention of a possible resurgence in Southern drama in a 1925 essay, but it wasn't until Dorothy had dramatized *Porgy*, bringing him fame and fortune, that DuBose had begun to be seen, and to see himself, as a playwright. *Porgy* had brought him two Hollywood screenwriting jobs, and he had enjoyed working with Gershwin on *Porgy and Bess*. Now, despite the failure of *Brass Ankle* and the poor critical reception of the play version of *Mamba*, but possibly because his last two novels had been lackluster, he began to concentrate on playwriting, with his native city offering him a salary and an opportunity.

Dorothy spent these years in the background, working on the Vesey play and trying to raise a difficult child while DuBose was in the local limelight due to his involvement with the Dock Street Theatre.

Built with Federal Emergency Relief Administration funds in a public works drive during the Depression, this jewel-box reproduction of an eighteenth-century London theater stood on the site of the earliest purpose-built theater in the colonies, now incorporated within and beyond the walls of a nineteenth-century hotel. The original theater had opened in Charleston in 1735 on Dock Street presenting the play *The Recruiting Officer*, and in 1937, some two hundred years later, it had been restaged with a witty prologue written and recited by DuBose. The event merited national attention, with many Charlestonians, including Dorothy, photographed on opening night, splayed across the pages of *Life* magazine.[1]

The city now had a magnificent theater, and the Carolina Art Association, the organization whose board administered the art museum in town under the directorship of Robert N. S. Whitelaw, took an interest in it. Whitelaw volunteered to lead the charge of coming up with a program worthy of the splendid structure. In the spring of 1938, the association received a Rockefeller Foundation grant to study the feasibility of creating a plan, and a second grant made possible the putting of policies and procedures into action. DuBose, who had been elected a member of the association's board, along with fellow board member Josephine Pinckney, were designated as liaisons to work with an amateur community theater group, the Footlight Players, to address the issue. The fact that Dorothy, the true dramatist, was neither put on the board nor tapped in a professional capacity reveals the institution's loyalty to locals, in lieu of outsiders. DuBose and Josephine, in fact, were coupled on three committees, perhaps again fueling the great divorce rumor gossiped about in the city. DuBose and Josephine had worked together on founding the Poetry Society of South Carolina in 1920, which had resulted in a blossoming of poets in the region, and now two decades later, they were back again, hoping to make Charleston a theatrical capital.

Heyward had been fairly successful dodging office-holding in the Poetry Society, and now he gladly resigned his position on the Carolina Art Association board to lead the project as resident dramatist, with a grant-paid salary of $2,600, allowing "him to continue his own creative writing" while "stimulating and developing an interest in playwriting." Even before the Rockefeller grant, just as soon as the theater had opened, Claire Boothe Luce, Broadway playwright and one of the wealthy Northerners who wintered in Charleston with her husband, Henry Luce, founder of *Time* magazine, had put up $200 for a best one-act play award, the winner to be produced on the Dock Street stage. While it was national in scope, an award for a local playwright was announced simultaneously.[2]

The national award went to William Rose Benét; his play *Day's End* was produced in May 1938. In June 1938 College of Charleston professor Paul Weidner had his play *The Fourth Watch* produced. *The Happy Journey*, by Thornton Wilder, Dorothy's friend from the MacDowell Colony, was thrown in for good measure. In this new development in their lives, Dorothy kept her habitual silence, although she was far better suited to speak on dramatic writing and theatrical production than her husband. Whether by choice, habit, or desire to build up her spouse, she stayed in the background—literally so in a photograph and news story about the contest, seated behind DuBose and Benét.

In November 1939, once all had been formalized, DuBose delivered a speech about the new program. Dorothy must have been gratified to hear her husband, who years before had not been "handicapped by ever having read a book or taking a course in playwriting," finally acknowledge how exacting a craft it was; "having served my apprenticeship in most forms of creative writing as practiced today," he said, "I feel qualified to state that in my opinion the technique of the drama is far the most difficult to master.... Writing for the theatre therefore requires not only a higher order ... but one that has applied itself to the labor of mastering a difficult and elaborate technique." He continued, boldly appropriating both his wife's profession and her experience. Making no reference to her, he lectured his audience about George Pierce Baker at Harvard, and how students of his once had the rare opportunity to write plays, have them critiqued, and possibly see them performed. Now, he announced, he was going to adapt that process to a group of hopeful playwrights in Charleston. Writers would send their plays in, and the one best suited for production would be chosen and its author brought to town to shape it for staging. There is no suggestion that Dorothy did anything but silently watch this act of professional ventriloquism as he spoke and the plan went forward; only after his death would she link her association with Baker and the Dock Street. Announcements of the prize competition, one national and one local, went out and entries poured in.[3]

DuBose picked *Danbury Fair*, by Albert Carriere, as the national winner, and Barrett Clark, the executive director of Dramatists Play Service, gave the local award to *Portrait of a Gentleman*, by Marian Murdoch. Caroline Sinkler, who had always aided DuBose in his projects, even paying for his hospitalization as a young man, provided funding. Both one-acts were duly produced at the Dock Street Theatre in the late spring of 1940. Brimming with a sense of fulfillment, DuBose submitted his resident dramatist annual report on May 16, complete with text and statistics. Under his direction, ten local writers had been recruited; they had written six three-act plays and six one-act plays; four one-acts were produced, and one play, he reported, was getting some professional interest in New York. Seventy-five locals had been recruited to act as a collaborative group of critics and audience members. Like a farmer proud of his bountiful crop, excited and full of new ideas for the next season, DuBose took off with his family to North Carolina before the heat set in. Dawn Hill had been sold to support Follywood and the house on the Battery; and now, sadly, without Janie for the very first time, the Heywards were to stay with friends, the Matthews, who had an apartment for them.[4]

But up in the mountains, DuBose seemed out of sorts. In their seventeen years together, Dorothy had often seen him depressed, and she hoped he could gather his strength before they made their annual pilgrimage to the MacDowell Colony. After feeling some pain for a couple of days, he gave in to Dorothy's suggestion to go see his cousin, Dr. Allen Jervey, in Tryon. But that day it was raining; the next day, they didn't make plans. On June 16, DuBose saw Jenifer off in a car to visit a friend, and Margaret Matthew drove him down to the doctor in Tryon. That afternoon Dorothy had his cocktail ready for his arrival, but when no one returned in time, she poured it out.

In Tryon, Jervey had taken a cardiogram, suspecting heart trouble, and had sent DuBose back home; but five miles into the twenty-mile return trip, gaining altitude, DuBose experienced sudden severe pains. Matthew immediately turned the car around. She left Heyward in Jervey's care and sped back for Dorothy. But by the time they returned, DuBose had died, likely of a coronary thrombosis. He was two-and-a-half months shy of his fifty-fifth birthday, his death coming just over a year after Janie's.

"I never saw DuBose ill," a shocked Dorothy repeated endlessly to friends and family for weeks. "When he left for Tryon he was his own self. He was gone when I reached the hospital." And she had seen no signals, had "not the slightest misgiving." Her ignorance of his condition appalled her. Stunned, she could not think. DuBose had once told her what he wanted for a funeral, but she could recall none of it. Grabbing up a very confused Jenifer, who had seen her father seemingly well that morning, she returned "addlepated" to Charleston; she had forgotten that the South Battery house had been closed up. Mother and daughter arrived to rooms sheeted and ghostly, silent as a tomb, making the experience even more dreadful.

The funeral was held two days later in St. Philip's cemetery, a few buildings north of the Dock Street Theatre. The city turned out, and it was national news. The service was graveside only; there were no hymns. The rector read Heyward's early poem, "Epitaph for a Poet."

Later that night, June 18, Dorothy and Josephine Pinckney, who had helped with all the arrangements, "sat in the grave yard together. She had driven me there to see the flowers. They were very beautiful. We sat on a low coping together looking at them."

Dorothy would always remember how Josephine

> suddenly began telling me of a time she had been deeply in love. I thought then, & I still believe, she was saying to me, "I want you to know the truth because I suspect that people told you it was DuBose I loved."
>
> She was right. I remember so clearly the first time I heard it. Lawrence [sic] and Helen Stallings were in Ch[arleston] & DB & Jo & I drove with them to Middleton Gardens. Jo, Lawrence & DB decided to walk around the lakes.
>
> Helen & I sat down on a bank by a lake. She said, "So that is J. P. Charming, isn't she? I've heard about her all my life. And of course [you] know what I've heard. That she has never married because she has always been in love with DB."
>
> I was startled. It seemed such an odd thing to say. . . .
>
> Jo & DB were devoted friends for a good ten years before I came into the picture. . . . Though I've never thought of it before, my guess is that if Jo had wanted to marry DB she could have had him.
>
> I am no wiser today than I was then.[5]

If not wise back then, she was not worried. Dorothy had never doubted DuBose's devotion to her or Josephine's constancy as a friend; she could be depended upon for anything, from unsheeting a closed house to doubling as family. Within weeks of DuBose's death, Dorothy was considering Jo, Jenifer's godmother, as a possible legal guardian if Dorothy got ill or died or could not care for her daughter.

Her first choice had been her "twin cousin," Charles Hartzell, with whom she had spent her childhood in Puerto Rico, but that would "break bonds" with Charleston, against DuBose's wishes. Sending Jenifer to DuBose's sister, Jeannie, Dorothy believed, would be "tragic." "Jo is next," she wrote her attorney. "But she is not family." An elderly cousin, Elizabeth DuBose Miller, was considered, but she seemed too fragile; "maybe a joint [custody] between Junior and Jo" was what Dorothy proposed.

She had been named resident playwright immediately after DuBose's death. Her designated salary was $2,000, a trifle less than he had been paid, but enough to allow her to pay the mortgage on the house on the Battery. And money was now an issue. She had met with attorneys and bank officers to look over the finances, which DuBose had always managed. She'd have to rent the house on Folly Beach. There was some cash, and some investments, but not much.[6]

Along with shock and grief, there was a life for her and Jenifer to figure out. Dorothy also needed to learn how to make a living.

CHAPTER 15

War and Worries

Dorothy and DuBose had planned to go the MacDowell Colony later that summer; Jen had been enrolled in the nearby Sergeant camp. Dorothy, at a loss, carried on with both plans.

The return must have been bittersweet to the site where she claimed that her life began, where her playwriting career commenced, and where DuBose had proposed. "Poor little Dorothy Heyward is here, so brave," Mrs. MacDowell wrote upon her arrival less than a month after the sudden death; "and though associations make it hard for her, her many friends help her." Those friends were William Rose Benét, who had won the first playwriting award at the Dock Street Theatre; Marjorie Flack, illustrator of *The Country Bunny*; popular editor, poet, and folklorist Carl Carmer with his wife, Betty; and playwright Thornton Wilder. Those three, Wilder, Carmer, and DuBose, according to one source, were among the artists Mrs. MacDowell favored most at the Colony. The Benéts, Wilder, and the Carmers banded together to help Dorothy, convincing her that getting back to work would be her salvation.

Closest to her heart was the play about Vesey. She and DuBose had shared "embryonic" scenes with actor Paul Robeson, who was enthusiastic. Robeson had worked with Heyward on *The Emperor Jones* and had briefly played Crown on Broadway. He was ready to start before the authors were. To keep busy, he had taken the role of John Henry on Broadway, the show debuting and dying in January 1940, and then kept tabs on how the script was progressing.[1]

That summer, her friends suggested that although she had worked on it for over three years and it was still not finished, the play, in their opinion, was far enough advanced for her to give a reading of the script at the Colony, an event considered momentous enough for a *Life* magazine photographer to be present to record it, although the images were never published. After the reading,

Thornton Wilder, wildly enthusiastic, recommended that Dorothy work with Jed Harris, who had produced Wilder's *Our Town* on Broadway to Pulitzer Prize–winning results. Harris read it and was enthusiastic, too, but wanted changes: Vesey's drive to free his people and his family was a straightforward story of a man obsessed by a single idea of self-liberation. Both Harris and Wilder were more intrigued with the enslaved George Wilson, who revealed the plot to the white authorities. What had it been like for him, conflicted between freedom for his people and his personal loyalty to a white man he did not want to see murdered? That, they felt, could expand the story. Playwright Esther Wilbur Bates, who was also at the reading, wrote Dorothy that "even without any changes, it is still a perfectly wonderful piece of playwriting, and you are too close to it to know how magnificent it is." She agreed it might be a sound idea to have George "torn between the irreconcilable impulses."

Dorothy was amenable, but pinning down Harris was difficult. If she had had issues with Mamoulian, and had been horrified by McClintic, she found Harris, often called the most loathsome man in the American theater, baffling. "Dorothy, no one in the world has ever wanted to be responsible for anyone else in the world's knowing Jed," Thornton warned her, yet Harris, in Wilder's opinion, was "not only the best director in the U.S.A., but the only one. . . . Distrust the charm," he went on to tell her. "Beware of the run around—the endless dickering with no money down, the great big Friendship and the then disappearing into air. Get the Dramatist's Guild contract as soon as his interest appears genuine."[2]

Wilder's predictions proved true; for even though Harris said he loved the play, and said he loved her, he would not respond to Dorothy's queries, and he did not follow through with his promise to option it. As soon as he did, she'd get on with the suggested rewriting. But she waited and waited.

It was at this juncture that the Theatre Guild expressed an interest in the play. Lawrence Langner thought it "one of the finest . . . that has come into our hands in the last five years." Yet Dorothy kept trying for Harris, until Langner won her over with a deeper connection to Robeson, whom everyone believed would be perfect for Vesey. Robeson was a friend of the "reddish," communist-leaning Lee Strasberg, whom the Guild decided to hire as director for the play.

Dorothy signed, and the Guild immediately put the pressure on, wanting to get the play staged by January 1942, before its option lapsed and Jed Harris would swoop in. Dorothy wanted more time to rewrite, as correspondence with Robeson went back and forth, and other Black actors deluged Dorothy with résumés and letters expressing their interest. Dorothy was in New York in December 1941, seeing to casting and preparing for rehearsals, when Pearl Harbor was bombed, and America's point of view changed overnight. A play about American division, whites and Blacks pitted against one another in a deeply flawed country that could not live up to its democratic ideals, was now seen, not just as unprofitable, but unpatriotic.

"We feel it would be bad to open a play of rebellion and race feeling and tragic mood at this moment when the public feeling is so strong for every sort of solidarity and the necessity of sacrificing individual freedom for the time being" was Theresa Helburn's judgment, shared with Dorothy ten days after the bombing. Casting stopped, rehearsals did not start, and the contract lapsed, the Guild deciding to mount it at a later, more propitious, time. Dorothy had no choice but to agree and hope that, maybe after all, Jed Harris would reappear. Her play's fate might have been different had it been produced then, instead of years later with a different Guild, a different script, and a different mood in the country.[3]

Although disappointed, she had plenty to keep her busy with what was fast becoming a full-time job at the Dock Street Theatre, dedicated to realizing DuBose's last goal in life. Against the advice of Clare Boothe Luce, Dorothy changed the contest from one-act plays to full three-act works. Luce warned it would be too difficult, but Dorothy disagreed. Nevertheless, she gratefully accepted Luce's suggestion that the award be renamed for DuBose. Luce helped fund the $500 award, along with contributions from Josephine Pinckney, her new beau/friend Wendell Willkie, Caroline Sinkler of Philadelphia, Huntington Hartford, and Charleston and Hollywood scriptwriter and playwright John MacGowan.

The first annual DuBose Heyward Playwriting Contest, as it was now called, was too successful. Dorothy was immediately swamped with applicants, over 140 scripts in hand a few days before the deadline and about 100 more by the time it arrived, requiring heroic and frenzied work on her part and that of others drafted to prevent a disaster. Dorothy was overwhelmed not just by the sheer number, but the need to stick to the deadline of announcing the winner by March 1. "Mrs. DuBose Heyward, the judge of the contest, is busy day and night reading the manuscripts," the local press announced, explaining that she was also calling on all her literary friends, soliciting help from

Poetry Society founder and old friend Laura Bragg, Frank Durham (a Citadel professor later to write the first biography of DuBose), Huntington Hartford, Helen McCormack, future director of the Gibbes Gallery Museum of Art, writer Katherine Drayton Mayrant Simons, and J. Waties Waring, eventually to be the first federal judge to rule that segregation is inequality. Further help was "solicited from Memminger high school, Ashley Hall [another local all-girls school], Charleston Day school [the one Jenifer attended], College of Charleston and the Citadel. The head of the English department in each one of these institutions has given cooperation in the work of reading and judging the plays."[4]

The first winner was *Museum Piece*, by Peggy Lamson, a lighthearted look at masterpieces and forgery, centered on a museum buying, displaying, and then doubting the authenticity of a Donatello sculpture. The young woman got the opportunity to come to town, see her script through rehearsal, and watch its vast cast present it in late April 1941. The local reviewer raved, and Lamson's second play, *Respectfully Yours*, was almost immediately optioned and bought by the Theatre Guild, which was then deferring Dorothy's own play on Vesey, ironically. Dorothy was her advocate, and Lamson became a lifelong friend.

The second (1941–42) season proved just as busy. The winner that year was engineer Thomas Conger Kennedy, whose *Song of the Bridge* dramatized a construction crew. He had previously played small parts on Broadway, but now, as a civilian in munitions war work, he could not commit the time to see his play through production, managing instead only a few hours of conference with Dorothy on his way to Texas. She silently rewrote it with help from Theresa Helburn from the Theatre Guild.

The rules changed for the 1942–43 contest, requiring a two-dollar submission fee to help pay for the work of professional script reader Edward Eager. Kirke Meacham and his play *Lilac Lake* tied with Robert M. Savage's *Mike the Angel*, splitting the $500 award and each getting a production in the spring, an event deemed interesting enough to inspire a syndicated photo and wire story. This season also saw fourteen radio scripts written by local playwrights in their "People in Defense" series, focusing on home front and war issues, broadcast locally. The scripts were then sent on to the national Office of Emergency Management to be used in communities across the country.[5]

War work was changing the city, and Dorothy ventured into a new field when Somerset Maugham, then staying at his publisher Nelson Doubleday's estate near Yemassee, South Carolina, came to town to give a live radio broadcast in support of books for sailors. He accepted an invitation from Dorothy, bringing younger writer Glenway Wescott with him, straining Dorothy's meager hostess skills. "I usually tried to persuade my guests that I was just having informal potluck—to cover my deficiencies," she confessed, not the best qualities for Maugham's visit, as he was then considered something like literary royalty.

Dorothy said she nearly rebuilt the house preparing and served champagne for the first time. It went to her head, as Jenifer, now a preteen, rushed in with her injured dog bleeding profusely. The evening was only saved by the more sophisticated and "always abstentious" Josephine Pinckney, who got the guests up to the Dock Street Theatre in time for an interview and then hosted a flawless reception for the writers at her house, adding to her august reputation and also to "Dizzy Dorothy" lore.[6]

In 1942 Dorothy's hopes for *Vesey* revived when the play caught the attention and intense interest of Canada Lee, whom Dorothy might have remembered from *Mamba's Daughters*; Ethel Waters certainly did, not caring for Lee's lack of professionalism. In that production, in trying to get other actors to crack up on stage, he had often disregarded blocking and refused to follow wardrobe rules, resulting in his pants falling down onstage one evening. Waters had been forced to upstage him one night when he tried to do it to her. Lee, however, was now electrifying audiences on Broadway in the dramatic adaptation of Richard Wright's *Native Son*. Playing Bigger Thomas, Lee was being hailed as a young Paul Robeson, for his engagement in left-wing politics, his acting chops, and his personal magnetism. While he did not sing, he had been a prizefighter, and making the story local, his mother was from South Carolina. Lee was the star of the moment, and his interest in the play could mean everything. But on December 7, 1942, exactly a year after the attack on Pearl Harbor, which canceled the play, Audrey Wood telegraphed Dorothy that Lee had changed his mind and was now "fearful" of doing *Set My People Free*. But he was still on the lookout for a vehicle to follow up his triumph in *Native Son*, and a possible candidate for a script had just crossed Audrey's desk. Its young author, Howard Rigsby, away in the army, had done it hurriedly. Was Dorothy interested in taking a look at it and possibly fixing the script?[7]

Its premise was intriguing. Sam Johnson, a Black merchant marine, survives a torpedo strike and is washed up on an island in the Pacific occupied by the Japanese. The natives, people of color, take him in, and for the first time in his life, Johnson, a Black everyman, finds himself part of a society where he is neither a minority nor the subject of prejudice. Instead, he is accepted in a world where his white shipmate now has to fear being hunted by the Japanese. Even the name of the island, New Georgia, reinforces the reversal theme. Sam's choice is at the center of the play: Should he pursue personal contentment or fight the Japanese for a cause and country that never included him?

Within a week, Canada Lee, sensing its important and timely themes, committed to the play, as unfinished as it was; and neophyte producer David Lowe became part of the deal. They had tried to get Mamoulian and Elia Kazan interested, but both rejected it, one reason being that it was not a full script. Wood pressed Dorothy for a decision.

The timing could not have been worse. With her rheumatism and tonsils flaring up, she was administering a national playwriting contest, raising a daughter starting to present with emotional problems, and she had just been contacted by her old friend and coauthor of *The Cinderelative*, Dorothy DeJagers, now in crisis. Not only did DeJagers need help with a play of her own, but she lacked funds for hospitalization for her increasingly evident mental illness. Ever-loyal Dorothy helped her out on both counts. "Having a play . . . produced this year is a necessity," Dorothy confided to DeJagers, "if Jenifer is to continue to attend [the] best camp and school. And she would be broken-hearted at leaving her school because all her friends go there. So Mama must work." The Howard Rigsby play was a godsend and, if a tad inconvenient, nevertheless a possible source of income. She said yes to Rigsby, Wood, David Lowe, and Canada Lee.[8]

The contract was signed in January 1943, and Audrey Wood suggested Dorothy get 50 to 60 percent of royalties along with top billing. Even though she needed the money, Dorothy protested, insisting on getting a smaller percentage, affording the younger writer a break to advance his career, as she was doing with DeJagers and with all the hopeful playwrights sending in their work to the Dock Street Theatre. She also insisted that Rigsby, with whom she had only corresponded, precede her in the credits.

Her self-effacing altruism would once more prove self-defeating. In early 1943, questioning some of the author's scenes, she concluded that Rigsby was the more poetic writer. While he favored grandiose speeches, she considered them talky and preachy; and although he gave her complete authority to rewrite, she nevertheless hesitated to cut his words, perhaps remembering how distraught she had been seeing her own scripts travestied. She did not want to gut parts that would break his heart, such as an apparent scene with ghosts of the ancestors present. "I have a fondness for ghosts," Dorothy admitted before cutting them, later lobbying unsuccessfully with her agent and the director to put them back in a final, pivotal scene where Sam believes he hears them, convincing him to do the right thing.[9]

Complicating the adaptation further was that she could not come to New York to work with producer Lowe and actor Lee: there was Jenifer, who needed much attention, and she was in the midst of the current prizewinning play, *Mike the Angel*, being produced, its author expecting to collaborate with her. She would come in an instant, she wrote Audrey Wood, but her commitment to DuBose's last project was sacrosanct.

That brought David Lowe to Charleston, briefly. Most of their discussions, however, like George and DuBose's on the opera, took place through the mail, as she and Lowe searched for a more dramatic motivation for Sam to take a stand for his country despite its disrespect of him. She accepted Lowe's idea of having the little boy who looks up to Sam die at the hands of the Japanese, which she did not like, still favoring the ghosts; the critics would not like the new idea either. In an attempt to learn more about the Solomon Islands, she did research at the Charleston Library Society and created a new character, the Lelaini, a folk leader, perhaps thus taking the place of the ghosts. In doing so, she created a role for Frank Wilson, her original Porgy, knowing he would walk off in any scene he was in. In trying to come up with a new ending and new scenes, Dorothy bounced ideas off the Dock Street Theatre's apprentice playwriting group.[10]

When the season was over, Dorothy headed to New York, barricading herself in the air-conditioned Gotham Hotel to focus on the script and make up for lost time. "I'm bubbling over with unabashed enthusiasm for the first time in months," David Lowe wrote to her on August 20, seeing her rewrites. "Time is definitely of the Essence," Dorothy summarized to DeJagers. "In a few short months . . . my play that was timely a year ago seem[s] like something by Thomas Nelson Page. Yet this change . . . makes this the time of all times for my play which happens to be about race prejudice, a plea for true freedom for all men."

Lee Strasberg, who had been considered for the Vesey play (and later founded the Actors' Studio, the home of method acting), was hired to direct.

He, along with David Lowe, a first-time producer, never really to succeed on Broadway but to do well in television, pressed Dorothy to finish the script to keep abreast of changes going on in the war. "But I have never before written a play in less than a year," she replied. "In signing up with you I had memories of my 47 Workshop days when I remembered accomplishing wonders when Professor Baker would demand that I finish an act by Wednesday. I overlooked the little fact that that was twenty years ago. While by no means detracting from Mr. Rigsby's fine beginning, I now feel that this has been almost as much work as the writing of a complete play. [It would become two-thirds hers, she'd say eventually.] Indeed I have sometimes felt slowed down by having ideas not my own to cleave to."[11]

Events were relentless. She woke up one morning to read that *New Georgia*, in the Solomon Islands, which had been the play's name, had been liberated, outpacing Rigsby's plot and making a title and place change necessary. She renamed it *South Pacific*, years before James Michener's Pulitzer Prize–winning book was published and became the basis of a Broadway hit. The rechristened work, with incidental music by Paul Bowles, was rushed into production, opening on December 29, 1943, just a few weeks after the one-year anniversary of Dorothy having first heard of it.

All three acts take place in the government community house on a now-unnamed island. Ruth, a young teacher, and her intellectual and ineffectual suitor, St. John, hide Sam and a white sailor named Dunlap after they survive their ship's sinking by the Japanese. Sam is lusty and content, while Dunlap, an articulate Princeton graduate, and St. John lecture him about the evils of their enemy. St. John leaves and Sam makes a move on the rather prim Ruth.

Act 2, a month later, shows Ruth in love with Sam, who is getting along well with everyone on the island. The Japanese threat is only conveyed by bullhorn announcements and reports of offstage atrocities, weakening the play, whose drama would have been much more effective as a film. Dunlap and St. John try to recruit Sam to prevent the Japanese from shelling the U.S. Navy to free the island, but he refuses to fight for a country that treated him so abysmally. The N-word is used frequently.

In act 3, Dunlap and St. John have been killed, and many on the island have turned against Sam for his selfish view of life, most especially the young boy Daniel, grandson of the tribal chief, the Leilani. By the end of the play, both of them have also been killed, finally prompting Sam to action. The curtain falls as he goes off to fight. Sam's change of heart reflects not so much a philosophical decision to support democracy, with all its faults, as much as it does melodrama, revenge, and sentimentality, showing Dorothy, too rushed and sacrificing nuance, taking the trite way out.

The reviews, resultingly, were mixed, while even those that condemned it never failed to praise the play for its basic moral integrity. "Without question, 'South Pacific' has many good qualities," Lewis Nichols began his *New York Times* review. "In the first place, Howard Rigsby and Dorothy Heyward, who wrote it, have brought to the play a sincerity which is not usual along Broadway. . . . The basic idea of a Negro shoved around at home and feeling no overpowering urge to help those who had shoved him, is unquestionably excellent. But the motivation of this particular one smacks too much of the theatre. His love for the girl, which is one of the reasons he decides to go after the Japanese, brings the whole thing down to the level of fifty plays a season—a level with which 'South Pacific' should not be content. Another of the reasons is the regard in which he had been held by a young native boy who was killed by the Japanese; that, too, is garden variety plot."

Critic Louis Kronenberger agreed. "Howard Rigsby and Dorothy Heyward have had something to say, and they have tried to say it as honestly as possible. That they have said it clumsily and confusedly at times is to their disadvantage but not to their discredit." Most did not like the pacing of the play, and Strasberg's direction was deemed leaden; but just about everyone agreed on the superlative performance of Canada Lee. *The New Yorker* noted that "as long as he is portraying a Negro in sullen rebellion against the white man's ways, he is magnificent, and even when he is asked to become an entirely different man for no dramatically valid reason, his honest intelligent struggle with the part is impressive to watch."[12]

Too impressive, Dorothy believed. She saw him still upstaging everyone and drawing attention to himself, making it a star vehicle at the expense of the ensemble and the script. "I had written a long speech about people who had nothing to be proud of except the color of their white skins. Everyone agreed that it was too long a preachment just at the end of the play. It was cut over Canada Lee's protest. On opening night, he 'forgot.' He apologized, but somehow he forgot every night that the short-lived play ran." That, with lackluster reviews, and with beginner David Lowe lacking the finances to keep the play on the stage to do rewrites, while most of the cast suffered the flu, caused *South Pacific* to close after five performances.

Yet its strengths lingered in many a critic's memory. In an article a month or so later, George Jean Nathan reflected, "That the play had its faults is no denying, but with all its faults it was nonetheless so superior to some such still running" on Broadway. "A flimsy comedy or romance could succeed despite its faults" was a later scholar's assessment. "But a flimsy play on race, war, and patriotism—touchy subjects ripped from the morning headlines—was asking for big trouble."[13]

Howard Rigsby, who'd go on to publish many novels but no more plays, waxed philosophic about it. "What has irritated and depressed me is that we both made a sincere and worthy effort—not for money," he wrote Dorothy. "I don't mean to condemn David as an entrepreneur; just don't think it was his type. Either that or had too much time [or not enough] to fiddle with it." On the other hand, Rigsby had nothing but praise for Dorothy. "You won't ever get away from the Rigsby clan," he warned her. She had made a friend but had failed to make any money.

Her return to Charleston brought her back to pressing problems; Jenifer was lovely; Jenifer was bright, finally settling into her schoolwork. But Jen, as she was called, puzzled Dorothy. She had been devoted to her father, but after his death she refused to speak of him, take flowers to his grave, or even enter the cemetery. Dorothy thought Jen would grow out of it, but her erratic behavior continued; as Dorothy herself grew more and more devoted to DuBose's memory, her daughter's act of turning any picture of her father to the wall was disturbing. Did Jen feel betrayed? Was she angry? DuBose had seen her go visit friends a few hours before he went to consult his doctor and had never returned. Grandmother Janie, also devoted to her, had died and deserted her almost just as suddenly. Dorothy worried that this might have somehow shocked and undermined Jenifer emotionally, forgetting that she herself had lost her father quite young, and later her grandfather and mother in succession.

Dorothy decided to send off the fourteen-year-old, who said she wanted to be a dancer. Since Charleston offered no such opportunities, Jen left for boarding school in Northampton, Massachusetts. The odd step Dorothy took next perhaps can only be explained by her continuing need for funds, including those for Jenifer's schooling.

In October 1944, still smarting from the failure of *South Pacific*, Dorothy signed a contract with actress, and later television writer, Claiborne Foster, and local Summerville, South Carolina, author Glenn Allan to cowrite a play based on his "Boysi" short stories. Allan had been filling the pages of *The Saturday Evening Post* with his "picture of American family life and the saga of a real American character," based on the antics of his eponymous Black hero, the cook and "[s]elf elected manager of the [white] Oates family." While not as overtly racist as Octavus Roy Cohen, Allan's stories still clung to stereotypes, enough to keep middle-class white Americans chuckling, his Boysi about as far away as possible from Sam Johnson in *South Pacific* and Denmark Vesey.[14]

Details are few, but it appears that Dorothy was again brought in as a script doctor to fix a work Foster had already begun, her vaunted "understanding of the Negro" recommending this white woman for the task. The finished play was called *Eighty Minutes to the Hour*, and although a script by that name was logged into the copyright office at the end of December 1945 under Foster's name first, with Allan's and Dorothy's trailing, it appears never to have been produced, a possible blessing. With Denmark Vesey in limbo, Sam Johnson gone, and Boysi never materializing, Porgy was now again claiming her attention.[15]

CHAPTER 16

Legacies

DuBose had lived long enough to see glimmers of his labor of love's eventual success. In 1937, after George Gershwin's death, excerpts of the opera had been staged to enthusiastic crowds at New York's Lewisohn Stadium; a full production was mounted in Los Angeles, leading to a tour of the West Coast in 1938, cut short by floods. Artists as varied as Billie Holiday and Bing Crosby were recording "Summertime," the royalties giving Dorothy a much-needed financial boost, since they accrued to her alone; "it was my lucky day when Ira failed to change a word of that lyric. . . . I have almost lived on that song," she'd write. "Summertime" was an instant classic, and interest in the opera ratcheted up in 1941 when Cheryl Crawford sought to revive it. Having stage-managed the Broadway play, supervised the actors in London, and worked on the opera, Crawford was on her way to becoming a major Broadway producer.

After many discussions with Ira and Dorothy, Crawford obtained permission to stage *Porgy and Bess* in a theater she operated in Maplewood, New Jersey. To make it profitable and palatable to a broader public, she reduced it to a middle ground between high opera and a Broadway musical. She also cut the number of musicians in the orchestra, with Ira's grudging permission, as well as many, but not all, of the recitatives. She also repurposed some of Dorothy's dialogue from her play script, which most critics approved. There was much fanfare when the opera/play transferred back to Broadway. George's mother, Rose, having changed her tune about the piece, was now one of the revival's financial backers. Todd Duncan returned to reprise his role of Porgy, and Anne Brown returned as Bess. When he sang "I Got Plenty o' Nuttin," the audience burst into applause—the songs were now well known, having been popularized through radio broadcasts after the opera's initial run.

Dorothy was torn; she thought the set design of Porgy's room in pink with a big gold frame on the wall silly, yet audiences came in droves for the performances. Crawford's stripped and dumbed-down version was a smashing success, becoming the longest-running Broadway revival at that point in history, before taking off on the road to crisscross America. But despite the fanfare and the financial rewards, Dorothy disliked it. "Indeed I found it an ordeal to sit through the revival," she'd note.[1]

The most horrific aspect of the production, however, was what she did *not* see. For although Crawford had gone back to Dorothy and DuBose's script to make the production more than ever a Heyward work, Crawford had blatantly broken with precedent and legal formalities to cash in on the glamour of the Gershwin name. She billed the opera solely as "George Gershwin's *Porgy and Bess*," and while the program had a full-page biography of George, and a smaller bit on Ira, DuBose was only mentioned in passing.

Try as she might to hide it, Dorothy had still not recovered from DuBose's sudden death ("I never saw him ill"), and now she felt Crawford was further erasing him. While those who had evaluated Gershwin's estate at his death thought the performance rights to *Porgy and Bess* only of "nominal" interest, Dorothy knew better. Seeing what Crawford had done, she, along with her agent, the Century Company, with rights to the play, and the Theatre Guild, joined forces to mount a united protest. According to Dorothy, Crawford only backed down on her false advertising when the copyright holders threatened to shut down the production. Dorothy forced Crawford to sign a new contract that demanded DuBose's name (and to some lesser extent, her own) be restored. *Porgy and Bess* would henceforth be credited as founded on the play by DuBose and Dorothy Heyward, with music credited to George, libretto to DuBose alone (despite Dorothy's acknowledged legal claim as coauthor), and lyrics by DuBose and Ira, in that order. Wherever names were to be used, the opera would be called George Gershwin's and DuBose Heyward's *Porgy and Bess*. (And new programs were printed proclaiming just that.) Dorothy's attorneys saw to it that "neither Dorothy Heyward nor Ira Gershwin's name need to be used in newspaper advertising." The signs around New York's Majestic Theater, "which mentioned DuBose Heyward's name in tiny type at the bottom," were changed, new programs were printed, and all signs around New York state, "which carry no credit to Mr. Heyward at all," had to be altered. "*Porgy* has become a part of Americana," Dorothy wrote; "no one has the right to take it away from DuBose."

While playing on Broadway and nearby, the advertising and contract language could be monitored. Dorothy feared that in the small towns across America where the opera was giving thousands of Americans their first exposure to it, Crawford would revert to her simplistic advertising and again call it Gershwin's *Porgy and Bess*. "Apparently Cheryl's disservice can never be wholly undone," Dorothy sadly concluded more than a dozen years later. It was not just the general public being duped; "before long people who had known DuBose well were speaking of G. Gershwin's opera."[2]

She faced a similar fading of DuBose's name and contributions back in Charleston at the Dock Street Theatre. The war had not only impacted her Vesey play and *South Pacific* but also the DuBose Heyward playwriting contest. "Personally, I would be willing to make any sacrifice within my power to see this work carried forward," DuBose had written in 1940, and in September 1943, to perpetuate his wish, Dorothy volunteered to keep on as resident playwright and donate her time for free, but the Carolina Art Association and Robert Whitelaw, with no more Rockefeller funds, now saw it as a money-losing proposition. The funding for the award was transferred to the National Theatre Conference Play Contest for men and women in uniform.[3]

If the life and legacy of DuBose and Dorothy's Dock Street Theatre work was not as long lived or as long lasting as George Pierce Baker's, the program did have an impact on its participants. Peggy Lamson, winner of the first playwriting award, was getting notice. Her next play, purchased but not produced by the Theatre Guild, would appear on the Dock Street Theatre stage, with legendary actress Dorothy Gish starring. Samuel French would publish and license it under the title *Respectfully Yours*, and it would be staged off-Broadway and later adapted for live television. Dorothy would join Lamson as cowriter in revisions of her first play, *Museum Piece*; and Lamson not only would publish a novel, a memoir of working in public television, and biographies of progressive leaders and American feminists, but, probably thanks to contacts with Dorothy, she'd also author the highly regarded first biography of a South Carolina African American politician, Robert Brown Elliott. In it, Lamson wrote against the grain and the then-standard beliefs about the corruption and ineptitude of Blacks in Reconstruction, just as Dorothy stood up for a heroic vision of Denmark Vesey.[4]

Thomas Conger Kennedy, the second prizewinner, would see his play staged in the Midwest. More prizes were awarded in 1946 and 1947, but none in 1948 due to the entries' lack of merit; then the program folded entirely. The 1946 winners, Walter Doniger and Malvin Wald, coauthors of the play *Father Was President*, would advance in their fields, Doniger as a film and television director and Wald when he was nominated for an Academy Award for his screenplay for the film *Naked City*. George Bellak's 1947 award-winning play, *Edge of the Sword*, would be staged internationally. Going to work in television, he'd be nominated for an Emmy.[5]

Participants in the local playwriting group, like John Zeigler, who published poetry and an autobiography and was a beloved cultural leader in town, would also succeed after Dorothy's first encouragement. Frank Durham would publish a play or two and become the first DuBose Heyward scholar and an expert on the early years of the Poetry Society. Theater director Philip Clark would produce two lauded mysteries set in the Lowcountry, and Katherine Drayton Mayrant Simons would not only publish a number of historical novels but write plays as well, produced locally under the directorship of another member of that group, Emmett Robinson, who'd keep live theater a reality in Charleston for decades, mentoring his wife, Patricia, author of well-received local plays, and helping launch the career of Walterboro, South Carolina, composer Mel Marvin, who would go on to write for Broadway.

Paul Metcalf, one of the younger members of the group of those who, upon occasion, literally sat at Dorothy's feet, would, with time, become a highly esteemed, if not particularly well-known, experimental writer. A great-grandson of Herman Melville (his mother found the manuscript of *Billy Budd*), Metcalf, after dropping out of Harvard, settled in Charleston in the early 1940s and worked in the theater. Later in his career, he'd employ a variety of genres, including "cut-up" juxtapositions. In a collection of his works titled *Appalache*, he'd place sections of newspaper articles about discrimination and racial attacks on Blacks in Monroe, North Carolina, in 1961 next to sections of the sources Dorothy and DuBose Heyward had utilized researching Denmark Vesey back in the 1930s. His fifteen-page "Telemaque" is a riveting and disturbing view of the continuing tragedy of race relations in this country. No doubt he first encountered the historical figure working with Dorothy, when she first thought her Vesey play would be produced. By the time the moment did come for the play to appear on Broadway, Metcalf had left the city.[6]

This is an agreement for the composing and writing of an opera based on the play and novel PORGY.

It is agreed that Mr. George Gershwin shall write the music; Mr. DuBose Heyward shall write the book and Mr. DuBose Heyward and Mr. Ira Gershwin the lyrics. The authors agree to finish the book, music and lyrics on or before June 1st, 1934. Within thirty days thereafter the Theatre Guild will either enter into a Dramatists Guild Contract with the authors or relinquish its option. If the Theatre Guild accepts the opera all parties to this agreement will enter into a contract for the play at the following terms:

> One Thousand Dollars ($1,000.) advance which is to be paid upon the signing of this agreement, receipt of which is hereby acknowledged, against royalties of five per cent (5%) to Mr. George Gershwin, Four Per Cent (4%) to Mr. DuBose Heyward and Dorothy Heyward and One Per Cent (1%) to Mr. Ira Gershwin. The picture rights in the dialogue and music for this opera shall be divided Thirty Per Cent (30%) to Mr. George Gershwin, Thirty Per Cent (30%) to Mr. and Mrs. DuBose Heyward, Six and Two Thirds Per Cent (6--2/3%) to Mr. Ira Gershwin and Thirty-three and One Third Per Cent (33-1/3%) to the Theatre Guild, it being understood that the silent motion picture rights to the novel have already been sold. All other terms shall be the standard musical comedy terms as outlined in the Dramatists Guild Contract.

If the Theatre Guild does not accept the opera by July 1st and sign a contract, the Thousand Dollars ($1,000.) paid herewith shall be forfeited and remain with the authors. If the authors do not submit the completed opera by June 1st, 1934, and the Theatre Guild so elects, they shall refund the Thousand Dollars ($1,000.) advance, $500. of which has been paid to Mr. George Gershwin and $500. to Mr. and Mrs. DuBose Heyward.

If the Theatre Guild relinquishes its right to produce the opera, it agrees also to relinquish the operatic rights in the play.

The signatures of the various parties to this agreement will serve as a contract between all.

New York, N.Y.
October 26, 1933.

THE THEATRE GUILD, INC.

Porgy and Bess contract. Courtesy of the South Carolina Historical Society.

George and Ira Gershwin and DuBose Heyward. Courtesy of the South Carolina Historical Society.

The hurricane scene, *Porgy and Bess*, 1935. Courtesy of the South Carolina Historical Society.

Rouben Mamoulian (*left*) and Samuel Goldwyn (*right*), ca. 1934, photo by Acme. Courtesy of the author.

Jenifer Heyward, ca. 1939. Courtesy of the South Carolina Historical Society.

Dorothy and DuBose Heyward, ca. 1930s. Courtesy of the South Carolina Historical Society.

Program of the 1942 production crediting only George Gershwin. Courtesy of the author.

A *South Pacific* promotional brochure. Courtesy of the author.

The MAJESTIC THEATRE

DIRECTION - MESSRS. LEE AND J. J. SHUBERT

SMOKING IS PROHIBITED IN ANY PART OF THIS THEATRE
Thoughtless persons annoy patrons and distract actors and endanger the safety of others by lighting matches during the performances and intermissions. This violates a city ordinance and renders the offender liable to a summons from the fireman on duty.

FIRE NOTICE: The exit indicated by a red light and sign nearest to the seat you occupy is the shortest route to the street. In the event of fire please do not run — WALK TO THAT EXIT

PROGRAM WEEK OCTOBER 4, 1948

THE THEATRE GUILD *presents*

Dorothy Heyward's New Play

CHARLESTON, 1822

with JUANO HERNANDEZ • JOHN ~~MARRIOTT~~ Canada Lee

Mildred Smith • Blaine Cordner • Frank Wilson • ~~Leigh Whipper~~

Directed by MARTIN RITT

Settings by Ralph Alswang

Costumes by ERNEST SCHRAPS

Production under the supervision of
LAWRENCE LANGNER and THERESA HELBURN

Associate Producer, Allyn Rice
Choral Direction and Arrangements by JOSHUA LEE

GEORGE, Head Slave—Property of Captain Wilson .... ~~JOHN MARRIOTT~~ Canada Lee
ROSE—Property of Captain Wilson .... MILDRED JOANNE SMITH
DENMARK—Property of Captain Wilson .... JUANO HERNANDEZ
CAPTAIN WILSON .... BLAINE CORDNER
PHYLLIS, his wife .... MARION SCANLON
ELIZA, his daughter .... GAIL GLADSTONE
GULLAH JACK, a conjur doctor .... LEIGH WHIPPER
TRADER HENRI .... SOMER ALBERG
MORRIS BROWN, Preacher (later Bishop) .... FRANK WILSON
PATROLMAN .... TYLER CARPENTER
THE MAUMA—Property of Captain Wilson .... BERTHA T. POWELL
POMPEY—Property of Captain Wilson .... ALONZO BOSAN
TINA—Property of Captain Wilson .... EDITH ATUKA-REID

A *Charleston, 1822* program reflecting the sudden change of actors. Courtesy of the author.

Marian MacDowell at a ninety-fifth birthday celebration, 1952, United Press Association photo. Courtesy of the author.

Dorothy meeting the cast of a Robert Breen production, ca. 1950s. Courtesy of the South Carolina Historical Society.

Dorothy and Jenifer at the *Porgy and Bess* film premiere, 1959. Courtesy of the South Carolina Historical Society.

Dorothy Heyward, date unknown. Courtesy of the South Carolina Historical Society.

CHAPTER 17

The Tragedy of Denmark Vesey

Two years after it was initially postponed due to the outbreak of war, Bretaigne Windust—the celebrated director of *Life with Father*, the longest-running nonmusical play on Broadway—toyed with mounting the Vesey play. Dorothy had titled it *Set My People Free*, and many who read it proclaimed it her "major opus," the crowning work of her career. Robert Milton, who had dodged the opportunity after being the first director chosen to direct *Porgy*, giving Mamoulian his big break, also thought of purchasing it. The Guild, however, continued to believe "that now is no time—while the war is on—to put on a play which emphasizes the bad treatment of negroes by the whites." The producers feared it "would tend to foster disunity in the war effort." That had prompted Dorothy to wonder "will the time [ever] again be right? . . . And, if the racial turmoil after the war, which many people expect, comes to pass, possibly the right time for this play has gone by forever." To catch the mood of the times, she rewrote the play, hoping to prove to nervous producers "that violence was in 1822 the wrong solution for the Negro problem, and still will always be the wrong solution."[1]

The next year (1944) brought what she called "a definite offer, guaranteeing a first-class production" from producers Robert McCann and T. Edward Hambleton, arriving just in time to satisfy her "yen to see the play produced in my lifetime." But the offer vanished before pen was put to paper. Jed Harris was still saying he was interested, even as Allyn Rice, a theatrical enthusiast who had been in an ensemble of Shakespeare's *As You Like It* on Broadway, optioned the play in 1947. Audrey Wood, Dorothy's agent, a stalwart through it all, called it "the only play in my career that I have worked on as an agent for a full ten year period." *Set My People Free*, she noted, "is a play in which the leading characters are negroes; is not looked upon as a picture-sale property; and in addition is a play that needs tremendous care from a director as well as from a managerial hand."[2]

While laboring for Dorothy, she also was encouraging a neophyte playwright named Tennessee Williams. It was her fondness for Dorothy and DuBose, in fact, that prompted Wood to lure the young Williams down to Charleston to speak with producer Irene Selznick, meeting in secret in the hotel just across the park from Dorothy's house. It led directly to the 1947 landmark staging of *A Streetcar Named Desire*. The very next year, Wood once more sold the Vesey play to the Theatre Guild, just about the time Dorothy was hit by a car crossing 72nd Street at Park Avenue, breaking a hip and nearly dying.

As the play moved toward production and Dorothy healed, she realized to her dismay that the times had changed, and the Theatre Guild had, too. The first inkling came in a letter from Jo Mielziner, acclaimed Broadway set designer, regretting that the Guild thought his fees too high for him to do the set for her "beautiful" play. "I know that the financial situation has changed *so* drastically since 1927," Dorothy immediately wrote Theresa Helburn, still recalling "the day when the Guild directors said to DuBose and me: 'We fully expect to lose money on *Porgy* but that does not deter us from doing a play when we believe it is a play the Guild should do.'" Helburn fired right back, taking umbrage, and Dorothy, always conflict-avoidant, immediately backtracked and apologized, yet she and others went on record saying the scenery was "shoddy," with images in the program making it look like backgrounds for a high school production. Allyn Rice, who had bought the rights before the Guild, stayed on to coproduce, contributing $16,500 of the estimated $60,000 production costs. Dorothy offered to invest as well, with proceeds expected from productions of *Porgy and Bess*.

Casting calls went out early, in February 1948, even before contracts were signed. "The reason for the early start of production activities . . . is the fact that the play calls for thirty-six to forty characters [thirty-eight would be named in the program], some of whom must be 'noble' in appearance." Robeson was no longer available or interested; prophetically mentioned in news articles as casting possibilities were Canada Lee, Juano Hernandez, and Rex Ingram.[3]

In her original version, Dorothy had presented Vesey "as history recorded him. . . . A single-idea man, whose single purpose was the Freedom of his people . . . but there were too many howls of protest [from readers and possible producers]. They pointed out that the audience can take only so much ruthlessness from its hero." So, she had "toned him down" while never surrendering her view of him as a heroic leader and martyr. And due to the changes in race relations after the war—the "turmoil" Dorothy had foreseen— even more whitewashing was deemed necessary. In 1946 Isaac Woodard, a returning Black serviceman, had been beaten and blinded by police in Batesburg, South Carolina, and the cry for justice had been taken up across the country, prompting Dorothy's friend, Federal Judge J. Waties Waring, to issue a series of landmark civil rights rulings. Now even the title, *Set My People Free*, was seen as menacing. For previews in New Haven on September 30, 1948, before going on to subscription audiences in Boston, Philadelphia, and New York, it was rechristened *Charleston, 1822*, hoping to push the story out of the headlines back into history.

African American actor Rex Ingram was cast as Vesey, and Puerto Rican Juano Hernandez followed as George Wilson, the enslaved man who informs on him. They would carry the main arguments of the play, each trying to convince the other of his point of view, the drama carried by two strong male leads, a thought-provoking scenario, not unlike *South Pacific*, still new territory for a playwright more at ease in densely plotted farces and comedies. In this case at least, the play was her own and not another's (except DuBose's) idea. Rehearsals inevitably brought changes, even in casting: although Hernandez had been picked to portray Wilson, his bulk and size compelled the director to ask Ingram, as Vesey, to switch parts. Also in the ensemble were Frank Wilson, who, a decade earlier, had performed a dramatic monologue he had written on Vesey, and Leigh Whipper, both from *Porgy* days, along with Leigh Whipper Jr. William Warfield, who'd become the reigning Porgy in operatic productions in the 1950s, was also cast as was Charleston native Urylee Leonardas, destined to sing Bess alternately with Leontyne Price in the future.[4]

When the play's staging during the war had seemed likely, Dorothy had written a prologue, involving two servicemen, one white, one Black, caught in a race-baiting fracas. Called to task by their white superior officer, all realize they hail from the Carolina Lowcountry; the Black soldier, upon questioning, reveals he's named George Wilson for his ancestor who saved the white citizens of Charleston; the white captain recalls his civilian life as a historian, when he tried to solve the conundrum of one of "the most amazing episodes in all history." Had the original George Wilson been "a great and good man or just a fawning lick-spittle"? Was Vesey "a rabble rouser thirsting for power or a great and selfless prophet"? With the white and Black servicemen smarting from the wounds inflicted on each other, the captain promises to tell a story of freedom being hard bought, leading to the curtain rising.

With this prologue now discarded, and with less than a week before the opening in New Haven, Rex Ingram, cast as Wilson, did not turn up for rehearsals one morning. A telephone call revealed he had been arrested by federal authorities, charged with violation of the Mann Act, taking a minor, a white girl of fifteen, over state lines for sex, not just an explosive action in these Jim Crow years, but the death knell for an actor in a play about Black men plotting violence against white men and women. But his attorney argued differently. Since there were no morals clauses in Broadway contracts as there were in Hollywood, as long as Ingram showed up for court dates and rehearsals, he should be allowed to act. But when the press broke the story, the Guild panicked, warning that audiences in New Haven and Boston would boycott the play if Ingram appeared onstage. Ingram was fired, and legal wrangles ensued over wages he was due, adding expenses and necessitating a last-minute search. John Marriott, one of the actors seeking employment in the play back in 1941, was cast. He was only given a two-week contract, and at the end of it he resigned, seeing the handwriting on the wall in the person of Canada Lee, suddenly in the wings, watching his every move just before the Boston opening. Lee had lost interest in the play when he was not cast as Vesey; changing his mind, he decided playing George Wilson was better than nothing.

It was a huge blow to lose a major actor right before opening, and to have to replace the replacement, too. Time was lost in getting Canada Lee up to speed. "As a result, instead of our being able to spend our time in working on the rewriting of the play . . . we had to spend it on replacing actors," ran a Guild report. And Lee, realizing the Guild needed him, drove a hard bargain over his fees, crippling the budget further when the Guild could not afford it.

"I had great respect and liking for the young director," Dorothy said of Martin Ritt, who ironically had begun his acting career in blackface as Crown in what had to have been an unauthorized production of *Porgy* in the Borscht Belt. Soon to be accused of being a communist, Ritt had also helped her shape the script, wanting to stick to Vesey as a radical and a voice of left-leaning propaganda. "He wanted to kill sympathy for George and all understanding of the slave owner. I had never intended the play for propaganda. . . . Vesey must have been . . . about the greatest leader the Negro Race has ever had. But when I first began to write the play it seemed that not one Negro in a hundred thousand had ever heard of him."[5]

Although Ritt looked like a prizefighter, his nerves were more collapsible than hers, Dorothy reflected. He would be lauded decades later for leading actors to Oscar-winning performances, but at this point in his life he "could not control his two feature players" or tamp down the onstage rivalries simmering between Hernandez who, as Vesey, would not speak the lines Dorothy had written, and Lee, as Wilson, who followed suit.

There was some hope. "The producers kept telling me that Elia Kazan would arrive any day to advise and work with" Canada Lee. She knew, due to her experience with *South Pacific*, that he might upstage everyone, and she had also been warned by New York friends similarly that "Juano Hernandez would be praised by the critics acting something I had never written and that the play itself would be destroyed by his flamboyant performance."

Her gut reaction in New Haven was to either step in herself to mediate the issue or halt the production entirely. But always conciliatory and fearful of offending anyone, she did neither, later regretfully realizing that "if I had taken action on that first night in New Haven, I could have won. But I believed in Mr. Kazan's miracles; [and] I shrank from throwing hopeful actors out of work and hurting the director. Mr. Kazan never came. . . .

> Daily I saw the play getting farther and farther from what I had intended. Yet I lacked the courage to speak up and say, "I demand that this play be closed."
>
> Instead I only protested at the nightly conferences after the performances. Once I wept and Lawrence [Langner] sent me white orchids with a note, "Think nothing of it. Everyone drinks too much at times." This really raised my ire as drink had nothing to do with my despair.
>
> In Boston it grew worse. By the time we played Philadelphia Canada and Juano were refusing to rehearse. Canada refused to take curtain calls unless he could step forward for his bow last, and alone.

Hernandez, in turn, would not appear at all after the final curtain fell, puzzling audiences when a spotlight showed a vacant stage.

> I practically went to on my knees to Canada and to Juano but they sulked in their tents—or dressing rooms—while the precious days flew by.
>
> At long last I insisted that the Guild not take the play into New York. Lawrence said, "You can write every newspaper in New York saying we are opening this play

over your protest." ... I got a lawyer. He said, "You can't close the play at this late date, but I advise you to insist the actors speak only the lines you have written." By that time, Juano was saying almost nothing I had written. If he could have relearned the original lines in the short time left to us, he would have been giving unfamiliar cues to the rest of the cast, and it would have been a shambles.

I know now that on that first grueling night in New Haven Theresa Helburn saw the handwriting on the wall as clearly as I did. But Lawrence Langner seemed never to lose faith.

Dorothy could not avert her eyes from the disaster. The play opened at the Hudson Theater on November 3, 1948, with a ticketed formal after-party, not for Hernandez, who had top billing, but for Lee, whose name was in a larger font. The script itself was a mess, far from the original concept conceived nearly twenty years before: a historical chronology of the rise and fall of Denmark Vesey, with some parallels to DuBose's *Emperor Jones* script, without doubting Vesey's nobility. After Thornton Wilder and Jed Harris had encouraged her to focus more on George Wilson, she had, but Martin Ritt had walked her back from that. "I took a middle ground," Dorothy reminisced,

> seeing it as a conflict between Vesey's and George's point of view. Martin was at the opposite pole; he wanted Vesey to speak continuously in a loud clear voice for the right. I agreed to try out his ideas. When Thornton [Wilder] saw the result he protested that I once had a play which was excellent propaganda because it was a play about human beings in which the propaganda was inherent but never obvious; he contended that when the human values were played down and the speech-making played up it not only became less effective as a play but also lost its punch as propaganda.

Not of a philosophic bent, and unable to articulate the nuances of such a charged drama, Dorothy reverted to her old pattern of not sticking to her convictions, instead deferring to others who were more forceful.

The play as produced, a pastiche of various versions, featured songs provided by the Society for the Preservation of Spirituals, which had provided them previously for *Mamba* and *Porgy*. This time, however, the locals were miffed that their work was being used in a play that had more liberal views on race than they liked to see, ironic since Dorothy had discovered Vesey in researching her husband's essay for the Spiritual Society's book *The Carolina Low-Country*.[6]

The curtain rises on the white household, with Captain Wilson celebrating his marriage in 1810; he is noted for kindness to all and hints at his long relationship with George, the head of his enslaved house workers. Among the enslaved is Rose, who also wants to marry and who assumes that Wilson will grant permission. But her intended groom, Denmark, is enslaved by a man who purchased him in the Caribbean islands and brought him to Charleston. Denmark recalls his cruel upbringing, and he tells Rose's enslaver that he is saving up his money to buy his freedom. Wilson refuses Rose's request, hardening Vesey's resolve, determined more than ever to become a Moses to his people. Dorothy had bowed to the inevitability of the perceived need for there to be a "love interest" in the plot, but she wanted to cut the next scene in which the plot does not advance: A slave trader named Henri is murdered, showing slavery's cruelty and Vesey's ruthlessness. In this scene, which remained in the play, he meets the real-life character conjurer Gullah Jack, to become a coleader in the plot.

Scene 3 of act 1 is set in the African church in Charleston where the minister, Morris Brown, exhorts his congregation to keep their mind off temporal temptations like gambling and lotteries, focusing instead on holier beliefs. Word comes that Vesey has won a lottery, enabling him to buy his freedom and merge his daily life with a sacred mission to lead. (In actuality, the man won the lottery back in 1799.)

Act 2's first scene, set twelve years later in 1822, is in Denmark Vesey's room. Morris Brown and others are plotting with Vesey to overthrow the whites and free the enslaved; some followers want the endorsement of George Wilson, "the leading negro of Charleston." George conveniently comes in, looking for Brown, in need of him to officiate at his son's christening; Rose is his wife and the child's mother. Vesey invites him into the conspiracy, but George declines because his master has been nothing but kind to him; he does not want blood on his hands or his conscience.

In the next scene, back in the Wilson household, George, knowing of the conspiracy, tries to get his enslaver to move up his date of departure to leave town in the summer to avoid the massacre. It ends with George realizing Wilson does not really respect him at all, seeing him fit only for slavery. While this development was not commented on by critics at the time, the realization weakens George as a character. Why should he continue to be loyal to someone who believes in his inferiority?

Scene 3 reverts to Vesey's cabin. Rose enters and tells Denmark of George's dilemma, torn between freedom and culpability. Vesey asks Rose to send

George to a meeting the next night on Wadmalaw Island, to help convince him of the mission. Scene 4 is dramatic, featuring drums and chanting. While the discussion between Wilson and Vesey is repetitious, the tension mounts as consequences of the violence are spelled out. Dorothy wanted the scene longer; the Guild trimmed it.

In the first scene of act 3, the white Wilsons have postponed their departure and so George is frantic. In extremis, he confesses that a rebellion is imminent. Back in Vesey's room, in scene 2, just before the midnight rising, Vesey is with his men, who panic hearing white troops marching in the streets. George Wilson has betrayed them.

The final scene made no one happy. Dorothy did not believe the meeting between the two men necessary. "I am sorry I seem incapable of writing a final exciting clash between Vesey and George," she told the Guild. "God knows I tried, but they seem to have nothing important or exciting to say to each other." But Thornton Wilder did, and the Guild agreed. In one version, she had Vesey come to George's quarters to find Rose alone; he tells her to keep freedom alive and then goes off to his heroic end. In another, Vesey and George meet, but there is no need for revenge, for George is doomed to be known among the enslaved as the one who betrayed the plans for freedom.

Her preferred ending, which Audrey Wood also agreed was the best, would take place in the Wilson family's dining room after the failed uprising, with George the center of attention. Now freed, but with Rose still enslaved, he knows he has lost his place with both Blacks and whites, as in the background Vesey and his lieutenants are passing to be hanged, Vesey to become a hero in death, George, still living, to be vilified.

She fought for this version, and the cast tried it out, but only in a reading, not with blocking, and neither they nor director Martin Ritt liked it. So, against her wishes, the final scene mashed together pieces of the other versions. George returns to his cabin, where Vesey is in hiding. George informs Rose that because of what he has done, he has been freed by a grateful city, but not her or their children. Vesey appears, and after seeing George acknowledge his own defeat, he tells Rose to keep his story alive and is caught as he flees. The end comes offstage with mob noises and Blacks singing. Mamoulian thought the audience should see the mob converging on Vesey. On opening night in Philadelphia, the verdict was that the ending, as staged, was weak.[7]

Method actor E. G. Marshall took in one of the performances, and he understood what Dorothy had been reaching for. He likened the play to *Macbeth*, or "not unlike some of the ancient Greeks." It was not modern, for it did not give audiences someone to root for, or someone in whom to believe. "We cannot identify ourselves with Denmark's cause nor can we applaud his actions.... We cannot strongly hope he fails because [the] 'other side' is not really ours.... The high point of the play, and this is truly tragic, is when George stands with the deed to his freedom in his hand and realizes that he is a prisoner of his freedom, truly a slave at last."

Brooks Atkinson, dean of critics, similarly moved, wrote a *New York Times* review that was keen and penetrating. After recapping its history of being unproduced for years and referring to the "quivers of excitement about it ... passing up and down Broadway" every time it was rumored for production, he wondered how such an "intelligent and interesting drama" had to "wait so long [for] a public hearing." He applauded Dorothy for focusing on the conflicted George Wilson, giving the audience an opportunity to hear "original and provocative ideas" and giving Black actors roles rarely offered on Broadway. He called Hernandez's acting heroic, and Lee's superb, praising Mildred Joanne Smith who played Rose and Frank Wilson, who portrayed Morris Brown, as well as Gullah Jack. "Played with so much vividness and honesty, 'Set My People Free' is one of the best theatre experiences that has come along this season," he concluded. "The material is vital and the viewpoint provocative. Yet most of us are vaguely aware of imperfections in the drama that scatter or soften its final impact."

It could have been the unscripted interpolations of the actors, but it's likely Atkinson was on to something when he theorized that "Possibly Mrs. Heyward has unconsciously written it in different styles—melodrama for the story of the rebellion, character analysis in the case of George Wilson, and Negro mumbo-jumbo" for the Trader Henri murder plot and Wadmalaw Island scenes. (Those were mostly DuBose's.) "Jumping from place to place in ten separate scenes, 'Set My People Free' seems diffuse." Howard Barnes for the *Herald Tribune* concurred, writing, "It is possible the author, who wrote the piece some time ago, became too intrigued by her material." She "unquestionably grew too close to her themes ... to see it in sharp perspective," he reiterated in a different review. Despite the flaws, Atkinson called the play "one of the most genuine works of the season and a credit to the Theatre Guild."

Yet audiences stayed away, as they had with *South Pacific*, possibly for the same reason, not wanting to deal with the hard racial issues dividing the country. The play also had the bad luck to premiere just a day after the unexpected presidential election upset of Harry Truman, more liberal on race issues, over Thomas Dewey. Perhaps, Guild reports note, if the play had been capitalized enough, and funds had not been diverted to keep paying Rex Ingram and honoring an inflated salary for Canada Lee and weeks not lost in casting, the play could possibly have succeeded. But Dorothy's muddled script needed rewriting, and audiences were not ready for the story of Denmark Vesey. It closed within a month.

E. G. Marshall's words to Lawrence Langner, shared with Dorothy, might have softened some of the sting of defeat: "you all attempted something *great* and were not completely successful, for many obstacles were in your way—insurmountable I believe. To fail in a high endeavor is true success. To succeed in a petty undertaking is disgraceful."[8]

On the night the play closed, Allyn Rice, production associate, served champagne to the cast on stage. Half an hour after the audience's departure, Langner was sitting alone in the dark theater. Dorothy reminisced, "I went down to urge him to join the party. He shook his head. There were tears in his eyes."

Although it was he who had believed in it wholeheartedly, even as she had sought legal advice to keep him from opening it, Dorothy was the tiny tower of strength who comforted him, despite seeing ten years of her professional life and an opportunity of crowning her career going down with the final curtain. All along she had known Martin Ritt was the "wrongest" person to direct, yet "I respected him too much to allow his dismissal, even when I knew it meant death to the play." Conflating being truthful with being unkind, she had assured her own defeat.

"I was proud of myself at the Colony with all of you," she later wrote Marjorie Benét, "just after DuBose's death—when I was determined not to be a drag—and after the failures of *S. Pacific* and *Set M[y] P[eople] F[ree]*. The T. Guild had such high hopes for 'Porgy' as they had for *S.M.P.F.* . . . but when it had come and failed, after the long years of work I had put into it, . . . I helped give the gay backstage party, and never allowed myself a quarter-hour's grief." She had come to believe in the carefree persona she had crafted for herself, the woman others always saw as lighthearted, fey, and frivolous, never one to take failure to heart too deeply. "If I felt licked and defeated I kept it buried so deep that I did not know it myself."

As always, the only antidote for a failed play was to start writing a new one, so she decided to help the first winner of the DuBose Heyward Award, Peggy Lamson, revise *Museum Piece*. Yet something was amiss and had been for a long time. "When DuBose died I behaved almost too well, but all the time I felt that I was walking on the edge of an abyss and if I once looked over the edge I'd topple into it. But I kept putting off looking." Until she couldn't. Although she would soon tumble into the dark abyss of near death and madness, it wasn't really a fall. She was pushed.[9]

CHAPTER 18

A Candle for St. Jude

Dorothy would never be able to remember the exact chronology of events precipitating her downfall, and she would refuse to acknowledge her daughter's involvement in it. In 1949, when the perfect storm was brewing, Jenifer was almost twenty. From boarding school, she had gone to Sarah Lawrence for a year, then embarked "hellbent" on a career in ballet. To fund that, Dorothy had leased both Charleston houses, living instead in rented and borrowed apartments, in hotels, in New York and New England, often in Pigeon Cove, Massachusetts, near her friends, the Benéts.

When Jenifer had been at Sarah Lawrence, staff had written her mother just as Dorothy dreaded they would. Dorothy replied saying she had long encouraged Jen to see a psychiatrist, but the young woman had refused to bare her soul to a stranger. The issue, which Dorothy dubbed Jenifer's "vagueness," had manifested itself as far back as grammar school. When "the Dean of Sarah Lawrence College sent for me . . . I knew what to expect. The Dean was baffled by a girl, capable of meeting their high scholastic requirements, who showed up for Monday's classes on Tuesday, who signed up for riding, got into her riding togs, and went for a walk. (Of course, she never meant to go for a walk. She wandered about while waiting for her horse and wandered too far.)"

There were many other similar examples. Although hating to babysit, Jenifer would nevertheless do it to earn enough for ballet tickets. Having purchased them, however, she'd forget the performance and get angry at herself. When mother and daughter were desperate to find an apartment together, Jenifer accepted the call that informed her that one was available but neglected to tell her mother, so they lost it—all examples, Dorothy wrote, of a "puzzling mental block that prevents her from carrying out her intentions." Years later it could possibly have been diagnosed and treated as attention deficit disorder.

In Dorothy's view, there were multiple Jenifers (up to six)—one quiet and shy, another vivacious, the Jenifer wanting to get married, dating men who looked like her father, whose grave she still refused to visit; she grew uneasy even when his name was mentioned. Dorothy was now verbalizing thoughts that had occurred to her years before. "There were three Heywards who believed Jen was the center of the Universe—with no warning, she was told one day her adored grandmother was dead. A year later, almost to the day, her father drove her to town to play with her friends, saying he would return for her in a few hours. When she was brought home she was told that DuBose was dead. She kept saying she was too young." Was it possible, Dorothy asked the dean of Sarah Lawrence and prominent psychologist Karen Horney, that Jenifer could have suffered "a psychic shock at the time of her father's death"?

It was not mere frustration on Dorothy's part. "It seems I have parented something I wot not of," she confessed, "and . . . I have grown a little frightened of offending her. You have seen her with our mutual friends: Patti Whitelaw, Betty Carmer, Rosemary Benét," Dorothy wrote an associate. "As their children all call me Dorothy or Dotty, I had no luck in training J. to reverence." Jenifer was dismissing her mother just as producers, publishers, and actors had.[1]

The issue creating a crisis and driving Dorothy to seek professional help centered on an impending trip to England. As she told Horney in a desperate plea (there is no trace of the psychologist's reply), she needed to go abroad for six weeks to get a great amount of work done swiftly. If successful, Dorothy might be able to get not just her professional life back on track after a disheartening string of failures, but Jen's as well, by securing her a small role as a dancer in a play she was cowriting. Jen was eager to go, but Dorothy was afraid of telling her no.

She desperately needed someone to take care of details: tickets, bookings, and secretarial work. Jen had a friend perfect for the task, and Dorothy wanted to hire her. Jen insisted, instead, that she could do it, but Dorothy knew it would not work, and there would be scenes, crises, and consequences. A compromise of sorts was worked out; Jen was allowed to come, with Patti Whitelaw, wife of the director of the Gibbes Museum, coming along, at least for a while, as Jen's watcher and chaperone.

Despite all the stress Jenifer unwillingly caused her, Dorothy would never consider her daughter a contributing factor in her looming disaster, just as she had never been able to blame or get angry at DuBose for things done to frustrate her. If, when younger, hiding her own desires and bowing to the wishes of her family had been Dorothy's survival mechanism, she had not outgrown it. Nor had she learned the lesson of being honest instead of being kind—behavior that had prevented her from replacing Martin Ritt as director of *Set My People Free*. "When will you learn the fine art of insulting?" DuBose had asked her once in a courtship letter, accusing her of being unable of saying anything negative of anyone. As "a woman of good will," she could not express anger toward someone she respected or loved and so took blame upon herself. Her downfall, she finally realized, began with her trying to help her friend, the young playwright Peggy Lamson.

It started so innocuously: Lamson and Dorothy had a mutual acquaintance in Julia Clayburgh, who worked for the up-and-coming Broadway producer David Merrick. At first impressed, Dorothy came to see Clayburgh as more of a dilettante doing stenographic jobs, while dreaming of producing. When Lamson's play *Bee in Her Bonnet* debuted off-Broadway, Dorothy wanted to mark the occasion with a dinner party, and she asked Lamson for a guest list, which her landlord limited to fifteen. Clayburgh, who had been trying to get Lamson to write a play for her, had not made the cut, angering her to no end, so much so that she began telephoning Lamson and screaming insults at her.

Trying to make peace, Dorothy took Clayburgh to lunch to explain how her landlord's restriction had inadvertently caused the problem. It went well, and conversation drifted to Jenifer and her passion for ballet. A few days later Clayburgh telephoned with an idea about a popular, recently published novel by British writer Rumer Godden, *A Candle for St. Jude*, set in a ballet school. The story revolves around two elderly sisters' travails keeping a private London ballet school functioning. The push and pull between the performers and Madame, their ballet mistress, comes to a crisis at the school's fiftieth-anniversary performance after which Madame is set to retire. Would Dorothy write a play based on the book, Clayburgh asked, if rights could be secured?

Dorothy declined; she first had to finish working with Lamson on *Museum Piece*, and she wanted to collaborate with Bill Benét. When Clayburgh persisted, Dorothy read the novel a couple more times and became enchanted with it for its own merits and for what it could mean to Jenifer. Suddenly, "it seemed to me that I had never loved any play so much in all my life; and had never felt so assured that I could make of it something unique and lovely." *Cygnets*, young swans, is what she would call it.[2]

Rumer Godden, the novel's author, "came to America in June. We met with our agents, the two prospective producers, Julie Clayburgh and David Merrick.... I told Rumer that I so completely understood any misgivings she might have about turning her beautiful book over to a stranger.... I told her I loved her book ... but could only undertake the dramatization on the clear understanding that I was to finish it.... Rumer suggested that she join with me as collaborator and I accepted as I had great admiration for her as a writer and liked her on sight."

Dorothy began to adapt the novel on July 1, 1949, at the MacDowell Colony. As she had with *Porgy*, she went through the text to break it down into individual scenes. "'Candle for St. Jude' in which much of the drama is in the minds of the characters and in which the narrative does not follow a beginning-to-end time sequence, could be made into a dozen ... or five dozen ... different plays," she realized. "I tried it a dozen different ways; out of these many patterns I picked three and worked them into three widely different scenarios. I chose the one that seemed to me best, and ... it was ... the main foundation on which the play was built."

While working on the adaptation, she was alarmed when a close friend advised her to avoid any contact with Clayburgh. The friend reported that, when drinking, Clayburgh underwent a transformation and expressed a violent hatred of Dorothy. The story was so disturbing that Dorothy notified her agent, Audrey Wood. Clayburgh "has a very queer streak" and "a screw loose," she wrote. "After deep cogitation I have decided you should be burdened with these items, that you should know that our producer is capable of going completely berserk"; on second thought, however, being that woman of goodwill, Dorothy sealed, but did not send, the letter. Her discovery of it months later brought her comfort, seeing that her instincts had been right. Warned, she did keep her distance from Clayburgh, and when the latter sent her ideas, Dorothy refused to read them.

While Dorothy was working on *Cygnets*, Godden was in California consulting with the acclaimed French filmmaker Jean Renoir on his adaptation of her brief, vivid novel *The River*, assisting on the screenplay and becoming more and more confident of her burgeoning career. Before returning to England, she stopped in New York, then proceeded to the MacDowell Colony to work with Dorothy. They had the month of August to produce a draft for Merrick and Clayburgh.

In New Hampshire, arrangements were made for Godden's "peculiar diet." Now "quieted down and soothed" after her intense time in Hollywood, Godden found Dorothy "delightful, little and dried up and fragile." In return, Dorothy found Rumer a "near genius," perhaps forgetting her previous definition of a genius being someone who would change her mind endlessly, frustrating all around her. "I assumed that Rumer . . . a far finer writer than I but an inexperienced playwright . . . would want me to take the lead here. [Godden's one play had bombed on Broadway.] Nevertheless, I was eager to lead or be led. Rumer's idea was that we would sit at opposite sides of the table and compose each line together."

Dorothy, on the other hand, thought it might be better if one of them wrote a scene and the other critiqued it. Her way of working included walking around, pacing, and thinking out loud, hesitating and rewriting, but Godden would jot things down, rush to the next page or scene, never returning or rewriting. "I have to grind my thumbs with impatience," Godden felt about Dorothy, "but I believe we shall make a play."[3]

"Our work together was unsatisfactory because her mind is much quicker than mine," Dorothy recalled. "While I would be writing, re-writing, discarding and trying again two lines, she would have gone two pages ahead." The fact that Godden believed that they could finish and polish a three-act play in just over three weeks astonished Dorothy. But as a courtesy to the novelist, ignoring her better judgment again, she followed her lead. "On our next to last night at the Colony I urged on Rumer that we have a Colony play-reading."

It was a ritual there, and a date was set, even though the script was nearly nonexistent. Thornton Wilder, one of the country's premiere playwrights, was in residence and could help immeasurably. But while Godden agreed to the reading, she "refused to have the Colony's one bona fide playwright present fearing he would be brutal. (He was deeply hurt by his exclusion and he undoubtedly would have been brutal.) . . . What I hoped was that hearing . . . not merely seeing . . . our words would be of help to Rumer," Dorothy thought, "because the difference between words-to-be-spoken and words-to-be-read is not instinctive with her."

Dorothy understood what Colony responses meant. "Polite appreciation instead of brickbats usually indicates that the audience has not been roused to enough interest to take sides." And so, when "The brickbats thrown at our play were far below the accustomed number" and those attending were mildly kind,

Dorothy understood that most thought the play terrible; "the listeners sensed Rumer's shrinking from criticism and we had invited only polite people."

"Clayburgh and Merrick drove from New York to confer with us the day after the reading, Rumer's last day at the Colony." Again, Godden suggested an odd way to proceed, to which Dorothy unwillingly agreed. Godden just wanted to share little bits of scenes she liked. This confused the producers, who wanted "a sort of musical comedy but with a difference." Dorothy wanted to explain to Merrick and Clayburgh what needed to be done but was constrained. "A day or two before her departure, she [Godden] proposed to me a pact that, no matter how much we might differ between ourselves, we would speak 'always as one' to all others." Linking fingers together, "Promise?" Godden had asked Dorothy, looking her in the eye. "Promise," Dorothy replied, looking back.

"Damn that pledge," Dorothy later wrote in a piece she titled "Dirty Doings at the Crossroads," an homage to melodramatic silent films where heroines were tied to railroad tracks. "It has changed my whole life, and apparently it was only a casual thing with Rumer."

With nothing settled in New Hampshire but still having a few months to deliver a script, Merrick and Clayburgh got ready to depart. "As Rumer and C[layburgh] & M[errick] were leaving the Colony the same day . . . it would greatly simplify Rumer's trip if they could drive her to Westport." In her suggestion to simplify transportation and help others, Dorothy was betrayed by everyone in the car.

"Rumer's strange combination of insecurity and conceit . . . would make her the perfect receptacle for skillful suggestions that perhaps her fine work was being handicapped by an unworthy collaborator." In the car, Clayburgh became "a viper." She prodded Godden to speak out against her collaborator. Then, despite the pledge to act as one, Godden broke her word and betrayed Dorothy, agreeing that Dorothy was the stumbling block. "Julie must have had a lovely drive. Merrick would of course go along with Julie. He is an opportunist, equally happy to play ball with me or with Rumer; he only wants to be sure he is on the winning team." Saying nothing to Dorothy about this conversation, Godden returned to England and her children and was soon remarried, having been divorced a few years before. She then set out to India for filming of *The River*.[4] Instead of working on the script herself, Dorothy had capitulated to Rumer's request that she, Godden, be allowed to write a first draft alone. With her South Battery house rented, staying with her friend Ferdi Legare Backer at Old Town Plantation outside Charleston, Dorothy fiddled with individual scenes, eagerly awaiting Rumer's draft. "My high esteem for all Rumer's books, the delightful skips and jumps of her mind as we worked together last summer, gave me high hopes for the script." But she was aghast when it arrived, and she wrote back honestly, noting, "it was a keen disappointment. There was in it not one little glimmer of the glow or the gleam that I had learned to expect from Rumer.

"In February [1950] I wrote offering to set her free. . . . Rumer wrote most kindly that she was only the navigator and could not do without her pilot. And I have tried hard to pilot by remote control. I could have written the play (I think) in the time I have spent analysing, arguing, suggesting. When Rumer's second draft came it had rearrangements, innovations, yet in all essentials it was so like the first that I hardly knew which script I was reading. It was then I decided that I must either give up my dream of a wonderful play, my year of little writing and much frustrated waiting, or scrape the barrel for my last cent and get to England."

Which is exactly what she did, feeling an obligation to the producers, who had expected the script in January. Godden would later tell Dorothy that the reason she was not honest with her is that she did not want to hurt her feelings. "I was not the cause" of it, Godden would declare. Even as Patti Whitelaw in England witnessed some of it happen and thought Dorothy was not the problem, Godden disagreed, noting collaboration "is an intimate affair," essentially telling Dorothy that she was too fragile to be told the truth, which meant she had led her on, allowed her to come to England and do it all for naught.[5]

Unaware of all the backstories, still believing in the best of everyone—except Clayburgh—Dorothy, paying her own way, took Jenifer along, her daughter incorrectly assuming that she could just turn up and take classes with the Sadler Wells Ballet Company. "On coming to London, I had greatly hoped that, now that Rumer had had her long, long turn, she would work with me as DuBose worked: I taking the lead, and DuBose, who knew his characters far better than I, rewriting dialogue that was not in character, reworking scenes and giving a touch of brilliance I do not possess. Rumer has this brilliance," she was sure.

Rumer was all kindness and flowers, begging Dorothy to put off a collaboration for a week, while she, Godden, finished yet another version.

"It would be hard to explain my acquiescence to anyone who does not know Rumer. This time of her enthusiasm was no time to tell her the things I had to say. I was simply incapable of saying, 'St[o]p it, Rumer. It will be more of the same.' . . . After her week's solo flight she moved to the St. Ermin's [Hotel] so that we could confer constantly."

But it was bedlam there; "a madhouse," she told Audrey Wood. "I was put off my stride by this and utterly confused by her London pace." Godden had hired three secretaries to be ready to take down every word she uttered, sometimes giving dictation as she lay in a hot bath. Every word had to come from her, she said, so the play would flow evenly. "Rumer's speed, and my inability to appraise what she had written as fast as she could write it, had me in a state of utter confusion. I felt as though I were collaborating with a polite and solicitous steam roller, and I had a dazed feeling that out of the great activity must come progress."[6]

Yet deep down, she knew this was insane. The script produced was shared, via the mail, with Dorothy's agent, Godden's agent, and with Clayburgh and Merrick. "The four criticisms that I thought would put her into a mood to weigh my words of wisdom did not work out as expected." "Audrey Wood sent what seemed to me a fair and well-considered criticism; it was adverse but [she] evidently struggled to be kind. Rumer was offended, and rejected the criticism in toto. She was less offended by her own agent's advice to throw the whole thing away. . . . The Merrick letter was a puzzler. Julie had spoken to me by phone about the script quite bitterly, but even without this hint of their attitude, it would have seemed most improbable that two theatre-wise people could be sincere in praising the script. I warned Rumer—and she agreed—that they were probably trying to encourage us." It seems Merrick and Clayburgh were sticking by their plan to praise Godden and throw off Dorothy. "I later told Merrick that . . . if he had been as honest as Wood and [Godden's agent Alan] Collins, this might have a different ending."

When Merrick came to London and met with them, he confirmed his letter of praise was false. Once more Dorothy longed to tell Merrick the truth about the collaboration but again deferred, honoring her earlier pledge with Godden to act as one. "A promise is a promise," Dorothy could quote from the novel. "It is prrinciple," Madame, the erstwhile prima ballerina and head of the school, enunciates in her idiosyncratic accent. "When it's most difficult to keep a promise, that is the time you should, that is its *proof*."

Merrick scolded them in the vituperative manner for which he would become famous. (*The Abominable Showman* would be the title of the biography written about him only after his death, when he could no longer sue and browbeat.) His reversal and his excoriation of the play, Dorothy believed, would finally show Godden that the script was no good, and now maybe, finally, she would allow her to take the lead. But as luck would have it, it was just then that Godden received news that a novel of hers, which her agent had disliked, had just been selected by the Book of the Month Club in the States, guaranteeing sales and giving her a boost of self-confidence. Nevertheless, they set up another appointment to meet without Merrick.[7]

On June 24, 1950, Dorothy's apartment doorbell rang, and expecting Godden, she found Merrick instead. Godden, he said, wanted to cease all collaboration. He fired Dorothy on the spot. She was stunned but tried to take it with grace. It was business after all, and producers had the right to do what they wanted, but why, she wondered, hadn't Godden, whom she considered a friend, not told her that herself? "It's all very puzzling: My collaborator wants to try it alone. She writes entirely unhampered by me; she fails; she fails again and decides that the cause of her failure must be me," Dorothy concluded. She who had perfected the art of farce now found herself trapped in one that was no longer funny.

Sometime after Merrick left, Godden and Dorothy met face-to-face, and it was only then that the former spoke to her of the drive from the Colony to Connecticut back in August 1949 when Merrick and Clayburgh had suggested she drop Dorothy as her collaborator. Dorothy saw in an instant that Godden had played her false for months. Jenifer witnessed a bit of the fallout between the two women and became upset. Dorothy tried to make peace with this blow to her career and possibly her daughter's, but it was hard, stung again by yet another failure after Boysi, *South Pacific*, and *Set My People Free*. Yet it was the betrayal by a woman she had admired and truly liked that hurt most. (It's unknown whether she realized the irony of the situation: Godden was doing to Dorothy what Dorothy did to others, refusing to tell the truth in order to be kind.)

She managed to stay calm until four days later when Merrick, "an odd, odd character," begged Dorothy to see him one more time. She declined, explaining she was on her way to a cocktail party being given in her honor. But he seemed penitent, contrite, and earnest, and so she agreed to give him the hour he requested, one that ended up being very "expensive," an hour that changed her life.[8]

In the future, Merrick would become famous not just for his many successful prizewinning plays on Broadway, but also for his cruelty and indifference to the unhappiness and suffering he caused, getting a perverse joy from destroying those in his way. Frail, vulnerable, and distressed Dorothy gave this Abominable Showman one of his first victims. "You were right about that man Merrick," she wrote Peggy Lamson. "He has two faces—or six."

After apologizing for firing her, he began screaming and ranting. Why hadn't she fought back? Why hadn't she secretly written a draft without Godden's knowledge and sent it to him months before? He also asked "why I had not warned him that Rumer was a 'ham' playwright who could not possibly write the play alone. I was still too loyal to Rumer to allow him to talk this way about her in my flat." Merrick shouted that he and Dorothy were the real victims of Rumer Godden's manipulations and deceptions. He was so vituperative that after she showed him out, Dorothy felt caught up in a whirl of emotions.

She "was more than an hour late to my own party—and after I got there I had to slip off for a private collapse. In fact this was one of the turning points of my life." Dorothy could not conceive of someone so sadistically enjoying creating havoc and suffering.

"Until his visit I had been putting up a good fight not to let this thing get under my skin, but I suppose semi-suppressed unhappiness had made me vulnerable. I don't know why I should have believed Merrick nor why Rumer's ethics should be any concern of mine but with Merrick's visit I stopped sleeping and eating."[9]

CHAPTER 19

A Case for St. Jude

Dorothy's inability to comprehend Merrick's and Godden's behavior continued unabated, as her lack of sleep and loss of appetite escalated. Jenifer had been insisting on a holiday. Her friend William (Bill) Banks, who seemed a promising beau, was visiting, and instead of resting in the sun as she had hoped, Dorothy trooped along with them to Canterbury and Stonehenge, but "it's as though Merrick's two visits, more particularly the second, had caused some tangible physical change in my brain that had taken my thinking out of my control and had started a record playing in my head that I seem powerless to stop. . . . I am so utterly weary of it, yet the music goes 'round and round,'" she realized. "What is troubling me is fear I may be swiftly on my way to permanent mental invalidism."[1]

Never before in her life had she been at such a loss or so lethargic. She saw a doctor at Godden's suggestion. Not thinking clearly, Dorothy, perhaps even a bit masochistically, still thought Godden a friend, lacerating herself for being weak, and for letting the situation get to her. How could this one little upset trip her, in her own words, into "a screwball collapse"? The doctor replied that the triggering event was insignificant; the issues it brought up were. Yet, undone by Merrick, unable to blame Godden, she kept blaming herself, believing if she just had a bit more courage, she could stop her decline. "Six months ago I was leading a life so full that I was always breathless trying to keep up with it. Now I have got lost—which could not have surprised anyone more than me." St. Jude, she knew, was the patron saint of lost things.[2]

In a role reversal, Jenifer grew angry, not alarmed, when Dorothy kept forgetting things as a sort of mental fog rolled in. There were "islands" of reality she remembered such as visiting Stonehenge, but not Canterbury. Of a trip to Antwerp where DuBose's sister was visiting her daughter and son-in-law, John Fishburne, the American consul general there, she had no recall at all. And when Bill Banks, to evolve more into an escort for Jenifer than a boyfriend, asked Dorothy what happened with the play, she started trembling and suffered another collapse.

How she ended up in the Greenway "rest home," she never recalled, but she vaguely remembered being in an ambulance and having an operation to remove two large cysts in her buttocks, apparently a complication from her hip surgery three years before; another cyst was removed later.[3]

Her confusion and depression were so deep that her team of physicians, between some seven and nine of them, ordered ECT—electroconvulsive therapy—shocks to her brain twice a week to restore memory and equilibrium and get Merrick's words out of her head. "An aenesthetist [sic] knocks me cold, then the dr. applies the electricity, and when I at length come to, I all but have to be told who I am." Utterly confused and afraid, wondering if she was going to die and even considering suicide, Dorothy wrote desperate letters, worrying who would accompany Jenifer home with her corpse should she die. When she found carbon copies of such notes written to friends like Rebecca West, Thornton Wilder, and Peggy Lamson, she not only did not remember writing them, she had no idea whether she had sent them. She feared she might be like Dorothy DeJagers who, when institutionalized, had bombarded Dorothy with long, incomprehensible, and demented screeds. When worrying, for instance, if she had thanked the British author Marjory Sharp, first met in Charleston, for flowers, a note arrived from Sharp thanking Dorothy for her three thank-you notes. One doctor had encouraged her to keep writing down her memories to try to organize them, and oftentimes she cast them in letter form.[4]

While "I have faith in the excellent intentions . . . of the young doctor," she noted in a moment of clarity, "My doubts concern the drastic effects of the treatments. The doctor told me that they would render me temporarily unaccountable. I have recently registered a mild protest that, since unaccountable people are unaware of their unaccountableness, I should have been restrained from taking any action immediately after the treatment. My most frequent offence is the writing of goofy letters. On one occasion I sent an urgent appeal for my former collaborator to come at once; then apparently said things that caused her great distress—things that I would never have dreamed of saying if in control of my mind." Apparently, Dorothy had told Godden how much she had hurt her, but characteristically, when Godden objected and replied stiffly, Dorothy walked her comments back, even apologizing for actions done under mental duress.

After one especially traumatic shock session, she called Jenifer in agony, but the young woman said she had a dance lesson and could not come, another stinging blow to Dorothy, who had brought Jen along just to keep from hurting her feelings. Jenifer later denied knowing her mother was so ill.

But she was; and to Dorothy, it was that abyss she had been avoiding for years. "I wandered in very dark places," she concluded. After the conclusion of ECT, she slowly started getting bits of her memory back, and with it some of her old optimism. "I think I shall come out of this," she hoped. "For a while I seemed to be losing ground so rapidly that I thought perhaps I was down in the depths to stay. When I do come through I think that my life may be richer, for I now see that I have never before known deep and prolonged unhappiness. And surely everyone should know it once. Bitterness and despair are hardly to be coveted, but it seems as though every human who has lived as long as I should at least know what they feel like."

With more time for reflection, she came to realize she was better off than the woman who had caused so much of her pain. "I had DuBose, success and great happiness," she repeated in her ramblings. Although Godden was liked by so many people, Dorothy thought she might really be lonely, an amazing show of compassion (or incomprehension) for a woman whose betrayal had precipitated so much chaos.[5]

She had arrived in England in April 1950, had collapsed in June, the second conversation with Merrick having taken place on the 28th, the date Dorothy saw as the beginning of her breakdown; she started to get a sense of self back around Christmas. She would not leave London until after the new year; yet most of her time abroad would remain a blur, recalled, if at all, imperfectly. She longed to get back home, perhaps grateful that Jenifer was staying on to continue her ballet lessons with a private teacher.

When doctors determined it was safe to fly back, Dorothy, still weak and frightened, did not feel strong enough to undertake the journey alone. Rumer Godden, perhaps feeling guilty, volunteered to accompany her, instigating a series of letters on Dorothy's part to find and secretly pay for a place for Godden in New York City. She, the woman of goodwill, if not the best judgment, eventually absolved Godden of any responsibility for her breakdown, even going so far as to conclude that if given the chance to live that year over, she would have still gone through the madness to have met Rumer.

The two were met in New York by Marjorie Flack Benét and a host of other women friends who took care of her when Godden flew back to England. It was Benét, Josephine Pinckney, Patti Whitelaw, and the "appallingly young" Peggy Lamson who became her caregivers and confidantes.

After a few days in New York, Marjorie (or Marge) Benét went down to Beaufort, South Carolina, with Dorothy for two weeks, recuperating at the inn, Tidalholm, where they met up with Henry Seidel Canby and his wife, Marion, and where Dorothy participated in a concert by the Society for the Preservation of Spirituals. "I love this sea-island country," she wrote Rumer. "I do so yearn to have a house again. My house in Charleston means home to me." But it was rented, so when Dorothy returned to Charleston she went back to Old Town Plantation, again staying with friend Ferdi Legare Backer, now remarried as Ferdi Waring.[6]

Her "guest cottage by the lake" at Old Town was "all wisteria, azalea and jessamine," its beauty bracing. Yet still, "I am a little afraid," she confessed, feeling a ghostly presence, "as I did most of my work on *Candle* there." It was a place to be alone, but "in two minutes I can get to the big house and friends." "My friend who owns the plantation is growing flowers commercially: acres and acres of them. I am working with her. We have been stripping, clipping, sizing, grading, etc. hundreds and hundreds of dozens of Iris." The weather changed, and the late and early flowers were blooming simultaneously. "Now we are starting on Snap Dragon. It is wonderful for me. Some days I work until I think I am going to drop, but I don't drop, and I sleep better than in many a day; I have at last recaptured an appetite and, in spite of the strenuous work, I am up to ninety-five pounds." The skin of her arms, a friend remarked, no longer "looks like that of her granddaughter's pet toad just before its yearly skin-shedding."[7]

She had been forbidden to write by her doctors, either because of her habit of sending out "goofy" letters or because playwriting was now seen as disruptive to her mental health; yet she took up communicating again, through dictation, keeping up with Godden, if for no other reason than to come up with a cover story to explain her nearly a year away with nothing to show for it. "People who know me little seem to know I went abroad to work on a play. It will be worse at the Colony. Sometimes I have truthfully said that you found my work unsatisfactory but that is not a good subject-closer, and if questioned persistently enough I succumb to the urge to justify myself, all mixed-up with the urge to protect you. . . .

"I have been asked by the press but have so far managed to beg off from making a statement. . . . I should then like my version to agree with yours—or not to differ materially from any statement given out by the Alan Collins Office."

"The plans for the production fell through," was the report that appeared in the local press, on April Fool's Day, its editor, Thomas R. Waring Jr., a good friend, "and Mrs. Heyward, becoming ill, spent a lot of her time in a nursing home." With mental illness seen as shameful in this era, Dorothy, unwilling to tell the truth, kept mum. She'd make no mention of *Cygnets*, Godden, Clayburgh, or Merrick in her autobiography. And when Godden came to write her own, although she confessed to often hurting those for whom she cared, she omitted Dorothy completely. Her biographer, however, did not; but in referring to the cocktail party where Dorothy first collapsed, she attributed it, not to Merrick or Godden, but instead described an unnamed collaborator's "alcohol-fueled nervous breakdown." Clayburgh would garner a single mention in Merrick's biography with no reference to Dorothy. Poet Margaret Widdemer, after Dorothy's death, seems to be the sole one to have published anything about it, noting that she "had had a nervous breakdown, and they [Dorothy and Rumer] had found each other not easy to work with."[8]

Back at home, Dorothy came to believe, or pretended to, that she had made a complete recovery. Although able to eat and sleep and laugh, she'd never totally recover her self-confidence. Her days of a life in the theater were mostly behind her now.

CHAPTER 20

Operatic

Back in New York, however, those unaware of Dorothy's breakdown kept seeking her services. Affecting a breezy, everything-is-fine manner, she wrote Rumer Godden: "I seem suddenly and amusingly to be surrounded by operas." As always there was *Porgy and Bess*, now with new "kinks and twists" arising from dueling producers, Robert Breen and George Brandt, each vying to mount it. "The rival[s] . . . have taken it to court where [they] are charging each other with bribery and sabotage," she reported, tying her up like a "pretzel." She revealed her authorship when she wrote, "I want to redo the book, striving for the quality of its original [Theater Guild production] and the brevity of the [Cheryl Crawford] revival." She was now also considering a request to write a libretto for a children's opera based on the Jean de Brunhoff stories of Babar and Celeste, king and queen elephants, and another team sought her to craft "a musical based on *The Semi-Attached Couple*," a light novel from the early nineteenth century about lovers who marry but then are at a loss as to how to go forward. Just as she turned that down, there came yet another proposal from Douglas Moore, who had played her love interest in the play *His Blue Serge Suit* back at the MacDowell Colony in 1922. Now with a Pulitzer Prize for music to his credit, Moore wanted to base an opera on *Set My People Free*. Dorothy's letter to Jed Harris trying to determine if he was still interested had come back unopened, but the Karamu Players in Cleveland, the oldest African American theater company in the country (and the only company, in Dorothy's opinion, to successfully stage Porgy's flight from the police in his goat cart), had just triumphantly revived it.[1]

Latent in her letter to Godden was a subtle rebuke. "See how many other creative people desire me as a collaborator, despite your actions?" was the implication. Dorothy debated Moore's request, but finding his music "dull," she and her agent Audrey Wood demurred, losing the chance to give new life to the story of Vesey through a composer who'd come to be well regarded for his works on American themes. Author and agent were pursuing instead the young up-and-coming composer Ned Rorem, who was interested in an operatic version of *Mamba's Daughters*. (When Dorothy had tried to interest George Gershwin's friend Kay Swift, she had declined, replying that her work might be too "Gershwiny.") That's exactly what the "motherly" Dorothy Heyward desired, Ned Rorem believed. He discussed *Mamba* with James Baldwin, a fan of *Porgy and Bess*, staged arias for Dorothy, and even used the Eva Jessye Choir, veterans of *Porgy and Bess*, to help. Although he ultimately decided against it, the story lived on, the New York City Opera announcing years later it would do a *Mamba* version with music by Rorem and a libretto by Arnold Weinstein.[2]

One venture did pan out. "To my surprise, I have become the author of a libretto (sans lyrics) for a children's opera based on the Babar books," she reported to Rumer. "When first asked . . . we both thought, you remember, that I would be wise to work independently, but, when asked to reconsider, I sat down one morning and it wrote itself." If DuBose could write about a bunny for children, then she could follow suit with elephants. "It is commissioned for production in the fall of 1952. I have asked to be allowed not to enter in a hard-and-fast written agreement [once burned, twice shy apparently]. I think I shall be without anxieties so long as I know that my partner is free as air. Now he [the composer at the MacDowell Colony with her] is at the stage where he goes into ecstasies over all I write, but . . . I myself am far from sure that I am a wise choice," she concluded, still doubting herself.

The Russian composer Nicolai Berezowsky had sung as a child in the czar's choir and had thrown spitballs at Rasputin. Later he had been first violin for the New York Philharmonic and worked as a conductor for CBS. It was his wife, Judith Randal, who wrote the lyrics for Dorothy's one-act scenario in five scenes.

Starting with a gunshot, the opera follows the young Babar fleeing the jungle to the city, where he is taunted for being different. The Old Lady schoolteacher brings him back to the jungle, where it is discovered that the old king has died, and Babar is to marry the king's daughter Celeste. Both, however, are kidnapped and made to perform in a circus, till the Old Lady returns and, through a trick of hypnosis, frees the animals, who return permanently to the jungle.

At *Babar the Elephant*'s premiere on February 21, 1953, at Hunter College, *The New York Times* called it "inventive and delicately charming," and the *Herald Tribune* praised Dorothy's libretto for its "tight little plot line." She missed the performance, however, and it would rarely receive another. At the time she had returned to London to check on Jenifer, who had mostly ignored Dorothy's letters for over a year. There, Jen's teacher, Audrey DeVoss, secretly allowed the proud mother to slip in the back of a hall to see her daughter perform. Dorothy, transfixed and charmed with Jen's loveliness, still worried over her lack of focus and obsessed over Jen's failure to deliver a present to Godden. It was June 1953, and mother and daughter joined the throngs watching Queen Elizabeth II's coronation parade; Jenifer was whisked off to a whirl of landed gentry house parties, fueling Dorothy's hopes that her daughter would settle down and marry.[3]

But there was no Prince Charming. Boyfriends, supposedly three in three different cities, tended to be friends like Bill Banks, who, a perennial bachelor and seemingly gay, became her escort. While Dorothy found a place to live on Gramercy Park that she'd keep for the rest of her life, it was not large enough for two; so, Jen, returning to New York, lived nearby—chaotically. She had almost been evicted for not paying rent and had to move in with her mother when no electrician could figure out how to get her power back until it dawned on them that Jenifer had never paid her electricity bills. In 1954, however, Jen had a breakthrough. While everyone believed she had started ballet too late to become a professional, she had auditioned for and won a spot in the Ballet Russe de Monte Carlo, split from the original ballet troupe founded in 1938. (The other offshoot survived under the name the Original Ballets Russes.) Overjoyed, Dorothy dedicated herself to dotingly following the peripatetic group's grueling schedule, as the dancers crossed the continent by bus for one-night stands in small towns and large cities, proceeding down the West Coast into Mexico. "When I saw Jen in Philadelphia, she looked awful," Dorothy wrote "Mother MacDowell," Jen's godmother. "I wanted to snatch her out of that company. Also, she was so exhausted that she hated it and seemed downright terrified of the long stretch of one-night stands ahead. For Christmas week, they settled down in Chicago. . . . And what a difference! Jen had got the swing of it. She still loathes the interminable bus rides but loves the ballet. . . . She says that a daze of exhaustion is the habitual state of everyone and that she is getting used to it."[4]

Keeping news of her illnesses from her daughter, or making light of them, Dorothy suffered a series of accidents and hospitalizations, many stemming from rheumatism or arthritis. Discharged from Harkness Pavilion in 1952, she was in a taxi when its driver, suffering a heart attack, died at the wheel. The car careened up a steep embankment, veered back on the road, crossing lanes of traffic and skidding before rolling over and then finally righting itself, sending Dorothy immediately back to the hospital with broken vertebrae. For weeks afterward, she'd have to lie immobilized on her back in a heavy metal brace. When she tried to sue and collect her medical fees, she lost her case, prompting some vaguely anti-Semitic remarks from her about the Jewish attorney and a Jewish jury prone to side with him. If not for the income from *Porgy and Bess*, she said, she would have been in the charity wing.[5]

A plan to produce the play in Charleston seemed imminent. Back in the 1930s, three principals had been engaged from New York, a director hired, and everything seemed set for annual productions during tourist season "when the City Fathers said that it would not be good for the Charleston negro to learn that white people would come to see him in a play." Dorothy, always frank in her assessment of the city and its racial views, wrote to actress Helen Hayes to seek her help in publicizing the new production plans. "Thinking, even in Charleston, has changed so much in the last twelve years," she saw, "that it would now be possible to produce *Porgy* . . . to blacks and whites alike. . . . [S]ome Charlestonians would stay at home but the production would count on the thousands of visitors who go yearly to Charleston in the garden season." Ever loyal to the Dock Street Theatre, she found "the idea of performing it there a very comforting one," for it would also satisfy her "yearning to have a part of *Porgy* given back to DuBose." But that venue would not work. Memminger High School was not ready to integrate its auditorium, and the College of Charleston's gymnasium was not suitable, leaving only County Hall, the largest auditorium in town. One half of the seating would be reserved for Blacks, separated from the other for whites. Rehearsals began with local actors, and while the Charleston branch of the NAACP gave its blessing, when the national office heard of it through an article in *Jet* magazine, there was pushback. The local branch changed its stance, and the production was scuttled.[6]

While that was being debated, a local reporter doing research on Sammy Smalls turned up details of his life. Dorothy on her own would engage retired Charleston police officer Henry F. Church to investigate him, too.

Astonishingly, relatives, including his mother, were found living in poverty, and the story was widely covered. Dorothy was moved and wanted to help, but she was out of town. Needing a go-between, she unfortunately relied on Tom R. Waring Jr., the segregationist editor of the daily paper, to work out the delivery. Waring had been very useful to her in helping publish her white lie alibi about her mental breakdown in England, and in the coming years, he'd wield his cudgel in Dorothy's fight to restore credit to DuBose for *Porgy and Bess*. Waring would also cover her testimony before a Senate subcommittee where U.S. senator from South Carolina Strom Thurmond, for some reason, introduced her as the mystery writer Nero Wolfe, and she spoke on music broadcasting and copyright, a situation now giving her income from royalties of "Summertime" and the like a "terrible wallop."[7] Insensitive at best, Waring was suspicious about the integrity of some of the Smalls family, which they returned in equal measure, feeling Waring was insulting their dignity. Dorothy had learned to keep her advanced views to herself and was distressed when her good intentions were misunderstood and came to nothing. But she did join forces with Josephine Pinckney who, while believing in integration, still wanted schools to delay the federal mandates. Together they paid the tuition for a young African American woman named Jennie Pyatt to attend segregated Claflin College.

Dorothy was equally generous with others in these years. With continuing cash gifts to the MacDowell Colony in DuBose's name from *Porgy and Bess* royalties, Mrs. MacDowell finally overcame her reservations about Dorothy and now welcomed her and her contributions warmly.

In fact, "*Porgy and Bess* has become my life," Dorothy would soon state. As interest in the opera grew, it consumed more of her time, angst, and attention, coming close to endangering her hard-won sanity.[8]

CHAPTER 21

Porgy and Business

Ever since Cheryl Crawford's 1941 revival, *Porgy and Bess* had showed no signs of slowing down. In Europe, it had premiered during World War II in Denmark. In the postwar era, as America helped rebuild the ravaged continent, the opera's fame and popularity grew, giving it a luster and status abroad it had not enjoyed on its native turf.

George Gershwin had died without a will, so his estate went to his mother, Rose, who never was a fan of *Porgy*, and when she died, her estate, and thus the rights to the opera went to her three children in various fractions, and factions, many of the clan pointedly making sure Lee Gershwin, Ira's wife, would never get a share. But the siblings worked that out, and the Gershwin grandchildren had their interests included as well. At one point, Dorothy would count twenty-seven people in a room dickering over rights, trying her patience.

But it wasn't just the Gershwin clan; there was the Theatre Guild as well. And as Dorothy had discovered with *Set My People Free*, the Guild was "now less of an organization dedicated to originality and excellence in theatre than a group of managers, led by Langner and Helburn, in commercial competition with other Broadway producers. . . . It was now more interested in solid returns on investment."

With passion, tact, and great financial backing, and perhaps a tad bit of subterfuge, one of the many suitors wanting to produce the opera finally emerged the winner. Entrepreneur Robert Breen had the charm and know-how to get his way while his business partner, Blevins Davis, had the finances.

From Independence, Missouri, and a friend of President Harry Truman, Davis had married great wealth; and when his wife died soon after the marriage, he inherited it, using it to finance theatrical and dance productions, encountering Robert Breen along the way. While working in Europe, leading a tour of the American Ballet Theatre with U.S. State Department funds, Breen had conceived the idea of something similar for *Porgy and Bess*. He had worked with Cheryl Crawford and, aware of her association with the opera, believed she would be a trump card and bargaining chip in winning the rights.

But it was a misstep. "I have very pleasant memories of Cheryl in the far-off days when she took 'Porgy' to London," Dorothy wrote her agent, "and I think I have since seen her only twice: I shall go right on liking her personally, but I should greatly prefer not to do business with her." She would never stop blaming Crawford for being the first to start the trend of stripping DuBose's name from the opera. Due to Crawford's involvement, "I vote we call the whole thing off."[1]

The Gershwins agreed; they had not cared for her scaled-down, poor man's, middlebrow version of the opera either. Breen, so in love with the opera, with the full support of millionaire Davis, revised his strategy and took Crawford's name off contracts, while possibly planning to use her in some unarticulated manner. It worked. Davis put up the money, and contracts were signed on January 24, 1952, giving the duo the rights to mount a full-scale production of the opera and take it on the road. Mamoulian was thought of as a director, but again, Dorothy was not pleased. Breen found him charming, but "whenever he gets into a theatre he thinks he invented the stage and that he superseded the Greeks," Breen wrote Davis, confirming many others' opinions of the man who would later aggrandize his role in shaping the opera.

When Mamoulian pulled out, Breen got his chance to direct. He courted Dorothy, calling her "Duchess" or "Darling," probably ironically, since that was not at all the way she presented, and when he wanted extra dialogue in his production, he pleased her by going back to her script to get it. She was also at casting auditions, present when Leontyne Price, at the beginning of her career, sang. Dorothy and Breen were transfixed, but Ira Gershwin was not; they talked him out of his objections. William Warfield became Price's Porgy, and their marriage soon after sparked much coverage in the press. Cab Calloway assumed the role of Sportin' Life, continuing the type of miscasting that Dorothy disliked, and John McCurry, from Cleveland's Karamu Theatre, became Crown.

Alexander Smallens, who had wielded the baton in 1935, returned to conduct; he so believed in the work, and always had, that he told Dorothy, "It will run the rest of your life." The comment came soon after her taxi accident, and "trussed up in a brace and corset with big straps over my shoulder," she wryly remarked to Jen, "I don't know how much time he gives me."[2]

Rehearsals began on May 5, and Dorothy attended them, noting where pauses were needed, where music stepped on lines, and many other small points. Plans for its premiere at the Metropolitan Opera were part of Breen's idea, but the deal fell through due to scheduling and bookings. The opening came at the State Fair in Dallas, Texas, a huge success that Dorothy missed due to yet another hospitalization.

Audrey Wood and her husband, William Liebling, went in her stead, and their report back prompted Dorothy to write Breen immediately. Even though Audrey had "worked in the theatre all her life, and her playwrights often incorporate scenes relating to cannibalism, castration or people being torn to pieces by dogs [reference to her client's Tennessee Williams's work]," Wood nevertheless told Dorothy, "in all her experience [she] had never seen anything like Robert Breen's production" of the scene on Kittiwah Island in particular. "Breen had a bold conception of how to do the seduction scene," another associated with the production wrote, "bold because you didn't do those things in those days. He had Crown run his hands over her arms, her breasts, down her thighs. Breen had found the music notes for the action in the score, even though the scene had not been played that way before." So said Ella Gerber, who had first been chosen to direct the play when it was to have been staged in Charleston about this time. Breen replied to Dorothy, "But, darling, you wrote the words yourself." "Well, yes, I did write the words," she replied, "but I didn't expect them to be acted out so graphically," revealing a bit of prudery and, simultaneously, her claim of authorship. It was Dorothy who had inserted those words of dialogue into the play script.

Audiences, however, loved this version that Dorothy called "the Hot *Porgy and Bess*." Such graphic sensuousness was not expected in such "high" art, yet when it played in Washington, D.C., President Truman went backstage to congratulate the cast.

In August, still trapped in the iron contraption for her broken vertebrae, Dorothy dictated a letter to Breen, thanking him for his work, reminding him that the hurricane scene still needed attention, but telling him it was the final scene she found most worrisome. It was the tone she objected to—the actors' exuberance, the upbeat tempo and jazzy riffs, none of which were true to the spirit of the piece. She entreated Breen to stop directing the actors to play against the lines and instead cleave to what she and DuBose had intended. "I want the heartbreak put back. Let's have all the laughs we can, and all the excitement, and gaiety," but not at the ending, an ending she had crafted. With the crowd scenes and the swelling of the music, it all seemed to suggest that Porgy was off for a jaunt and that New York City was just around the corner. Everyone seemed so joyous, she said, it was as if they all believed he'd be back, triumphant, in a year or two, with Bess on his arm. One reviewer agreed, prompting Dorothy, aghast, to compare it to making *Romeo and Juliet* happy instead of tragic.

"Could I respectfully beg . . . could you someday try 'I'm On My Way' my way—George's and DuBose's way, and I assume Ira's—centered here on Porgy? . . . What I am trying to describe is a scene quieter in physical movement and therefore with far more impact in the one vital movement: Porgy's measured, singing exit." But Breen never did it that way, going for the broader, big bang sort of Broadway show bonanza ending, instead of something more subtle and poignant, the final notes dying on an exit that was doomed but yet somehow magnificent, like Greek tragedy. (And if that ending bothered her, it's probably good she never learned of an unsanctioned adaptation of it as a children's ballet by some New York high school students wherein "Crown wins Bess and Porgy dies of a broken heart.")[3]

The troupe embarked for Europe on September 1, 1952, and went from triumph to triumph in standing-room-only packed houses in Vienna, Berlin, London, and Paris; it traveled on Davis's money and sometimes that of the State Department, funneled through the nonprofit Everyman Opera set up by Breen when it represented the United States in international festivals, or was sent to foreign countries as part of a cultural exchange. While the work was being acclaimed as a world classic and the best possible cultural ambassador for the United States, some discerning critics, like Kenneth Tynan of the British *Evening Standard*, echoed Dorothy's unease, remarking on the lack of subtlety in the characterizations. He felt there was too much "indiscriminate stomping abandon, too much is happening all the time, all over the stage and we lose focus." But his was a minority opinion, and the tour ended in triumph, returning to the United States on March 1, 1953, to open in New York at the Ziegfeld Theatre.

There had been an election, and now Dwight Eisenhower was president. Through the machinations of South Carolinian statesman Bernard Baruch,

Breen got access to the White House, and now Eisenhower, like Truman before him, poured forth presidential praise on the director and cast. "I cannot emphasize too strongly how serious and enduring the work seems to me. You and your company are making a real contribution to the kind of understanding between nations that alone can bring mutual respect and trust. You are, in a real sense, ambassadors of the arts."

With the growing civil rights movement, however, there was disagreement on some fronts, due primarily to the lack of other major artistic vehicles on Black life. Major plays like *A Raisin in the Sun* and films like *The Defiant Ones* had yet to appear, so in the United States the opera was a lightning rod attracting attention as the object about which Black representation in high culture could be seen and discussed. Ironically, however, because the United States was getting negative world press about its lack of progress on civil rights, the opera was being used by the State Department to counter that story, showing what heights African American artists could reach, despite their portraying impoverished Blacks who live menaced by drugs and murder in a slum. Dorothy was distressed; propaganda had been far from her husband's mind as he had begun *Porgy*, and she and the Gershwins had not intended that either.

Comments from the cast members themselves about the opera and its characters acting out their fates in a particular historical moment in time, no doubt, comforted her. Charleston native Urylee Leonardos, who alternated with Leontyne Price as Bess, told the press, "You can find Catfish Row in New York, [or] Chicago," explaining that the work expressed universal truths through the lives of particular African Americans.

Breen, not content to sit on his laurels, kept working on production details, changing action on stage, and keeping the show alive. In New York, he took the opera from its traditional three acts to two; and in the time saved from a second intermission, he had at least one of DuBose's lyrics, "The Buzzard Song," which had been cut from the original production, put back in, albeit in a different place. Breen was always careful to keep Dorothy informed of such things; and no doubt he was behind including her picture and biography in the program along with those of DuBose, George, and Ira, acknowledging her role to a greater extent than anyone had done before. (Ten years before, however, even as she fought for DuBose and against Ira, she unaccountably had outright lied to a journalist saying, "The opera is the work of George Gershwin, DuBose

Heyward, and Ira Gershwin. My sole contribution was the typing.") Breen knew better than that, however. While sincerely liking her, he was still shrewd enough to keep her on his side, especially as he decided to maneuver for the movie rights.

DuBose had sold the silent rights to the novel back in the 1920s, but nothing had come of it. The 1935 opera contract had given the Theatre Guild one-third of the sale of the film rights; Dorothy and DuBose's share, now all hers, was pegged at 30 percent, with the same amount for George Gershwin, allotting Ira a mere 6⅔ percent share. If all the Gershwin heirs pooled their percentages, they would have a large interest, but with the many factions in the family, that was not likely, which left Dorothy as the person with the largest individual share, close to the Theatre Guild's, and obviously in a position of power, shocking the people who were dickering for a sale. Breen, aware of this, convinced Dorothy to assign him all her television and film rights in the novel, play, and opera for $5,000 for five years. That, he said, would enable him to deal with agents, interested buyers, and the "Gershwin clan." Dorothy, always grateful to him for promoting *Porgy* around the world, consented gladly. Breen, however, still had no funds of his own, and his backer, Davis, was becoming reluctant to advance any more, having rarely been paid back any of his investment.

The stakes grew higher when the Hollywood agent, Swifty Lazar, who introduced himself to Dorothy over the telephone as the Devil, entered the picture. "The *Porgy and Bess* story grows more and more fabulous and the producers more and more temperamental," Dorothy reported to Josephine Pinckney in February 1955. "It seems to me I spend half of my time listening to phone messages telling me what I must be sure . . . not to say." And as the opera proved more popular across the world, the stakes rose even higher. After 305 performances in New York, the company set off to Paris, Zagreb, Belgrade, Venice, Athens, Venice, Tel Aviv, and Alexandria. Dorothy grew excited as the most exalted opportunity for any opera loomed, a production at the premiere opera house in the world, where no American opera had ever played: La Scala in Milan, Italy. She worked to gather the art wanted for an exhibit to be held at the performance. It included George Gershwin's portrait of DuBose, which she did not like, preferring instead the one by Charleston artist and friend Haskell Coffin (although DuBose himself said it made him look like a "Harvard man"). "It may be an inferior piece of art, but at least not quite as fearsome as the Gershwin portrait," was Dorothy's verdict. Work by Anna Heyward Taylor was to travel as well, along with a sketch done of Sammy Smalls given to DuBose by Henry F. Church, the detective who had tried to ferret out his history. So rare, it was insured for $5,000, and it never came back, stolen at La Scala or lost.[4]

Opening night was another triumph. "We had sung gloriously," Maya Angelou, then a member of the chorus, recalled. "We performed *Porgy and Bess* as never before, and if the La Scala patrons loved us, it was only fitting because we certainly performed as if we were in love with one another."

Later that same year, 1955, Dorothy Heyward, in a wheelchair, flew with Josephine Pinckney and Jenifer to take in the performance in Lima, Peru. The trio also planned another trip for early January 1956, when the production was set to make history again by playing behind the Iron Curtain in Soviet Russia. The State Department had declined to pay for the trip, but the Russian government itself had stepped in and offered to assume all costs, paying in rubles. When the Cold War was at its most frigid, before Van Cliburn won the Tchaikovsky competition, this first cultural exchange with the West started a thaw. Accompanying them on this once-in-a-lifetime opportunity, with so few outsiders allowed in Russia, would be William Banks, Jenifer's friend. She decided to take a brief break from the Ballet Russe de Monte Carlo to do it.

Dorothy's health, as always, was an issue. She was hospitalized on Christmas day, hoping this would build up her strength. "I thought I was going there until within thirty-six hours of the takeoff. Then the doctors said they wanted me to know that if I went it would be with their strict disapproval. I thought I would go anyway, and then I got to thinking what a nuisance I would be to everyone if I got sick over there."[5]

Ironically, visas arrived only for Jen and Dorothy, not Banks or Josephine Pinckney. Jen, alone and unchaperoned in Russia, prompted nightmares for Dorothy; but when Ella Gerber, whom Dorothy liked, got her visa, a solution presented itself. Gerber had worked as the troupe's acting coach, and her husband had one of the few white roles in the opera; she, Dorothy sighed, could help look out for Jenifer. Going along as well was Truman Capote, contracted to write an article for *The New Yorker*. Although *Life* magazine would also cover the historic event, Capote's longer article was much more highly regarded.

Unfortunately—because it was mostly about Capote and backstage gossip and not about the opera—DuBose's name was not mentioned once, even as Capote tried to trap Jenifer into saying something negative about the production. Breen wrote Dorothy that Capote was appalled that neither Leningrad nor Moscow was chic, and that no one there had heard of him. He was acting like a spoiled child because he was not the center of attention. The Russians called him Popov, and no one knew why until Breen attended the circus and saw that its main clown by that name bore an uncanny resemblance to Capote: same hairdo, some walk, same velvet jacket. Capote took an especial dislike to Lee Gershwin, and Jen, in one of her infrequent letters home, passed on some off-color gossip about her as well, prompting Dorothy's, "Poor, crazy Lee! And poor, poor Ira! . . . I should think he would bop her over the head and drop her in the swimming pool. I always thought he was very much in love with her. . . . I do hope there is not too great a tragedy ahead."[6]

More worrisome than that, however, was Jenifer's behavior. She had originally planned to be in Russia for just a few days and then return to her dancing; but when the opera troupe invited her to go along through Poland and other Soviet satellite countries, she tagged along. Dorothy, not hearing from her, first was alarmed and then appalled when she realized Breen was paying Jen's expenses—with Davis's money, no doubt—and she vowed to reimburse him.

While in Russia, Jen and Ella Gerber conceived the idea of collaborating on a play about the troupe's adventures to be called *The Red and the Black*. Jenifer also wrote an article about her own adventures, but the piece, along with photos taken by Gerber's husband, the official photographer, also went unpublished, despite Dorothy's bringing it to the attention of Charlestonian Ashley Halsey Jr., now associate editor of *The Saturday Evening Post*.

When she returned, Dorothy was relieved and exasperated. "Jenifer had reluctantly gone to Russia for one week," she noted, "but she stayed abroad for three and a half months. When she finally returned, I inquired about her sacred [dancing]. She said, 'Oh, did I forget to tell you? I've given up the ballet.'"

"I can hardly keep up with her careers," Dorothy was soon reporting. "She yearned to be a ballet dancer until she got a job in a professional company, and then she yearned to get out of it. A year ago she was working at Doubleday from nine till five, studying speed-writing from six till nine and working with a collaborator from nine till twelve on an account of their Iron Curtain experiences. I begged her to drop one activity, but she wouldn't. Then she dropped all three. Now she is studying for the stage—which could be fine, if it lasted." She would act in a number of regional theaters, and Dorothy would try to get her work through the Theatre Guild; Jenifer would take the stage name of Jenifer DuBose, instead of Jenifer DuBose Heyward. A photo of her, noting her as an aspiring actress, would eventually appear in *Holiday* magazine.[7]

Perhaps oversimplifying it, Dorothy thought that Jen, falling in love at sixteen and disillusioned at nineteen, would be happy if she married. Jenifer "is completely frank in admitting this is her greatest desire. There is no dearth of run-of-the-mill beaux, but Jen avoids them whenever possible. Three times she has been in love with a man who looked like DuBose." She still would not speak of her father or visit his grave, however. "So, the marriage problem is difficult; men who do not look like DuBose need not apply." Aside from a neighbor who was a psychiatrist, Dorothy only had Jenifer's two godmothers, Marian MacDowell and Josephine Pinckney, in whom to confide. She also kept Pinckney up to date as negotiations for the film sale of the opera escalated to new heights, becoming another pitched battle involving DuBose.

Sometime "before the [*Porgy and Bess*] lawyers, executor and producers drove me raving," as Dorothy put it, she had fled to the Carolina Inn, in Summerville, South Carolina, to spend time with Josephine. Her friend was recuperating from an illness and trying to finish a novel away from the many friends and well-wishers who demanded her time throughout the year and especially in tourist season. She and Audrey Wood, she told Josephine, were often the only women in a "conference room . . . always filled with men. They always stood gallantly when Audrey and I entered and immediately resumed hurling epithets at each other."[8]

A February 1956 "jamboree" session had lasted seven hours and featured "nine men present [who] shouted at each other steadily, no one listening to anyone else," with Dorothy said to be a calming influence. In another meeting, recalling the episode with Guthrie McClintic, someone threw a briefcase. Audrey Wood, used to complex bargaining, admitted she was shocked at such behavior. "I can truly say that in all my years I have been representing writers, I have never seen the negotiations for the sale of the motion picture rights take this amount of time from so many people," she reflected, an experience parallel to her work on *Set My People Free*.

The negotiations became even more complex through the continuing machinations of Swifty Lazar, an ever-present player in the bidding war for film rights. Dorothy was rooting for Breen, with funding by Davis, to acquire the rights, partially because he had vaguely promised her the chance to work on the screenplay and because she knew that he, more than anyone else, was responsible for making the opera a global phenomenon. He still had the option he had purchased from her, which he could use as a bargaining chip. But the prices offered for the rights were skyrocketing with Hal Wallis, Otto Preminger, Louis B. Mayer, and others jockeying for control, one offer of about a million dollars coming from Columbia Pictures. And with Breen and Davis now having issues, Breen was losing his chance.[9]

The various competing and often fractious factions at the table included Dorothy, who owned 30 percent of the film rights but had 40 percent of the Breen-Davis royalties; the Theatre Guild; and the Gershwin heirs, who were far from unified, with Ira and Lee Gershwin sometimes dissenting. John Rumsey of the Century Play Company told Dorothy that Ira, even with his small percentage, was willing to kill the deal to keep his sister's children from getting anything. He also told her that Ira had been willing at one point to change the libretto and lyrics for a sale back in 1953, infuriating Dorothy further, for she knew Ira had had little or nothing to do with the former, which was mostly hers. As George's brother, Ira, despite his minority share, was perceived as the "owner" of the opera in the negotiations, and Dorothy, the major shareholder, was ignored because she was a woman. It only got worse when someone repeated an overheard conversation to her about Ira claiming to have written the opera's spirituals.[10]

Relations deteriorated even further when Ira asked Dorothy if, once Breen's option ran out in 1958, she would side with him and go for that million-dollar sale to Columbia. Not interested in the money yet needing it more than Ira, she stayed loyal to Breen, who acquired sole rights from Davis, but there was no stopping Swifty Lazar. Lazar had taken on Ira Gershwin as a client, even as he began secret talks with Samuel Goldwyn, who wanted to crown his career with a production of *Porgy and Bess*. It was a conflict of interests for Lazar to represent both the buyer and one of the sellers, one with a particularly small fraction of the rights. (Such double-dealing had earlier appalled Ira when he discovered similar behavior in the handling of his mother's estate.) In his autobiography, wanting to clean up his image—Lazar died before it was published—he called Ira a father figure. And his way around that ethical question was to make sure there was no paper trail to convict him. One day as Goldwyn and Lazar were driving around Hollywood, Lazar spotted a Rolls Royce he liked. Goldwyn bought it for him in lieu of payment for representation. Lazar would later alter that story in his autobiography, ascribing it to another deal instead.

Dorothy, ignorant of the conspiracy, refused to sign with Goldwyn unless Breen was part of the deal. Hearing that, the crafty producer approached Breen and promised him he could coproduce; Goldwyn also dangled the possibility of directing. Without telling Dorothy, and without legal advice, Breen transferred the option he held from Dorothy for unnamed considerations to Goldwyn.

Dorothy was appalled and felt betrayed. Breen, however, ecstatic that he was to be the one to bring the opera he so admired to the screen, immediately began to draft his own version of the screenplay, without Dorothy, and started discussions with Goldwyn about casting. But then Goldwyn revealed his ploy. Theirs had been only an oral agreement, as valueless as the paper it was not written on. Goldwyn, with Lazar, had outmaneuvered and talked Breen out of his and Dorothy's rights through malevolence, deviance, and a façade of charm. And in his lawsuit against him for breach of contract, Goldwyn loyalists would vouch for the latter's sterling qualities. Breen would lose his case, dying almost penniless. "Ethics is not necessarily a word you associate with Hollywood," Lazar would write. "But during the Golden Era most of these men did deals on a handshake and more often than not lived up to their commitments." This obviously was one of the exceptions.[11]

In all this maddening turmoil, after a gap of about fifteen years of living in New York, New England, and England, Dorothy had enough. She sought refuge again in DuBose's, and now her, hometown.

CHAPTER 22

Home

In June 1957 Dorothy retook occupancy of Follywood, the Folly Beach house where much of the opera had been written and where, almost as soon as she moved in, Hollywood came calling; attorneys asked if they could fly down, contracts in hand, for her to sign.

Dorothy demurred. Reading through the over fifty-page opus, she found that documents mentioned were not included and others were referenced that she had never seen. She discovered that others involved, including Ira, had made stipulations and demands before signing. She decided to join their company, responding that her signature was going to "stand or fall" on one item and one item only: the film that Samuel Goldwyn, who had emerged as the leading contender, wanted to make would honor her husband with the same credit "in accordance with the agreement between [DuBose] and George Gershwin." She had been put off by the dickering leading up to this point in which DuBose had been ignored. She had too, to some extent; had she shown them the contract proving she was coauthor of the libretto, she might have been respected more. Just a short time before, in a debate over some royalties due her, she had stood up for herself by signing a deposition, stating, "I, Dorothy K. Heyward . . . being duly sworn declare that in collaboration with my late husband, I wrote the libretto of the operetta entitled PORGY AND BESS, that I am entitled to 20% (twenty percent) of all the royalties." Her greatest concern, however, was "that, though the terms may look all right in the contract, advertisers might get around them. The Crawford . . . revival of P&B gave me a suspicious mind. They repeatedly broke the contract notwithstanding repeated threats from the Dramatists Guild that they would close the show."

The negotiations had become so acrimonious that they were being handled by a legal arbitrator. To one of the attorneys, she reiterated, "On this I stand.

Ira didn't like our million dollar offer and he held us a year and a half. Now it's my turn to be balky. You know I want to be cooperative but I have learned the hard way that the 'inadvertencies' will far out-number the cases in which the contract is strictly complied with."

It was not cash, but credit, that concerned her. She demanded the omission of the clause that said that "inadvertent dropping" of Heyward's or anyone's name would not constitute a breach of contract, insisting instead that new language be inserted ensuring that "Neither the name of George Gershwin nor of DuBose Heyward may be used alone." It was maddening. Ira, holding only a small percentage of the rights, was going to get complete control over the music, while she, with a larger stake, despite a 1935 contract and a later sworn statement noting she was coauthor of the libretto, would be granted no control over the text. Furthermore, it had always been the custom that DuBose's name precede Ira's, but now an attorney was contesting that, and it galled her. That was not the Ira she remembered. That Ira "was always modest and retiring about his contributions and DuBose was the one who was insisting that Ira's work was by no means as unimportant as Ira protested." She couldn't understand why Ira was not joining her in giving her husband credit that was due, when "DuBose ... had the greatest admiration for Ira and said that he was one of the most fair-dealing people he knew."

When she found out that the attorneys seeking top billing for Ira over DuBose were doing so at Lenore's insistence, Dorothy was livid and could not understand why Ira's wife was saying she "would never sign" a contract that so insulted her husband, despite Ira's much smaller contribution to the opera than either Dorothy's or DuBose's. To Dorothy this was a matter of principle; she would not back down, and this time, the "woman of good will" refused to be steamrolled as she had been previously. Standing up for her husband as she never had for herself, she saw to it that language was inserted that George's name could not appear without DuBose's, and they were to be in the same size font.

"I have a feeling that Lazar is the critter we are dealing with," Dorothy wrote her own agent, "and that he will do all in his power to raise the prestige of *his* client—and to heck with yours!" Jenifer had been with Ira in Russia, and she reported him to be "such a retiring and unhappy-seeming man that no doubt Lazar can do anything he likes with him. DuBose would certainly have been surprised . . . and because of DuBose's affection for Ira, I should hate to have any arguments with him."[1]

So, while she never faced him or Lee, she nevertheless constantly told others of the truth as she saw it. As individual songs were published and copyrighted, with sheet music and lyrics being sold, money now entered the equation. Ira was now getting profits (and credit) from songs she thought were DuBose's except for a slight correction or two by Ira; but the songs DuBose had helped in a similar way were mostly in Ira's name, she claimed, depriving DuBose of credit and Dorothy of income. Dorothy once wrote to Ira about which lyrics were his and which ones were DuBose's, but he did not answer, even as he himself felt bitter about the lack of credit given him on songs he had written for another musical show.

Ira, no doubt, heard of her disappointment, and he had no problem confronting Dorothy in correspondence, tartly blaming her for her loyalty to Breen, for holding up the signing of the contracts, ignoring the fact that Lazar, his agent, had been double-dealing, and that she owned almost five times the amount in the deal than he did, and that she was fighting for her husband's name, while he knew his would always take precedence. Whether he knew it or not, he would soon be rubbing salt in her wounds when he said he received no money for all the advice he gave Goldwyn, having been involved, he claimed, in at least fifty conferences with the filmmakers. She had never been consulted and would have loved to have had the opportunity to weigh in. She was horrified that, when talking to Goldwyn on the phone, the producer told her that he had heard that DuBose might have had something to do with the opera's lyrics.

With no control over content, she had no veto over the writer, and the ones being considered were worrisome. Ketti Frings had done a scenario, going back to the novel, adding somewhat racist and denigrating scenes that Dorothy had wisely left out. Playwright N. Richard Nash was chosen eventually. He stuck fairly closely to Dorothy and DuBose's libretto, and she told Audrey, "I wish I had some control over the cast. [Sidney Poitier reluctantly would take the lead as Porgy, Dorothy Dandridge as Bess, with Sammy Davis Jr. as Sportin' Life, Pearl Bailey as Maria, Diahann Carol as Clara, and Brock Peters as Crown, with all but Peters's and Bailey's voices dubbed by 'ghosts.'] But I do not have Ira's (or Lazar's) insouciance about blocking other people's plan indefinitely."

It was getting time to surrender. "In spite of my best efforts to take it in a relaxed mood, I always get excited and then can't sleep. So, I have about reached the conclusion that I will step out and make Jenifer the head of the family. I don't mean by that that I am going to change the ratio of our percentages but will let her make the decisions, and whoever . . . calls up I'll simply say, 'You'll have to speak to Jen. I know nothing about it.'"

That would have been revenge on all the attorneys as well as Jenifer. The contract first presented to Dorothy in June was finally signed in October 1957, and when it was all over, she gave Jenifer her power of attorney. Then, over her doctor's advice, she went to Hollywood with Jen to meet Samuel Goldwyn and see some of the filming.[2]

He had been gracious over the telephone; she wanted to give him a talking to about DuBose's versus Ira's role, but upon arriving, she "learned that Mr. Goldwyn does the talking." Not only did he not meet her, but he stuck her in an un-air-conditioned hotel room when Los Angeles was experiencing a heat wave pushing temperatures near one hundred.

He had been having problems with his movie. His massive set had burned under mysterious circumstances the night before filming was to start; and his actors were refusing to use the informal Black English in the script, instead enunciating their dialogue in perfect English, while singers, dubbing their voices, used the slang and dropped "g"s. Mamoulian, who had been hired to direct, wanted to film in Charleston but had been overruled, and he hated the vast sound stage Goldwyn had built, exploding Catfish Row to massive proportions. Goldwyn didn't like Mamoulian's attitude or the fact that the latter had hired his own press agent to satisfy his ego and to build up his contribution to *Porgy and Bess*. Brooking no rival, Goldwyn fired him during production and replaced him with Otto Preminger, who treated Poitier and Dandridge disrespectfully. Leigh Whipper, who had created the role of the Crab Man in the original play version and who was cast in the film, quit over the replacement of Mamoulian, starting the rumor that Preminger was racist, which he was not. He just berated and maltreated anyone he wanted to, regardless of race or gender.

Dorothy didn't fare much better. Promised access to the film set, she found the door locked against her, and she furiously beat on it crying out that she was the author of the words they were speaking. When Bill Banks, Jen's longtime escort, got wind of that and her un-air-conditioned rooms, he threatened to share the story with *Time* magazine. Goldwyn relented; they got air-conditioned rooms, and he allowed Dorothy to see rushes of certain scenes and to listen into the stereophonic score. He told her it was Preminger's orders that had closed the set, but at a premiere, Preminger chided her for not coming to visit. In Los Angeles, Dorothy and Jen also spent time with Ira and Leonore.

No one on the set had been happy, and everyone was unimpressed with the little bent woman who hobbled around. Pre-premiere, she had been interviewed on television and asked unaccountably if she liked sunbathing. She replied honestly that she did not and then was admonished because that show's advertiser was a suntan lotion, no one having thought to tell her that beforehand. (Long after her death, in another production, Broadway hawkers would create a "Summertime and the Living Is Easy" sunscreen.) She attended the New York City premiere, and at the one in Boston she was trotted out for Goldwyn to kiss her, and then she was dismissed.[3]

As for the movie itself, while it got some acclaim, including an Academy Award for its musical score conducted by André Previn, and the Golden Globe for best film musical, most critics dismissed it as tediously slow and overblown, much of it due not just to the director's plodding pacing but Preminger's insistence on long shots, with very few closeups, losing intimacy with the actors. And worse, because the NAACP wanted to use it to integrate theaters in the South, Goldwyn pulled it from distribution and so it was never shown, as the play and opera had never been, in Charleston, its home. Dorothy, in later correspondence, chided Ira for holding up a million-dollar sale for the one that went to Goldwyn's inept hands for $650,000 paid over time, and he taunted her back that he had never really wanted a film in the first place, reminding her that she had put out a statement that she had liked the film. In fact, both of them had been pressured by the studio's publicity department to do that. Ira had praised it lavishly, but to others privately, he lambasted it. Dorothy kept her opinions to herself.

Yet she refused to sit by silently when the novel was reissued as a movie tie-in. It had been republished in hardback with her introduction, and now it appeared in paperback with a scene from the film on the cover with the statement calling it, "The poignant novel from which came the world-famous George and Ira Gershwin folk-opera." "It is not strange that you should make the mistake," she wrote the publisher, "as it now seems to me that all the world believes Ira Gershwin wrote the 'Porgy and Bess' lyrics. He did write several of the best (the ones sung by Sportin' Life) and collaborated with DuBose on others. He was DuBose's close friend and there was never anything but harmony between both Gershwins and DuBose. Nevertheless, Ira was not included in the original plans.... DuBose would be greatly astonished if he could see the Bantam 'Porgy' I now have ... [so] to call 'Porgy and Bess' 'the George and Ira Gershwin opera' simply isn't so." No changes were made, however, despite her legal claims, and no books were pulled from the shelves. The only way to counter it was to write her own book on DuBose and the opera.

The idea had developed over time, the original kernel prompted by a suggestion by Robert Breen. He felt no amount of publicity was ever enough and encouraged Dorothy to write vignettes of her experiences with it over the years. While she agreed it was a good idea, she still sometimes doubted her talent as well as her sanity. Even letter writing was torturous, each of which she composed and recomposed endlessly, a habit begun back in the London rest home when putting words together seemed a constructive way back to health.

Sitting in front of a blank piece of paper, she felt paralyzed. She had wanted to start writing for Breen when she had joined Josephine Pinckney finishing her final novel in Summerville some years before, but she found herself fretting over not just what to write, but how to write it, torn between the lighthearted, frothy style for which she had a natural flair and the darker, serious tone of *South Pacific, Set My People Free*, and truth telling. While her intent to get her husband's name back on the opera was deadly serious, she chose to affect a breezy style instead. She believed that a light touch would be more welcoming to readers as well as to the one writing it.

Once she began, it was as if she was "hypnotized" or in a trance, dashing off a first draft of an essay she thought was pretty good; but then confidence failed her. "A psychiatrist would tell you that my touchiness about this story is that it is supposed to be one of a series—and that I have a subconscious conviction that if the first were turned down it would doom the whole series." Unable to go on, she turned to other writers, "ghosts" as she called them, to help her. Her friend Peggy Lamson, apparently her first choice, turned her down, and others who accepted were disappointing. "I suppose it is an impossibility to have anyone else write what is in your own mind," she confessed to Audrey Wood. Those helping her seem to have included her friend Margie Neeson, a local journalist whose husband briefly ran the Dock Street Theatre and whom Dorothy had approached on other topics. She also considered Phoebe Wilson, a friend of Jenifer's who needed money. To Neeson, she had apologized for being "psycho," explaining, "I have lost completely, and I suppose, permanently, the gift of normal sleep." This was when negotiations for the film were ratcheting up and Jenifer was a cause for concern. "When I lead a quiet life, I sleep. . . . Any pressure, especially any pressure I try to put on self, the more dope it takes for me to drop off at all. I suppose the amounts I am taking now are of dope fiend proportions."[4]

"The first ghost wrote something that I could hardly recognize as having any relation to my story—a complete rewrite on which I am afraid she spent much work," Dorothy summarized. "The second ghost did not make quite such drastic changes but still it did not seem to me like anything I had written." She preferred the work of a new acquaintance, the young Harry Whipple, recommended by Wood's husband and business partner Bill Liebling. Whipple had tried to mimic Dorothy's "spark and humor," and she credited him with about half of the finished product.[5]

Off it went to *The New Yorker* just when Truman Capote's *Porgy and Bess* essay was accepted, and so it was declined, and then it went off to *Colliers*. Dorothy missed a luncheon with the editor, and soon after the magazine ceased publication. While it's impossible to be totally sure, it seems that this ghosted essay was the one published as "Porgy's Goat" in *Harper's Magazine* in December 1957. It relates her dramatizing of the novel, only "two jumps" ahead of DuBose as he wrote it. She either made up a false chronology, the ghost confused it, or she might have actually forgotten it. She gave currency to the belief that Gershwin supposedly signaled his interest to DuBose while she was still dramatizing the novel, flushing her out in the open. Most of the scenes, she claimed in the article, had included the goat, not apparent in her drafts, and had to be rewritten as impractical. She then shared anecdotes of various goats that had been used in different productions. Despite her light touch, there were expressions of her true and less happy feelings. The rueful ending includes a reference to the negotiations over the movie. "In theater agreements, there is always a phrase such as 'The director and cast must be satisfactory to Ira Gershwin and Dorothy Heyward.'" She had hoped for that in the film, but she realized it was probably going to be more like: "The director and cast must be satisfactory to Ira Gershwin. The goat must be satisfactory to Dorothy Heyward."

The article was not followed by others, despite her desire to publish more.

In May 1958, however, she attended a ceremony honoring the Carolina Art Association's centennial anniversary, held along with a meeting of the American Association of Museums, the speaker being *Harper's* chief editor, John Fischer. "There was a long, long receiving line. And I managed to pull off the biggest surprise I've ever given Charleston. When I was introduced to him in the line—with a couple hundred lined up to meet him—he stepped out of place and conducted me to a corner in full view of the hosts and other guests of honor and held a hurried conference. He said *Harper's* would like to publish all my Porgy articles, but would have to publish them consecutively like a serial—and how soon could I get them in?"

So, now with ghostly help, Dorothy rushed to produce chapters on DuBose's writing of the novel and her dramatization of it. The essay "Thursday" referred to the Guild's initial production of *Porgy* magically becoming a success while she and DuBose were shut in a hotel room rewriting. An "Enter George" chapter focused on their collaboration, with others about Cheryl Crawford, Bob Breen, Swifty Lazar, and Samuel Goldwyn, all lighthearted, and all portraying her as a woman befuddled at the ways of the world, the pieces entertaining and devoid of any of the witty bitchiness of Capote's spin on his time behind the Iron Curtain. While the chapters have good lines, polish, and drive, they do not necessarily hang together, and perhaps that is what doomed them, or maybe they were not delivered promptly enough. Dorothy never explained why they were not published. Yet there was still hope, perhaps due to the diligence of her agent. With *Porgy and Bess* still a national and international phenomenon, a publisher offered Dorothy a contract for an entire book on the subject.

A scholarly biography of DuBose by Frank Durham, who had worked with Dorothy and DuBose at the Dock Street Theatre, had appeared in 1954. In it, he sketched Heyward's life, his works, and was analytical on the Ira Gershwin issue. In his dissertation upon which the biography was based, he had quoted a letter from Ira saying that he, Ira, had rarely changed a word of any of DuBose's lyrics, and that they rarely needed polishing. He further confessed that many of Ira's lyrics had been bolstered by words "borrowed from the text [by Dorothy]." Durham nevertheless credited the opera to the three men, "with Heyward and George Gershwin shaping the whole work and Ira Gershwin playing an integral part in the writing of the lyrics."

While some of this might have soothed Dorothy and some not, Durham's book, due to its publishing date, did have limitations. It had come out before the opera had gone to Russia, and before it was filmed, and while a loyal cadre of friends read it, its scholarly nature probably limited its popularity. Hers was going to be different.

She signed the contract in September 1960 to deliver a work of eighty thousand words by October of the next year, a tight deadline for an author in doubt of her ability to focus. "It started out to be a sort of biography of DuBose, centering largely on adventures with 'Porgy' and 'Porgy and Bess,'" she explained. "But two editors have protested to me that they want an autobiography featuring DuBose but told in the first person."

That meant she'd have to do something very uncharacteristic—write about herself, which she usually avoided. To meet the deadline, she used Dictaphones and employed secretaries, focusing mostly not on her life, but just on her life in the theater, referring a bit to her youth, but leaving great gaps about her past, zeroing in on some on her works. She put in a reference or two to her mother-in-law, Janie, and, slipping up, included some troubling thoughts about Jenifer, but mostly she censored herself and focused on positive and amusing anecdotes, never shy of including self-deprecating ones. While touching on her disappointments with *South Pacific* and *Set My People Free*, she steered clear of any mention of Rumer Godden, Julie Clayburgh, and David Merrick. Oddly, the provisional title she chose was "I Am Too Young," the comment she attributed to the ten-year-old Jenifer upon being told of her father's death. (Was it perhaps, instead, a twisted reference to her line in the book that she was young at a rather mature age?) She missed the deadline.[6]

Ill health was one factor; her crippling arthritis had prevented her from going to the MacDowell Colony where she could have concentrated on writing. She had not been there since 1959 but had been donating generously in DuBose's name and had chaired Marian MacDowell's ninety-fifth birthday celebration committee. She had become very much like "Mother MacDowell" herself; both were tiny, indominable women with canes, each working in their way to keep the memory of their husbands alive.

In August 1961 she was asked to join the board of trustees of the off-Broadway theater company the Phoenix, founded by T. Edward Hambleton, who had once owned rights to *Set My People Free* and where, earlier, Jenifer finally landed an acting job.[7]

In November 1961, a month after the manuscript deadline, Dorothy went into the hospital for a routine appendectomy. It was successful, and gallstones that had been troubling her were also removed. She was cheery when Jenifer visited her, but by the time Jenifer got back to her apartment, the phone was ringing. Dorothy, well a minute before, had lapsed into a coma and was fighting for her life.

Other phones started to ring; telegrams went flying.

Ella Gerber, a friend of Jenifer and always to be involved with *Porgy and Bess*, telephoned Bob Breen, who tried to locate Blevins Davis. It was Breen who supplied the details. He explained that Dorothy died that evening, Sunday, November 19, having been in great health moments before. ("I never saw him ill," she had said of DuBose over twenty years previously.) "They had no idea what caused her to go at the time," Breen noted; she was felled by a coronary thrombosis, the same cause of DuBose's death. "Jenifer is leaving this afternoon with Dorothy's body for Charleston and there will be no service of any kind here—only in Charleston."

It was fitting. The city had determined her personal and professional destiny, through her husband and her works on Porgy, Mamba, and Denmark Vesey; she had learned to call Charleston home. Her emotional lodestone certainly lay in St. Philip's cemetery. That's where the ceremony took place the afternoon of November 22. It echoed DuBose's simple funeral, graveside with no religious rites. Her modest tombstone, with just name and dates, would be a close match to his, once more mirroring their many similarities. There were few contemporaries left: Josephine Pinckney had died a few years before; Marian MacDowell was gone, as was Marjorie Flack Benét. The pallbearers were young relatives from DuBose's family and some younger men with whom she had worked at the Dock Street Theatre. The editor of the *News and Courier*, Tom Waring Jr., was among them, and he likely was the author of an editorial that eulogized her. "Though she was fragile in appearance as a Dresden china shepherdess, Dorothy Heyward, in intellect was keen as steel and as strong in spirit," it began. Her marriage, he noted, had brought a Southerner and Northerner together, and with that, he apparently could not resist taking a segregationist stand, something Dorothy would have abhorred, as he deplored "the militant forces that ignored its human elements and tried to turn 'Porgy' into an item of race propaganda." He knew of her struggles with those who stood in her way, but in which category he apparently did not include himself, noting, "It fell on her to negotiate with agents of show business, both on Broadway and in Hollywood. In a notoriously tough field, she held her own while remaining the lady that she always was." Perhaps he did not know the full story of her self-inflicted failures or her mental breakdown; if he did, he only emphasized her turning the other cheek. "Kind, gentle, but equipped with a reporter's discerning eye that saw straight through worldly subterfuges, Mrs. Heyward was an interesting figure on the national scene. She was also a dear friend to those fortunate enough to know her personally. Charlestonians especially have reason to cherish her memory."

In 1951, when she had donated DuBose's papers to the South Carolina Historical Society, its president, Samuel Gaillard Stoney, who had helped with Gullah in the 1927 production, linked Dorothy and DuBose to the city, quipping that not "since the firing on Fort Sumter has there been such general [good] news of the community . . . as came with . . . 'Porgy' [and] 'Porgy and Bess.' . . . We have DuBose and Dorothy Heyward to thank for the great deal of the best . . . publicity . . . since then." And at her death, she did enjoy a brief, sudden fame. While the Gershwin name was inevitably trumpeted in her obituary in *The New York Times* and in others throughout the country, she nevertheless managed to achieve what she had always avoided.[8]

For the first time in her life, at the end of her life, Dorothy Heyward got what she never wanted: top billing.

AFTERWORD

Of course, it did not last. But *Porgy and Bess* did.

In 1970 the opera was staged in Charleston, thirty-five years after its debut, and after it had reached all other inhabited continents. It was a historic event in many ways because it was a crowning event of the celebration of the three hundredth anniversary of Charleston's founding. The year before had been marked with civil and racial unrest due to unfair hiring practices and treatment of mostly African American women at the Medical College, and the staging of the opera in front on an integrated audience, after so many years of segregation, helped in a healing process across the racial divide, perhaps the sort of "propaganda" Dorothy might have approved. The city she called her home was changing.

In 1976, in America's bicentennial year, the opera was seized upon as a national treasure, produced and embraced as an American icon. The next year, the Houston Grand Opera production received a Tony Award on Broadway as the year's best revival, and the cast album won a Grammy. In 1985, when *Porgy and Bess* was celebrating its fiftieth anniversary, it was restaged in Charleston, at the same time I arranged a conference marking the hundredth anniversary of DuBose's birth. Income from the production went to support minority and other charities, and it debuted at the Metropolitan Opera house that same year. (In 2021 the Met's recording of the 2019 production would also win a Grammy.)

DuBose continued to receive attention. Two more biographies of him appeared in the decades after Dorothy's death, she herself receiving some mention but no rigorous attention. (On visiting her grave, Ira Gershwin's attorney, Leonard Saxe, wrote that he believed she had gotten the Gershwin story wrong.) DuBose was the focus of a chapter in a book on Southern playwrights, despite the fact he had only written one play by himself; the others with his name on them were mostly her work. While he was acknowledged for his attempt to revive theatrical arts in the South at the Dock Street Theatre, Dorothy, in fact, had carried the torch longer and more successfully than he.

And, predictably, when a book on overlooked and neglected Southern women playwrights appeared, Dorothy was not included (due perhaps to her Ohio birth, or her having cowritten many plays with a man, or maybe just from ignorance). While Lillian Smith and the dramatization of her antilynching novel *Strange Fruit* and its failed Broadway production were discussed, Dorothy's attempt to dramatize racism at roughly the same time via *Set My People Free* was not. Another chapter focused on Carson McCullers's play *The Member of the Wedding*, starring Ethel Waters, who had made her debut as a dramatic actress thanks to Dorothy. Another Charleston link came in the chapter on African American playwright Alice Childress. A native of the city, she had set *Wedding Band* in the era of *Porgy and Bess*, and there were some echoes of the work in it, focusing on a doomed (interracial) love affair, set in a slum, with references to the Jenkins Orphanage Band, and a tragic end with one of the lovers going off to New York City. Dorothy merited not a single mention.[1]

In March 1984, after marrying briefly and divorcing, Jenifer DuBose Heyward Wood died of cancer; like her father, she was not quite fifty-five years old. She was buried with her parents in St. Philip's cemetery, a place she foreswore visiting. Her obituary listed her as a sculptress.

It was after her death that Jenifer's papers, and those of her mother, along with some more of DuBose's, came to the South Carolina Historical Society, where like Dorothy herself, they were mostly ignored. And even when a graduate student valiantly reassembled Dorothy's unpublished autobiography to get its various versions of numerous chapters into a readable format, the thesis, if quoted, was taken at face value, and those reading it accepted Dorothy's version as fact. If researchers had looked further, they would have found other chapters, such as those on Dorothy and DuBose's courtship, her description of Charleston's disappointment with DuBose writing about Blacks, and others that had not been included in the thesis.

Executors going through the several linear feet of her papers sold off most of the correspondence and items that could bring money. Letters from the likes of Rebecca West, Osbert Sitwell, Judge J. Waties Waring, and other distinguished men and women were scattered. (There are no letters from Ira present in her papers. Yet, likely due to the fact that Dorothy misfiled some important and valuable items, including an inscribed photograph from George and Ira to DuBose, it and other treasures escaped the auctioneer's hammer and are now in the collections of the South Carolina Historical Society, where I first encountered them.) Someone had boxed up her autobiography, two bulging folders with various lists of what was to be included, along with other chapters she had cut, in numerous variant versions.

On those tortured pages you can read editorial comments in unknown hands, voices of her "ghosts" asking for more information. In her chapter on *Set My People Free*, for instance, one ghost asks for more details about Jed Harris. Who was the actor arrested and imprisoned during rehearsals? is another query. She wrote that she had "great respect and liking for the director . . . who could not control his featured actors," but she did not name him, so the curious ghost asked for that, too.

It was Martin Ritt (she never answered), who himself had refused to name names in the McCarthy hearings of the 1950s. Not for political reasons, but out of politeness and that inability to speak ill of someone, she kept silent, writing that she was glad he had gone on to prominence, which she had not.

In those sometimes nearly obliterated and poignantly overwritten pages, she succeeded all too well in channeling DuBose but not herself. Instead, for a reason she alone understood, she portrayed herself as she had her heroines Paulette, Jonica, and Nancy Ann. And so, the Dorothy Heyward figure that emerges from those pages is a slightly bewildered but plucky young girl going through farcical situations to arrive, manipulated by circumstance, at a dénouement she always wanted. Even so, she did break her own code and, in a scattered paragraph or two, revealed something of her true self, as when she spoke of "dreaming of seeing a curtain rise on a play of mine that is as I had envisioned—acted, directed, designed and produced as I had meant it to be." That was only granted her in the cases of *Porgy* and *Porgy and Bess*, which show her genius.

Concerning the others, "there are certainly those who will say, 'Since you specialize in flops, perhaps your troubles are with the play.' To them I answer 'Nonsense.' I won't settle for that. It's the director, producer and actors who [turned] my lovely plays into something monstrous—something at which I can't bear to look." Even doing this, she kept those deserving of blame nameless.[2]

In all this, Dorothy Heyward achieved a very odd and a very personal victory. "Today, many people—even Charlestonians—believe that there was once a crippled beggar whose name was Porgy, [and] that he lived in old

Cabbage Row when the ancient mansion had become a Negro tenement. . . . And they believe that *Porgy* and *Porgy and Bess* is the beggar's true life story," she had written in 1957.[3]

Similarly, she, who lived in Porgy's shadow, shared a similar fate by creating a fictional character others came to believe as real: she created a frail, befuddled, innocent Dorothy Heyward muddling along, instead of the true, "interesting lady on the national scene" who was strong in spirit and had an intellect "keen as steel"; most of her public—historians, critics, and biographers—confused the actress with her performance.

Ironically, however, a fiction writer did not.

Best-selling author Dorothy Benton Frank, a Charleston native, focused on Dorothy Heyward in her 2011 novel, *Folly Beach*. Dottie (as we called her) was drawn to Dorothy, she said, by the similarity of their given names (Dorothea) and the fact that at one point, they had lived at the same New York address. In her book based very loosely on the truth, Cate Cooper, a woman needing to stand on her own, returns to her hometown and comes to terms with life while residing in Follywood, Dorothy and DuBose's beach house. Cooper, following the outlines of Dorothy's short story "The Young Ghost," feels a force in the house calling out for recognition. (*I Am Too Young* Dorothy had titled her autobiography; was it the young ghost she was referencing?)

While the story is unabashedly made up, Dottie got something right. At the end of the book, the heroine Kate has come into her own by writing a play about Dorothy Heyward, giving her the credit she did not get, or even ask for, in her life. As the play is performed and the curtain descends, Dorothy Heyward makes an appearance—ironically, as a ghost—hovering over the Dock Street Theatre stage.[4]

The image is heartbreakingly apt; for in Frank's fiction, as in real life, Dorothy Heyward remains a ghost, the ghostwriter of the opera who flits past the audience to haunt *Porgy* and *Porgy and Bess*. Whether visible or not, and whether credited or not, her specter is present whenever the curtain goes up, and it is most especially present when it goes down on the transcendent ending she crafted for it, an ending so vastly different from the self-effacing one she fashioned for herself.

But that, in the end, is how she wanted it.

ACKNOWLEDGMENTS

As Dorothy Heyward well knew, works with a single name on a title page are likely, more often than not, collaborations, and this book is certainly no exception. My work would not have been possible without the help of countless individuals who contributed to its, and my, development in many ways over the decades. First of all, I have to credit the late Mrs. Granville (Mary Elizabeth Barbot) Prior for graciously ignoring the condescending attitude of a jejune young researcher who entered the Fireproof Building, the home of the South Carolina Historical Society (SCHS) in the early 1970s, and who airily remarked on the interesting collection of DuBose Heyward books seen on a shelf. When she turned to me and asked me if I would like to catalog the papers of DuBose Heyward, neither of us could have realized the impact that invitation would have on my life. Not only did Mrs. Prior start me on a career path as an archivist that lasted nearly fifty years, she also started the chain of events that ultimately led to the writing of this book. When Gene Waddell succeeded her as director, he continued to allow me to find and define myself professionally and to pursue my scholarly passions. I cannot thank either of them enough for all those gifts.

The staff at the historical society, over the years, have carried on the traditions of collection stewardship and the encouragement of scholarship in an exemplary manner. Due to past director Faye Jenson and current director Elizabeth Chew, and the remarkable professionals such as Virginia Ellison, Molly Silliman, Sidney Derrick, and Brandon Reid there today, the SCHS remains a beacon to historians and researchers and an incubator for scholarly work and projects. That it adheres to such high and rigorous professional standards redounds to its credit and increases my gratitude. I also thank the College of Charleston for granting me a sabbatical during which a draft of this work was written. Addlestone Library's interlibrary loan staff, under the cheerful and winning directorship of Brandon Lewter, have enriched this work and my intellectual life to no end. Thank you all.

Gershwin archivist Michael Owen, author of the landmark biography of Ira Gershwin, personifies generosity and scholarly integrity, and while relations between Ira and Dorothy were not always the best, I am happy to say that our connection did not mirror theirs. I would also like to thank the late Michael Strunsky and his wife, Jean, for generously sharing the script of the 2012 Broadway production of *Porgy and Bess* with me. Thanks are due as well to the family of the late Dr. Billy Arant for allowing me to purchase items from his massive DuBose Heyward and Charleston Renaissance collection, containing information not before available to scholars. Collectors certainly do their part.

I wish I could recall and name all the other archivists and library professionals at other institutions such as the Library of Congress and the Beinecke Library at Yale University whose promptness, professionalism, and eagerness made my work easier and less prone to mistakes, which remain all my own. All the authors of articles and books cited in my bibliography were contributors as well and created a foundation upon which I could build. Included in that is the work of the late Dr. Arnold Schwab, whose biography of Marian MacDowell was not published but who generously shared his research notes with me decades ago. No less important have been the anonymous readers who commented on my manuscript; copyeditor extraordinaire Daniel Simon; as well as Editor-in-Chief Nate Holly; Assistant Director for Editorial, Design, and Production Jon Davies; and their distinguished and dedicated staff at the University of Georgia Press, who believed in this project from the beginning and decided to take a chance on the story of a woman who had been forgotten and who wanted to remain that way.

Naming names (or not) has always been part of the *Porgy and Bess* saga and also part of the era that took it to the stages of the world. Those of you who read notes will see the names of particular people who enlightened me on particular points. And as for my friends and family—you know who you are—I apologize for ghosting myself on so many occasions for so many years, and I thank you for listening to my endless tirades, even as you supported me for often choosing the past over the present. And here's to you, Jonathan Ray, the most tolerant and loving of husbands, for quelling my fears, encouraging my curiosity, putting up with my ways, and giving me a home, shelter, and love. Writers know when words fail . . . thank you, Jonathan, for never failing me.

NOTES

Preface. Naming Names

1. Alpert, *Life and Times*; Noonan, *Strange Career*; Thompson, *The Gershwins*.
2. Durham, *DuBose Heyward*; Slavick, *DuBose Heyward*; Hutchisson, *DuBose Heyward*.
3. Horowitz, *On My Way*.
4. Barranger, *A Gambler's Instinct*; Crawford, *One Naked Individual*.
5. Fordham, "Samuel Smalls," 25–31.
6. Coven, "Heyward, Dorothy Hartzell," 112–13. It lists only three sources: a 1932 entry in *Contemporary American Playwrights*, her obituary, and an entry in *Who Was Who in America*, 1968. The most complete summary, with some errors of fact and omissions, however, is in Shafer, *American Women Playwrights*, 395–402. In it, she ranks Dorothy Heyward with the third tier of playwrights, placing her among those who "made a particular contribution to the American theatre [who] . . . will be remembered for at least one significant play which moved audiences, challenged conventional ideas, or broke new ground in the theatre" (458).
7. Dorothy K. Heyward, Autobiographical writings, Dorothy K. Heyward Papers (hereinafter cited as DKH Papers), South Carolina Historical Society (hereinafter cited as SCHS), folder 180.01.04.03.03-18.

Chapter 1. Dorothy Kuhns of Canton, Ohio

1. Elizabeth Hanna, "'Tiptoeing in Their Footsteps': Dorothy Heyward's Unpublished Autobiography," College of Charleston, 2005, 15, herein afterwards cited as "Tiptoeing"; Dorothy Heyward birth certificate, DKH Papers, SCHS folder 180.01.04.03.03-29; "Captain Herman L. Kuhns Will Take Charge of the Garlock in Cleveland," *Canton, Ohio, Repository*, January 17, 1901; "Captain Kuhns Dies of Apoplexy at San Juan Puerto Rico," *Repository*, May 15, 1904; Hanna, "Tiptoeing," 25. Dorothy wrote that her mother was so talented that she was offered a position at the Metropolitan Opera.
2. Hanna, "Tiptoeing," 24–32, passim. Article with no headline, *Washington, D.C., Evening Star*, June 11, 1902, 5; "Death of Dr. L. M. Kuhns," *Evening Star*, December 15, 1903, 10; comment on Negro plays: DKH Papers, SCHS, folder 180.01.03.02-03. That blithe statement is belied by the fact that early in her career, pre-*Porgy*, others did seek her out as a collaborator on non-Negro-themed works, and others would do so after *Porgy*'s success as well.
3. "Captain Kuhns Dies," *Cleveland, Ohio, Leader*, May 15, 1904, 39; niece: DKH Papers, SCHS, folder 180.01.04.03.03-29; Hanna, "Tiptoeing," 24; Kuhns, "My Favorite Character in History."
4. Hanna, "Tiptoeing," 25, 28–29, 95; "Bluebeard's: Wives Impersonated at Friday Evening Entertainment," *Repository*, July 14, 1908, 6; "Cantonian in Play," *Repository*, April 22, 1923, 4.

5. "Captain Kuhns Is Dead," *Evening Star*, May 21, 1904, 7; "Letters from Quartermaster Kuhns," *Repository*, July 22, 1898, 1; Hanna, "Tiptoeing," 30–31. "History Resources: Confirming Governors for Territories of Cuba, Puerto Rico, and the Philippines, 1901," Gilder Lehrman Center for American History, www.gilderlehrman.org/content/confirming-governors-territories-cuba-puerto-rico-and-philippines-1901; Greene, *Mr. Skylark*, 184. There is a photo album documenting McKinley's funeral in Dorothy Heyward's papers.
6. "Captain Kuhns Is Dead"; Hanna, "Tiptoeing," 26; "W. H. Kuhns Is Dead," *Repository*, May 13, 1905, 10; Hanna, "Tiptoeing," 26.
7. Hanna, "Tiptoeing," 25, 31; social notices mentioning Dorothy at her aunt's in Washington, D.C., are in the *Evening Star*, June 11, 1902, and February 5 and 9, 1911, among others; Dorothy Heyward to Peggy Lamson, January 21, 1951, DKH Papers, SCHS, folder 180.01.003.04(c)04-27; Hanna, "Tiptoeing," 25, 26–28; Durham, *DuBose Heyward*, 7; DKH Papers, SCHS, folder 180.01.04.03.03-20.
8. *Evening Star*, January 26, 1913, 61, an event that President and Mrs. Taft attended; articles referencing Dorothy's proficiency at tennis appear in *The Repository*, September 22, 1912, 15, August 16, 1914, 3, and elsewhere; "D.A.R. Play to Aid Nursery Fund," *Repository*, April 29, 1916, 3; "Sees Needs of Suffrage," *Repository*, September 5, 1914, 4; "Former Canton Girl Back from the Orient," *Repository*, March 24, 1911, 3.
9. See the 1914–15 diary of Dorothy Kuhns, DKH Papers, SCHS folder 180.01.05(D)01-02; Hanna, "Tiptoeing," 4, 31; kissed and proposed: autobiographical writings, DKH Papers, SCHS, folder 180.01.04.03.03-19; "curbed": notes on *Nancy Ann*, DKH Papers, SCHS, folder 180.01.03.04(Misc.)01-04; Hanna, "Tiptoeing," 31.

Chapter 2. Apprentice Playwright
1. Biographical sketch, DKH Papers, SCHS, folder 180.01.04.04.01-01; Dorothy Heyward, "'Nancy Ann' and Some Others"; *The Ghost of Moorsdown Manor* scenario, DKH Papers, SCHS, folder 180.01.03.04(G)01-01.
2. For information on women playwrights of the era, see Shafer, *American Women Playwrights*. Biographical sketch, DKH Papers, SCHS, folder 180.01.04.04.01-01; notes for autobiographical chapter "My Calamitous Career," DKH Papers, SCHS, folder 180.01.04.03.03-18; Hanna, "Tiptoeing," 97.
3. Beeston, "Christina," 587–95. For a typescript of the play, see DKH Papers, SCHS, folder 180.01.03.04(C)01-01; George Pierce Baker to DKH, July 12, 1918, and September 10, 1918, DKH Papers, SCHS, folder 180.01.01(B)01-01.
4. For more information on Baker and the development of English 47 classes, see Kinne, *George Pierce Baker*. Despite the fact that she was one of his most successful female students, Dorothy Heyward is not mentioned, although the fellowship and prize she won are. Very few of Baker's women students are discussed. George Pierce Baker to DKH, September 10, 1918, DKH Papers, SCHS, folder 180.01.01(B)01-01. Her correspondence in 1916 with the author's agent is in DKH Papers, SCHS, folder 180.01.03.04(C)01-02. In his letter of November 8, 1916, to "Miss Kuhns," Francis Arthur Jones wrote, "The sum you offer for the dramatic rights of Mr. Beeston's story would not interest us."
5. Hanna, "Tiptoeing," 17, 18, and 16–23, passim; Heyward, "'Nancy Ann.'" For her appearance in a play, see "Cantonian in Play," *Repository*, April 22, 1923, 24.
6. Autobiographical notes, DKH Papers, SCHS, folder 180.01.04.03.03-17; *Jonica* fragments and various versions are in DKH Papers, SCHS, box 12. Hanna, "Tiptoeing," 2.
7. Hanna, "Tiptoeing," 2; Helburn, *A Wayward Quest*, 14.
8. Autobiographical notes, DKH Papers, SCHS, folder 180.01.04.03.03-18; Hanna, "Tiptoeing,"

3. Wolfe was there in her second year. Not as successful in drama, Wolfe would write a biting portrait of Baker in his novel *Of Time and the River* as Professor James Graves Hatcher. *Peg*: Autobiographical notes, DKH Papers, SCHS, folder 180.01.04.03.03-18; Hanna, "Tiptoeing," 97; Bennett, *Year Book*, 57; photocopy of broadside from Town Theatre, Columbia, S.C., in author's possession; see also Ambrose Gonzales to Dorothy Heyward, April 24, 1925, DKH Papers, SCHS, folder 180.01.01(Misc.)01-01; Heyward, *Love in a Cupboard*; Hanna, "Tiptoeing," 3, 1–15, passim.
9. Hanna, "Tiptoeing," 7, 5, 7–9, 4–15; "The Average Woman," February 6, 2023, https://en.wikipedia.org/wiki/The_Average_Woman.
10. The contract is in DKH Papers, SCHS, folder 180.01.03.04(J)02-05. Despite the lack of production, Klauber would impact her life later as the producer of the 1933 film of Eugene O'Neill's play *The Emperor Jones*, with a screenplay written by her husband, DuBose.
11. "Kissing Time," May 11, 2023, https://en.wikipedia.org/wiki/Kissing_Time; Hanna, "Tiptoeing," 22–23, 3, 33–34.

Chapter 3. The MacDowell Colony
1. Autobiographical notes, DKH Papers, SCHS, folder 180.01.04.03.03-19. Biographical sketch of Dorothy Heyward, written by her in the third person, DKH Papers, SCHS, folder 180.01.04. 04.01-01. Heyward, *Mamba's Daughters*, 128.
2. The police report on Heyward's death, filed at 3:30 a.m., May 20, 1888, recorded that he "accidentally got caught mashed and killed by falling into the gearing of [the] Rice Mill foot of Laurens Street." Day Book, Charleston Police Records, Charleston Library Society. The newspaper article, "A Dreadful Death," *Charleston News and Courier*, May 22, 1888, 8, noting that the details of his death were too grisly to relate, nevertheless gave them, describing how his clothes got caught in the mill's turning screw and whirled his body around at the speed of 150 times a minute, slamming his legs against the nearby framework. The biographical details of DuBose Heyward and his mother, Janie, in this chapter and others, are from the three biographies of him: Durham, *DuBose Heyward*; Slavick, *DuBose Heyward*; and Hutchisson, *DuBose Heyward*. For Janie, see also Greene, "Charleston Childhood," 154–67.
3. Autobiographical notes, DKH Papers, SCHS, folder 180.01.04.03.03-20; Greene, "Charleston Childhood," 160.
4. For information on John Bennett and his impact on DuBose Heyward and Charleston, see Greene, *Mr. Skylark*; Heyward, *Porgy*, 11.
5. Clark, *Innocence Abroad*, 244.
6. Biographical sketch of Dorothy Heyward, written by her in the third person, DKH Papers, SCHS, folder 180.01.04.04.01-01; Hanna, "Tiptoeing," 31; Widdemer, *Golden Friends*, 68. Dorothy supposed they were fourth or seventh cousins: autobiographical notes, DKH Papers, SCHS folder 180.01.04.03.03.20.
7. For a list of the cast, etc., see Richie, *His Blue Serge Suit*, 12; Clark, *Innocence Abroad*, 238.
8. Autobiographical notes, DKH Papers, SCHS, folders 180.01.04.03.03-21 and 180.01.04.03.03-19; DuBose Heyward to "Dear Little Dorothy," Saturday [n.d.] on Clyde Line stationery, and letter dated "The Office, (but it is nine o[']clock at night, and everyone has gone home) Time, Monday evening," DuBose Heyward Papers (subsequently cited as DBH Papers), SCHS, folder 1172.01.01(H)03-02. In the same folder, his letter to "My Dear Dorothy" datelined Friday on his letterhead listing his two addresses, mentions their

"insubordination" and another letter to "My Dear Dorothy" dated "Wednesday," states that they "both caught the Devil's own time of it."
9. Most of his letters to Dorothy with their various farewells, all in DBH Papers, SCHS, folder 1172.01.01(H)03-02, are undated, just noting the day of the week. For heat and business see his letter, October 6, 1922, to "Dorothy Dear"; engagement: undated letter to "Dear Little Dorothy" on United States Casualty Company letterhead; African American: letter to "My Dear Dorothy" on Poetry Society of South Carolina letterhead, "Saturday." Jane Heyward's letter to "Dear Dorothy" is dated February 22 [1923], in which she sends a brochure showing her picture, inquiring of her health and work, etc., DBH Papers, SCHS, folder 1172.01.01(H)03-01.
10. Hanna, "Tiptoeing," 37, 39; McKee, *Valiant Woman*, 54–55.
11. Bennett's letter is quoted in Greene, *Mr. Skylark*, 184; autobiographical writings, DKH Papers, SCHS, folder 180.01.04.03.03-19.
12. For information on Josephine Pinckney, see Bellows, *A Talent for Living*; autobiographical writings, DKH Papers, SCHS, folder 180.01.04.03.03-15; Hanna, "Tiptoeing," 39.

Chapter 4. *Nancy Ann*
1. "Society," *Evening Star*, September 24, 1923, 8. Whitall: photocopy of DuBose Heyward to "My Dear Mr. Waring," September 20, [1923], DBH Papers, SCHS, folder 1172.01.01(Misc.)01-01; telegram Josephine Pinckney to DuBose Heyward, n.d., DBH Papers, SCHS, folder 1172.01.01(H)03-03; Laura Bragg (1881–1978), an associate and mentor of DuBose Heyward, repeated the story about Dorothy dyeing her hair to the author several times in the summer and fall of 1976. Hanna, "Tiptoeing," 40.
2. Barry would go on to write a play based on socialite Gertrude Sanford Legendre, who'd later befriend Dorothy and promote *Porgy and Bess*, sponsoring the fiftieth anniversary of the opera in 1985, in its Charleston production; "Dorothy H. Kuhns Wins Drama Prize," *Boston, Mass., Herald*, September 14, 1923, 11; for meeting Burke, see miscellaneous writings, DKH Papers, SCHS, folder 180.01.03.04(Misc.)01-06. Contract for *The Dud* is in DKH Papers, SCHS, folder 180.01.03.04(N)01-02; Hanna, "Tiptoeing," 40.
3. Greene, *Mr. Skylark*, 184, 192; undated letter to "Dearest Mother Janie," DBH Papers, SCHS, folder 1172.01.01(H)03-01.
4. A joke going the rounds then told of a local woman who rented her home to a Northerner; the renter complained about the state of the kitchen. The Charleston woman was supposed to have been aghast, replying in horror, "You mean you actually went into it?" Heyward, "Porgy's Native Tongue," x2.
5. See "Nixon's Apollo Theatre Program, Atlantic City, N.J.," DKH Papers, SCHS, folder 180.01.03(N)01-06. Heyward, *Nancy Ann*, 3; while stating that its original name was *The Dud*, an original copyright date of 1912 is an obvious mistake for 1922; autobiographical notes, DKH Papers, SCHS, folder 180.01.04.03.03-18.
6. Miscellaneous writings, DKH Papers, SCHS, folder 180.01.03.04(Misc.)01-06; Heyward, "'Nancy Ann' and Some Others."
7. Hanna, "Tiptoeing," 37; "Francine Larrimore," May 9, 2023, https://en.wikipedia.org/wiki/Francine_Larrimore; writings on *Nancy Ann*, DKH Papers, SCHS, folder, 180.01.03.04(N)01-08.
8. Rowena Tobias, "Dramatist That Put 'Porgy' and 'Mamba' on Broadway Works on Original Play Now," *Charleston News and Courier*, March 5, 1939. *Nancy Ann* lecture notes, DKH Papers, SCHS, folder 180.01.03.04(Misc.)01-04.
9. Alexander Woollcott, "'The Reviewing Stand' by Alexander Woollcott," *Buffalo News*,

April 12, 1924, 46; an unnamed local paper reprinted it under the title "Mrs. Heyward's Play," DKH Papers, SCHS, folder 180.01.03.04(N)01-10.

10. Clipping from the *Baltimore American*, May 20, 1924, DKH Papers, SCHS, folder 180.01.03.04(N)01-10; undated clipping from *Life*, DKH Papers, SCHS, folder 180.01.03.04(N)01–07; Percy Hammond, "Oddments and Remainders: 'Nancy Ann,' a Harvard Prize Play," *New York Herald Tribune*, April 6, 1924, DKH Papers, SCHS, folder 180.01.03.04(N)01-08.

11. Typed quotes extracted from reviews of *Nancy Ann* from *Chicago Evening Post* and *New York Telegram and Evening Mail*, DKH Papers, SCHS, folder 180.01.03.04(N)01-08; the folder also has the April 1 clipping of Woollcott's review, unattributed, but according to "'The Reviewing Stand' by Alexander Woollcott," *Buffalo News*, April 12, 1924, 46, it was published first in the *New York Sun*.

12. *Christian Science Monitor* review clipping, April 7, 1924, DKH Papers, SCHS, folder 180.01.03.04(N)01-10; miscellaneous writings, DKH Papers, SCHS, folder 180.01.03.04(Misc.)01-06.

13. See correspondence with Fred Ballard, DKH Papers, SCHS, folder 180.01.03.04(N)01-02; "Nancy Ann," www.ibdb.com/broadway-production/nancy-ann-9496; "Nancy Ann's Author Sees Changed Play," *Charleston Evening Post*, February 21, 1925, 9; Greene, *Mr. Skylark*, 326n.62; "'Nancy Ann' by the Thalians," *Charleston News and Courier*, May 4, 1934, 2-B; Hanna, "Tiptoeing," 52.

Chapter 5. *Porgy*: Origins

1. "Son" is how she often addressed him in letters: See DBH Papers, SCHS, folder 1172.01.01(H)03-01. For more on the era before the renaissance, see Greene, *Mr. Skylark*, 147–68 passim; Clark, *Innocence*, 247. Heyward told a student who wrote her thesis on him that Dorothy had encouraged him as well: See Creighton, "DuBose Heyward," 16; Bellows, *Talent for Living*, 123; Greene, *Mr. Skylark*, 328n.2.

2. Heyward, "Introduction" to *Porgy: A Play in Four Acts*, xi. No one mentioned Heyward's physical link to Sammy Smalls until after the former's death: See Greene, *Mr. Skylark*, 315n.27; Gershwin, Heyward, and Gershwin, *Theatre Guild Presents*, 51, hereinafter abbreviated as Gershwin and Heyward, *Theatre Guild: Porgy and Bess*, the original publication of the score and libretto.

3. Greene, "'The Little Shining Word,'" 75–81; Smith, *Where the Light Falls*, 23. Smith unaccountably puts DuBose and Dorothy's daughter Jenifer there at the MacDowell Colony that summer; she would not be born for another six years.

4. Heyward and Heyward, *Porgy: A Play*, xii; see dedication pages of Heyward and Allen, *Carolina Chansons* (according to an autobiographical promotional essay written by Allen in the author's collection, it was winning a coin toss that led to Heyward's name preceding Allen's on the title page, despite the latter's contribution being the greater); Heyward, *Skylines and Horizons*; and Heyward, *Porgy*.

5. "Miss Alice" chapter notes (not included in the Hanna version of Dorothy Heyward's autobiography), DKH Papers, SCHS, folder 180.01.04.03.01-02; photocopy of letter to Robert Molloy, December 22, 1957, DKH Papers, SCHS, folder 180.01.01.01(W)02-01, original in Thomas Waring Jr. Papers, SCHS, folder 23-405-3; she repeats the story in autobiographical notes in folder 180.01.04.03.03-14. Molloy, incidentally, would include this bit—how white Charlestonians cooled toward DuBose Heyward for his empathy for Blacks—in a novel of his own; Molloy, *Reunion*, 219.

6. Typescript petition submitted to the Charleston (S.C.) City Council by residents of Church Street in Charleston, South Carolina, SCHS manuscript number 43-16; Hicks, *In Darkest South Carolina*, 128, 241–42; Cabot presented Dorothy a mounted black-and-white photograph of the portrait, DKH Papers, SCHS, folder 180.02.08-01. The painting, with a presale estimate set between $20,000 to $30,000, was sold on October 6, 2017, by Sotheby's, New York. This is the first time the subject of the painting has been identified.
7. Letter to "Dear Mr. Uoenson ??," DKH Papers, SCHS, folder 1172.01.03(P)01-20 (the typing makes it unclear as to the name); Hanna, "Tiptoeing," 51–52.
8. Letter to "Dear Mr. Uoenson ??"; typescript on *Porgy* enclosed with letter to Thomas R. Waring, November 25, 1952, DKH Papers, SCHS, folder 180.01.01.01(W)01-01; much of this is recycled almost verbatim in Hanna, "Tiptoeing," 52–53; letter to Uoenson; the information on two miscarriages come from a letter of John Bennett to Hervey Allen, October 25, 1929, John Bennett Papers, SCHS, 21-144-11.
9. Hanna, "Tiptoeing," 54. From at least December 1925 through March 1926, the Heywards were staying in the Confederate Home, titularly a home for widows and orphans of Confederate soldiers, but also the place where the Poetry Society had offices and artists had studios: "DuBose Heyward Works on Novel," *Charleston News and Courier*, December 24, 1925, 8; undated letter to "Dear Little Dorothy" on United States Casualty Company letterhead, DBH Papers, SCHS, folder 1172.01.01(H)03-02; Hanna, "Tiptoeing," 54; Letter to "Dear Mr. Uoenson ??"; the typescript of *Angel* shows some of Dorothy's corrections, DBH papers, SCHS, folders 1172.01.04.02(A)01-11/13; autobiographical notes, DKH Papers, SCHS, folder 180.01.04.03.0-21. In her "mad" writings in the aftermath of her disastrous collaboration with Rumer Godden, she'd also note percentages and suggest it was nearly all her work, DKH Papers, SCHS, folder 180.01.03.04(C)04-22.
10. DKH to Alma Klaw, n.d., DKH Papers, SCHS, folder 180.01.03.04(C)03-07; Hanna, "Tiptoeing," 54; autobiographical notes, DKH Papers, SCHS, folder 180.01.04.03.0-21; crap scene: autobiographical letters and notes re: Rumer Godden, DKH Papers, SCHS, folder 180.01.03.04(C)04-22.
11. Durham, "DuBose Heyward," 336; autobiographical notes, DKH Papers, SCHS, folder 180.01.04.03.0-21; Durham, "DuBose Heyward," 335.
12. All biographies of Heyward describe the collaboration with Allen; for the collaboration with Pinckney, see Bellows, *Talent for Living*, 158–59; quote is from Dorothy Heyward to Thomas R. Waring Jr., October 9, [1960], Thomas R. Waring Jr. Papers, SCHS, folder 23-405-3; for Ira Gershwin, see the discussion in chapter 12.

Chapter 6. *Porgy*: Novel to Play
1. Heyward, *Porgy*, 196; Heyward and Heyward, *Porgy: A Play*, 1–2, 11; Heyward, *Wild Roses*; Schiff, "The Man Who Breathed," section 2, 35.
2. Hanna, "Tiptoeing," 69; Heyward, *Star Spangled*; Heyward, "And Once Again," 39–42; for Dorothy's disapproval of vulgarity, see the *Jonica* discussion in chapter 10.
3. For a photo of DuBose and Hervey Allen, taken by John Bennett's son, see Greene, *Mr. Skylark*, images following page 168; he mentions her "physical handicaps" in his letter to "Dear Little Dorothy," datelined "Monday" on United States Casualty Company letterhead, DBH Papers, SCHS, folder 1172.01.01(H)03-02; Janie notes the difficulty Dorothy faces "To have ambition and be handicapped" in her letter of November 16, 1922, DBH Papers, SCHS, folder 1172.01.01(H)03-01. "We are here because we are here, because we are here," Heyward had written a graduate student inquiring about his philosophy of life; Creighton: "DuBose Heyward," 27.

4. Heyward, *Porgy*, n.p., leaf after dedication page and image before part 1. Many reviews, some noting the difference between the play and the novel, are summarized and quoted in Cooper, "A Comparative Study of *Porgy*, 57–61; typescript on *Porgy* enclosed with letter to Thomas R. Waring, November 25, 1952, DKH Papers, SCHS, folder 180.01.01.01(W)01-01.
5. Durham, *DuBose Heyward*, 113, 58; story of *Porgy and Bess* by DKH in Thomas R. Waring Jr. Papers, SCHS, folder 23-405-2; in a letter to Audrey Wood, June 30, 1950, writing of how she had collaborated with DuBose, she noted that she had written "so much of 'Porgy' that DuBose protested against the inclusion of his name," DKH Papers, SCHS, folder 180.01.03.04(C)04-26; it was copyrighted as *Porgy*, and not as *Catfish Row*, as she said they intended: DBH Papers, SCHS, 1172.01.04.03(P)01-06; Hanna, "Tiptoeing," 55; "Though I wrote ninety-five percent of 'Porgy' I have always known that DuBose's part was the more important," she jotted down in her autobiographical notes regarding her collaboration with Rumer Godden, DKH Papers, SCHS, folder 180.01.03.04(C)04-22.
6. Contract with the Actors' Theatre, author's collection; "Equity Theatre" entry in Bordman and Hischack, *Oxford Companion*, 208; "Actors' Theatre Plans to Extend Its Activities," *Portland, Oregon, Journal*, October 6, 1925, 52. DuBose Heyward to Paul Green, February 2, 1927, Paul Green Papers, Southern Historical Collection, University of North Carolina at Chapel Hill, box 1, folder 84. In her autobiography, Dorothy wrote that all three producers wanted the play but that she and DuBose chose the Guild; Hanna, "Tiptoeing," 55.
7. *Jonica* notes and correspondence, DKH Papers, SCHS, folder 180.01.03.04(J)02-06; the original of Dorothy's letter to Gertrude Workman of the Century Play Company describing this is on the reverse of a letter of Harper's Brothers Publishers to her husband, October 23, 1929. DBH Papers, SCHS, folder 1172.01.04.03(P)01-10; a photocopy of it is in DKH Papers, SCHS, 180.01.03.04(J)02-106.
8. Dorothy Heyward and Alma Klaw, of the family that owned most of the commercial theaters, would collaborate on a play titled *Clinkers*, DKH Papers, SCHS, folders 180.01.03.04(C)03-01/07; Helburn, *Wayward Quest*, 70; Hanna, "Tiptoeing," 55.
9. Heyward and Heyward, *Porgy: A Play*, xiii; Hanna, "Tiptoeing," 54; Williams, *Devil and a Good Woman*, 176–80; "Octavus Roy Cohen's Comedy of Negro Life Well Acted by All 'Black Face' Cast," *New York Times*, July 20, 1920, 16.
10. George Gershwin, "Rhapsody in Catfish Row," X, 1–2, reprinted in Wyatt and Johnson, *George Gershwin Reader*, 219; Hanna, "Tiptoeing," 51; Dorothy noted that the actor who played "darky" butler Binner could double as another (white) person in the play, Heyward, *Nancy Ann*, 6, 4. The January 1927 *Bookman* article is referenced and quoted as "Soon to Produce 'Porgy' on Stage: Now Being Dramatized: Mr. and Mrs. Heyward Are Preparing His Story for the Theater," *Charleston News and Courier*, January 7, 1927, 10.

Chapter 7. Stops and Starts
1. Hanna, "Tiptoeing," 59; "menace": DKH autobiographical notes, DKH Papers, SCHS, folder 180.01.04.03.03-12; Dorothy wrote that Gershwin had first contacted DuBose by letter (Hanna, "Tiptoeing," 53), and many scholars have searched for it fruitlessly. White, *Tastemaker*, 162–64; "An Interview with DuBose Heyward," 6; an earlier story, "George Gershwin to Compose Music in Operatic Version of 'Porgy,'" appeared in the January 1934 issue, 3. Heyward would also later contradict the Laurence Stallings version and say Gershwin contacted him by letter.

2. Hanna, "Tiptoeing," 54; Shirley, "Porgy and Bess," 98; Hanna, "Tiptoeing," 61; George Gershwin, "Rhapsody in Catfish Row," in Wyatt and Johnson, *George Gershwin Reader*, 219; Theresa Helburn to DuBose Heyward, June 27, 1927, DBH Papers, SCHS, folder 1172.01.04.03(P)01-16.
3. Edith to Mrs. W. S. [Stanley] Garretson, Thursday, April 6, 1927, author's collection; the letters to his mother, April through June 1927, with the fishermen singing letter dated April 18 and the "gentry" letter dated June 5, are in DBH Papers, SCHS, folder 1172.01.01(H)03-01.
4. Dorothy's story is mentioned in his letter of June 10, DBH Papers, SCHS, folder 1172.01.01(H)03-01; autobiographical notes mention a "Rose" and her predicament, DKH Papers, SCHS, 180.01.04.03.03-22; Cohen, *Out of the Shadow*; Cohen is mentioned as being at DuBose's reading of *Porgy* at the MacDowell Colony, note 3, chapter 5 above; Heyward, "Young Ghost," 22–24, 101–2; Yezierska, "Wild Winter Love," 485–91.
5. "Hot Water" would eventually become her novel *Three-a-Day*, published years later, but she was contracting for it as a possible story or serial in 1927; see DKH Papers, SCHS, folder 180.01.03.04(T)02.08; Theresa Helburn to DuBose Heyward, June 27, 1927, DBH Papers, folder 1172.01.04.03(P)01-16. "Charleston Visit Delights Theatre Guild's Director," *Charleston News and Courier*, August 16, 1927, 2.
6. Mamoulian's 1958 statement is quoted in Horowitz, *"On My Way,"* 41; Alpert, *Life and Times*, 150; Theresa Helburn to DuBose Heyward, June 27, 1927, DBH Papers, SCHS, folder 1172.01.04.03(P)01-16.
7. DuBose Heyward to Hervey Allen, May 28, [1927], and DuBose Heyward to Hervey Allen, September 25, [1927], both DBH Papers, SCHS, folder 1172.01.01(A)01-04.

Chapter 8. *Porgy*: Revisions

1. All of these changes are seen in the version of the play that would be published in 1928: Heyward and Heyward, *Porgy: A Play*. With the same text, but lacking DuBose's introduction, the play was first published for the Theatre Guild, in orange wraps, as "The Theatre Guild Edition": Heyward and Heyward, *Porgy: A Play*. "DuBose" was finally capitalized correctly in the British edition published by Ernest Benn, London, in 1929. These formats have been called the "acting" edition (although that term was dropped from the title page of the London edition), and although all known Theatre Guild and amateur productions through the 1930s followed the three-act structure, most scholars only know the play in this format.
2. As explained in the note above, all of these textual changes and cuts are from the 1927/28 published "acting" version play. The cutting of the end of the scene alluded to here is present in the prompt script; see note 7 below.
3. For information on Ralph Bennett, whom Charlestonians realized was the basis for the honey man, see the articles regarding his death, which note that fact and which transcribe the lyrics of his song: "'You Got Honey?' Never Again; Death Comes to 'De Honey Man,'" *Charleston News and Courier*, December 28, 1927; "'Honey Man' Is Traffic Victim," *Charleston Evening Post*, December 27, 1927, which notes that he was about seventy-five, that he carried his honey in a tray balanced on his head, and a basket on his arm with "'magic' roots" in it. African American artist Edwin Harleston, upon whom DuBose Heyward would base Frank North, a character in *Mamba's Daughters*, painted him with the baskets on his arms; see https://gibbesmuseum.pastperfectonline.com/webobject/BB386002-BF54-4895-A216-204568953756. There is a photograph of him (possibly used by Harleston for his painting) in Rhett and Gay, *Two Hundred Years*

of *Charleston Cooking*, 224–25, claiming he was ninety and clairvoyant, making this minor character one of the most documented persons upon which a character in the play and opera was based. For his marriage to a younger woman, named Zola Davis, she fifty-six, he about sixty-nine, giving him a birth year in the 1850s, see "'Honey' Will Be Benedict," *Charleston Evening Post*, November 5, 1925, 5; DuBose Heyward to "Dearest Mother," datelined "Manger, Wednesday" [September 21, 1927?], DBH Papers, SCHS, folder 1172.01.01(H)03-01; "children": Woods, "The Negro on Broadway," 75; Waters, *His Eye Is on the Sparrow*, 238.

4. Nugent would meet his lover Richmond Barthe, who saw him in performance in a roadshow production and he, Barthe, would create a statue of Rose McClendon as Serena that would end up at Frank Lloyd Wright's Fallingwater. West's first novel, *And the Living Is Easy*, would take its name from the future opera's lyrics, showing how far the ripples of *Porgy* would travel from Broadway; van Notten, *Wallace Thurman's Harlem Renaissance*, 188–92. According to his obituary ("This Week's Census," *Jet*, February 10, 1955, 49), Perry toured in *Porgy and Bess* in a USO version in World War II, making him and Georgette Harvey, also gay, the only actors to appear in both the play and the opera; Harvey's partner Musa Williams would appear in a revival of *Porgy and Bess* and in Dorothy Heyward's *Set My People Free*.

5. Heyward and Heyward, *Porgy: A Play*, xiii–xiv; DuBose Heyward to Janie Heyward, September 18 [1927], DBH Papers, SCHS, folder 1172.01.01(H)03-01; for labor laws, see DuBose Heyward to "Dearest Mother," datelined "Wednesday" [September 14, 1927?], and another letter, with a similar address, datelined "Thursday" [September 29, 1927?], DBH Papers, SCHS, folder 1172.01.01(H)03-01; for more on the band, see Greene, *Mr. Skylark*, 213–14; "Krazy Kat Klub," March 22, 2023, https://en.wikipedia.org/wiki/Krazy_Kat_Klub. Throckmorton was instrumental in starting the Howard University Players; Shafer, *American Women Playwrights*, 159.

6. Typescript on *Porgy and Bess* by DKH sent to Thomas R. Waring Jr., Thomas R. Waring Jr. Papers, SCHS, folder 23-405-2; see also Hanna, "Tiptoeing," 61; DuBose Heyward to "Dearest Mother," datelined "Manger, Wednesday" [September 21, 1927?] and DuBose Heyward to "My Dear," datelined Friday [September 9, 1927?], DBH Papers, SCHS, folder 1172.01.01(H)03-01.

7. Heyward, *Mamba's Daughters*, 303, 304–5, 302. All the citations regarding script changes are from the *Porgy* prompt script, Theatre Guild Archive, Beinecke Rare Book and Manuscript Library (hereinafter Beinecke Library), Yale University (YCall Mss 436, Series III), digitized here: https://archives.yale.edu/repositories/11/archival_objects/630545.

8. Autobiographical notes, DKH Papers, SCHS, folders 180.01.04.03.03-19 and 180.01.04.03.03-21; Gershwin, *Lyrics*, 149; Heyward and Heyward, *Porgy: A Play*, xviii–xix; "Leigh Whipper," November 26, 2022, https://en.wikipedia.org/wiki/Leigh_Whipper; "Leigh Whipper," www.imdb.com/name/nm0924181.

9. Alpert, *Life and Times*, 53; Woods, "Negro on Broadway," 74–76; Heyward and Heyward, *Porgy: A Play*, xviii. Following his musical bent, Whipper would eventually publish sheet music and lyrics with collaborator Porter Grainger; and as for the crab man's cry, it apparently was once such a well-known feature that a novelist noted that it "has been a familiar sound in Charleston for two centuries": See Stovall, *Son of Carolina*, 7.

10. Hanna, "Tiptoeing," 63; Horowitz, *"On My Way,"* 1–2, 57–60, 42; see Dorothy's letter to John Rumsey, May 27, 1957, DKH Papers, SCHS, folder 180.01.01(R)02-03, and her letter to her cousin "Junior" and his wife, Annie Hartzell, April 14, 1958, DKH Papers, SCHS,

folder 180.01.01.01(H)01.01; Joseph Horowitz, "Porgy and Bess at the Met," *American Scholar* (web only), October 9, 2019, https://theamericanscholar.org/porgy-and-bess-at-the-met; George Gershwin wrote DuBose Heyward, December 17, 1934, acknowledging Heyward's negative feelings about Mamoulian, and years later Dorothy annotated the letter, "Please do not quote." DBH Papers, SCHS, folder 1172.01.01(G)01-01.
11. Horowitz, *"On My Way,"* 64; Hanna, "Tiptoeing," 63; J. Brooks Atkinson, "Negro Lithography," *New York Times*, October 11, 1927, 26; soar and stumble: Joseph Wood Krutch, "Black Ecstasy," *The Nation*, October 26, 1927, quoted in Cooper, "Comparative Study," 58; "electrifying": John Mason Brown, "Broadway in Review," *Theatre Arts Monthly*, December 1927, quoted in Cooper, "Comparative Study," 52; typescript on *Porgy* enclosed with letter to Thomas R. Waring, November 25, 1952, DKH Papers, SCHS, folder 180.01.01.01(W)01-01.
12. DuBose Heyward to "Dearest Mother," typescript on Hotel Manger stationery, DBH Papers, SCHS, folder 1172.01.01(H)03-01; as for scene changes, Dorothy wrote, "The house would stay dark for a minute or two—it seemed like ten—and then the house lights would come on. After another minute, the house lights would dim again, and everyone expected the curtain to go up. It finally did, but in no less than three dark minutes, which seemed like twenty"; Hanna, "Tiptoeing," 63; DuBose Heyward to "Dearest Mother," on Hotel Manger stationery, datelined "Saturday," DBH Papers, SCHS, folder 1172.01.01(H)03-01.
13. The program, with the insert, signed to John Bennett but in DuBose's papers, is dated "10-10-27" and lists four acts; every other program, including the one just a week later, dated "10-17-27," shows the play in three acts, DBH Papers, SCHS, 1172.01.04.03(P)01-07; "'Porgy' Light Plot," 8, *Porgy* prompt script, Mss 436, Theatre Guild Archive, Beinecke Library, Yale University, box 360, folder 7236, contains a page that outlines lighting for act 4, apparently inadvertently left in the script once it was retyped into three acts. This confusion between three and four acts is mirrored in Mantle, *The Best Plays of 1927–1928*; the lengthy synopsis, 212–53, notes it is four acts while a brief summary of all the plays on Broadway that year notes it as three, 383. When the Theatre Guild published an anthology of its best plays, *Porgy* was included, and although Dorothy got first billing, only DuBose was discussed and put in the league with dramatists such as Eugene O'Neill, Bernard Shaw, and Maxwell Anderson (*Theatre Guild Anthology*). When the Theatre Guild was again celebrated in 1955, the text of the play, in four acts, with "Dubose" as the primary author, was published: *Theatre Arts*, October 1955, 35–64; and DuBose was again given first billing in Macgowan, *Famous American Plays*, a paperback reprinted for decades. DuBose Heyward to "Dear," on Hotel Manger stationery, datelined "Thursday," DBH Papers, SCHS, folder 1172.01.01(H)03-01.
14. Macgowan, *Famous American Plays*. On the letter from Leeds to "My beloved dear," datelined "Sunday before church," Dorothy wrote "Leila Leeds to J. S. H. re Porgy," DKH Papers, SCHS, folder 1172.01.04.03(P)01-19; Hanna, "Tiptoeing," 67.

Chapter 9. *Porgy* Abroad
1. DuBose Heyward to Hervey Allen, March 15, [1928], and July 23, [1928], DBH Papers, SCHS, folder 1172.01.01(A)01-04; Susan Bennett to her family, May 6, 1928, John Bennett Papers, SCHS, 21-159-12; DuBose Heyward to Hervey Allen, July 23, [1928], DBH Papers, SCHS, folder 1172.01.01(A)01-04.
2. "Mamoulian, 'Porgy' Director, Delights in Insectless City," *Charleston News and Courier*, January 15, 1929, 9; "Heywards to See London's 'Porgy,'" *Charleston News and Courier*,

January 16, 1929, 2; DuBose Heyward to Janie Screven Heyward, January 28, 1929, DBH Papers, SCHS, folder 1172.01.01(H)03-01. John Bennett wrote to his family about DuBose's wish to avoid "complications along the color line" in New York, October 17, 1928, John Bennett Papers, SCHS, folder 21-141-13.

3. Letters to "Dearest Ma," datelined "S.S. Providence" and "Dearest Ma" datelined "Wednesday," "Dearest Ma," datelined Monday, and "Dearest Mother," datelined Sunday, March 10, DBH Papers, SCHS, folder 1172.01.01(H)03-01.

4. Mitchell and Davis, *Literary Sisters*, unpaginated photograph between 114 and 115; the goat is, unaccountably, called a donkey. DuBose Heyward to "Dearest Mother," April 6, [1929], DBH Papers, SCHS, folder 1172.01.01(H)03-01. Dorothy Heyward, "Porgy's Goat," 37–41.

5. The London program reads "His Majesty's Theatre, by arrangement with the Daniel Mayer Company and the Theatre Guild, Inc., New York City, Charles B. Cochran and Crosby Gaige Have the honour to announce the original Theatre Guild cast and production of *Porgy, a Folk Play*, by DuBose & Dorothy Heyward"; Dorothy Heyward to Mr. Miller, May 7, 1958, DKH Papers, SCHS, folder 180.01.01(Misc.)01-3. All other contracts present in DuBose Heyward's papers, except for the original Theatre Guild production, show his name before Dorothy's, DBH Papers, SCHS, folder, 1172.01.0403(P)01-10.

6. Noonan, *Strange Career*, 118–24; Blanche Prener to DuBose Heyward December 24, 1931, DBH Papers, SCHS, folder 1172.01.04.03(P)01-25. Hanna, "Tiptoeing," 67. West, *Ending in Earnest*, 66–68; DuBose's attendance at the party was noted by Clark, "Dubose [sic] Heyward."

7. Hanna, "Tiptoeing," 68. DuBose Heyward to "Dearest Mother," March 17, [1929], DBH Papers, SCHS, folder 1172.01.01(H)03-01; Hanna, "Tiptoeing," 68; specifications and contract for the building of Dawn Hill, DBH Papers, SCHS, folder 1172.01.02(D)01-01; Gertrude Workman to Dorothy Heyward, May 8, 1929, DKH Papers, SCHS, folder 180.01.03.04(C)02-10.

8. John Patton Russell to Dorothy Heyward, December 8, 1924, DKH Papers, SCHS, folder 180.01.03.04(C)02-10. "Harry Frazee," May 13, 2023, https://en.wikipedia.org/wiki/Harry_Frazee.

Chapter 10. Three-a-Days

1. Contract and correspondence in DKH Papers, SCHS, folder 180.01.03.04(T)02-08; "Porgy, Now on Stage, to Be Made into a Screen Story," *Charleston News and Courier*, January 1, 1928, 2.

2. Heyward, *Three-a-Day*, 135, 136, 154, 279, 298, 300.

3. Thyra Samter Winslow, "In Vaudeville," *New York Herald Tribune*; "In Vaudeville," *New York Times*, undated articles in DKH Papers, SCHS, folder 180.01.03.04(T)02-11; Hanna, "Tiptoeing," 66 (characteristically, Dorothy wrote a few sentences about DuBose's books but not a word about hers); *Three-a-Day* correspondence and notes, DKH Papers, SCHS, folder 180.01.03.04(T)02-109. Contract with Warner Brothers, February 25, 1936, DKH Papers, SCHS, folder 180.01.03.04(T)02-09.

4. The original of Dorothy's letter to Gertrude Workman of the Century Play Company describing this is on the reverse of a letter of Harper's Brothers Publishers to her husband, October 23, 1929, DBH Papers, SCHS, folder 1172.01.04.03(P)01-10; a photocopy of it is in DKH Papers, SCHS, 180.01.03.04(J)02-06. The contract is dated only 1929 and is in DKH Papers, SCHS, folder 180.01.03.04(J)02-05.

5. Gertrude Workman to Dorothy Heyward, April 12, 1930, DKH Papers, SCHS, folder 180.01.03.04(J)02-05; Gertrude Workman to Dorothy Heyward, April 18, 1930, DKH Papers, SCHS, folder 180.01.03.04(J)02-06; autobiographical notes, 180.01.04.03.03.17; Hanna, "Tiptoeing," 67; Bach, *Dazzler*, 57, 59, 60; Brown, *Moss Hart*, 32–33.
6. All the quoted reviews are in DKH Papers, SCHS, folder 180.01.03(J)02-08: E. De S. M., "From the Front Row: Reviews and News of Washington's Theatres," *Evening Star*, March 30, 1930; Char, "Jonica," *Variety*, April 8 [?], 1930; Stephen Rathburn, "'Jonica' at Craig: Friedlander Presents Lively Amusing Musical Comedy," *New York Sun*, April 9, 1930; Arthur Ruhl, "'Jonica': Musical Comedy at Craig Adapted from Dorothy Heyward Story," *New York Herald Tribune*, April 8, 1930; *Variety*, May 14, 1930; Robert Garland, "'Jonica' Gives . . . [rest of headline missing]: Production Has Its Merits, but Will Be Even More Engaging When Ironing Out of Which He Is Confident Has Been Done, He Asserts," *New York Evening Telegram*, April 9, 1930; *Jonica* correspondence, DKH Papers, SCHS, folder 180.01.03.04(J)02-06.
7. Daniel Reed to Dorothy DeJagers, June 11, 1930, DKH Papers, SCHS, folder 180.01.03.04(C)02-10; complicated wordplay was DeJagers's forte, her stories in the *Saturday Evening Post* full of frenzied verbal high jinks, language calling too much attention to itself in the absence of character development and plot. Eichler to Dorothy Heyward, March 31, 1930; see also the March 1930 Harrisburg Community Theatre News Program of *And Arabella*, DKH Papers, SCHS, folder 180.01.03.04(C)02-02.
8. Dorothy Heyward to Miss Eichler, September 1, 1930, DKH Papers, SCHS, folder 18001.03.04(C)02-02; "The Average Woman," February 6, 2023, https://en.wikipedia.org/wiki/The_Average_Woman; Thomas Kane, Century Play Company, to Dorothy Heyward, August 28, 1930, DKH Papers, SCHS, folder 180.01.03.0(C)02-10; in the letter to Miss Eichler, Dorothy said she felt the play was best suited for amateur productions; Heyward and DeJagers, *Little Girl Blue*.
9. Dorothy Heyward to Miss Eichler, September 1, 1930, DKH Papers, SCHS, folder 18001.03.04(C)02-02; Thomas Kane, Century Play Co., to Dorothy Heyward, August 28, 1930, DKH Papers, SCHS, folder 180.01.03.04(C)02-10; "Hyman Bros Have Theatre Club Plan: First Play of Season, 'Cinderelative,' Due This Thursday Eve," unnamed newspaper, September 14, 1930, DKH Papers, SCHS, folder 180.01.03.04(C)02-08.
10. Undated letter to DuBose Heyward, DKH Papers, SCHS, folder 180.01.03.04(C)02-11; Dorothy DeJagers to Dorothy Heyward ("Dear Lamie"), August 27, 1930, DKH Papers, SCHS, folder 18001.03.04(C)02-02; Thomas Kane, Century Play Co., to Dorothy Heyward, August 28, 1930, DKH Papers, SCHS, folder 180.01.03.04(C)02-10.
11. Telegram from DuBose Heyward to Dorothy Heyward, September 19, 1930, DKH Papers, SCHS, folder 180.01.03.014(C)02-10; Robert Littell, "The New Play," *New York World*, undated clipping; Rives Matthews, "Comedy: Cinderelative," *Billboard*, September 27, 1930; Gilbert Gabriel, "'Cinderelative': Something Simple in the Comedy Line," unidentified New York paper, n.d., all preceding citations in DKH Papers, SCHS, folder 180.01.03.04(C)02-08; Dorothy DeJagers to Dorothy Heyward, October 16, 1942, DKH Papers, SCHS, folder 180.01.01.01(D)02-02; although written years afterward, DeJagers seems to be referring to the time when Jenifer was an infant, and DeJagers was seeing Dorothy often, which is likely this time. She wrote that she should have sent Dorothy to a doctor (perhaps she was also suffering postpartum depression, undiagnosed then), but realizing that both DuBose and the doctor were men, they would not have understood. Telegram, Dorothy Heyward to DuBose Heyward, September 19, 1930, DKH Papers, SCHS, folder 180.01.03.04(C)02-10. Dorothy dedicated *Three-a-Day* to Jenifer.

Chapter 11. "Our Next Play"

1. DuBose Heyward to "Dear Mother MacDowell," n.d., DuBose Heyward to Mrs. Edward MacDowell, 28 March, 1930, and Dorothy Heyward to "Dearest Mother MacDowell, n.d. (ca. April 1, 1930), all in Mrs. Edward MacDowell Papers, Library of Congress; Hanna, "Tiptoeing," 69–70.
2. Standard DuBose Heyward biographies discuss the *Emperor Jones* film; the best source is a biography of the director: Delson, *Dudley Murphy*, 122–50; publishing contract, September 18, 1931, DKH Papers, SCHS, folder 180.01.03.04(P)05-02.
3. All scholars, including the author, believed that the novel was based on Charleston etcher Alfred Hutty because the main male character is an etcher. Dorothy warned DuBose that people would assume that, and her husband replied that he would squelch the rumors by having Alfred Hutty design the dust jacket, which just confirmed suspicions by most readers; autobiographical notes, DKH Papers, SCHS, folder 180.01.04.03.03-22; "'Porgy,' Now on Stage, to Be Made into Screen Story," *Charleston News and Courier*, January 1, 1928, 2.
4. "Mrs. DuBose Heyward will not only be one of the members present but is a silent member [her fate always] of the central committee," James Southall Wilson wrote to DuBose Heyward, August 4, 1931, James Southall Wilson Papers, University of Virginia Libraries. Heyward, *Pulitzer Prize Murders*, 285; Anderson, "New Mystery Stories," 49; Mortimer Quick, "Best Mystery Tales of Year Are Named," *Toledo Times*, December 18, 1932; typed transcript of review from *Chicago Evening Post*, May 6, 1932; untitled review, *Charleston, W.V., Gazette*, May 22, 1932; untitled review, *Newark, N.J., News*, June 4, 1932, DKH Papers, SCHS, folder 180.01.03.04(P)05-01; typescript on *Porgy* enclosed with letter to Thomas R. Waring, November 25, 1952, DKH Papers, SCHS, folder 180.01.01.01(W)01-01.
5. Dorothy Heyward wrote of participating in one of the concerts in the 1950s in a letter to Jenifer Heyward, April 12, 1951, Jenifer Heyward Wood Papers, SCHS, folder 181.01.01.02; Heyward, "Negro in the Low-Country," 171–87; Heyward wrote scholars to help him with research; a reply of August 9, 1930, from Ulrich B. Phillips is in DBH Papers, SCHS, 1172.01.01(Misc.)01-01; Delson, *Dudley Murphy*, 122–50; Heyward, "Denmark Vesey"; Hanna, "Tiptoeing," 88.
6. Nathaniel Heyward (1766–1851) was one of the judges at the trial; he was the son of Daniel Heyward (1720–1777), as was Thomas Heyward Jr. (1746–1809), signer of the Declaration of Independence, DuBose Heyward's direct ancestor; Dorothy Heyward to Douglas Moore, July 30, 1951, DKH Papers, SCHS, folder 180.01.01(Misc.)01-01; see the "Merrivale" manuscript, DBH Papers, SCHS, folders 1172.01.04(Misc.)02-02/04.
7. Vorse, *Strike!* The Hergesheimer story was originally published in the July 9, 1927, edition of *Saturday Evening Post*, 10–11, 44, 46, 49, but it was also heralded in the Charleston press, and in another article he mentioned knowing the Heywards: "'Charleston' Is the Theme of Joseph Hergesheimer Story," *Charleston News and Courier*, July 8, 1927, 6; "Charleston Is Ideal Spot," *Charleston Evening Post*, February 4, 1926, 2. One of her characters in *The Cinderelative* refers to one of his novels. Hergesheimer, *Quiet Cities*, 287–354.
8. De Graff, "Searching for 'Authenticity,'" 187–211; Kramer, *Denmark Vesey*. Hille's oratorio is mentioned in the reprint, Higginson, "Denmark Vesey," facing page 1; see also Aaron Kramer and Waldemar Hille correspondence, University of Michigan Libraries, and Reuss, "American Folksongs," 89–111.

9. Heyward, "Negro in Low-Country," 178–79; DuBose Heyward to George C. Tyler, April 20, 1932, DBH Papers, SCHS, folder 1172.01.01(T)01-01; George Gershwin to DuBose Heyward, March 29, 1932, DBH Papers, SCHS, folder 1172.01.01(G)01-01; George C. Tyler to DuBose Heyward, April 25, 1932, DBH Papers, SCHS, folder 1172.01.01(T)01-01.

Chapter 12. Credit and Credibility

1. Hutchisson, *DuBose Heyward*, 141; contract for *Porgy and Bess*, October 12, 1933, DBH Papers, SCHS, restricted vault; the author is grateful to Gershwin archivist Michael Owen for sharing a copy of the Gershwin contract, lacking Dorothy's signature, reproduction in author's files; Dorothy Heyward to Audrey Wood, August 16, 1957, DKH Papers, SCHS, folder 180.01.01.01(W)07-02.
2. George Gershwin to DuBose Heyward, March 29, 1932, DBH Papers, SCHS, folder 1172.01.01(G)01-01; see citation for 1933 contract, note above; for naming, see DuBose Heyward, "Porgy and Bess Return on Wings of Song," *Stage*, October 1935, 25–28, citation on 28; Hanna, "Tiptoeing," 61; the author thanks Gershwin archivist Michael Owen for sharing a copy of the October 16, 1934, contract with the Gershwins and Munsell, reproduction in author's files.
3. October 16, 1934, contract with the Gershwins and Munsell, see note immediately above;. Alpert, *Life and Times*, 76; DuBose Heyward to George Gershwin, March 2, 1934, DBH Papers, SCHS, folder 1172.01.01(G)01-01; Mamoulian, "I Remember," 47–57, citation on 48.
4. Alpert, *Life and Times*, 134; Porgy prompt script, 1–3, Mss 436, Theatre Guild Archive, Beinecke Library, Yale University, box 360, folder 7236; Gershwin and Heyward, *Theatre Guild*, 23–24; Gershwin, *Lyrics*, 360; DuBose Heyward to George Gershwin, November 12, 1933, DBH Papers, SCHS, folder 1172.01.01(G)01-01.
5. All the quotes are from "DuBose Heyward Shunned Ovation on Opera Stage: Author of 'Porgy,' Paged by Charleston's Contingent in Audience at Boston, Stays Modestly in Background," *Charleston News and Courier*, October 6, 1935, 18; contract photostat, June 28, 1935, DKH Papers, SCHS, folder 180.01.03.01-18; the original contract was first advertised at auction in June 2022, www.liveauctioneers.com/item/125318948_contract-for-the-first-production-of-porgy-and-bess, and was sold for $16,000 in February 2023, www.liveauctioneers.com/item/144501435_george-gershwin-signed-contract-for-1st-production-of-porgy-and-bess-also-signed-by-dubose-heyward.
6. The *Charleston News and Courier*, October 11, 1888, reported, "Mr. [A. E.] Gonzales also furnished a novel and mirth-provoking male in a Gullah oration—'Ooman is a sometime ting,' by the Reb. Nepchne Kinlaw." The author thanks Steve Hoffius for bringing this to his attention. Some of the actors in the play acknowledged they had used Gonzales's *Black Border* book to help with the Gullah and loaned the book to Dorothy: autobiographical notes, DKH Papers, SCHS, folder 180.01.04.03.03-19.
7. Autobiographical notes, DKH Papers, SCHS folder 180.01.04.03.03-19; Dorothy Heyward to Thomas Waring, April 28, 1953, DKH Papers, SCHS, folder 180.01.01(W)01-01; for George's comment to Ira re credit see Owen, *Ira Gershwin*, 118; Durham, "DuBose Heyward," 375; Dorothy Heyward to Thomas Waring, April 28, 1953, DKH Papers, SCHS, folder 180.01.01.0(W)01-01; for Ira Gershwin's description of sharing credit with DuBose for "I Got Plenty o' Nuttin,'" see Gershwin, *Lyrics*, 360. Dorothy is not mentioned.
8. Gershwin and Heyward, *Theatre Guild*, 244–46; Gershwin, "Rhapsody in Catfish Row," x, 1–2; Shirley, "Porgy and Bess," 101–2, notes that the libretto is in "the pre-Ira state"; Dorothy Heyward used the term herself in a version of the opera she and DuBose had

worked on: see DBH papers, SCHS, folder 1172.01.04.03(P)02-06, the notation in her handwriting; Hutchisson, *DuBose Heyward*, 156; Ira discusses the creation of this song in Gershwin, *Lyrics*, 147–50.
9. Durham, "DuBose Heyward," 375; "assists": Dorothy Heyward to R. P. Edmunds, March 1, 1957, DKH Papers, SCHS, 180.01.01.01(E)02-01; Dorothy Heyward to Richard Roberts, n.d. (ca. January 1959), DKH Papers, SCHS, folder 180.01.01.01(Misc.)01-03; Ira Gershwin to DuBose Heyward, August 2, 1937, DBH Papers, SCHS, folder 1172.01(G)01-01. George Gershwin, in his own notes in the first draft of the *Porgy and Bess* libretto at the Library of Congress, credited her husband with "Summertime," "A Woman Is a Sometime Thing," "My Man's Gone Now," the "Train Song in the saucer burial scene," "It Take a Long Pull to Get There," "The Buzzard Song," "Street Cries," and the finale, "I'm on My Way" (and not Mamoulian, who claimed to have authored it); he gave joint billing to DuBose and Ira for "Plenty o' Nuttin'" (with which Dorothy disagreed), "I Loves You, Porgy," "A Boat Leaving for New York" (which now is totally credited to Ira), and "Where's My Bess." He gave Ira sole credit for "I Can't Sit Down" (a phrase used repeatedly in the play), "I Got No Shame," "It Ain't Necessarily So," and "A Red Headed Woman." In his list he left out Bess's song with Crown, "What You Want with Bess," mostly words from a scene she had moved around in various versions of the play and which is credited to Ira, DuBose and, rightly, to her, and "Bess, You Is My Woman Now," which would be eventually credited totally to Ira, despite his confession that it was one of their "collaborative efforts, rather than my exclusive work." Photo: Gershwin, Heyward, and Gershwin, *Porgy and Bess: Vocal Score*, unnumbered leaf following title page.
10. "Gershwin Coming Back Here for Atmosphere for 'Porgy,'" *Charleston News and Courier*, June 5, 1934, 10; Hanna, "Tiptoeing," 71–77 passim; "DuBose Heyward Shunned Ovation on Opera Stage," *Charleston News and Courier*, October 6, 1935, 18. That Dorothy was part of the treks into the surrounding Lowcountry is proved in an article that states she went along to Wadmalaw Island with her husband, Gershwin, and his cousin, the painter Henry Botkin, to hear local Blacks, associated with the pageant *Plantation Echoes*, sing; Gershwin also played the piano there, "Gershwin, Heyward Visit in Rockville: Plantation Negroes Sing for Composer, Working on Music for 'Porgy,'" *Charleston News and Courier*, July 17, 1934, 12. The author thanks historian Heather Hodges for helping track down this citation.

Chapter 13. *Mamba's Daughters*

1. Autobiographical notes, DKH Papers, SCHS, folder 180.01.04.03.03-18; Lewisohn, *The Golden Vase* (1931). Lewisohn, a few years older than Heyward, had immigrated to America with his family, and although he had left Charleston, he garnered much national attention, often mentioned in the Charleston press, making it possible that Heyward was aware of the book; or, being of the same age, they could have both been experiencing the same sort of doldrums. *The Golden Vase*, a much more cerebral work, focuses on the pressures on an artist to be more commercial at the promptings of his wife, Katherine, instead of following his muse, and *Lost Morning* follows suit, with Felix Hollister at the mercy of his wife, Miriam. Heyward's Hollister and Lewisohn's John Ridgevale have grown children and find a spiritual muse in a young woman, young enough to be a daughter, a relationship not erotic, but inspirational to each: Leslie Morgan for Felix, Lisl Schönbrunn for Ridgevale. In the latter's case, he leaves her, taking inspiration for his greatest work from her. Leslie Morgan, through her accidental death, leaves Hollister,

who gives up on his marriage to Miriam, determined to embark on a new phase of his career. Hanna, "Tiptoeing," 69; Bellows, *Talent for Living*, 173–76.
2. Dorothy Heyward to Karen Horney, April 10, 1950, and Dorothy Heyward to Mrs. Brebner, March 3, 1949, DKH Papers, SCHS, folder 180.01.01.01(H)01-01; DuBose Heyward, pictures by Flack, *Country Bunny*; Bryan Collier, "Tale of 'The County Bunny' Was Made Just for Jenifer," *Charleston News and Courier*, April 10, 1955, 34; DuBose Heyward to Mary [Matthew], June 20, [1939?], DBH Papers, SCHS, folder 1172.01.01(Misc.)01-01; Jack McGowan to DuBose Heyward, n.d., and Bertha Case (of Liebling-Wood, Inc.) to DuBose Heyward, April 17, 1940, DBH Papers, SCHS, folder 1172.04.03(A)01-07; the unfinished manuscript is in DBH Papers, SCHS, folders 1172.01.04.03(A)01-01/03.
3. DuBose Heyward to Hervey Allen, August 22, 1933, DBH Papers, SCHS, folder 1172.01.01(A)01-05; Bailey, "DuBose Heyward," 25, 95. The material he gathered was used for his last novel, *Star Spangled Virgin* (1939). Dorothy stated that Kurt Weill and Arthur Schwartz were both interested in collaborating with Heyward, with work begun with the latter and later abandoned; Hanna, "Tiptoeing," 86–87.
4. Autobiographical notes, DKH Papers, SCHS, folder 180.01.04.03.03-20; Hanna, "Tiptoeing," 51; Waters, *His Eye*, 237–38; "Daughter of Mamba," 97; Shirley, "Porgy and Bess," 100; Waters, *His Eye*, 238–39.
5. Heyward, *Mamba's Daughters*, 27, 163, 173; Dorothy Heyward to Audrey Wood, June 30, 1959, DKH Papers, SCHS, folder 180.01.03.04(C)04-26; DuBose Heyward to Warren Munsell, August 7, 1937, DBH Papers. SCHS, folder 1172.01.04.03(M)01-24.
6. Waters, *His Eye*, 239, 240, 241–43; Waters wrote that it was a man named Greenwald who pulled the funding, but a letter to DuBose Heyward suggests that it was the Broadway producer Sam Grisman instead; the news that Louis Simon, a director, had "read the play and is crazy about it," came to Heyward one day while walking in front of the office building his insurance office had once; Simon's uncle, P. Leroy Pinkussohn, had told him the news: P. Leroy Pinkussohn to DuBose Heyward, May 2,1938, DBH Papers, SCHS, folder 172.01.04.03(M)01-24.
7. DuBose Heyward, *Star Spangled Virgin*; for more on the operatic version, see note 3; McClintic, *Me and Kit*, 313; Waters, *His Eye*, 243–45; the cast is listed in Dorothy and DuBose Heyward, *Mamba's Daughters*, second unnumbered page after the title page.
8. "Notes on Mamba," typescript with Dorothy Heyward holograph note "Who wrote it," DBH Papers, SCHS, folder 1172.01.04.03(M)01-20; autobiographical notes, DKH Papers, SCHS, folder 180.01.04.03.03-20. For more on McClintic's behavior, his relationship with his wife, and his sexuality, see Mosel, Macy, and Graham, *Leading Lady*, passim; for her abortion, 156–57; for her liking of violence and bad plays, 236, 238, 240, 247.
9. Marian MacDowell to Nina Maud Richardson, January 2, 1939, Marian MacDowell Papers, Library of Congress; in Dorothy and DuBose Heyward, *Mamba's Daughters: A Play*, 85, verso of third unnumbered leaf after the title page; DBH Papers, SCHS, folder 1172.01.04.03(M)01-19 contains "Typescript (carbon) of the 1939 New York playing version of *Mamba's Daughters*."
10. Waters, *His Eye*, 247, 248–49; Perry Watkins: Hughes and Meltzer, *Black Magic*, 196; Waters quotes the advertisement in *The New York Times*, January 6, 1939, DBH Papers, SCHS, folder 1172.01.04.03(M)01-21; Brooks Atkinson, "'Mamba's Daughters Put on by Equity Community Troupe at De Wit Clinton in the Bronx," *New York Times*, March 21, 1953, 12; staff writers, "Obie Honors to Foreman Plays," *Variety*, May 20, 1998, https://variety.com/1998/legit/news/obie-honors-to-foreman-plays-1117471065; Marian

MacDowell to Nina Maud Richardson, January 7, 1939 and January 15, 1939, Marian MacDowell Papers, Library of Congress.

11. The *Life* magazine article "Mamba's Daughters" features sixteen photographs, in chronological order, explaining the plot; quoted in Durham, "DuBose Heyward," 398. Mosel, Macy, and Graham, *Leading Lady* (see also note 8); letters from Audrey Wood to DuBose Heyward, February 16, 1939, and March 7, 1939, and undated note from DuBose to Audrey Wood, agreeing to reduced royalties, DBH Papers, SCHS, folder 1172.01.04.03(M)01-24; quoted in Hutchisson, *DuBose Heyward*, 185; DuBose Heyward to Sarita, November 16, 1939, DBH Papers, SCHS, folder 1172.01.04.08-04.

Chapter 14. The Dock Street Theatre

1. Durham, *DuBose Heyward*, 12; script of "1773: An Historical Interlude," DBH Papers, SCHS, folder 1172.01.04.03(S)01-01; DuBose Heyward, "The New Note in Southern Literature," *The Bookman*, April 1925, 153–56, included in Hutchisson, *DuBose Heyward Reader*, 22–26; "First U.S. Theatre Is Restored: Charleston Blue Bloods Give It a Gala Opening," *Life*, December 20, 1937, 49–50; Dorothy Heyward is captioned in one of the images.

2. For more on the history of the theater and the Carolina Art Association, see the Dock Street Theatre Collection Papers, SCHS, 1177.00, and DBH Papers, SCHS, cited below. Heyward and Pinckney were on the theater production committee, the operating committee, and the advisory committee; *Dock Street Theatre*, 15; "DuBose Heyward Appointed Resident Playwright Here," *Charleston News and Courier*, November 8, 1939. According to a letter from R. N. S. Whitelaw to Luce, February 21, 1941, the grant was for $5,000 a year for three years, DBH Papers, SCHS, folder 1172.01.04.08-10. $200 award: "Fifty Associate Members of Playwright School to Be Sounding Board," unnamed newspaper, undated clipping, DBH Papers. SCHS, folder 1172.01.04.08-09.

3. *Dock Street Theatre*; "Benét Prepares for Play Opening Here Next Monday," unnamed newspaper [*Charleston Evening Post*?], May 3, 1939, clipping in DBH Papers, SCHS, folder 1172.01.04.08-09; autobiographical notes, DKH Papers, SCHS, folder 180.01.04.03.0-21; his lecture from November 1939 is in DBH Papers, SCHS, 1172.04.08-12; see also clipping there, R[owena] W[ilson] T[obias], "Playwrights Cut Teeth on Small Audience," *Charleston News and Courier*, November 19, 1939; "Awards Cost Dorothy Heyward Midnight Oil," clipping in DuBose Heyward vertical file, Charleston County Public Library, ascribed to the *Christian Science Mentor* [sic] *Magazine*, 1943.

4. DBH Papers, SCHS, folder 1172.01.04.08.12; his report is in DBH Papers, SCHS, folder 1172.01.04.08.24.

5. The quotes and details are from Dorothy Heyward to her family, June 27, 1940, DKH Papers, 180.01.01(Misc.)04-01; she wrote various versions of the letter to different people; Durham, *DuBose Heyward*, 139. Autobiographical notes, DKH Papers, SCHS folder 180.01.04.03.03-15. According to her biographer, as a young woman Pinckney had fallen in love with and proposed to a man named Richard Wigglesworth who turned her down; Bellows, *Talent for Living*, 86–89.

6. Dorothy Heyward to her family, June 27, 1940, DKH Papers, and Dorothy Heyward to Joseph McGee, July 10, 1940, both in DKH Papers, SCHS, folder 180.01.01(Misc.)04-01.

Chapter 15. War and Worries

1. Mrs. Edward MacDowell to Elizabeth White, July 14, 1940, Marian MacDowell Papers, Library of Congress; McKee, *Valiant Woman*, 54–55; Dorothy Heyward to Lawrence

Langner, November 11, 1941, Mss 436, Theatre Guild Archive, Beinecke Library, Yale, box 32, folder 2391, which also contains the information on Paul Robeson.
2. Hanna, "Tiptoeing," 88–91; Dorothy Heyward to Douglas Moore, July 30, 1951, DKH Papers, SCHS, folder 180.01.01(Misc.)01-01; three years: Dorothy Heyward to David Lowe, March 20, 1943, DKH Papers, SCHS, folder 180.01.03.04(S)02-19; Esther Bates to Dorothy Heyward, September 19, 1940, DKH Papers, SCHS, folder 180.01.03.04(S)01-97; Thornton Wilder to Dorothy Heyward, November 6, 1940, folder 180.01.01.01(W)05-01; Wilder notes Harris being loathed by many.
3. Lawrence Langner to "Essie" [Eslanda] Robeson, October 25, 1941, and Theresa Helburn to Lawrence Langner, September 29, 1949, both Mss 436, Theatre Guild Archive, Beinecke Library, Yale, box 92, folder 2391; for casting, see DKH Papers, SCHS, folder 180.01.03.04(S)01-96 and Mss 436, Theatre Guild Archive, Beinecke Library, Yale, box 92, folder 2389; contract: Theresa Helburn to Dorothy Heyward, December 17, 1941, Mss 436, Theatre Guild Archive, Beinecke Library, Yale, box 92, folder 2389.
4. Clare Boothe Luce to Dorothy Heyward, January 4, 1941, DBH Papers, SCHS, folder 1172.01.04.08-10; "Theatre Offers Award to Honor DuBose Heyward," *Canton, Ohio, Repository*, January 24, 1941; "142 Plays Entered in Dock St. Contest," unnamed newspaper, n.d., DBH Papers, SCHS, folder 1172.01.04.08-09. For more information on the contest and how the playwriting program worked, see "Awards Cost Dorothy Heyward Midnight Oil," clipping in DuBose Heyward vertical file, Charleston County Public Library, ascribed to the *Christian Science Mentor* [sic] *Magazine*, 1943.
5. Rowena Wilson Tobias, "Lively Comedy at Dock Street," *Charleston News and Courier*, April 25, 1941; "Mrs. Heyward Invites Playwrights to Charleston," undated, unidentified clipping of an AP story dated November 1, DBH Papers, SCHS, folder 1172.01.04.08-09. The Theatre Guild did not produce it; it was first staged at the Dock Street Theatre with the veteran actress Dorothy Gish in the lead. It was read by various producers under various names, such as *Her Lord and Master* and *Bee in Her Bonnet*, for a number of years and was eventually broadcast by Kraft Theatre on television in 1949.
6. Luelle M. Clark, "Double Success Stunned Playwright," *Charleston News and Courier*, March 29, 1942, clipping, DBH Papers, SCHS, folder 1172.01.04.08-09; announcement and entry form, DBH Papers, SCHS, folder 172.01.04.08-03; "Dock Street Playwrights Winning New Recognition," *Charleston News and Courier*, February 26, 1942, 16; Wide World syndicated photo with captions, dated March 9, 1943, author's collection; "OCD to Use Local Plays," *Charleston News and Courier*, August 15, 1942, 5. Autobiographical notes, DKH Papers, SCHS, folder 180.01.04.03.03-29. One wonders if Dorothy knew that these men were gay; she would share an agent with Tennessee Williams and seemingly was aware of the subtext in some of his plays; nevertheless play number 197, *A Sure Foundation*, in the 1940–41 contest was considered not fit for the Dock Street Theatre due to its homosexual content, the notation in Dorothy Heyward's handwriting, DBH Papers, SCHS, folder 1172.01.04.08-26.
7. Waters, *His Eye*, 250; the best source of information on Lee is Mona Z. Smith, *Becoming Something*; telegram of Audrey Wood to Dorothy Heyward, December 7, 1942, DKH Papers, SCHS, folder 180.01.03.04(S)02-18.
8. Audrey Wood to Dorothy Heyward, December 13, 1942, January 4, 1943, DKH Papers, SCHS, folder 180.01.03.04(S)02-18. The correspondence with DeJagers, some dated and some not, notes Dorothy working on her play, *The Emperor's Shirt*, and DeJagers's growing mental illness and need for hospitalization at Johns Hopkins: DKH Papers, SCHS,

folders 180.01.01.01(D)02-01/04; Dorothy Heyward to Dorothy DeJagers, July 1942, DKH Papers, SCHS 180.01.01.01(D)02-02.
9. Contract: DKH Papers, SCHS, folder, 180.01.03.04(S)02-17; correspondence of Dorothy Heyward and Audrey Wood, December 1942–March 1943, DKH Papers, SCHS, folder 180.01.03.04(S)02-18; Dorothy Heyward to David Lowe, March 20, 1943, and February 16, 1943, DKH Papers, SCHS folder 180.01.03.04(S)02-19. With there being no complete script for the play in her papers, and none found elsewhere, Dorothy's letters can be used to track changes she made.
10. Dorothy Heyward to Audrey Wood, March 18, 1943, DKH Papers, SCHS, folder 180.01.03.04(S)02-18; Lowe was back in New York by February 23, 1943, when he wrote her commenting on Sam Stoney, whom he met in Charleston: DKH Papers, SCHS, folder 180.01.03.04(S)02-19; Dorothy Heyward to David Lowe, February 16, 1943, DKH Papers, SCHS, folder 180.01.03.04(S)02-19. She did not want the boy Daniel to die, but just to spurn Sam.
11. David Lowe to Dorothy Heyward, August 20, 1943, DKH Papers, SCHS, folder 180.01.03.04(S)02-19; Dorothy Heyward to Dorothy DeJagers, undated letter [summer 1943 when she was in New York], DKH Papers, SCHS, folder 180.01.01.01(D)02-04; Dorothy Heyward to David Lowe, March 20, 1943, DKH Papers, SCHS, folder 180.01.03.04(S)02-19; two-thirds: Dorothy Heyward to Audrey Wood, June 30, 1950, DKH Papers, SCHS, folder 180.01.03.04(C)04-26.
12. As noted in note 9 above, there is no complete script available to ascertain with certainty the exact dialogue, plot, and motivations; Lewis Nichols, "The Play," *New York Times*, December 30, 1943; Louis Kronenberger, "An Honest Try on a Good Theme," unnamed newspaper, December 30, 1943, and "Native Son in the Solomons," undated *New Yorker* article, all in DKH Papers, SCHS, folder 180.01.03.04(S)02-24.
13. Autobiographical notes, DKH Papers, SCHS, folder 180.01.04.03.02-03; George Jean Nathan, "Some of the Year's Best Theatregoing Might Be Done in Storehouse," unnamed newspaper, n.d., clipping, DKH Papers, SCHS, folder 180.01.03.04(S)02-24; M. Smith, *Becoming Something*, 163.
14. Howard Rigsby to Dorothy Heyward, March 25, 1944, DKH Papers, SCHS, folder 180.01.03.04(S)02-21; Dorothy Heyward to Mrs. Brebner, March 3, 1949, DKH Papers, SCHS, folder 180.01.01.01(H)01-01; *Boysi* contract, DKH Papers, SCHS, folder 180.01.02(B)02-01; Allan, *Boysi Himself*, front flap dust jacket copy.
15. H. G. Walker, "Glenn Allan's Boysi Stories Being Prepared for Dramatization by Mrs. Dorothy Heyward," *Charleston News and Courier*, November 12, 1944; the copyright entry reads: "Eighty minutes to the hour by C. Foster, based upon the Boysi stories by G. Allan (c) 1c, Dec. 27, 1945, D96554, Claiborne Foster, New York, Glenn Allan, Summerville, S.C. & Dorothy Heyward, New York," 6592, Library of Congress, Catalog of Copyright Entries 1945 Dramatic Compositions New Series Vol 18 Pt 1, 204, https://archive.org/details/catalogofcopyrig181libr/page/204/mode/2up.

Chapter 16. Legacies

1. See Alpert, *Life and Times*, for a full history of productions; Dorothy Heyward to Thomas R. Waring Jr., April 28, 1953, DKH Papers, SCHS, folder 180.01.01.01(W)01-01; for specifics on this revival, see Lynch, "Cheryl Crawford's *Porgy and Bess*"; Dorothy Heyward to Lawrence Langner, March, 8, 1950, Mss 436, Theatre Guild Archive, Beinecke Library, Yale, box 92, folder 2392; Dorothy Heyward to "Dear Terry" [Helburn], n.d. [1948], on

her stationery, giving an address of 85 Granite Street, Pigeon Cove, Mass., DKH Papers, SCHS, folder 180.01.03.04(S)01-97.
2. See the souvenir booklet from the production: "Cheryl Crawford Presents George Gershwin's Immortal 'Porgy and Bess,'" n.d. (1942), author's collection; making matters worse, the text notes that Ira Gershwin wrote the lyrics with DuBose in Charleston. Wyatt and Johnson, *George Gershwin Reader*, 280; Dorothy Heyward to John Rumsey, June 4, 1957, DKH Papers, SCHS, folder 180.01.01(R)02-03; "Heyward's Name Left off Billing: Widow Insists Producer of 'Porgy and Bess' Credit Creator of Character," *Charleston News and Courier*, July 12, 1942, 26; Dorothy Heyward to Dorothy DeJagers, July 3, 1942, DKH Papers, SCHS, folder 180.01.01(D)02-02; Dorothy Heyward to John Rumsey, June 4, 1957, DKH Papers, SCHS, folder 180.01.01(R)02-03.
3. Robert N.S. Whitelaw, quoting DuBose Heyward, to Henry Luce, January 21, 1941, DBH Papers, SCHS, folder 1172.01.04.08-10, original in 1172.01.04.08-02; Robert N.S. Whitelaw to Dorothy Heyward, September 1, 1943, DBH Papers, SCHS, folder 1172.01.04.08-19; printed announcement, Dock Street Theatre Collection, SCHS, box 21-201, Carolina Art Association Folder 1943-44.
4. A production history of the play is given in Peggy Lamson, *Respectfully Yours*; "MIT News: Memorial Set for Peggy Lamson, May 22, 1996," https://news.mit.edu/1996/lamson-0522; Lamson, *The Glorious Failure*.
5. "Omaha Theater to Give Local Award Play," *Charleston News and Courier*, February 26, 1948, 6; "Dock St. to Resume Heyward Award, Interrupted by War," *Charleston News and Courier*, March 1, 1946, 16; "Heyward Award Will Not Be Made This Year," *Charleston News and Courier*, November 3, 1948, 10; "DuBose Heyward Playwriting Award Won by New York Man," *Charleston News and Courier*, November 2, 1947, 8; "Walter Doniger," April 4, 2023, https://en.wikipedia.org/wiki/Walter_Doniger; "George Bellak," February 24, 2022, https://en.wikipedia.org/wiki/George_Bellak.
6. Rowena Wilson Tobias, "Young Playwright, Like His Ancestor Who Created 'Moby Dick,' Won't Bend to Popular Taste," *Charleston News and Courier*, January 7, 1940, 17; "Paul Metcalf," August 15, 2022, https://en.wikipedia.org/wiki/Paul_Metcalf; Metcalf, *Appalache*, 75–91.

Chapter 17. The Tragedy of Denmark Vesey

1. Autobiographical notes, DKH Papers, SCHS, folder 180.01.04.03.03-18; Audrey Wood to Dorothy Heyward, January 21, 1943, DKH Papers, folder 180.01.03.04(S)02-18; Dorothy Heyward to Theresa Helburn, n.d., Mss 436, Theatre Guild Archive, Beinecke Library, Yale, box 92, folder 2389; Lawrence Langner to Dorothy Heyward, December 30, 1943, and Dorothy Heyward to Lawrence Langner, March 8, 1944, both Mss 436, Theatre Guild Archive, Beinecke Library, Yale, box 92, folder 2391.
2. Heyward to Lawrence Langner, March 8, 1944, Mss 436, Theatre Guild Archive, Beinecke Library, Yale, box 92, folder 2391; memo from Kenneth Rowe to Theresa Helburn and Langner, April 25, 1926, and DKH to Theresa Helburn, April 23, 1946, both Mss 436, Theatre Guild Archive, Beinecke Library, Yale, box 92, folder 2389; Audrey Wood to Dramatists Guild, July 8, 1948, DKH Papers, SCHS folder 180.01.03.04(S)01-97.
3. Wood, *Represented by Audrey Wood*, 153; "Dorothy Heyward Struck by Auto, Has Broken Hip," *Charleston News and Courier*, January 13, 1948, 7; Jo Mielziner to Dorothy Heyward, July 8, 1948, Dorothy Heyward to Theresa Helburn, July 22, 1948, and Dorothy Heyward to Theresa Helburn, July 14, 1948, DKH Papers, SCHS, 180.01.03.04(S)01-97;

"shoddy": L. Arnold Weissberger to Theresa Helburn, October 11, 1948, Mss 436, Theatre Guild Archive, Beinecke Library, Yale, box 92, folder 2392; production costs: Fitelson and Mayers memo to Lawrence Langner, August 6, 1948, Mss 436, Theatre Guild Archive, Beinecke Library, Yale, box 92, folder 2392.

4. Dorothy Heyward to Allyn Rice, March 24, [1948], Dorothy Heyward Papers, SCHS, 180.01.03.04(S)01-97. For the Woodard case, see Gergel, *Unexampled Courage*; *Charleston, 1822* program, author's collection; Smith, *Becoming Something*, 263; Dolinar, *Black Cultural Front*, 40.

5. The prologue is in DKH Papers, SCHS, folder 180.01.03.04(S)01-09; Smith, *Becoming Something*, 263–65; "Rough Draft: He Set My People Free," December 21, 1948, Mss 436, Theatre Guild Archive, Beinecke Library, Yale, box 92, folder 2392. Dorothy misidentified Ritt, calling him Langner in her autobiography (Hanna, "Tiptoeing," 92); Miller, *Films of Martin Ritt*, 6; Dorothy Heyward to Douglas Moore, July 30, 1951, DKH Papers, SCHS, folder 180.01.01.01(misc.)01-01. One who had heard of Vesey, possibly through Dorothy herself, was African American radio script writer Richard Durham, who wrote a historically inaccurate but dramatic installment on Vesey for the Chicago-based "Destination Freedom" radio series, see McDonald, *Richard Durham's Destination Freedom*, 47–62. It was broadcast in July 1948, as stories about Vesey and *Set My People Free* were appearing as early as February of that year, including Louis Calta, "Guild Co-Sponsor of Heyward Play: Organization to Join Allyn Rice in Doing 'Set My People Free' Next Season," *New York Times*, February 21, 1948, 8.

6. Hanna, "Tiptoeing," 92–3; Smith, *Becoming Something*, 265; Hanna, "Tiptoeing," 93; opening night party invitation, Mss 436, Theatre Guild Archive, Beinecke Library, Yale, box 92, folder 2392; Dorothy Heyward to Mrs. Jelliff (associated with Karamu House Theatre, which later produced the play), December 3, 1949, DKH Papers, SCHS, folder 180.01.03.04(S)01-97; Dick Reeves to Dorothy Heyward, October 5, 1948, DKH Papers, folder 180.01.01(R)01.01.

7. Dorothy Heyward, *Set My People Free* (final script), DKH Papers, SCHS, folder 180.01.03.04(S)01-103, 2-1-2; Dorothy Heyward to Lawrence Langner, n.d., Hotel Holley letterhead and "*LL's* [Lawrence Langner's] *memorandum re SET MY PEOPLE FREE – to be placed in the files*," November 3, 1948 (dictated November 1), both Mss 436, Theatre Guild Archive, Beinecke Library, Yale, box 92, folder 2392; Wood's agreement: Dorothy Heyward to Douglas Moore, February 15, 1957, DKH Papers, SCHS, folder 180.01.01(Misc.)01-03; "Audience Responds to Mrs. Heyward's Play on Charleston," *Charleston News and Courier*, October 20, 1948.

8. E. G. Marshall to Lawrence Langner, November 19, [1948], Mss 436, Theatre Guild Archive, Beinecke Library, Yale, box 92, folder 2388; Brooks Atkinson, "'SET MY PEOPLE FREE': Theatre Guild Stages Historical Negro Drama with Some Superb Players," *New York Times*, November 14, 1948; Howard Barnes, "The Theatres," attributed, in an unknown hand, to *New York Herald Tribune*, November 5, 1948; Howard Barnes, "The Theatre Guild's Play about Slaves in Revolt," *New York Herald Tribune*, November 7, 1948, DKH Papers, SCHS, folder 180.01.03.04(S)01-98; Smith, *Becoming Something*, 267–68.

9. Hanna, "Tiptoeing," 94; Dorothy Heyward to Marjorie Benét [dear Beloved Marge], December 21, n.d. [ca. 1950], DKH Papers, SCHS, 180.01.03.04(C)04-28; Dorothy Heyward to Peggy Lamson, January 21, 1951, DKH Papers, SCHS, folder 180.01.03.04(C)04-27; autobiographical notes re. *Cygnets*, DKH Papers, SCHS, folder 180.01.03.04(C)04-28.

Chapter 18. *A Candle for St. Jude*

1. Dorothy Heyward to Helen Hayes, April 27, 1951, DKH Papers, SCHS, folder 180.01.01(Misc.)01-01. Dorothy Heyward to Karen Horney, April 10, 1950, Jenifer Heyward Wood Papers, SCHS, folder 181.01.91.01; Dorothy Heyward to Rumer Godden, November 30, 1950, DKH Papers, SCHS, folder 180.01.03.04(C)04-27. Although she wrote "Rosemary Benét" in her letter, she may have meant her brother-in-law's wife, Marjorie Benét. In this period of her life, Dorothy constantly rewrote narratives, sometimes in letters and sometimes just to herself; the same exact wording of phrases, sentences, and paragraphs is repeated verbatim in many texts, this explaining the designation of "autobiographical notes re *Cygnets*" in the notes below, along with specific letter references. Confusing the matter further is that papers from this era of her life are present in two places in her collection, some in the works series under *Cygnets* and some in the correspondence series under Godden.
2. "Mrs. Heyward Visits City, Reports on Doings of Herself and Daughter," *Charleston News and Courier*, April 1, 1951; DuBose Heyward to "Dorothy Dear," Saturday, United States Casualty Company stationery, DBH Papers, SCHS, folder 1172.01.01(H)03-02. Dorothy summarized much of this in a document she called "Dirty Doings at the Crossroads" in her autobiographical notes re *Cygnets*, DKH Papers, SCHS, folder 180.01.03.04(C)04-23; Dorothy Heyward to Peggy Lamson, January 21, 1951, DKH Papers, SCHS, folder 180.01.03.04(C)04-27.
3. Autobiographical notes re *Cygnets* beginning "FIRST MEETING," DKH Papers, SCHS, folder 180.01.03.04(C)04-24. All subsequent quotes in this note citing this folder are from this document; Dorothy Heyward to Audrey Wood, July 17, [1949], DKH Papers, SCHS, folder 180.01.01.0(W)07-03; Chisolm, *Rumer Godden*, 219–20; Autobiographical notes, DKH Papers, SCHS, folder 180.01.03.04(C)04-24; Chisolm, *Rumer Godden*, 220.
4. All quotes are from autobiographical notes, DKH Papers, SCHS, folder 180.01.03.04(C)04-24; fingers: autobiographical notes, "Prologue: Dirty Doings at the Crossroads," DKH Papers, SCHS, folder 180.01.03.04(C)04-23; Chisolm, *Rumer Godden*, passim.
5. Autobiographical notes re *Cygnets*, DKH Papers, SCHS, folder 180.01.03.04(C)04-24; Dorothy Heyward to Audrey Wood, July 3, 1950, and Rumer Godden to Dorothy Heyward, October 18, 1950, both DKH Papers, SCHS, folder 180.01.01.01(G)02-01.
6. Autobiographical notes re *Cygnets*, DKH Papers, SCHS, folder 180.01.03.04(C)04-24; Dorothy Heyward to Audrey Wood, July 3, 1950, DKH Papers, SCHS, folder 180.01.01.01(G)02-01.
7. Dorothy Heyward to Marjorie Benét ["Beloved Marge"] February 11, [1950], DKH Papers, SCHS, folder 180.01.03.04(C)04-22; Godden, *Candle for St. Jude*, 211; Kissell, *David Merrick*; Dorothy Heyward to Marjorie Benét, December 21, [1950], DKH Papers, SCHS, folder 180.01.03.04(C)04-28.
8. Autobiographical notes re *Cygnets*, DKH Papers, SCHS, folders 180.01.03.04(C)04-24 and 180.01.03.04(C)04-22; Jen: Dorothy Heyward to Rumer Godden, November 30, 1950, DKH Papers, SCHS, folder 180.01.03.04(C)04-26; odd: autobiographical notes re *Cygnets*, DKH Papers, SCHS, folder 180.01.03.04(C)04-22; Dorothy Heyward to Peggy Lamson, July 15, 1950, DKH Papers, SCHS, folder 180.01.93.04(C)04-26.
9. Kissell, *David Merrick*, passim; Dorothy Heyward to Peggy Lamson, July 15, 1950, DKH Papers, SCHS folder 180.01.93.04(C)04-26; Dorothy Heyward to Marjorie Benét, December 21 [1950], DKH Papers, SCHS, folder 180.01.03.04(C)04-28; autobiographical notes re *Cygnets*, DKH Papers, SCHS, folder 180.01.03.04(C)04-22.

Chapter 19. A Case for St. Jude
1. Dorothy Heyward to Rumer Godden, n.d., DKH Papers, SCHS, folder 180.01.01.01(G)02-03; Dorothy Heyward to Peggy Lamson, January 21, 1951, DKH Papers, SCHS, folder 180.01.03.04(C)04-27.
2. Screwball: Dorothy Heyward to Rumer Godden, July 14, 1950, DKH Papers, SCHS folder 180.01.01.01(G)02-01; Dorothy Heyward to Rumer Godden, n.d., DKH Papers, SCHS, folder 180.01.01.01(G)02-03; Dorothy Heyward to Dr. Atchley, December 24, 1950, DKH Papers, SCHS, folder 180.01.03.04(C)04-26; Dorothy Heyward to Rumer Godden, November 30, 1951, DKH Papers, SCHS, folder 180.01.01.01(G)02-03.
3. Islands: Dorothy Heyward to Rumer Godden, November 30, 1951, DKH Papers, SCHS, folder 180.01.01.01(G)02-03; Dorothy Heyward to Dr. Atchley, December 24, 1950, DKH Papers, SCHS, folder 180.01.03.04(C)04-26; Dorothy Heyward to Peggy Lamson, January 21, 1951, DKH Papers, SCHS, folder 180.01.03.04(C)04-07; Dorothy Heyward to Marjorie Benét, December 12, [1950], DKH Papers, SCHS, folder 180.01.03.04(C)04-28.
4. She claims nine physicians in her letter to Peggy Lamson, March 17, 1951, DKH Papers, SCHS, folder 180.01.01.01(C)01-01; DKH to Marjorie Benét, December 12, [1950], DKH Papers, SCHS, folder 180.01.03.04(C)04-28; her corpse: DKH to Rumer Godden, November 30, 1950, DKH Papers, SCHS, and DeJagers: DKH to Peggy Lamson, July 15, 1950, both DKH Papers, SCHS folder 180.01.03.04(C)04-26; Sharp and encourage: Dorothy Heyward to Rumer Godden, December 17, 1950, and Dorothy Heyward to Rumer Godden, November 30, 1951, both DKH Papers, SCHS, folder 180.01.01.01(G)02-03.
5. Dorothy Heyward to Dr. Atchley, December 24, 1950, DKH Papers, SCHS, folder 180.01.03.04(C)04-26; Dorothy Heyward to Rumer Godden, December 17, 1950, DKH Papers, SCHS, folder 180.01.01.01(G)02-03. Fragment of letter, Dorothy Heyward to Rumer Godden, March 8, 1951, DKH Papers, SCHS, folder 180.01.01(G)02-02. DuBose: Dorothy Heyward to Peggy Lamson, January 21, 1951, DKH Papers, SCHS, folder 180.01.03.04(C)04-27.
6. Dorothy Heyward to Marjorie Benét, February 11, 1951, DKH Papers, SCHS, folder 180.01.03.04(C)04-22; Dorothy Heyward to Rumer Godden, March 8, 1951, DKH Papers, SCHS, folder 180.01.01(G)02-02; "Mrs. Heyward Visits City, Reports on Doings of Herself and Daughter," *Charleston News and Courier*, April 1, 1951.
7. Dorothy Heyward to Rumer Godden, April 2, 1951, DKH Papers, SCHS, folder 180.01.01(G)02-02; Dorothy Heyward to Peggy Lamson April 26, 1951, DKH Papers, SCHS, folder 180.01.01.01(Misc.)01-01; Dorothy Heyward to Rumer Godden, March 8, 1951, DKH folders, SCHS, folder 180.01.01(G)02-02.
8. Dorothy Heyward to Rumer Godden, April 2, 1951, DKH Papers, SCHS, 180.01.01(G)02-02; "Mrs. Heyward Visits City, Reports on Doings of Herself and Daughter," *Charleston News and Courier*, April 1, 1951; Godden, *House with Four*; Chisolm, *Rumer Godden*, 241–42. Was Dorothy an alcoholic? She noted getting tipsy on champagne when entertaining Somerset Maugham, and Lawrence Langner accused her of drinking too much to explain her behavior during a crisis during *Set My People Free*. Only in one letter, and it is at this point of her life, does she describe being drunk; so delighted to be regaining her health, at her first dinner party after the rest home, she said she overindulged in drinking, thinking she was being clever as she described her collapse, but apparently her listeners found it disturbing: Dorothy Heyward to Peggy Lamson, March 7, 1951, DKH Papers, SCHS, folder 180.01.01.01(L)01-01. The evidence of her

having a drinking problem is not conclusive; instead, it seems more likely that being underweight and using pills to sleep, she quickly showed the effects of drinking small amounts. Ira Gershwin's biographer notes Ira's and many others' overuse of prescription drugs in this era (Owen, *Ira Gershwin*, 226); Widdemer, *Golden Friends*, 94.

Chapter 20. Operatic

1. Fragments of letters, Dorothy Heyward to Rumer Godden, DKH Papers, SCHS, folder 180.01.01(G)02-02; DKH to Audrey Wood, August 5, 1951, and Audrey Wood to Dorothy Heyward, August 16, 1951, DKH Papers, SCHS, folder 180.01.01(W)07-01; Dorothy Heyward to Thornton Wilder, February 12, 1951, DKH Papers, SCHS, folder 180.01.01(W)05-01, and earlier Karamu correspondence, with DKH's letter to Jed Harris, unopened and returned by the post office, DKH Papers, SCHS, folder 180.01.03.04(S)01-97.
2. Audrey Wood to Dorothy Heyward, August 16, 1951, DKH Papers, SCHS, folder 180.01.01(W)07-01; "Kay Swift to Dorothy Heyward, August 2, 1959," https://onlineexhibits.library.yale.edu/s/swift/item/6720; Rorem, *Settling the Score*, 12–13; untitled squib, *Charleston News and Courier*, September 25, 1961, 6.
3. Dorothy Heyward to Rumer Godden, July 25, 1951, DKH Papers, SCHS, folder 180.01.01(G)02-02; https://en.wikipedia.org/wiki/Nicolai_Berezowsky, December 25, 2022; for information on the opera and correspondence, see DKH Papers, SCHS, folder 180.01.03.04(B)01-05; the quotes from the newspapers are reproduced in "Babar the Elephant: Opera for Children in One Act," promotional brochure, author's collection; Berezowsky, *Babar the Elephant*.
4. Dorothy Heyward to Jenifer Heyward, n.d., DKH Papers, SCHS, folder 180.01.01(H)01-04; Dorothy Heyward to Margaret Neeson, n.d., DKH Papers, SCHS, folder 180.01.01(N)01-01; Dorothy Heyward to Marian MacDowell, January 19, 1955, Marian MacDowell Papers, Library of Congress.
5. Dorothy Heyward to Jenifer Heyward, June 27, 1952, Jenifer Heyward Wood Papers, SCHS, 181.01.01.03; Dorothy Heyward to "Jo" [Josephine Pinckney?], December 3, 1955, DKH Papers, SCHS, folder 180.01.01(Misc.)01-02; Dorothy Heyward to Marian MacDowell, December 8, 1955, Marian MacDowell Papers, Library of Congress.
6. Dorothy Heyward to Helen Hayes (Mrs. Charles MacArthur), April 27, 1950, DKH Papers, SCHS, 180.01.01(Misc.)01-01; Bryan Collier, "Dock Street Theatre to Stage DuBose Heyward's Play 'Porgy,'" *Charleston News and Courier*, May 8, 1952; "Dock Street Cancels Production of 'Porgy,'" *Charleston News and Courier*, March 17, 1954, 1; "Seating 'About Face' Shocks Fourteen Members of 'Porgy' Cast," *Charleston News and Courier*, March 21, 1954, 4; "'Porgy' Cancelled over Segregation," *New York Times*, March 23, 1954, Thomas R. Waring Jr. Papers, SCHS, folder 23/405/2.
7. Washington Correspondent, "Verbal Slip Has Mrs. Heyward as Mystery Writer," and "Broadcasters' Music Policy Attacked by Mrs. Heyward," both *Charleston News and Courier*, May 20, 1958; Dorothy Heyward to Burnet Maybank, October 16, 1951, DKH Papers, SCHS, folder 180.01.01(Misc.)01-02; Dorothy Heyward to Annie and Junior Hartzell, May 18, [1958], DKH Papers, SCHS, folder 180.01.01.01(H)01-01.
8. Josephine Pinckney to Dorothy Heyward, February 7, n.d.; and June 26, [1951], DKH Papers, SCHS, folder 180.01.01(P)02-01. Dorothy is cast in more racist light in Noonan, *Strange Career*, 249–52, although Noonan's suggestion that Dorothy is incredulous about the claims really refers to her wondering why the family did not support him in his life but were doing so after his death. Her letters to Marian MacDowell in the 1950s have constant references to her contributing to the Colony, with her even chairing Mrs.

MacDowell's ninety-fifth birthday celebration; in her letter of May 29, 1955, she refers to more contributions in DuBose's name. Marian MacDowell Papers, Library of Congress. Dorothy Heyward to Annie and Junior Hartzell, August 25, 1959, DKH Papers, SCHS, folder 180.01.01.01(H)01-01.

Chapter 21. *Porgy* and Business
1. For a fuller description of the opera's peregrinations, see Alpert, *Life and Times*; heirs, Guild, etc.: Alpert, *Life and Times*, 147–48; Dorothy Heyward to Audrey Wood, September 14, 1951, DKH Papers, SCHS, 180.01.01.01(W)07-01; Alpert, *Life and Times*, 152, 150.
2. Robert Breen correspondence, DKH Papers, SCHS, folders 180.01.01.01(B)05-01/10, especially 05-06. Alpert, *Life and Times*, 163, refers to Breen going back to the novel for dialogue, but with not much dialogue there, it had to have been the play (153, 155). Dorothy Heyward to Jenifer Heyward, March 17, 1952, Jenifer Heyward Wood Papers, SCHS, folder 181.01.01-03.
3. Alpert, *Life and Times*, 157; Hanna, "Tiptoeing," 110; Alpert, *Life and Times*, quoting Ella Gerber, 162; Hanna, "Tiptoeing," 110; Dorothy Heyward to Robert Breen, August 12, 1952, DKH Papers, SCHS, folder 180.01.01.01(B)05-02; "Dance Version of 'Porgy': Young N.Y. interracial ballet group scores hit with show," *Ebony*, September 1958, 99–100.
4. Alpert, *Life and Times*, 177, 180, 183, 243, 185; Hanna, "Tiptoeing," 115; lie: "Awards Cost Dorothy Heyward Midnight Oil," clipping in DuBose Heyward vertical file, Charleston County Public Library, ascribed to the *Christian Science Mentor* [sic] *Magazine*, 1943; Dorothy Heyward to Josephine Pinckney, February 11, 1955, DKH Papers, SCHS, folder 180.01.01.01(Misc.)01-02; Dorothy Heyward to Patti Whitelaw, February 11, 1955, DKH Papers, SCHS, 180.01.01.01(Misc.)01-02.
5. Alpert, *Life and Times*, 203; Dorothy Heyward to Marian MacDowell, December 8, 1955, DKH Papers, SCHS 180.01.01.01(Misc.)01-02; Dorothy Heyward to Marjorie Neeson, June 2, 1956, DKH Papers, SCHS folder, 180.01.01.01(N)01-01.
6. Dorothy Heyward to Ashley Halsey, n.d., Jenifer Heyward Wood Papers, SCHS, folder 181.01.01.06; Robert Breen to Dorothy Heyward, September 22, 1956, DKH Papers, SCHS, folder 180.01.01.01(B)05-05; Dorothy Heyward to Jenifer Heyward, March 14, 1956, Jenifer Heyward Wood Papers, SCHS, folder 181.01.01.05.
7. Dorothy Heyward to Junior and Annie Hartzell, March 14, 1956, DKH Papers, SCHS, folder 180.01.01.01(H)01-01; Dorothy Heyward to Ashley Halsey, December 6, 1956, Jenifer Heyward Wood Papers, SCHS, folder 181.01.01.05; Dorothy Heyward to Robert Breen, March 10, 1956, DKH Papers, SCHS, folder 180.01.01.01(B)05-06; Hanna, "Tiptoeing," 156; Dorothy Heyward to Dana, October 2, 1957, Jenifer Heyward Wood Papers, SCHS, folder 181.01.01.06; her image appears on page 76 in William Francis Guess, "South Carolina," *Holiday*, December 1956, 75–81, 124–25, 127–30, 132–33.
8. Dorothy Heyward to Marian MacDowell, June 20, 1956, DKH Papers, SCHS, 180.01.01.01(M)01-01; Dorothy Heyward to Dana, October 2, 1957, Jenifer Heyward Wood Papers, SCHS, folder 181.01.01.06; Dorothy Heyward to Josephine Pinckney, February 25, 1956, DKH Papers, SCHS, folder 180.01.01.01(P)02-01; Hanna, "Tiptoeing," 108.
9. Dorothy Heyward to Josephine Pinckney, February 25, 1956, DKH Papers, SCHS, folder 180.01.01.01(P)02-01; Dorothy Heyward to Robert Breen, November 17, 1957, DKH Papers, SCHS, folder 180.01.01.01(B)05-06; Audrey Wood to Robert Breen, February 14, 1955, DKH Papers, SCHS, folder 180.01.01.01(W)07-02; Alpert, *Life and Times*, 253, 244.

10. Robert E. Dustin, general manager, *Porgy and Bess* Company, to John Rumsey, American Play Company, July 19, 1956, DKH Papers, SCHS, folder 180.01.01.01(B)05-06; (50 percent went to the estate of Rose Gershwin, 10 percent to Ira, 20 percent to Dorothy and another 20 percent to her, being DuBose's heir); John Rumsey to Dorothy Heyward, December 11, 1956, and December 15, 1953, DKH Papers, SCHS, folder 180.01.0101(R)02-01; "owner": Owen, *Ira Gershwin*, 253; Dorothy Heyward to Thomas R. Waring Jr., April 28, 1953, DKH Papers, SCHS, folder 180.01.01.01(W)01-01.
11. Alpert, *Life and Times*, 244, 250; Owen, *Ira Gershwin*, 221; Lazar and Tapert, *Swifty*, 111–12; Alpert, *Life and Times*, 250–53, 284–85; Lazar, *Swifty*, 117–18.

Chapter 22. Home

1. Deposition, DKH Papers, SCHS, folder 180.01.01(R)02-03; Dorothy Heyward to Mr. Leavy, June 29, 1957; Dorothy Heyward to Eddie Colton, n.d. [late August 1957], DKH Papers, SCHS, folder 180.010.01.01(C)02-03; Dorothy Heyward to Audrey Wood, August 9, 1957, and August 16, 1957, DKH Papers, SCHS, folder 180.01.01.01(W)07-02; Owen, *Ira Gershwin*, 253.
2. Dorothy Heyward to Thomas R. Waring Jr., April 28, 1953, DKH Papers, SCHS, folder 180.01.01.01(W)01-0; Alpert, *Life and Times*, 286; Dorothy Heyward to Audrey Wood, August 16, 1957, DKH Papers, SCHS, folder 180.01.01.01(W)07-02; Alpert, *Life and Times*, 260; Dorothy Heyward to Audrey Wood, August 9, 1957, DKH Papers, SCHS, folder 180.01.01.01(W)07-02; fragment of letter of Dorothy Heyward to Audrey Wood, DKH Papers, SCHS, folder 180.01.01.01(W)07-03.
3. Hanna, "Tiptoeing," 109, 117; Alpert, *Life and Times*, 259–67; Hutchisson, *DuBose Heyward*, 168; Hanna, "Tiptoeing," 118–19, 121, 118; the suntan lotion was one of the promotional items produced for the 2012 musical (nonoperatic) revival of *The Gershwins' Porgy and Bess* with actress Audra McDonald (author's collection).
4. Alpert, *Life and Times*, 276–82, 286; Dorothy Heyward to Richard Roberts of Bantam Books, n.d. (January 1959), DKH Papers, SCHS, 180.01.01.01(Misc.)01-03; Dorothy Heyward to Audrey Wood, April 2, 1956, DKH Papers, folder 180.01.01.01(W)07-02; Dorothy Heyward to Margaret Neeson, August 2, 1956, DKH Papers, SCHS, folder 180.01.01.01(N)01-01.
5. Harold E. Whipple to Dorothy Heyward, April 6, 1956, and Dorothy Heyward to Harold Whipple, June 2, 1956, DKH Papers, SCHS, folder 180.01.01.01(W)03-01; Dorothy Heyward to Josephine Pinckney, February 25, DKH Papers, SCHS, folder 180.01.01.01(P)02-01.
6. Heyward, "Porgy's Goat," 41; Dorothy Heyward to Jenifer Heyward, May 11, (1958), DKH Papers, SCHS folder 180.01.01.01(Misc.)01-03; Durham, *DuBose Heyward*, 126; Dorothy Heyward to Sue Hastings, August 25, 1959, DKH Papers, SCHS, folder 180.01.01.01(Misc.)01-03; the contract is in Dorothy Heyward Papers, SCHS, folder 180.01.04.03.03-31.
7. Dorothy Heyward to Marian MacDowell, April 3, 1952, Marian MacDowell Papers, Library of Congress; Dorothy Heyward to Mary [Howe], October 4, 1949, and letter from National Phoenix Theatre Company to Dorothy Heyward, August 16, 1961, DKH Papers, SCHS, folder 180.01.01.01(MISC)01-03.
8. "Mrs. Heyward Visits City, Reports On Doings of Herself and Daughter," *Charleston News and Courier*, April 1, 1951, 27; "Dorothy Heyward," *Charleston News and Courier*, November, 22, 1961, 10; "Heyward and Other Papers Donated to Historical Society," *Charleston News and Courier*, June 13, 1951, 19; "Mrs. Heyward, 71, Playwright, Dies: Co-Author of Drama That Became 'Porgy and Bess,'" *New York Times*, November 20, 1961, 31. The *NYT* was one of the few papers (and possibly the only one) to mention her unfinished autobiography.

Afterword
1. Owen, *Ira Gershwin*, 285; Watson, *History of Southern Drama*, 122–32; McDonald and Paige, *Southern Women Playwrights*.
2. Hanna, "Tiptoeing," 105.
3. Dorothy Heyward, "Foreword," in Heyward, *Porgy*, n.p.
4. Frank, *Folly Beach*.

WORKS CITED

Archival Collections

Aaron Kramer Papers, University of Michigan Special Collections Research Center
Author's Collection
City of Charleston Police Records, Charleston Library Society
Dock Street Theatre Papers, South Carolina Historical Society
Dorothy K. Heyward Papers, South Carolina Historical Society
DuBose Heyward Papers, South Carolina Historical Society
George and Ira Gershwin Papers, Library of Congress
James Southall Wilson Papers, University of Virginia Libraries
John Bennett Papers, South Carolina Historical Society
Marian MacDowell Papers, Library of Congress
Miscellaneous Manuscript Series, South Carolina Historical Society
Paul Green Papers, Southern Historical Collection, University of North Carolina–Chapel Hill
Theatre Guild Archive, Beinecke Rare Book and Manuscript Library, Yale University
Thomas R. Waring Jr. Papers, South Carolina Historical Society
Vertical Files, Charleston County Public Library, South Carolina Room

Published Works

Allan, Glenn. *Boysi Himself*. New York: Samuel Curl, 1946.
Alpert, Hollis. *The Life and Times of Porgy and Bess: The Story of an American Classic*. New York: Knopf, 1990.
Anderson, Isaac. "New Mystery Stories." *New York Times Book Review*, April 24, 1932.
Bach, Steven. *Dazzler: The Life and Times of Moss Hart*. New York: Knopf, 2001.
Bailey, Rosalie Vincent. "DuBose Heyward: Poet, Novelist, Playwright." Master's thesis, Duke University, 1941.
Barranger, Milly S. *A Gambler's Instinct: The Story of Broadway Producer Cheryl Crawford*. Carbondale: Southern Illinois University Press, 2010.
Beeston, J. L. "Christina," *Grand Magazine* 13, no. 77 (July 1911): 587–95.
Bellows, Barbara. *A Talent for Living: Josephine Pinckney and the Charleston Literary Tradition*. Baton Rouge: Louisiana State University Press, 2006.
Bennett, John, ed. *The Year Book of the Poetry Society of South Carolina, 1925*. Columbia: State, 1925.

Berezowsky, Nicolai. *Babar the Elephant Vocal Score: Story Based on the Babar Stories by Jean de Brunhoff, Libretto by Dorothy Heyward, Lyrics by Judith Randal*. Boston: Carl Fischer, 1952.

Bordman, Gerald, and Thomas S. Hischack, eds. *Oxford Companion to American Theatre*. 3rd ed. New York: Oxford University Press, 2004.

Brown, Jared. *Moss Hart: A Prince of the Theatre: A Biography in Three Acts*. New York: Back Stage, 2006.

"Cheryl Crawford Presents George Gershwin's Immortal 'Porgy and Bess.'" n.d. (1942).

Chisolm, Anne. *Rumer Godden: A Storyteller's Life*. London: Macmillan, 1998.

Clark, Emily. "Dubose [sic] Heyward." *Virginia Quarterly Review* 6, no. 4 (Autumn 1930): 546–56.

——. *Innocence Abroad*. New York: Knopf, 1934.

Cohen, Rose. *Out of the Shadow*. New York: George H. Doran, 1918.

Cooper, John Webb. "A Comparative Study of *Porgy*, the Novel, *Porgy*, the Play, and *Porgy and Bess*, the Opera." Master's thesis, Columbia University, 1950.

Coven, Brenda. "Heyward, Dorothy Hartzell (1890–1961)." *American Women Dramatists of the Twentieth Century: A Bibliography*, 112–13. Metuchen: Scarecrow, 1982.

Crawford, Cheryl. *One Naked Individual: My Fifty Years in the Theatre*. Indianapolis: Bobbs-Merrill, 1977.

Creighton, Nannie Elizabeth. "DuBose Heyward and His Contribution to Literature." Master's thesis, University of South Carolina, 1933.

"Dance Version of 'Porgy': Young N.Y. Interracial Ballet Group Scores Hit with Show." *Ebony* 13, no. 11 (September 1958): 99–100.

"Daughter of Mamba." *New York Times*, January 1, 1939.

De Graff, Melissa J. "Searching for 'Authenticity' in Paul Bowles's *Denmark Vesey*." In *Blackness in Opera*, ed. Naomi Andrei, 187–211. Urbana: University of Illinois Press, 2012.

Delson, Susan. *Dudley Murphy: Hollywood Wild Card*. Minneapolis: University of Minnesota Press, 2006.

Dock Street Theatre, Charleston, South Carolina, 1736–1939: Annual Playwriting Awards Program. Charleston: Furlong, 1939.

Dolinar, Brian. *The Black Cultural Front: Black Writers and Artists of the Depression Generation*. Jackson: University Press of Mississippi, 2012.

Durham, Francis Marion (Frank). "DuBose Heyward: The Southerner as Artist, a Critical and Biographical Study." PhD diss., Columbia University, 1953.

——. *DuBose Heyward: The Man Who Wrote Porgy*. Columbia: University of South Carolina Press, 1954.

"First U.S. Theatre Is Restored: Charleston Blue Bloods Give It a Gala Opening." *Life* 3, no. 25 (December 20, 1937): 49–50.

Fordham, Damon. "Samuel Smalls: The Man Who Inspired Porgy." In *Porgy and Bess: A Charleston Story*, ed. Harlan Greene, 25–31. Charleston: Home House, 2016.

Frank, Dorothy Benton. *Folly Beach*. New York: William Morrow, 2011.

Gergel, Richard. *Unexampled Courage: The Blinding of Sgt. Isaac Woodard and the Awakening of President Harry S. Truman and Judge J. Waties Waring*. New York: Farrar, Straus & Giroux, 2019.

Gershwin, George. "Rhapsody in Catfish Row: Mr. Gershwin Tells the Origins and Scheme for His Music in the New Folk Opera called 'Porgy and Bess.'" *New York Times*, October 20, 1935, X, 1–2.

Gershwin, George, DuBose Heyward, and Ira Gershwin. *Porgy and Bess: Vocal Score*. New York: Gershwin, [1935?].

———. *The Theatre Guild Presents Porgy and Bess*. New York: Gershwin, 1935.

Gershwin, Ira. *Lyrics on Several Occasions*. New York: Knopf, 1959.

Godden, Rumer. *A Candle for St. Jude*. New York: Viking, 1948.

———. *A House with Four Rooms*. New York: Quill / William Morrow, 1989.

Greene, Harlan. "Charleston Childhood: The First Years of DuBose Heyward." *South Carolina Historical Magazine* 83, no. 2 (April 1982): 154–67.

———. "'The Little Shining Word': From Porgo to Porgy." *South Carolina Historical Magazine* 87, no. 1 (January 1986): 75–81.

———. *Mr. Skylark: John Bennett and the Charleston Renaissance*. Athens: University of Georgia Press, 2001.

Guess, William Francis. "South Carolina." *Holiday* 20, no. 6 (December 1956): 75–81, 124–25, 127–30, 132–33.

Hanna, Elizabeth. "'Tiptoeing in Their Footsteps': Dorothy Heyward's Unpublished Autobiography." Master's thesis, College of Charleston, 2005.

Helburn, Theresa. *A Wayward Quest: The Autobiography of Theresa Helburn*. Boston: Little, Brown, 1960.

Hergesheimer, Joseph. "Charleston." *Saturday Evening Post* 200, no. 2 (July 9, 1927): 10–11, 44, 46, 49.

———. *Quiet Cities*. New York: Knopf, 1933.

Heyward, Dorothy. "Denmark Vesey—Whose Life Was a 'True Thriller.'" *New York Star*, October 31, 1948.

———. *Love in a Cupboard: Comedy in One Act*. New York: Samuel French, 1926.

———. "'Nancy Ann' and Some Others by Dorothy Heyward author of 'Nancy Ann.'" *New York Times*, April 6, 1924.

———. "Porgy's Goat." *Harper's Magazine* 215, no. 1291 (December 1957): 37–41.

———. "Porgy's Native Tongue." *New York Times*, December 4, 1927, X2.

———. *The Pulitzer Prize Murders*. New York: Farrar & Rinehart, 1932.

———. *Three-a-Day*. New York: Century, 1930.

———. "The Young Ghost." *McCall's* 55, no. 5 (February 1928): 22–24, 101–2.

Heyward, Dorothy, and Dorothy DeJagers. *Little Girl Blue: A Romantic Comedy in a Prologue and Three Acts*. New York: Samuel French, 1931.

Heyward, Dorothy, and DuBose Heyward. *Mamba's Daughters: A Play*. New York: Farrar & Rinehart, 1939.

———. *Porgy: A Play in Four Acts, from the Novel by Dubose* [sic] *Heyward* Garden City: Doubleday, Doran, 1927.

———. *Porgy: A Play in Four Acts from the Novel by Dubose* [sic] *Heyward: With an Introduction on the American Negro in Art*. Garden City: Doubleday, Doran, 1928.

Heyward, DuBose. "And Once Again—the Negro." *Reviewer* 4 (October 1923): 39–42.

———. *Mamba's Daughters*. New York: Doubleday, Doran, 1929.

———. "The Negro in the Low-Country." In *The Carolina Low-Country*, ed. Augustine T. Smythe, 171–87. New York: Macmillan, 1931.

———. *Porgy*. New York: George H. Doran, 1925.

———. *Porgy: A Novel* [with foreword by Dorothy Heyward]. Garden City: Doubleday, 1953.

——— "Porgy and Bess Return on Wings of Song." *Stage* 13, no. 1 (October 1935): 25–28.

———. *Skylines and Horizons*. New York: Macmillan, 1924.

———. *Star Spangled Virgin*. New York: Farrar & Rinehart, 1939.

Heyward, DuBose, and Hervey Allen. *Carolina Chansons: Legends of the Low Country*. New York: Macmillan, 1922.

Heyward, DuBose, and Marjorie Flack (illustrator). *The Country Bunny and the Little Gold Shoes: As Told to Jenifer*. Boston: Houghton Mifflin, 1939.

Heyward, Janie Screven. *Wild Roses*. New York: Neale, 1905.

Hicks, Brian. *In Darkest South Carolina: J. Waties Waring and the Secret Plan That Sparked a Civil Rights Movement*. Charleston: Evening Post, 2018.

Higginson, Thomas Wentworth. "Denmark Vesey." Los Angeles: John Henry and Mary Louisa Dunn Bryant Foundation, 1962.

"His Majesty's Theatre, by arrangement with the Daniel Mayer Company and the Theatre Guild, New York City, Charles B. Cochran and Crosby Gaige Have the honour to announce the original Theatre Guild cast and production of Porgy, a Folk Play, by DuBose & Dorothy Heyward." 1929.

Horowitz, Joseph. *"On My Way": The Untold Story of Rouben Mamoulian, George Gershwin and Porgy and Bess*. New York: Norton, 2013.

Hughes, Langston, and Milton Meltzer. *Black Magic: A Pictorial History of the African-American in the Performing Arts*. New York: Da Capo, 1990.

Hutchisson, James M. *DuBose Heyward: A Charleston Gentleman and the World of Porgy and Bess*. Jackson: University Press of Mississippi, 2000.

———. *A DuBose Heyward Reader*. Athens: University of Georgia Press, 2003.

"An Interview with DuBose Heyward." *Coastal Topics*, May 1935, 6.

Kinne, Wismer. *George Pierce Baker and the American Theatre*. New York: Greenwood, 1968.

Kissell, Howard. *David Merrick: The Abominable Showman: The Unauthorized Biography*. New York: Applause, 1993.

Kramer, Aaron. *Denmark Vesey and Other Poems, Including Translations from the Yiddish*. New York: n.p., 1952.

Kuhns, Dorothy. "My Favorite Character in History." *St. Nicholas Magazine* 30, no. 8 (June 1903): 758.

Lamson, Peggy. *The Glorious Failure: Black Congressman Robert Brown Elliott and the Reconstruction in South Carolina*. New York: Norton, 1973.
——— *Respectfully Yours: A Comedy in Three Acts*. New York: Samuel French, 1947.
Lazar, Irving, and Annette Tapert. *Swifty: My Life and Good Times*. New York: Simon & Schuster, 1995.
Lewisohn, Ludwig. *The Golden Vase*. New York: Harper, 1931.
Lynch, Christopher. "Cheryl Crawford's *Porgy and Bess*: Navigating Cultural Hierarchy." *Journal of the Society for American Music* 10, no. 5 (2016): 331–63.
Macgowan, Kenneth, ed. *Famous American Plays of the 1920s*. New York: Dell, 1959.
"Mamba's Daughters: Ethel Waters, Queen of the Blues, Makes Her First Dramatic Hit." *Life* 6, no. 4 (January 23, 1939): 49–51.
Mamoulian, Rouben. "I Remember." In *George Gershwin*, ed. Merle Armitage, 47–57. New York: Longmans, Green, 1938.
Mantle, Burns. *The Best Plays of 1927–1928*. New York: Dodd, Mead, 1928.
McClintic, Guthrie. *Me and Kit*. Boston: Little, Brown, 1955.
McDonald, J. Fred, ed. *Richard Durham's Destination Freedom: Scripts from Radio's Black Legacy, 1948–50*. New York: Prager, 1989.
McDonald, Robert L., and Linda Rohrer Paige. *Southern Women Playwrights: New Essays in Literary History and Criticism*. Tuscaloosa: University of Alabama Press, 2002.
McKee, Nancy. *Valiant Woman*. San Antonio: Naylor, 1962.
Metcalf, Paul. *Appalache*. Berkeley: Turtle Island Foundation, 1976.
Miller, Gabriel. *The Films of Martin Ritt*. Jackson: University Press of Mississippi, 2000.
Mitchell, Verner D., and Cynthia Davis. *Literary Sisters: Dorothy West and Her Circle: A Biography of the Harlem Renaissance*. New Brunswick: Rutgers University Press, 2012.
Molloy, Robert. *The Reunion*. Garden City: Doubleday, 1959.
Mosel, Tad, Gertrude Macy, and Martha Graham. *Leading Lady: The World and Theatre of Katharine Cornell*. Boston: Little, Brown, 1978.
Noonan, Ellen. *The Strange Career of Porgy and Bess: Race, Culture, and America's Most Famous Opera*. Chapel Hill: University of North Carolina Press, 2012.
Owen, Michael. *Ira Gershwin: A Life in Words*. New York: Liveright, 2025.
Reuss, Richard A. "American Folksongs and Left-Wing Politics, 1935–56." *Journal of the Folklore Institute* 12, nos. 2/3 (1975): 89–111.
Rhett, Blanche, and Lettie Gay. *Two Hundred Years of Charleston Cooking*. New York: Random House, 1934.
Richie, Belle MacDiarmid. *His Blue Serge Suit and Other Plays*. Boston: B. J. Brimmer, 1924.
Rorem, Ned. *Settling the Score: Essays on Music*. New York: Harcourt, Brace, Jovanovich, 1988.
Schiff, David. "The Man Who Breathed Life into 'Porgy and Bess.'" *New York Times*, March 5, 2000, section 2, 35.
Shafer, Yvonne. "Dorothy Heyward (1890–1961)." In *American Women Playwrights, 1900–1950*, 395–402. New York: Peter Lang, 1995.

Shirley, Wayne. "Porgy and Bess." *Quarterly Journal of the Library of Congress* 31, no. 2 (April 1974): 97–107.

Slavick, William. *DuBose Heyward*. Boston: Twayne, 1981.

Smith, Chard Powers. *Where the Light Falls: A Portrait of Edwin Arlington Robinson*. New York: Macmillan, 1965.

Smith, Mona Z. *Becoming Something: The Story of Canada Lee*. New York: Faber & Faber, 2004.

Stewart, Ollie. "An American Opera Conquers Europe." *Theatre Arts* 39, no. 10 (October 1955): 30–64, 93–94.

Stovall, Genie Orchard. *A Son of Carolina*. New York: Neale, 1909.

Theatre Guild Anthology. New York: Random House, 1936.

"Theatre Guild Program: *Porgy* by Dorothy and DuBose Heyward at the Guild Theatre." 1927.

"This Week's Census." *Jet* 7, no. 14 (February 10, 1955): 49.

Thompson, Robin. *The Gershwins' Porgy and Bess: A 75th Anniversary Celebration*. Milwaukee: Amadeus, 2010.

van Notten, Eleonore. *Wallace Thurman's Harlem Renaissance*. Amsterdam: Editions Rodopi, 1994.

Vorse, Mary Heaton. *Strike!* New York: Horace Liveright, 1930.

Waters, Ethel, with Charles Samuels. *His Eye Is on the Sparrow: An Autobiography*. Garden City: Doubleday, 1951.

Watson, Charles S. *The History of Southern Drama*. Lexington: University Press of Kentucky, 1997.

West, Dorothy. *The Living Is Easy*. New York: Feminist Press, 1996.

West, Rebecca. *Ending in Earnest: A Literary Log*. New York: Doubleday, Doran, 1931.

White, Edward. *The Tastemaker: Carl Van Vechten and the Birth of Modern America*. New York: Farrar, Straus & Giroux, 2014.

Widdemer, Margaret. *Golden Friends I Had: Unrevised Memories of Margaret Widdemer*. Garden City: Doubleday, 1964.

Williams, Susan Millar. *A Devil and a Good Woman, Too: The Lives of Julia Peterkin*. Athens: University of Georgia Press, 1997.

Wood, Audrey, with Max Wilk. *Represented by Audrey Wood*. Garden City: Doubleday, 1981.

Woods, Porter S. "The Negro on Broadway: The Transition Years, 1920–1930." PhD diss., Yale University, 1965.

Wyatt, Robert, and Andrew Johnson, eds. *The George Gershwin Reader*. New York: Oxford University Press, 2004.

Yezierska, Anzia. "Wild Winter Love." *Century Magazine* 113 (February 1927): 485–91.

INDEX

Abbey Theatre (Dublin), 48
Abominable Showman, The (Kissel), 160
Academy Award, 140, 187
Academy of Music (Charleston), 26
Actor's Equity, 65
Actors' Studio, 132
Actors' Theatre, 47, 49
Adams, Maude, 3
Adler family, 24
Agnes Scott College, 26
Allan, Glenn, 136
Allen, Hervey, 15, 18, 20, 43, 55, 72, 109, 119; *Carolina Chansons* (with DuBose Heyward), 16, 205n4; collaborating with DuBose Heyward, 31, 36, 88
Alvin Theatre (New York City), 105
American Association of Museums, 190
American Ballet Theatre, 173
American Scholar magazine, 68
America's Sweethearts (Dorothy and DuBose Heyward), 109, 118
Ames, Winthrop, 7
And Arabella (Dorothy Heyward, DeJagers, and Eichler), 85; *Little Girl Blue*, 86. See also *Cinderelative, The; Poor Paulette*
"And Once Again —the Negro" (DuBose Heyward), 42
Anderson, Judith, 117
Angel (DuBose Heyward), 35
Angelou, Maya, 178
Arliss, George, 47
Art Theatre, Inc., 76
"Artistic Triumph, An" (DuBose Heyward), 14

As You Like It (Shakespeare), 141
Ashley Hall (Charleston), 129
Ashton, Winifred, 75
Astor, Nancy, 75
Atkins, Zoë, 6
Atkinson, Brooks, 68, 70, 117, 118, 149
"Average Woman, The" (DeJagers), 86

Babar the Elephant (Berezowsky, Dorothy Heyward, and Randal), 167, 168–69
Backer, Ferdi Legare (Waring), 157
Bagnold, Enid, 75
Bailey, Pearl, 185
Baker, George Pierce, 7, 8, 12, 13, 17, 18, 20, 21, 36, 48, 122, 133; as teacher, 10–11
Baldwin, James 168
Ballard, Fred, 205n13
Ballet Russe de Monte Carlo, 169, 178
Bankhead, Tallulah, 117
Banks, William (Bill), 162, 163, 178, 186–87
Barber, Mary Saxton, 2
Barnard Studio (MacDowell Colony), 30
Barnes, Howard, 149
Barretts of Wimpole Street, The (Besier), 114
Barry, Philip, 20, 204n2
Barrymore, Ethel, 47, 49
Barthe, Richmond, 209n4
Baruch, Bernard, 175
Bates, Esther Wilbur, 127
Bayard, Theodore, 74
Bayly, Mrs. William Hamilton (aunt), 4, 20

235

Bee in Her Bonnet (Lamson), 154, 218n5
Beerbohm, Max, 75
Beeston, L. J., 7
Bellak, George, 140
Belmont Prize. *See* Harvard Prize
Belmont Production Company, 21
Benchley, Robert C., 21
Benét, Marjorie Flack, 108, 126, 150, 152, 165, 192, 222n1
Benét, Rosemary, 153
Benét, William Rose, 108, 122, 126, 152, 154; *Day's End,* 121
Bennett, John, 18, 21, 26, 28, 43, 61, 70, 72, 73; attitude on race, 31; *Master Skylark,* 15; as mentor, 15, 18, 15, 31, 93
Bennett, Ralph, 57, 208–9n3
Bennett, Susan Smythe, 28, 72
Berezowsky, Nicolai, 168
Billboard, 87
Billy Budd (Melville), 140
Black Broder, The (Gonzales), 63, 214n6
Blackbirds (Broadway review), 110
Book of the Month Club, 160
Bookman, The (magazine), 49, 75
Boston Post, 98
Boston Red Sox, 75
Botkin, Henry, 215n10
Bowles, Paul, 92, 133
"Boysi" stories (Allan), 136, 160
Bragg, Laura, 129, 204n1
Brandt, George, 167
Brandt and Brandt literary agents, 77
Brass Ankle (DuBose Heyward), 89, 114, 120
Breen, Robert, 167, 185, 188, 190, 192; director of *Porgy and Bess,* 172–82 passim
Brooke, Clifford, 22
Brown, Anne, 115, 137
Brown Jackets (Jane Screven Heyward), 21
Brunhoff, Jean de, 167
Bubbles, John, 102
Burke, Billie, 21

Calloway, Cab, 173
Canby, Henry Seidel, 165
Canby, Marion, 165
Candle for St. Jude, A (Godden), 154, 155, 165. See also *Cygnets*
Capote, Truman, 178–79, 189, 191
Carmer, Betty, 126, 153
Carmer, Carl, 126
Carnegie Hall, 105
Carol, Diahann, 185
Carolina Art Association, 121, 139, 190
Carolina Chansons (DuBose Heyward and Allen), 16, 205n4
Carolina Inn (Summerville, S.C.), 180
Carolina Low-Country, 93, 146
Carolina Playmakers, 119
Carothers, Rachel, 6
Carriere, Albert, 122
Carter, Jack, 63
CBS (Columbia Broadcasting System), 168
Cello, Harp, and Violin (Dorothy Heyward), 7, 8, 11, 36, 77
Century Magazine, 52, 77
Century Play Company, 76, 82, 86–87, 138, 181
Century Publishing Company, 73, 77, 78, 81
"Charleston" (Hergesheimer), 92
Charleston, 1822 (Dorothy Heyward), 143. See also *Set My People Free*
Charleston County Hall, 170
Charleston Day School, 108, 129
Charleston Library Society, 93, 130
Charleston Museum, 120
Charleston News and Courier, 77, 192
Chicago Evening Post, 25, 90
Childress, Alice, 196
Christian Science Monitor, 25
"Christina" (Beeston), 7, 11
Church, Henry F., 170, 178
Church of the Transfiguration (New York City), 20
Cinderelative, The (Dorothy Heyward

and DeJagers), 76, 77, 81, 88, 93, 131; production and synopsis, 84–87. See also *Poor Paulette*
"Cinderelatives" (G. Gershwin), 76
Citadel, The, 129
Claflin College, 171
Clark, Barrett, 122
Clark, Emily, 17, 29
Clark, Philip, 140
Clayburgh, Julia, 154, 155, 157, 158, 159, 160, 166, 191
Cliburn, Van, 178
Clinkers (Klaw and Dorothy Heyward), 207n8
Clyde Line (steamships), 17, 59
Cochran, Charles B., 74
Coffin, Haskell, 177
Cohan, George M., 8, 12; as character in play, 23
Cohen, Octavus Roy, 31, 136; *Come Seven!*, 33, 49
Cohen, Rose Gollup, 30, 89; *Out of the Shadow*, 52
College Hero, The (play), 4
College of Charleston, 121, 129, 170
Collier's magazine, 189
Collins, Alan, 159
Colonial Theatre (Boston), 105
Colum, Padraic, 17
Columbia Pictures, 181
Columbia University, 8, 9
Come Seven! (O. R. Cohen), 33, 49
Confederate Home (Charleston), 206n9
Connelley, Marc, 86
Cornell, Katherine, 47, 114, 115, 116, 118. See also McClintic, Guthrie
County Bunny and the Little Gold Shoes, The (DuBose Heyward), 108, 126
Crawford, Cheryl, x, 172, 173, 190; relationship with Dorothy Heyward, 138–39, 171. See also *Porgy and Bess* (opera)
Crosby, Bing, 137

Curtain Must Rise, The, 77. See also *Three-a-Day*
Cygnets (Dorothy Heyward and Rumer Godden), 154, 155–56, 157–60, 165, 166

Danbury Fair (Carriere), 122
Dandridge, Dorothy, 185, 186
Dane, Clemence, 75
Davis, Blevins, 172, 173, 177, 179, 180, 192
Davis, Sammy, Jr., 185
Davis, Zola, 208<–9n3
Dawn Hill (Heyward home), 75, 88–89, 113, 116, 123
Day's End (W. R. Benét), 121
Declaration of Independence, 15, 22, 120
Deep River (L. Stallings), 50
Defiant Ones, The (film), 176
DeJagers, Dorothy: attendance at MacDowell Colony, 11–12, 13; collaboration with Dorothy Heyward, 85, 86 131; mental health issues, 12, 131, 132, 163
—works: *And Arabella* (with Dorothy Heyward and Eichler), 85; "The Average Woman," 86; *Little Girl Blue* (with Dorothy Heyward), 86; *Poor Paulette* (with Dorothy Heyward), 12, 75, 84. See also *Cinderelative, The*
DeVoss, Audrey, 169
Dewey, Thomas, 150
Digges, Dudley, 47
Dock St. Theatre (Charleston), 120–21, 126, 130, 131, 170, 188, 191, 192, 198; Dorothy Heyward as resident playwright, 12, 128–29, 132, 139–40, 195; DuBose Heyward as resident playwright, 121–23, 139, 195
Doniger, Walter, 140
Doubleday, Nelson, 129
Doubleday, Russell, 74
Doubleday Publishing Company, 179
Dramatists Guild, 81, 82

Dramatists Play Service, 122
DuBose, Edwin (uncle of DuBose), 34
DuBose, Lou, 16–17, 18, 203n6
DuBose family, 30
DuBose Heyward Playwrighting Contest and Award, 128–29, 139–40
Dud, The (Dorothy Heyward), 17, 18, 19, 20, 22. See also *Nancy Ann*
Duncan, Augustin, 22, 23, 47
Duncan, Todd, 137
DuPont family, 47
Durham, Frank, 36, 129, 140, 190–91
Durham, Richard, 221n5
Dybbuk, The (An-Sky), 50

Eager, Edward, 129
Edge of the Sword (Bellak), 140
Edisto Island, 111
Eichler, Adele, 85
Eighty Minutes to the Hour (Foster, Allan, and Dorothy Heyward), 136
Eisenhower, Dwight, 176
Elizabeth II, Queen, 169
Elliott, Robert Brown, 139
Emmy Award, 140
Emperor Jones, The (DuBose Heyward screenplay), 47, 89, 91, 126, 146; similarity to *Porgy* (play), 89
Emperor Jones, The (O'Neill), 89
"Epitaph for a Poet" (DuBose Heyward), 123
Equity Players, 47
Erlanger Theatrical Syndicate, 48
Eva Jessye Choir, 168
Everyman Opera Company, 175
Excelsior Film Company, 6

Fallingwater (Frank Lloyd Wright house), 209n4
Farr, Joyce (pseudonym), 82
Farrar, John, 49, 117
Father Was President (Doniger and Wald), 140

Faulkner, William, 89
Federal Emergency Relief Agency, 120
Ferber, Edna, 6
Ferrer, José, 115
Fields, Dorothy, 110
Fishburne, John, 163
Flack, Majorie. See Benét, Marjorie Flack
Folly Beach, 96, 104, 108, 125, 183, 198
Folly Beach (Frank), 198
Follywood (Heyward home), 108, 125, 182, 198
Footlight Players, 121
Ford, Paul Henri, 92
Fort Sumter, 40
49th Street Theatre, 26
Foster, Claiborne, 136
Fourth Watch, The (Weidner), 121
Frank, Dorothy Benton, 198
Franken, Rose, 6
Frazee, Harry, 75, 76
Friedlander, William, 47, 81, 82, 83, 84
Frings, Ketti, 185

Gabriel, Gilbert, 87
Gale, Zona, 6
Galsworthy, John, 25
Gerald (servant), 109
Gerber, Ella, 178, 192; *The Red and the Black* (with Jenifer Heyward), 179
Gershwin, George, 46, 78, 109, 185, 187, 189, 196; "Cinderelatives," 76; collaboration on *Star Spangled Virgin* proposed, 114; death, 114, 137, 172; interest in *Porgy*, 50–51; *Of Thee I Sing* (with Ira), 114; *Oh, Kay!* (with Ira), 50; portrait of DuBose, 177; relationship with Dorothy Heyward, 104; social skills of, 104. See also Gershwin, Ira; *Porgy and Bess* (opera)
—collaboration on *Porgy and Bess*, 68, 94, 107, 108, 138, 183, 187–88, 190; with Dorothy Heyward, 93, 95–106 passim, 167, 174, 187; with DuBose Heyward,

36, 93–99, 102, 104, 105, 107, 108. *See also* Heyward, DuBose: writing habits: writing *Porgy and Bess*
Gershwin, Ira, 43, 51, 137, 173, 185, 187, 189, 195; collaboration on *Porgy and Bess*, 57, 58, 63, 64, 95, 96, 100, 101–3, 138, 187–88; letters of, 196; *Of Thee I Sing* (with George), 114; *Oh, Kay!* (with George), 50; *Porgy and Bess* (film) and, 181, 184; *Porgy and Bess* film rights, 179, 181, 190. See also *Porgy and Bess* (opera); *and under* Heyward, Dorothy: relationships; Heyward, DuBose: collaborations
Gershwin, Leonore (Lee), 51, 172, 179, 181, 184, 187
Gershwin, Rose, 104, 137, 172
Gershwin family, 172, 173, 177, 181
Ghost of Moorsdown Manor, The (Dorothy Heyward), 6
Gibbes Museum of Art, 129, 153
Gillespie, Heather, 118
Girl Behind the Gun, The (Bolton and Wodehouse), 12
Gish, Dorothy, 139
Glasgow, Ellen, 89
Glaspell, Susan, 7
Godden, Rumer, 154–61 passim, 163–64, 165–66, 167, 168, 191; *A Candle for St. Jude*, 154, 155, 165; *Cygnets* (with Dorothy Heyward), 154, 155–56, 157–60, 165, 166; *The River* (screenplay), 155, 157
Golden, John, 76
Golden Globe Award, 187
Golden Vase, The (Lewisohn), 107
Goldwyn, Samuel, ix, 181, 182, 183, 185, 186, 187, 190. See also *Porgy and Bess* (film)
Gone with the Wind (film), 26
Gonzales, Ambrose, 63, 214n6
Good Earth, The (DuBose Heyward screenplay), 89

Gotham Hotel (New York City), 130
Grace (aunt of Dorothy Heyward) 4, 5
Grainger, Porter, 209n9
Grammy Award, 195
Green, Paul, 119; *In Abraham's Bosom*, 50
Green Grow the Lilacs (Riggs), 34
Green Pastures, The (Connelley), 86
Greenwald, Mr., 216n6
Greenway rest home (London), 163
Grisman, Sam, 216n6
Guerry, Moultrie, 88
Gullah, 21, 35, 63, 74, 98, 110, 193

Half Pint Flask, The (DuBose Heyward), 57
Halsey, Ashley, Jr., 179
Hambleton, T. Edward, 141, 191
Hamilton, Clayton, 8
Hammerstein, Oscar, 117
Hammond, Percy, 25
Happy Journey, The (Wilder), 121
Harkness Pavilion (New York City hospital), 170
Harleston, Edwin, 208–9n3
Harper's Magazine, 189, 190
Harris, Jed, 127, 128, 141, 146, 167
Hart, Moss, 83
Hartford, Huntington, 109, 128, 129
Hartzell, Anne (Dorothy's cousin's wife), 13
Hartzell, Charles S. (Dorothy's uncle), 3, 4, 5
Hartzell, Charles S., Jr. ("Junior"; Dorothy's first "twin" cousin), 4, 5, 13, 88, 124
Hartzell, Dorothea (Dora) Virginia (Dorothy's mother). *See* Kuhns, Dorothea (Dora) Virginia
Hartzell, Hugh (pseudonym), 86
Hartzell, Josiah, 2, 3, 4
Hartzell, Ralph, 2
Hartzell family, 2
Harvard Book Shop Players, 17
Harvard Prize, 20, 25, 81
Harvard University, 7, 10, 122, 140
Harvey, Georgette, 74, 110, 115, 209n4

Haskell, Jeannie Heyward (Register; sister of DuBose Heyward), 15, 28, 108, 124, 162
Have a Good Time, Jonica (Dorothy Heyward), 9–10, 47, 81. See also *Jonica*
Hayes, Helen, 170
Heinemann Publishing Company, 74
Helburn, Theresa, 10, 48, 101, 128, 129, 142, 146, 172; producer of *Porgy* (play), 53–54, 61. *See also* Theatre Guild
Her Lord and Master (Lamson), 218n5
Hergesheimer, Joseph, 92
Hernandez, Juano, x; in *Set My People Free*, 142, 143, 145, 146, 149
Herndon, R. G., 21, 23, 26
Heyward, Daniel, 213n6
Heyward, Dorothy: alcohol consumption, 130, 145, 166, 223–24n8; anti-Semitic comment, 170; attendance at MacDowell Colony, 11–12, 14–17, 30–31, 126, 155–57, 168; attitude on race, 31, 32, 42, 44–45, 46, 49, 92, 105, 110, 134, 136, 139, 143, 145, 146, 170, 171; attitude toward homosexuality, 218n6; collaboration on *Porgy and Bess*, 93, 95–106 passim, 167, 174, 187; collaboration with Dorothy DeJagers, 12, 85, 86; courtship and meeting DuBose Heyward, 14–19; death, 192; definition of "genius," 65, 156; denying herself credit, 34–37 passim, 46–47, 49, 74, 79, 99–100, 103, 105, 106, 121–22, 131, 138, 176–77, 183, 198, 207n5; divorce rumor, 41, 107, 121; education, 4, 5; encouragement of DuBose, 29, 35–36, 122, 205n1; ghost writers and, 188, 189, 190, 197; ill health, 13, 28, 29, 30, 33, 45, 50–51, 72, 73, 88, 142, 163, 165, 170, 173–74, 178, 191, 212n11; immature looks and behavior, 5, 10, 12, 20, 37, 72, 74, 190, 197; lack of domestic skills, 21–22, 108, 130; learning Gullah, 21; miscarriages, 34, 72, 79; nervous breakdown / mental health, 151, 159, 161, 162–66, 188, 189, 193, 206n6, 222n1; nonconfrontationalism, 13, 81, 103, 116, 131–32, 137–38, 142, 145, 146, 148, 150, 152, 153–54, 156, 157, 159, 162, 164, 166, 185, 196; papers of, vii, 196–97; playwrighting student, 8–11; portrait of, 32–33, 206n6; pregnancy, 81, 87; proceeds from opera lyrics, 137, 171, 185; ranking with other women playwrights, 201n6; relationship to Charleston, 21, 32, 33, 121, 182, 193; as resident playwright at Dock St. Theatre, 12, 128–29, 132, 139–40, 195; travel, 51–55, 73, 108, 158–65 passim; wedding, 20; youth, 1–5

—relationships, personal and professional: with Breen, 172–73, 176–77, 182; with Crawford, 138–39, 173; with DuBose, 4, 17, 18, 27, 33, 35–37, 51, 53, 75, 77–79, 87, 91, 119, 122, 132, 138, 139, 153–54, 158, 164; with Friedlander, 47–48, 81–82, 83; with Gershwin, George, 104; with Gershwin, Ira, ix, 37, 40, 57, 58, 95, 100, 102–3, 105–6, 179, 181, 184–85, 187–89; with Gershwin, Rose, 104; with Godden, 155–66 passim, 167; with Goldwyn, 185, 186, 187; with Herndon, 24; with Heyward, Jane (mother-in-law), 17, 21, 45, 109, 191; with Heyward, Jenifer (daughter), 108, 152–54, 169, 191; with Hyman, Jack and Lionel, 85–87; with Lowe, 131–33; with MacDowell, 16, 17, 18, 118, 126, 171, 180, 191; with Mamoulian, 53, 60, 68, 102, 110, 173, 209–10n10; with McClintic, 116, 118, 119; with Merrick, 157, 159–61, 162, 164; with Pinckney, Josephine, 19, 123–24, 165, 171, 180; with Ritt, 144, 145, 146, 148, 150, 154, 156

—works: *America's Sweethearts* (with DuBose, unfinished), 109, 118; *And*

Arabella (with DeJagers and Eichler) 85; *Babar the Elephant* (with Berezowsky and Randal), 167, 168–69; *Cello, Harp, and Violin* 7, 8, 11, 36, 77; *Charleston, 1822*, 143; *Clinkers* (with Klaw), 207n8; *Cygnets* (with Godden), 154, 155–56, 157–60, 165, 166; *The Dud*, 17, 18, 19, 20, 22; *Eighty Minutes to the Hour* (with Foster and Allan), 136; *The Ghost of Moorsdown Manor*, 6; *Have a Good Time, Jonica*, 9–10, 47, 81; *I Am Too Young* (unfinished autobiography), 190, 191, 197–98; *Jonica* (with Hart), 81–84, 86, 88; *Little Girl Blue* (with DeJagers), 86; *Love in a Cupboard*, 11, 63; *Mr. Pygmalion* 8, 9; *New Georgia* (with Rigsby), 133; *Nightmare House*, 90; *Poor Paulette* (with DeJagers), 12, 75, 84; "Porgy's Goat," 189; *The Pulitzer Prize Murders*, 34, 89–90, *Siberia*ward, 7, 11, 23; *South Pacific* (with Rigsby), 130–35, 136, 139, 143, 145, 149, 150, 160, 188, 191; "The Young Ghost," 52, 89, 107, 198. See also *Cinderelative, The*; *Mamba's Daughters* (Dorothy and Dubose Heyward play); *Nancy Ann*; *Porgy* (play); *Porgy and Bess* (film); *Porgy and Bess* (opera); *Set My People Free*; *Three-a-Day*
—writing habits, 33, 35, 155, 156, 158, 165; writing *Cygnets*, 155–60; writing *I Am too Young*, 188–91, 197; writing *Mamba's Daughters* (play), 33; writing *Porgy* (play), 33–37, 40–46, 52, 53, 54–61, 62, 63–67, 69, 174, 189, 207n5; writing "Porgy's Goat," 188–89; writing *Set My People Free*, 90–94, 109, 120; writing *South Pacific*, 131–33
Heyward, DuBose: attendance at MacDowell Colony, 14, 15, 16–17, 30–31; attitude on race, 18, 31–32, 45, 60, 61, 64, 72–73, 114, 115; autobiographical elements of *Mamba's Daughters*, 62, 111; background, 14–15, 16; biographies of, 190–91, 195; comment regarding Jews, 59; courtship of Dorothy Kuhns, 14–19, 27; death, 123, 135, 138, 191, 192; divorce rumor, 41, 107, 121; ill health, 28, 30, 30–31, 39, 45, 51–52, 123, 205n2; papers of, vii, 193, 196–97; portraits of, 177; relationship with Charleston, 28, 30, 32, 108, 111, 120, 193; as resident playwright at Dock St. Theatre, 121–23, 139, 195; travel, 51–55, 73, 108, 109, 111; wedding, 20
—collaborations: with Allen, 31, 36; with Gershwin, George, 36, 93, 94, 95–96, 97, 98–99, 102, 104, 105, 107, 108, 215n9; with Gershwin, Ira, 36–37, 57–58, 64, 95–96, 100–103, 105–6, 116, 137, 181, 184–85, 187–89; with Heyward, Dorothy, 34–35, 36–37; with Pinckney, Josephine, 36; on *Porgy and Bess*, 95–106 passim, 107
—relationships, personal and professional: with Heyward, Jane (mother), 15, 17, 31, 119; with MacDowell, 18, 88, 116, 118, 126; with Mamoulian, 53, 60, 68; with Pinckney, Josephine, 18–19, 29, 121, 124
—works: *America's Sweethearts* (with Dorothy, unfinished), 109, 118; "And Once Again—the Negro," 42; *Angel*, 35; "An Artistic Triumph," 14; *Brass Ankle*, 89, 114, 120; *Carolina Chansons* (with Allen), 16, 205n4; *The County Bunny and the Little Gold Shoes*, 108, 126; *The Emperor Jones* (screenplay), 47, 89, 91, 126, 146; "Epitaph for a Poet," 123; *The Good Earth* (screenplay) 89; *The Half Pint Flask*, 57; *Lost Morning*, 89, 107, 109, 213n3, 214n1; "The Negro in the Lowcountry," 91; *Peter Ashley*, 90, 91, 94; *Star Spangled Virgin*, 42, 114, 216n3. See also *Mamba's Daughters* (DuBose

Heyward, DuBose: works (*continued*)
Heyward novel); *Mamba's Daughters* (Dorothy and Dubose Heyward play); *Porgy* (novel); *Porgy* (play); *Porgy and Bess* (opera)
—writing habits, 35; writing *Mamba's Daughters* (play), 113; writing *Porgy* (novel), 28–31; writing *Porgy* (play), 34–35, 52, 54–61, 62, 63–67, 69; writing *Porgy and Bess*, 95–98, 100, 103, 215n9; writing *Set My People Free*, 90–94, 109
Heyward, Edwin Watkins (DuBose's father), 15; death, 203n2
Heyward, Jane (Janie) Screven DuBose (DuBose's mother), 28, 34, 36, 51, 52, 54, 55, 59, 60, 61, 70, 75, 77, 87, 123; as character in *Mamba's Daughters*, 62; death, 119, 135; relationship with Dorothy (daughter-in-law), 17, 21, 45, 109; relationship with DuBose, 15, 17, 62; rumored author of *Porgy*, 30
—works: *Brown Jackets*, 21; *Wild Roses*, 40; writings, 15, 30, 31, 91, 107, 191
Heyward, Jeannie. *See* Haskell, Jeannie Heyward
Heyward, Jenifer DuBose (daughter), 123, 124, 126, 129, 130, 186, 189, 191, 192; actress, 179–80, 191; birth, 87, 88; christening, 88, 107, 108; dancer, 108, 152, 158, 164, 165, 169, 178, 179; death, vii, 196; papers of, 196; psychological issues, 108, 135, 152–53, 169, 180; *The Red and the Black* (with Gerber), 179; stage name, 179–80; suitors, 169, 180; travels with *Porgy and Bess*, 178–79; writings of, 179
Heyward, Nathaniel, 213n6
Heyward, Thomas, Jr., 22, 120, 213n6
Heyward and O'Neill Insurance Company, 29
Hill, Waldermar, 92
Hill, Wesley, 64
His Blue Serge Suit (Ritchie), 17, 167

His Majesty's Theatre (London), 73
HMS Pinafore (Gilbert and Sullivan), 1, 25
Hodges, Heather, 215n10
Hoffius, Steve, 214n6
Holiday magazine, 180
Holliday, Billie, 137
Horney, Karen, 153
Horowitz, Joseph, 67; *On My Way*, 68
Hot Water, 77. *See also Three-a-Day*
Hotel Manger (New York City), 55
House Un-American Activities Committee, ix
Houston Grand Opera, 195
Howard University, 65
Hughes, Heyward (pseudonym), 86
Hunter College, 169
Hutty, Alfred, 213n3
Hyman, Jack, 86
Hyman, Lionel, 86
Hyman brothers (producers), 85–87

I Am Too Young (Dorothy Heyward), 190, 191, 197–98
In Abraham's Bosom (P. Green), 50
Ingram, Rex, 142, 143, 144

Jenkins Orphanage Band, 42, 61, 64, 73, 196
Jervey, Allen, 123
Jervey, Sadie, 108
Jet magazine, 170
Jolson, Al, 95
Jonica (Dorothy Heyward and Hart): production, 81–84, 88; mentioned, 86. *See also Have a Good Time, Jonica*
Joseph Conrad (ship), 109

Karamu Players, 167
Karamu Theatre, 173
Kaufman, George, 83
Kaye-Smith, Sheila, 75
Kazan, Elia, 13, 145
Kennedy, Thomas Conger, 139; *Song of the Bridge*, 129

Kern, Jerome, 113
Kiawah Island, 43
Kissing Time (Bolton and Wodehouse), 12
Klauber, Adolph, 12
Klaw, Alma, 207n8
Klaw Theatrical Syndicate, 48
Kraft Theatre, 218n5
Kramer, Aaron, 92
Kramer Players (Charleston), 26
Krazy Kat Klub, 61
Kronenberger, Louis, 134
Kuhns, Dorothea (Dora) Virginia (Dorothy's mother), 1, 3, 4, 201n1 (chap. 1)
Kuhns, Herman Lyties (Dorothy's father), 1, 2; death, 3; Spanish American War service, 3
Kuhns, L. M., 2, 3
Kuhns, Louis (Dorothy's brother), 1, 3, 4
Kuhns, Wilbur (Dorothy's brother), 1, 2, 3
Kuhns family, 2
Kummer, Clare, 6–7

La Bohème (Puccini), 3
La Scala Opera House (Milan), 177, 178
Lamson, Peggy, 161, 163, 165; ghost writer, 188
—works: *Bee in Her Bonnet*, 154, 218n5; *Her Lord and Master*, 218n5; *Museum Piece*, 129, 139, 151; *Respectfully Yours*, 129, 139, 218n5
Langner, Lawrence, 48, 127, 145–46, 150, 172. *See also* Theatre Guild
Larrimore, Francine, 24, 25
Latham, Minor, 8
Lazar, Irving ("Swifty"), 177, 182, 185, 190
Lee, Canada: in *Mamba's Daughters*, 115, 130; in *Set My People Free*, 130, 142, 144, 145, 146, 149, 150; in *South Pacific*, 131, 132, 134; mentioned, x
Leeds, Leila, 70
Legendre, Gertrude Sanford, 204n2
Leonardas, Urylee, 143, 176

Lewisohn, Ludwig, 214n1; *The Golden Vase*, 107
Lewisohn stadium (New York City), 137
Library of Congress, 101
Liebling, William, 174, 189
Life magazine, 25, 118, 120, 126, 178
Life with Father (Lindsay and Crouse), 141
Lilac Lake (Meacham), 129
Literary Guild, 72
Little Girl Blue (Dorothy Heyward and DeJagers), 86; *And Arabella*, 85. *See also Cinderelative, The*; *Poor Paulette*
London Evening Standard, 175
Loray Mills, 92
Lost Morning (DuBose Heyward), 89, 107 109, 213n3, 214n1
Love in a Cupboard (Dorothy Heyward), 11, 63
Lowe, David, 131, 132, 133, 134, 135. *See also South Pacific*
Lowell, Amy, 15, 29
Lowndes, Marie Belloc, 75
Luce, Clare Boothe, 121, 128
Luce, Henry, 121

Macbeth (Shakespeare), 149
MacDowell, Marian, 11, 118, 126, 169, 180, 191, 192; attitude to Dorothy, 16, 17, 18, 118, 126, 191; attitude to DuBose, 18, 126; godmother to Jenifer, 88
MacDowell Colony, 1, 85, 89, 108, 121, 123, 171, 191; Dorothy Heyward's attendance at, 11–12, 14–17, 30–31, 126, 155–57, 168; DuBose Heyward's attendance at, 14, 15, 16–17, 30–31
MacDowell Fellowship, 7, 10, 11, 14–17
MacGowan, John, 128
Madison, Ella, 64
Majestic (Steam Ship), 51
Majestic Theatre (New York City), 138
Mamba's Daughters (Dorothy and DuBose Heyward play), 120; origins, 110–11; writing of, 111–17 passim; production,

Mamba's Daughters (continued) 117–19. *See also* McClintic, Guthrie; Waters, Ethel
Mamba's Daughters (DuBose Heyward novel), 45, 46, 52, 53, 54, 110, 111; autobiographical elements, 62–63, 72, 73
Mamba's Daughters (projected opera), 168
Mamoulian, Rouben, x, 88, 105, 127, 131, 137; directing *Porgy*, 53–54, 55, 59, 60–61, 63, 66, 67, 70, 72, 74; directing *Porgy and Bess* (film), 186; directing *Porgy and Bess* (opera), 97, 102, 105, 110; influence on *Porgy* (play), 53, 67–68; relationship with Dorothy Heyward, 53, 60, 68, 102, 110, 173, 209–10n10; revisions suggested for *Porgy*, 53–54, 55, 59, 63, 66, 67, 70, 72, 74, 95, 96, 101
Mann Act, 144
Maria (servant), 21–22, 63
Marriott, John, 144
Marshall, E. G., 148–49, 150
Marvin, Mel, 140
Master Skylark (J. Bennett), 15
Matthew, Margaret, 123
Matthew family, 123
Maugham, Somerset, 129–30
Mayer, Louis B., 181
McCall's magazine, 52
McCann, Robert, 141
McCarthy, Joseph W., 197
McClendon, Rose, x, 60, 74, 209n4
McClintic, Guthrie, 114–16, 118–19, 127, 180
McCormack, Helen, 129
McCullers, Carson, 196
McCurry, John, 173
McDonald, Audra, 226n3
McHugh, Jimmy, 110
McKinley, Ida Saxton, 2, 3
McKinley, William, 2, 3; funeral, 202n5 (chap. 1)
Meacham, Kirke, 129
Medical College of South Carolina, 195

Melville, Herman, 140
Member of the Wedding, The (McCullers), 196
Memminger High School (Charleston), 129, 170
Meredith, Burgess, 117
Merrick, David, 154, 155, 166, 191; relationship with Dorothy Heyward, 157, 159–61, 162, 164
Metcalf, Paul, 140
Metropolitan Opera (New York City), vii, 174, 195, 201n1 (chap. 1)
Meyer, Joseph, 83
Michener, James, 133
Middleton Gardens, 124
Mielziner, Jo, 142
Mike the Angel (Savage), 129, 132
Miller, Elizabeth DuBose, 124
Milton, Robert, 51, 141
Moll, William, 83
Molloy, Robert, 205n5
Moore, Douglas, 17, 167–68
Morgan family, 47
Moscow Art Theatre, 48
Mr. Pygmalion (Dorothy Heyward), 8, 9
Munsell, Warren, 95, 96
Murdoch, Marian, 122
Museum Piece (Lamson), 129, 139, 151
My Old Kentucky Home (Hendersonville, N.C.), 51

Naked City, The (Wald), 140
Nancy Ann (Dorothy Heyward), 29, 47, 49, 81, 83; plot and production details, 22–26, 27. *See also Dud, The*
Nash, N. Richard, 185
Nathan, George Jean, 135
National Association for the Advancement of Colored People (NAACP), 170
National Cathedral School, 4, 20
National Theatre (Washington, D.C.), 83
National Theatre Conference Play Contest, 139

Native Son (Wright), 130
Neeson, Margie, 188, 189
"Negro in the Lowcountry, The" (DuBose Heyward), 91
Negro's Actor Guild, 65
Nevin, Arthur, 17
New Georgia (Rigsby and Dorothy Heyward), 133. See also *South Pacific*
New York Herald Tribune, 80, 84, 98, 149, 169
New York Philharmonic, 168
New York Telegram and Evening Mail, 25
New York Times, 21, 80, 90, 134, 149, 169, 193
New Yorker, 134, 178, 179,
Newark (N.J.) News, 90
Nichols, Lewis, 134
Nightmare House (Dorothy Heyward), 90
Noonan, Ellen, 224n7
Nugent, Robert Bruce, 60, 209n4

Obie award, 118
Of Thee I Sing (Gershwin and Gershwin musical), 114
Of Time and the River (Wolfe), 202–3n8 (chap. 2)
Office of Emergency Management, 129
Oh, Kay! (Gershwin and Gershwin musical), 50
Ohio Volunteer Infantry, 3
Oklahoma! (Rodgers and Hammerstein), 34
Old Town Plantation, 158, 165
On a Balcony, Charleston, South Carolina (L. C. Perry), 32–33, 206n6
On My Way (Horowitz), 68
Once in a Lifetime (Kaufman and Hart), 83
O'Neill, Eugene, 119; *The Emperor Jones*, 89
"Orienta" (Heyward home), 28
Original Ballet Russe, 169
Our Town (Wilder), 127
Out of the Shadow (R. G. Cohen), 52
Owen, Michael, 214n1&2
Page, Thomas Nelson, 132

Paramount Pictures, 74
Peg o' My Heart (Manners), 11
"People in Defense" (radio scripts), 129
Perry, Edward G., 60, 209n4
Perry, Lilla Cabot, 34, 51; *On a Balcony, Charleston, South Carolina*, 32–33, 206n6
Peter Ashley (DuBose Heyward), 90, 91, 94
Peter Pan (play), 3
Peterkin, Julia, 49
Peters, Brock, 185
Phillips, Ulrich B., 213n5
Phoenix Theatre Company, 191
Pinckney, Camilla Scott, 19, 20
Pinckney, Josephine, 55, 121, 128, 165, 177, 178, 180, 188, 192; attitude on race, 31, 171; background, 18–19; 20; collaboration with DuBose Heyward, 36; godmother to Jenifer, 88; not marrying, 29, 217n5; possible source of divorce rumor, 41, 107, 121, 123, 130, 188, 192; relationship with Dorothy, 18–19, 21, 123–24; relationship with DuBose, 18–19, 29, 124; relationship with Willkie, 19, 108, 128; writings, 31
Pinkussohn, P. Leroy, 216n6
Plantation Echoes (Wilson), 215n10
Poe, Edgar Allan, 90
Poetry Society of South Carolina, 16, 72, 121, 204n9 (chap. 3)
Poitier, Sidney, 185, 186
Poor Paulette (Dorothy Heyward and DeJagers), 12, 75, 84; *And Arabella*, 85; *Little Girl Blue*, 86. See also *Cinderelative, The*
Popov (clown), 178
Porgy (novel), 16; origins, 29–30; synopsis, 38–40; writing of, 28–31
Porgy (play) 91, 93, 96, 98, 109, 113, 120; critical reception, 68–69; film rights, 89; gay presence in chorus, 209n4; goat, 40, 44, 45, 57, 58, 59, 73; Jenkins Orphanage Band and, 61, 64, 73; Karamu Players production, 167;

Porgy (continued)
 London production, 73–74; Mamoulian claims of influence on, 53, 67–68; Mamoulian directing, 59, 69–61; Mamoulian revisions, 53–54, 55, 59, 63, 66, 67, 70, 72, 74, 95, 96, 101; premiere, 66, 68; prompt script, 63–65, 66–67, 70; possible Charleston production, 170, 174; possible French production, 74; rights to, 172–73; royalties, 88; strike by chorus, 60; Theatre Guild production, 48–49, 51, 53–54, 142; writing of, 33–37, 40–46, 52, 53, 54–61, 62, 63–67, 69, 174, 189, 207n5

Porgy and Bess (film), 181, 185–87; rights and royalties, 95, 177, 180–86. *See also* Goldwyn, Samuel

Porgy and Bess (opera), vii, 107, 110, 170, 171, 190; based on Dorothy Heyward's work, 95–99, 101, 167, 174, 186; Charleston, S.C., productions, 195, 204n2; contracts with authors, 95–96, 99, 184; Crawford and, x, 172, 173, 190; Crawford production, 137–39, 167, 183; creation of, and Theatre Guild production, 95–106 passim, 167, 190; cuts, 102–3; Davis-Breen production and world tour, 167, 168, 171, 172–81 passim; deposition of Dorothy regarding authorship, 183, 184; film rights, 95, 177, 180–86; as Heyward-Gershwin collaboration, 93, 95–106, 167, 174, 187; lyrics attributed to DuBose, 215n9; premiere, 83, 105–6; race issues and, 176. *See also* Gershwin, George; Gershwin, Ira; Heyward, Dorothy: relationships, personal and professional: with Gershwin, Ira; Mamoulian, Rouben

"Porgy's Goat" (Dorothy Heyward), 189

Portrait of a Gentleman (Murdoch), 122

Preminger, Otto, 181, 186, 187

Previn, André, 187

Price, Leontyne, 143, 173

Providence (ship), 73

Provincetown Players, 7

Pulitzer Prize, 83, 114, 127, 133, 167

Pulitzer Prize Murders, The (Dorothy Heyward), 34, 89–90

Pyatt, Jennie, 171

Quiet Cities (Hergesheimer), 92

Radcliffe College, 7, 10, 20

Raisin in the Sun, A (Hansberry), 176

Randal, Judith, 168

Rasputin, Grigori, 168

"Raven, The," (Poe), 90

Recruiting Officer, The (Farquhar), 120

Red and the Black, The (Jenifer Heyward and Gerber), 179

Reed, Daniel, 85

Register, Edwin, 28

Register, Jeannie Heyward Haskell. *See* Haskell, Jeannie Heyward

Renoir, Jean, 155

Repository, The (Canton, Ohio), 2

Respectfully Yours (Lamson), 129, 139, 218n5

Return of the Soldier, The (West), 8

Reunion (Molloy), 205n5

Rhett, Alicia, 26

Rice, Allyn, 141, 142, 150

Riggs, Lynn, 34

Rigsby, Howard, 131, 133, 134, 135; *New Georgia* (with Dorothy Heyward), 133; *South Pacific* (with Dorothy Heyward), 130–35, 136, 139, 143, 145, 149, 150, 160, 188, 191

Rinehart, Stanley, 117

Ripley's Believe it or Not, 86

Ritchie, Belle McDiarmid, 17

Ritt, Martin, 144, 145–46, 148, 150, 154, 156, 197. *See also Set My People Free*

River, The (Godden screenplay), 155, 157

Robeson, Paul, 126, 127, 128, 130

Robinson, Edward Arlington, 12, 16, 20, 30
Robinson, Emmett, 140
Robinson, Patricia, 140
Rockefeller family, 47
Rockefeller Foundation, 121, 139
Romeo and Juliet (Shakespeare), 175
Roosevelt, Eleanor, 119
Roosevelt, Theodore, 3
Rorem, Ned, 168
Rourke, Constance, 30
Rumsey, John, 181
Russell, John Patton, 76
Ruth, George Herman (Babe), 75

Saddler Wells Ballet Company, 158
Saint Ermin's Hotel (London), 159
Saint James Palace (London), 75
Saint Michael's Episcopal Church (Charleston), 40
Saint Nicholas Magazine, 2
Saint Philip's Episcopal Church (Charleston), 119, 123, 192
Samuel French Publishing Company, 11, 86, 139
Sarah Lawrence College, 152
Sass, George Herbert, 28
Saturday Evening Post, 12, 86, 92, 136, 179
Savage, Robert M., 129
Saxe, Leonard, 195
Saxton, Ida (McKinley), 2, 3
Scarlet Sister Mary (Peterkin), 49
Schubert Theatrical Syndicate, 48
Schwartz, Arthur, 216n3
Selznick, Irene, 142
Semi-Attached Couple, The (Eden), 167
Sergeant camp, 126
Set My People Free (Dorothy Heyward), 126–28, 130, 139, 160, 172, 180, 188, 191, 196; as *Charleston, 1822*, 143; Karamu Players Production, 187; projected opera, 167–78; Theatre Guild production, 128, 142–50; writing of, 90–94, 109, 120. See also Ritt, Martin; Vesey, Denmark
Shakespeare, William: *As You Like It*, 141; *Macbeth*, 149; *Romeo and Juliet*, 175
Sharp, Marjory, 164
Shaw, George Bernard, 25
Shirley, Wayne, 51, 67, 110
Show Boat (Hammerstein and Kern), 73
Shuffle Along (Miller and Lyles), 33
Siberiaward (Dorothy Heyward), 7, 11, 23
Simon, Louis, 216n6
Simons, Katherine Drayton Mayrant, 129, 140
Simonson, Lee, 61, 62
Sinkler, Caroline, 122, 128
Sitwell, Osbert, 196
Smallens, Alexander, 102, 105, 173
Smalls, Ed, 65
Smalls, Sammy, x, 29–30, 31, 45; drawing of, 178; family of, 171
Smalls Paradise (New York City), 65
Smith, Alice Ravenel Huger, 32
Smith, Chard, 30
Smith, Lillian, 196
Smith, Mildred Joanne, 149
Society for the Preservation of Spirituals, 91, 113, 115, 146, 165
Solomon Islands, 132, 133
Song of the Bridge (Kennedy), 129
South Carolina Historical Society, vii, 196, 197
South Pacific (Rigsby and Dorothy Heyward), 130–35, 136, 139, 143, 145, 149, 150, 160, 188, 191
Stallings, Helen, 124
Stallings, Laurence, 124, 207n1; *Deep River*, 50
Stanislavski, Konstantin, 53
Star Spangled Virgin (DuBose Heyward), 42, 114, 216n3
Stern, Gladys Bronwyn, 75
Stevens, Alfred, 75

Stoney, Sam Gaillard, Jr., 63, 93, 219n10
Strange Fruit (Smith), 196
Strasberg, Lee, 127, 132, 133. See also *South Pacific*
Streetcar Named Desire, A (T. Williams), 142
Strike! (Vorse), 92
Swift, Kay, 168

Taft, Helen (Nellie), 202n8 (chap. 1)
Taft, William Howard, 202n8 (chap. 1)
Taylor, Anna Heyward, 177
Taylor, Deems, 104
Taylor, Paulette, 47
"Telemaque" (Metcalf), 140. *See also* Vesey, Denmark
Texas State Fair, 174
Theatre Guild, 10, 86, 114, 116, 129, 139, 172, 179–80; history of, 48; producing *Porgy* (play), 48–49, 51, 53–54; producing *Porgy and Bess*, 95, 96, 99, 138; producing *Set My People Free*, 127–28, 137, 142, 144–46, 150. *See also* Helburn, Theresa; Langner, Lawrence; *Porgy and Bess* (film)
Three-a-Day (Dorothy Heyward) 90, 92; other names for and evolution of, 77; synopsis, 78–80, 83, 86
Throckmorton, Cleon, 61
Thurman, Wallace, 60
Thurmond, Strom, 171
Tidalholm inn (Beaufort), 165
Time magazine, 12, 187
Toledo Times, 90
Tony Award, 195
Toots Ensemble, 77. See also *Three-a-Day*
Town Theatre (Columbia, S.C.), 11
Truman, Harry, 150, 172, 174, 176
Tyler, George C., 93
Tynan, Kenneth, 175

Uncle Tom's Cabin (play), 2
United States State Department, 173, 176, 178

University of Minnesota, 5

Van Vechten, Carl, 50, 117, 118
Variety, 83
Vesey, Denmark, x, 90–94, 120, 126, 136, 139; as subject of "Telemaque," 140. See also *Set My People Free*
Victory Theatre (Charleston), 26
Virgin Islands, 109, 114
von Arnim, Elizabeth, 75

Wald, Malvin, 140
Wallis, Hal, 181
Walpole, Hugh, 52
Warfield, William, 143, 173
Waring, Ferdi Legare (Backer), 157, 165
Waring, Julius Waties, 32, 129, 143, 196
Waring, Thomas R., Jr., 46, 166, 171, 192
Warner Brothers, 81
Waters, Ethel, x, 110–11, 130, 196; *Mamba's Daughters* and, 113–14, 117–18; opinion of *Porgy* (play), 60. See also *Mamba's Daughters* (Dorothy and DuBose Heyward play)
Watkins, Perry, 117
Wedding Band (Childress), 196
Weidner, Paul, 121
Weill, Kurt, 216n3
Weinstein, Arnold, 168
Wells, H. G., 75
Wescott, Glenway, 130
West, Dorothy, 60
West, Rebecca, 75, 163, 196; *The Return of the Soldier*, 8
Whipper, Leigh Rollin, 65–66, 74, 143, 174, 186, 209n9
Whipple, Harry (ghost writer), 189
Whitall, William Van R., 20
White Point Garden (Charleston), 108
Whitelaw, Patti, 153, 158, 165
Whitelaw, Robert N. S., 121, 139
Widdemer, Margaret, 166
Wiggins, Ella May, 92

Wigglesworth, Richard, 217n5
Wild Roses (Jane Screven Heyward), 40
"Wild Winter Love" (Yezierska), 52
Wilder, Thornton, 126, 146, 148, 156, 163; *The Happy Journey*, 121; *Our Town*, 127
Williams, Musa, 209n4
Williams, Tennessee, 174; *A Streetcar Named Desire*, 142
Willkie, Wendell, 19, 108, 128
Wilson, Frank, 130, 143, 149
Wilson, George, 127, 143–49 passim. See also *Set My People Free*
Wilson, Phoebe, 188
Windust, Bretaigne, 141
Wizard of Oz, The (film), 21
Wodehouse, P. G., 12
Wolfe, Nero, 171
Wolfe, Thomas, 10, 202–3n8 (chap. 2)

Woman's Home Companion magazine, 52
Wood, Audrey (agent), 14, 103, 130, 132, 142, 148, 155, 159, 168, 174, 185, 188
Woodard, Isaac, 143
Woollcott, Alexander, 24, 25
Workman, Gertrude, 82, 83
Workshop 47. See Baker, George Pierce
Wright, Frank Lloyd, 209n4
Wright, Richard, 130
Wylie, Elinor, 16

Yezierska, Anzia, 52
You and I (Barry), 20, 204n2
"Young Ghost, The" (Dorothy Heyward), 52, 89, 107, 198

Zeigler, John, 140
Ziegfield Theatre (New York City), 175

www.ingramcontent.com/pod-product-compliance
Lightning Source LLC
Chambersburg PA
CBHW031455121025

33828CB00004B/10